BUYING
AND
SELLING
A SMALL
BUSINESS

BUYING
AND
SELLING
A SMALL
BUSINESS

An Entrepreneurial Strategy for Success

Ernest J. Honigmann
with illustrations by Matt Kindt

Monnet Press
www.monnetpress.com

Editor and indexer: Christine Frank
Page designer, illustrator, cover designer, and print coordinator: Matt Kindt
Marketing consultant: Lance Tilford
Legal advisor: Intellectual Property Law Center, LLC (Mary Lu Sanders-Zinser)
Publicity researcher: Nancy Stranczek

Printer: RR Donnelley
Cover photos licensor: Corbis
Graphics: The Creative Group (Jay Babcock)

Printed on acid-free paper

Library of Congress Control Number: 2007901995

ISBN-13: 978-0-9793579-0-9
ISBN-10: 0-9793579-0-X

CONTENTS AT A GLANCE

CONTENTS IN DETAIL

LIST OF REAL-LIFE EXAMPLES

LIST OF FIGURES

LIST OF ILLUSTRATIONS

PREFACE

The genesis of this book was the day I went to the library to find something I could recommend to my students. When I came home that night empty-handed, I felt discouraged, but I didn't give up. I kept searching the catalogues and stacks at other libraries and I managed to find a scant handful of excellent books. But the excellent ones were for sale prices well outside the realm of small business, or for topics like venture capital and appraising that were too specialized for my students, my buyers, or my sellers. Finally, I did give up. That's when I decided to write this thing myself. The small business marketplace was in sore need of a detailed, comprehensive manual on solving its many difficulties, and somebody had to do it.

That was in 1992.

Now, in 2007, as this book goes to press, I'm still searching the libraries, and things haven't changed much. I've reviewed a total of about 40 books in the how-to genre with no significant improvements to report.

I've also reviewed several university textbooks on entrepreneurship. I found their qualities of writing and informing their readers to be at the usual high levels of academia, but dealing almost exclusively in starting a business. They tend to brush over buying with a single chapter or less, and they cover selling mostly with advice (like launching an IPO) ill-suited for the owners of small businesses. What's more, their advice tends toward the management level, like a branch manager's outline to his staff, while *Buying and Selling a Small Business* (BSSB) tends toward the detail level, like an engineer's blueprint for shop workers.

So here's how this book can be useful: depending on the aim of your entrepreneurship program, *BSSB* can serve as the text for a new course in buying a business, or as a complement to the text in an existing course in starting a business. However, since university professors generally do not have all of the right experience to teach the variety of topics in this book, you may have to supplement your staff with one or more instructors from outside your school. For example, you might hire a business broker to teach brokering (Chapter 5), a business owner for fact-finding (Chapter 6), and a mediator for negotiating (Chapter 8).

Of course, if you are simply a prospective buyer or seller of a small business, as opposed to a teacher or a student, this book will guide you through virtually every step in your deal.

To enhance your understanding of the text and add to your enjoyment, I've provided background and orientation below. Part 1 describes the small business marketplace including its meaning, its difficulties, and its history. Part 2 describes the benefits you should expect from reading this book. And Part 3 describes the organization and features of this book, its many examples, the disciplines and areas covered, and those not covered.

Whether you're a small business manager or a business school professor, I think you're in for a big surprise by the depth and complexity of what you are about to discover.

PART 1:
THE SMALL BUSINESS MARKETPLACE

The Meaning of a Small Business. In 1980, when I began my career as a business broker, I thought that buying a small business was just a way to invest, and that selling was merely an exit. I also thought that a small business was little more than a chattel or an offshoot of the job market.

I was so wrong about that.

The purchase and sale of a small business are major milestones in the lives of most entrepreneurs. For buyers, it is the beginning of a new, more fulfilling life. For sellers, it is often the end. In Maslow's Hierarchy of human needs, the buyer's purchase of a small business would score at the highest level, the one described by Maslow as self-actualization. That's when one becomes all that one can be. That's why the purchase and sale of a small business are on the same scale of life's most memorable events as graduations, weddings, divorces, and funerals. And that's why they are just as emotional.

The Definition of a Small Business. In contrast to definitions based on annual sales, number of employees, or other quantitative measures, I define a small business conceptually as one with only one tier of management, namely, the owner. That definition is not perfect but it more or less sums up what most small businesses actually are. Its importance will be brought out in Part 4 of Chapter 7, "Appraising."

The Scope of the Marketplace. There are some five million corporations in America. About 98% of them have fewer than 100 employees, and 89% have fewer than 20. I would guess that most of those in the 89% would fit the above definition of a small business. I would also guess that from 10 to 15 percent of them are for sale at any given time. (See http://app1.sba.gov/faqs/ for the latest information.)

How I Chose My Book Title. The title I really wanted was *Arcane World*. It summarized so perfectly the small business marketplace and all the difficulties of working in it. But that neat, nippy phrase, alas, was an alien in the world of search engines. Besides, for many folks, *arcane* itself was arcane. So that's how I came to the dull but practical title now on the cover. My gurus made me do it.

A Litany of Difficulties—Why the Small Business Marketplace Is Dysfunctional.
When you consider that these are small businesses we are talking about, this marketplace is surprisingly complex. For example, the typical deal is not a relatively easy sale of corporate stock. Instead, it is an asset sale requiring around 20 documents to close (see Appendix A on page 474).

Adding to the difficulty is that the marketplace is mostly unregulated. In Missouri, for example, the state does not require testing and licensing for business brokers as it does for real estate agents, certified public accountants, and lawyers. That means that anyone may become a business broker by simply so declaring. It also means that people are not being trained whose skills we can reasonably count on. The result is a marketplace where incompetence is much too common, and people are getting hurt. Details are provided in some of the real-life examples spread through the book. (The examples where people are getting hurt are summarized in Part 2 of Chapter 12, starting on page 448.)

In some states, regulation does exist but much of it is superficial, requiring only a real estate license or a simple registration with the state.

Because the market in most states is either unregulated or regulated superficially, with no licensed, well-trained advisors for guidance, buyers and sellers often turn to their accountants and lawyers for help. But these professional advisors lack the special training required to be effective in this marketplace. As a result, their good intentions notwithstanding, they often do more harm than good, and their clients are getting hurt. Those details too are provided in the above-mentioned real-life examples.

There are private organizations that train and certify business brokers and business appraisers, and they seem to be competent. But they are not widely recognized, so the help they provide is very limited.

Other sources of help are available, but the advice offered is usually aimed at business starters, only seldom at buyers and sellers, and it tends to be too basic to be helpful in this market. For example, the State of Missouri maintains a web site offering advice for entrepreneurs. That site is very informative and easy to read, and I recommend it to those newly interested in business. However, it doesn't begin to deal with the difficulties in this litany (see http://www.ded.mo.gov/business/pdfs/startuppacket.pdf). And the Small Business Administration (SBA), for another example, has a group known as SCORE (Service Corps of Retired Executives) providing volunteer advisors who are experienced in business and anxious to help. Yet, for all their good intentions, those volunteers seem to have little or no training for this marketplace.

What's worse is that the inadequate help we receive from otherwise trustable sources as the Missouri web site and SCORE obscures the need for advice that we can reliably count on. In other words, we can think we're being helped when we're really not.

Worse still, as if the marketplace were not difficult enough, the human condition, in all its diversity, exerts its dispiriting influence. Here are some of the problems that occasionally impede our deals: marital discord, idiosyncratic behavior (occasionally by in-house accountants, and by owners who do their own bookkeeping), dueling partners, hubris, myths (those with respect to financing are especially persistent), emotional blockages (like irrational resistance to hiring a lawyer), incivility, arrogance, autocracy (mainly by business owners), rudeness, skullduggery, and meanness of spirit. Of course, these are not the everyday stuff that deals are made of, but they appear often enough to remind us of our humanity, and to make an already tough market even tougher.

But worst of all is that for many, the biggest difficulty is when would-be buyers and would-be sellers attempt to find each other to simply get their deals started. That's because this marketplace, unlike the real estate marketplace, lacks a multiple listing service and because business brokers sometimes don't cooperate with one another. It is also because sellers tend to keep their businesses for sale a closely guarded secret. Because of this difficulty, the painstaking effort to find the right matchup—probably harder on buyers than on sellers—often amounts to months or even years of fruitless and frustrating searching, the kind of effort that some would describe as drudgery. One almost has to go through the experience to understand why each deal, once it gets started, should be thought of as precious to behold and worth fighting to preserve.

Amidst all the difficulties, however, there are two groups that stand tall. One is the SBA which does a great job working with the banking industry to finance the purchases of small businesses. The other is the banking industry itself which, despite imperfections, does an overall fine job financing those purchases.

The difficulties nevertheless prevail. Thus, working a deal successfully from start to finish requires technical skill, diplomacy, no end of patience, and a sensitivity to human emotions. It is something of an art, and it is always a challenge.

Continuing the Litany—A Difficulty of Another Kind. Based on my observations, most business owners do not report their true incomes. That makes business appraising a difficult and special art. Because cheating on taxes is rampant, and because it is done systematically in large amounts, I felt compelled to tell my readers, in exhaustive detail, how to deal with it. In fact, I've offered enough detail that my explanation may seem like an encouragement to cheat. You may even think of it as unethical. I will therefore remind you that a writer's first duty is to tell the truth, and that means the whole truth. It usually leads to a greater good. (See "Business Morality in America" on my web site: www.monnetpress.com.)

Why the Real Estate Marketplace Is Regulated, While the Small Business Marketplace Is Not. The marketplace's regulatory disparity—and some of the difficulties mentioned above—can best be understood by looking briefly at a special history of our culture.

The situation began more or less in 1215 when King John signed the Magna Carta and copies were distributed to some 20 boroughs around the kingdom. As a result of the distribution of that document, the laws introduced by it, and the judicial decisions arising from it, became common throughout the land. Thus, English common law was born and, through colonization, so was American law.

These early laws dealt more with ownership of land than with ownership of business because land was more important as a producer and store of wealth and as a badge of prestige. Businesses in those days consisted mainly of crafts connected to the land or to a fief (a feudal estate lived on and worked by vassals). Crafts rarely were marketed partly because they tended to be family affairs (although apprentices and journeymen sometimes were hired) but, more importantly, because the value of a craft mostly remains with the skill of the artisan and that skill cannot be sold. Further, many of the reasons we think of today for selling a business either did not commonly exist, did not exist at all, or were not socially acceptable or recognized. Such reasons included retirement in old age (most people died before reaching old age), divorce, moving to another city to be with family, burnout, and upward mobility.

Another factor explaining the disparity between real estate-marketing law and business-marketing law is that early advances in entrepreneurship were hampered by conservative laws tending to preserve the status quo. One English law passed in the 1500s, for example, limited the number of looms that could be maintained in the homes of country weavers. Gradually, however, such developments as specialization, technological improvements, marketing techniques, emerging social attitudes, and laws tolerating such changes came into being. Then the industrial revolution, beginning in the late 1700s, shifted emphasis from agriculture to production and from the skills of workers to the capabilities of machines. Even then, the vast majority of the people remained agrarian and rural and the need for laws dealing with the buying and selling of businesses remained slight.

Finally, the twentieth century unfolded, society became urbanized and complex, and businesses became numerous while the reasons for selling businesses became compelling and common. Thus, with a glimpse of history and the realization that the need for laws and regulations for the marketing of businesses developed suddenly and recently while the need for regulations governing the marketing of real estate developed centuries ago, the regulatory disparity between the two markets becomes understandable.

Still, there is another reason that significant regulatory control has not yet reached the small business marketplace. Most of the buy-sell transaction is so much more difficult than meets the eye that few individuals have been able to define it, especially in writing. That's why the small business marketplace is arcane. And that's why it will remain arcane unless it is subjected to intelligent regulation. The difficulty is partly because of the market's innate technicality and partly because whether one is a principal to the transaction or an advisor, the skills required are largely an art as well as a science. (See Chapter 12, Part 2 for my proposal to regulate.)

PART 2:
THE BENEFITS OF READING THIS BOOK

The Benefits for Buyers and Sellers. The primary benefit is that it will increase the probability of starting a deal and completing it. Towards those ends, I've urged buyers and sellers to use a fair-and-reasonable approach in all their dealings, particularly while negotiating the price and terms. (Failure to recognize the importance of the fair-and-reasonable approach is how accountants and lawyers most often hurt their own clients. That's how deals get killed.)

Other benefits include a smoother transaction, shorter time to attain success, better chance of survival for buyers after they take ownership, less chance of taking back a damaged business for sellers who finance, lower fees, and a variety of emotional enhancements including more self-confidence and better human relationships.

To encourage readers to follow the advice I've given, I've tried to explain why to do things as well as how. Understanding why is what moves people to do what they need to do.

I've also included business tips that I've learned through the years, partly from my general experience and partly from my discussions with business owners. Some of the tips were deliberately planned and written; they appear in Part 3 of Chapter 12. The others were written spontaneously as they came to mind and were woven into the text.

How This Book Qualifies for the University Classroom. Although I wrote in the how-to mode, my scope and depth took on the quality of a textbook. For example:

- Chapter 1, "Qualifications for Ownership," presents a comprehensive, detailed analysis of the skills and traits necessary to own and operate a small business.
- Chapter 2, "Business Terms and Concepts," is a combined primer and glossary which describes the world of business and serves as a prerequisite for the chapters that follow. It includes a brief but important analysis of illiquidity. Because this chapter is so basic, experienced business people may want to skip it. But no one should skip the section on illiquidity.
- Chapter 5, "Business Brokers," includes an analysis of the seemingly excessive fees that brokers charge their clients.

(I categorized the brokers' services into marketing functions to explain how the brokers truly earn their fees.)

- Chapter 7, "Appraising," includes a step-by-step description of preparing cash-flow projections. Many if not most CPAs will learn from it. (Note that none of the 40 books I've reviewed in this genre offered the step-by-step description I've provided. That's an interesting deficiency considering that it's so difficult to get bank financing without it, and almost impossible to get SBA participation.)
- And note that several of the chapters in this book directly serve starters of a business as well as buyers.

Collateral Uses of This Book. In addition to being a how-to book for buyers and sellers and a textbook or collateral reader for classes in entrepreneurship, this book may serve as follows:

- A reference book for professional advisors including accountants, lawyers, and commercial loan officers. (Those advisors will best benefit their clients by reading through the entire book.)
- A text for schools offering courses in business brokering.
- A text for real estate schools offering courses in business sales.
- A reference book for real estate agents selling businesses.
- A reference book for chambers of commerce and trade associations to lend to their members.

Note that libraries, even those with good collections in this genre, will find the comprehensiveness of this book a complement to the smaller books they presently have on their shelves.

PART 3:
THE ORGANIZATION AND FEATURES OF THIS BOOK

How This Book Is Organized. Exclusive of the front matter, it is organized into twelve chapters, three appendices, and an index.

Except for Chapters 1 and 2, the chapters are divided into two or more parts. These parts, in turn, are divided into sections identified by their bold-face titles. (The organization of this Preface is typical for the chapters.)

Each chapter is dedicated to a single topic—except Chapter 12, which has three topics—and can be read independently, but with three qualifications: First, the book is an organic whole, so there are threads of logic woven into all of the chapters which afford the book its continuity. Second, as mentioned above, Chapter 2, which describes business terms and concepts, serves as a prerequisite for those inexperienced in business. And third, in Chapters 6 through 9, there is a special continuity with respect to the Acme Widget Corporation.

In consonance with the how-to mode of the book, the chapters appear, more or less, in the natural, chronological order of a typical deal.

The appendices contain important material, some of which could appear in the chapters. I separated them, however, partly because of their length and partly because the material seemed more appropriate for back matter.

The Examples in This Book. There are three kinds of examples: first, there is the ordinary kind woven into the text, occurring copiously, and beginning with the words, "for example."

Second—as a special feature of this book—there are 55 real-life examples. These are snippets taken from actual cases showing how deals are done, both rightly and wrongly. They tend to show what life is like in the trenches. (Not always a pretty sight.) Thus, they are an aid to avoiding the mistakes of the past. Although they have been altered to maintain the confidentiality of the participants, they are, every one of them, actual cases with no added color or exaggeration.

Some of these real-life examples, in part or in whole, are second-hand accounts subject to the inaccuracies of such accounts. Nevertheless, please know that I have tried to get the facts as accurate as possible by listening closely as they were related to me and by asking reasonable questions. In any case, I feel confident that you will benefit from reading them. I also think you will enjoy reading them as much as I enjoyed writing them. In a way, they are the fun part of this book.

Third—also as a special feature of this book—there is a fictional case describing the purchase and sale of the Acme Widget Corporation. This example shows how things tie together going through fact-finding, appraising, negotiating, and financing (Chapters 6 through 9). It also provides a baseline for comparison with your own deals. Although fictional, this example is truer than truth. How can fiction be truer than truth? Because you can say things in fiction that you would avoid for fear of trouble if you told the bare truth. This example too is a part of the fun.

Disciplines and Areas Not Covered. Although I tried to provide virtually everything you will need to get you through your deal, there are three disciplines about which I have offered only minimal advice: taxes, law, and real estate. These disciplines are so extensive and so amply covered by the various experts in their fields that I could not possibly do justice to them nor is there reason for me to try. Moreover, the variances in customs and laws from one geographical or political area to another suggest strongly that you should have your own personal advisors help you with these disciplines. What I have tried to do, however, is offer enough basic information so that you will at least know when you need help, and why you need it.

Another area that I have barely touched on is franchises. That is a field in itself and you should look elsewhere for advice.

One area that I could have written about in greater detail than I have, but chose not to, was the Internet and its relationship to the small business marketplace. Even though, for the purpose of book publicity, I have my own web site—www. monnetpress.com—I still prefer to make connections with buyers and sellers through newspaper advertising, the postal service, the telephone, personal visits, and, of course, email. Nevertheless, I suggest that you log onto some of the sites offering businesses for sale and judge their usefulness for yourself.

Although the information in this book mainly reflects my experience with businesses selling for prices up through the low seven figures—virtually all of which were asset sales as opposed to stock sales—the principles, theories, procedures, and tactics presented here will generally apply to businesses of all types and sizes, including those in the Fortune 500. As a precaution, however, if you are dealing with businesses selling for prices much beyond my range of experience, it would be wise to seek additional advice from other sources. Along that line, I can recommend *How To Do a Leveraged Buyout or Acquisition* by Nicholas Wallner, Ph. D. and J. Terrence Greve, MBA, (Buyout Publications, Inc., San Diego, California, 1984).

Best Wishes and Grand Endeavors. And now, I offer my enthusiastic best wishes to you as you begin your endeavors in one of life's great events, the buying and selling of a small business.

ACKNOWLEDGMENTS

Several persons reviewed portions of the manuscript and offered suggestions. These included my friend and brokering colleague, Bud Howe (who reviewed the entire work); my lawyer, Tom Mendelson; bank vice president and commercial loan officer, John A. Novatny; and former publisher's editor, Amy Ost.

I enjoyed writing the book and, sometimes, even seeking a publisher. There were times, however, when my horizons seemed so far away. That was when the friendliness, advice, and words of encouragement I received were so helpful towards sustaining my spirit and getting the job done. To each of the above, I express my heartfelt appreciation.

CREDO

Treat Others as You Would Be Treated

CHAPTER 1
Qualifications for Ownership

At the beginning of every deal, no single concern is more important than the buyer's ability to own and operate the business. If that ability is not made immediately clear, the seller should politely dismiss the buyer. Otherwise, the seller will be wasting precious time and effort with a buyer who has little chance of obtaining bank financing or of leasing the premises.

Sometimes a poorly qualified buyer gets financed by a seller who doesn't know what he or she is doing. Then the seller is at great risk of taking back a damaged business. Also at risk if the business fails are the employees who may lose their jobs; the suppliers and landlord who may lose their receivables; the customers who may lose their deposits; the buyer who may lose his or her down payment, credit rating, and self image; and the whole community which may lose the income and prestige of a well managed business (see Real-Life Example 9.1, page 343).

For these key reasons, the buyer's qualifications rank first in importance, and first in the chronological order of the deal.

This chapter is dedicated to examining those qualifications, comparing their relative importance, and showing how they might apply in a variety of situations.

Basic Qualifications for Ownership. There are several factors contributing to a buyer's qualifications to own and operate a business. These include general education, general experience which contributes to overall wisdom and maturity, special training in the pertinent trade or industry, direct experience in the type of business being bought, and marks of excellence such as promotions and accomplishments which distinguish better performers from lesser ones. Some judgment is required to assign relative values to these factors but the most important is successful experience in the type of business being bought. That's because it provides the buyer with knowledge of the problems peculiar to the business and with knowledge of how to solve them. It also provides the buyer with the touch of reality so often required to rid a person of his or her illusions.

Some examples of how buyers qualify for the businesses they buy will help explain what is meant by the qualification factors mentioned above. These examples will also demonstrate how some weaknesses may be judged acceptable if offset by compensating strengths. The examples are actual cases with details altered to mask identities.

Example 1.1 The business for sale is a machine shop with no established product line (such shops are called job shops because they usually must bid for each job they work on), 20 employees, and gross sales of $1.7 million.

The prospective buyer has a master's degree in engineering. In just two years out of college, he joined a Fortune 500 company as Chief Industrial Engineer in a branch location. During the next eight years he won two promotions leading to quality control manager in charge of three QC supervisors, 75 hourly workers, all technical and administrative activities, and the development of working relationships with the customers. He also was charged with selection and installation of new equipment, in which capacity he traveled to and closely worked with several machine tool builders in the United States, Taiwan, and Japan. This buyer had exceptionally strong qualifications but with two shortcomings: relatively little experience actually operating a machine, and little cost-estimating experience in a competitive environment (cost-estimating skill is critical in a job shop). These shortcomings were acceptable because they were partly outweighed by his strengths and because the seller contractually agreed to stay for two years, allowing ample time for learning and transition.

Example 1.2 The business for sale is a fast-food restaurant with 45 employees and annual gross revenues in seven figures.

The buyer has a university degree in an unrelated field and ten years' experience in owning and managing a cafeteria. The fast-food restaurant differs from the cafeteria in several important respects, raising questions about the validity of the buyer's experience. It produces three times the revenues of the cafeteria, it has substantially longer hours, and it employs waiters to provide table service. Other circumstances, however, are closely similar: some menu items and prices are comparable and both the restaurant and the cafeteria have largely up-scale clienteles. An hourly employee, not a relative, operates the cafeteria cash register evidencing that the buyer knows how to manage cash. Turnover of the buyer's employees is almost nonexistent, evidencing his ability to hire and to supervise. Nearby competition is keen suggesting his ability to manage closely and to survive. Additionally, the buyer had not purchased the cafeteria. He had started with an empty storefront, negotiated an attractive long-term lease, and designed the layout with a consultant's help. He had also purchased the equipment, hired the employees, purchased the inventory of supplies, and advertised the opening of his cafeteria, all with considerable risk but also with obvious success. Thus, the ability of this buyer to take over the short-order restaurant is not certain but is so well evidenced that he can be judged well qualified and an excellent risk.

Example 1.3 The business offered for sale is a small neighborhood restaurant (28 seats) selling pizza, sandwiches, and beer. The owner makes a modest living but personal problems force a distress sale.

The buyer is a young man with ten years' experience in a popular gourmet restaurant who has resigned to spend full time searching for a restaurant of his own. He has relatively little cash and no credentials to speak of outside of his previous employment which, as it turns out, is a very good credential. There he had started as a bus boy and worked his way up to kitchen manager, with the entire kitchen staff, including the buyers, reporting to him. He had not controlled the dining area but had learned its operation through close association with the restaurant personnel. By virtue of his successful experience and his stability there is little doubt that he is qualified to own and manage a restaurant.

Example 1.4 The business for sale is a small manufacturing company with an established product line, about a third of which is patented. It is a high-quality line with a large potential market that the seller never tried to develop because of his aversion to selling. Sales in a good year approach seven figures but have dwindled recently to less than $200,000 because of the owner's failing health. After 30 years in business, the owner is forced to sell. Manufacturing is fairly simple and can be taught (although it possibly could be more difficult than it looks). Sales need to be improved sharply to make a turnaround.

The buyer is a husband-and-wife team. The husband has a bare modicum of manufacturing experience and no experience in supervising, but he has 20 successful years as a salesman and he knows how to make cold calls (in a cold call, a salesperson calls on a prospective customer without benefit of referral, prior announcement, or introduction of any kind). The wife has strong secretarial experience and is personable. She will run the office and the in-house retail shop and will provide general supervision for the shop workers while her husband is out on calls. This team is not ideal but is well matched to the main need of the business, and therefore qualified despite shortcomings in manufacturing and supervising. An important factor is that if manufacturing problems should arise beyond the capability of the buyer, a consultant could always be hired.

Example 1.5 The business for sale is a small bar in a rough neighborhood. The only food officially sold is prepackaged snacks such as potato chips and pretzels, but the owner keeps lunch meat in the refrigerator and will sell a sandwich to a hungry customer.

The buyer's only qualification is that he has been a bartender for 12 years at a lounge in a prestigious hotel. He obviously knows how to tap a barrel or mix a cocktail. When asked if he can handle the rough clientele he will be serving, he replies that if you can handle a soused CEO or a trial lawyer drowning his sorrows, you can handle anyone. This buyer's qualifications appear adequate.

Example 1.6 The business for sale is a small but well-established sewer-contracting company with a very good reputation.

The buyer is a plumbing-contracting company which will benefit synergistically from combining the overhead of the two companies and from being able to bid an entire sewer-and-plumbing contracting job without having to share the profit with a sewer company. The owner has never laid a sewer nor estimated a sewer cost but, with the help of subcontractors, he has bid any number of sewer jobs along with his plumbing jobs. His overall career success, the close similarity of his present business to the business being bought, and the availability of a consultant should he need one, qualify this buyer for ownership of this company.

The other factors important to acquiring a business (cash commitment and so on) will be dealt with later. For now, a buyer's abilities and character traits will be examined because those are more important than anything else and because they are chronologically a priority.

The Elements of Good Management. Small businesses, like everything else in life, require skill and hard work to manage successfully. Skill and hard work, however, do not always bring success. Small businesses are known for their high failure rates and these high rates lead to an inquiry as to their causes. The purpose of the inquiry is to better understand the importance of the qualifications for ownership. Although an itemized list of the causes of business failure could be made, all causes probably can be summarized into two categories, poor management or poor luck. Examples of causes sometimes thought of as poor luck but which can and usually should be attributed to poor management are undercapitalization, poor sales, employee theft, employee turnover, and equipment failure. Examples of causes which genuinely may be attributed to poor luck are customers' loss of jobs, cancellation of contracts beyond the business owner's foresight or control, wars, tornadoes, and major changes in regulatory control. The line between poor management and poor luck is not always clear but, for now, that is not important. What is important is that the elements of good management—at least some of them, anyway—be identified, and that their relationship to business success be recognized.

The elements of good management are simply the skills and character traits required to manage successfully. To determine those skills and traits, it is necessary to understand the tasks which a manager must perform or delegate. A few of these tasks have already been mentioned in the examples above. Following is a fuller sampling of such tasks (not all of these tasks would apply to all businesses):
- Hire employees.
- Supervise employees.
- Discharge employees.
- Evaluate the clientele.
- Design the goods, including prices, to suit the clientele.

- Design the decor to suit the clientele.
- Arrange the service to suit the clientele.
- Evaluate the competition.
- Adjust the goods, services, prices, and decor to the competition.
- Purchase materials to meet the requirements of quality and price.
- Manufacture or perform with consistently adequate quality.
- Assure full quality from suppliers.
- Assure full quantity from suppliers.
- Prevent or minimize employee theft.
- Prevent or minimize supplier theft.
- Comply with a variety of governmental codes.
- Manage finances.
- Manage cash.

Some of the skills and traits required to perform these tasks are obvious but some are not. For example, the hiring of an employee—a critical task for most small business owners—requires some knowledge of the job the employee is to perform and it also requires the ability to determine whether the prospective employee is capable of performing or learning that job. That much is obvious. What is not obvious is that hiring an employee also requires the ability to persuade a capable prospect, who by virtue of his or her capability has some choice in where he or she works, that employment at the business in question will be beneficial for the prospect as well as for the owner. Also not obvious is that hiring an employee requires enough patience to wait for the right prospect to apply, and enough mental toughness to reject poor prospects who show too little promise to risk employing.

The above example of hiring an employee illustrates the difference between the skills and traits that obviously are necessary and those that are also necessary but not obvious. Such hidden skills and traits are not mere touches of elegance occasionally useful and therefore only of marginal value. They are an integral part and requirement of the daily routine of managing a business and, therefore, an important and perhaps critical aspect of success.

Another example to illustrate hidden skills and traits is the task of purchasing quality supplies, particularly those that are perishable or that have limited shelf lives. This task requires patience to find acceptable quality, mental toughness to reject inferior quality, persuasion to get the best or at least appropriate quality from the suppliers, and enough skill of discrimination to know the difference. Moreover, there are other deeper, more hidden tiers of skills and traits necessary to successfully manage a business. Examples of such super-hidden skills and super-hidden traits are the ability to discern the difference between patience and excessive caution and the difference between mental toughness and recalcitrance.

Additional skills and traits of both obvious and hidden nature could be shown but the point is already established that the talents necessary to manage a business are more numerous and less apparent than meets the eye and that the failure to recognize them probably accounts for many if not most business failures. Now the obvious question is how to determine which prospective business owners are likely to possess these qualities and which ones are not. The answer, suggested above but which bears repeating, is that the buyer's record of success is the best evidence available.

Looking now at the question from a different view, one of the qualifications for ownership that usually escapes attention is a would-be owner's healthy state of mind. Although it is beyond the scope of this book to explore this factor in depth, it should be noted that a person in mental distress is not in the right state of mind to commit to something so complex and so risky as buying a business. Such situations as divorce, loss of a loved one, family dispute, or any other emotionally draining problem should be allowed to stabilize before thinking seriously about buying a business. Anyone involved in a transaction where doubt exists as to the state of the buyer's mind should gently inquire to determine if there actually is a problem. If there is and if the doubt persists, the buyer should be advised to see a professional counselor such as a psychologist or a social worker. If the advice is not accepted and/or the problem persists, the person providing the financing should be told of the possible problem, but only after checking with a lawyer to guard against committing a civil wrong.

One factor affecting a buyer's state of mind is his or her reason for wishing to buy a business. That's important not only for a mental check but also for a better understanding of the thinking involved and the goals that are set.

Reasons for Buying a Business. In light of all of the demands, aggravations, and financial risks of owning a business, a person's reasons for buying should be tested to be sure that they will hold up during ownership. There are three kinds of reasons for buying a business: right reasons, wrong reasons, and an arguable reason. Having the right reasons is a qualification for ownership while having the wrong reasons is a disqualification. In the following discussion, there are two underlying premises: one is that a person's primary motivation in life is to be happy. The other is that happiness is only partly a state of affairs; it is also a state of mind. Happiness, therefore, and, by inference, the type of business that will bring happiness, is as limitless as the variety of the human condition. So are the reasons for buying.

Right Reasons for Buying a Business. The following elaborations of some of the more important reasons will help determine whether owning a business will serve a buyer's needs and whether, therefore, the buyer is qualified for ownership.

One common reason for ownership is to attain financial independence. That can mean the ability to earn and save enough money to live without outside help, or it can mean the ability to earn a wage based on the business owner's own criteria of performance instead of the criteria of others. With respect to the former, attempting to attain such independence may result in success, failure, or something in between. The buyer therefore must keep in mind that the probability of success is largely related to the degree of success in his or her previous career. Attempting to achieve independence through business ownership in the face of a strong possibility of business failure suggests that a person may be better off with the security of stable employment, even though corporate or institutional employment itself has many risks. In any case, this form of financial independence is relative, not absolute.

With respect to the latter meaning of independence, business owners may set their own criteria of performance but they are graded by the criteria of their customers while their performance is dependent on the performance of their employees. Thus, this form of financial independence is also relative, not absolute. Relativity notwithstanding, financial independence in either of its forms is a valid reason for buying a business.

Another common reason for buying is to become autonomous, which means to be in control. Autonomy, however, is relative since a business owner is responsible in one way or another to customers, employees, suppliers, and the government. When the business runs smoothly, physical autonomy is real since the owner has much control over the entire range of activity. When problems occur such as the loss of a key employee or breakdown of equipment, the owner may have to work long hours. Then autonomy may seem like an illusion. Under such circumstances an owner may have to remind himself that the greatest value of autonomy may be little more than the sheer feeling of it. This will be especially true if one owns a business in which the daily activity is something that is loved and because loving it is the reason the buyer made the commitment to own. Then working shorthanded into the night to fill orders, do paperwork, or repair equipment becomes both a benefit and an expression of autonomy because the buyer is doing what he or she has chosen to do.

Another right reason is to hire employees—or contractors—to carry out one's orders. Having others to share the work magnifies the owner's capabilities while leaving him or her free to focus on other tasks, or simply to have more free time.

To work to one's own ethical standards instead of a former employer's is a very personal matter that the buyer must handle to his or her own satisfaction. In some industries, ethical standards are mandated, at least in part, by state or federal regulations. Certain types of hiring discrimination, for example, are prohibited by federal law. Thus, an owner's ability to set his own standards is relative, not absolute.

To gain the prestige of business ownership is partly real and partly imagined depending on the variety of human viewpoints and perceptions. That a person would seek ownership of a business to gain prestige in the eyes of family or friends may seem sad for its paucity of self-esteem but such feelings are a part of being human. An owner's improved self-image therefore is important and it constitutes a genuine benefit of buying a business. It is not quite a right reason, however, unless accompanied by other more substantial reasons such as having enough skill to run the business, justifying one's own high esteem.

To play a bigger role in one's daily affairs and to feel closer to and more a part of the community because of it, as compared to what one did and the way one felt as an employee, is a valid reason to buy a business if it really gives the buyer satisfaction. Note that such a motive might be compared to becoming a bigger fish in a smaller pond. There is some truth to that comparison. Still, one might tell others that the new pond, though smaller, is warmer, brighter, and cleaner and the fish therein more entertaining.

To serve the community is a noble reason to own a business if ownership itself expands one's effectiveness in that regard. Prospective buyers and everyone else should keep in mind, though, that the community is served by any and all persons who are lawfully occupied. A special case where service to the community might receive official recognition and certain benefits occurs when the business being bought would probably be forced to close because of such reasons as the owner's retirement or failing health. In some such cases where jobs are preserved or increased, the Small Business Administration offers special financing to encourage purchases. This financing, known as SBA type 504, is discussed in Chapter 9.

Buying a business to provide a family economic unit has benefits and dangers. Some of the benefits are the trustworthiness of family members as partners; the assured presence of at least one owner-manager when another is ill or vacationing or when a business operates two or three shifts a day; the lower turnover of owner-employees and the resultant benefits (such as reduced job training and better continuity of relationships with suppliers and customers); the greater dedication of owners; and the greater flexibility of payroll when sales are down.

Some dangers of a family economic unit are that family relationships may be strained or ruined; a departing owner-employee may be difficult or impossible to replace; a bright ambitious employee not part of the family may leave for lack of advancement; and the family may suffer greater economic devastation for lack of diversified income if the business should fail. Another danger, a subtle one since it is created by one of the more desirable benefits, is that a seemingly trustworthy blood relative can disappear along with the cash, equipment, and inventory. Such calamity is unlikely but can become less unlikely if the relative in question has been subordinated with perceived unfairness and has been left to brood about it.

Finally, to love what one is doing and to be all that one can be are the best and highest reasons to buy a business. In 1954, psychologist Abraham Maslow (1908-1970) published a landmark work posing a hierarchy of human needs. He described the most basic need as physiological: food, water, and shelter. He described successively higher needs as security, a sense of belonging, and esteem from oneself and from others. He called the highest human need self-actualization, the creative process whereby dreams become the goals that one strives to attain. It also means developing the special potential one has to lead, to create, to perform, to enhance, to coordinate, to serve the community, or to do whatever it is that one must do to bring out not just those finest talents that all human beings possess in one way or another, but those talents which will best serve a person's aspirations, desires, or dreams. That is when one loves what one is doing. And that is when one becomes all that one can be.

Owning a business is not the only path to high attainment. One may also rise to the top in such fields as the arts, entertainment, athletics, corporate or institutional employment, teaching, professional practices, the trades, and so on. But for some individuals, business ownership may be the only way to attain self-actualization, to love what one is doing, and to be all that one can be.

Of all the reasons one may have for owning a business—autonomy, wealth, prestige, and so on—love, or at least resolute fondness, of one's duties in the daily affairs of ownership counts most towards sustaining a balance of pleasure and profit. Whether one owns a business or not, love of one's daily activity is the basic stuff of happiness.

The importance of loving one's work rings true when low sales, loss of key employees, new competitors, technical problems, and other adversities steal the glamour and force an owner to work long, financially unrewarding hours while wondering if and when it will ever pay off. Buying a business, then, is like entering a marriage; it is for better or for worse. It is also what best enables a person to be all that he or she can be.

Wrong Reasons for Buying a Business. The reasons suggested here are wrong because they are unwise, not because they are immoral. Most of them become right reasons or at least secondary benefits when accompanied by one or more right reasons. Examples are to escape distressful employment, to shore up one's pride, to show one's family that one can also succeed, to satisfy the longing of one's spouse thereby attaining peace in the household, and to create a niche for a retarded person to occupy himself or herself with dignity.

These reasons are wrong because they lack the necessary love for the business that is so vital for success. They are wrong because the buyer's mind is handicapped by distress, unhappiness, or a disturbance of its peace and because overcoming such handicaps to think logically and objectively through all the complexities of buying a business and making it grow requires inordinate talent that most individuals do not have. One may escape from unhappiness only to find oneself in a losing business which is simply unhappiness in another form.

An Arguable Reason for Buying a Business. A reason seldom referred to overtly is the opportunity to systematically report less than one's true income when paying taxes. Following is a sampling of the justifications for cheating. It is drawn from the cultural ambiance of modern America, an ambiance that could be described as corrosive:

- To sustain a level playing field against competitors who, presumably, are cheating.
- The approval of it implied by hypocrisy at the national level.
- The approval implied by unreasonable partisanship, also at the national level.

- The inferred approval of greed established by legal gambling in all its forms including state lotteries with absurdly colossal prizes.
- The near-universality (as one may reasonably surmise) of cheating.
- The failure of the IRS (and of the United States Congress which sets the rules) to implement a meaningful program of discovery and prosecution.

Illustration 1.1

*"I know the corporate policy, Worthington. This is **all you can be.**"*

- The laxness and sometime corruption of traditional guardians including stock exchanges, accounting firms, and directors on corporate boards (not to mention their resistance to reform).
- The decline of religiously based absolute morality with nothing officially authorized to replace it.
- The decline of religiously based meaning to life along with the corresponding lack of a clearly stated national purpose at the

personal level, and the disorientation and spiritual impoverishment resulting from it.

- The seemingly unfair salary levels of corporate chiefs, movie stars, and professional athletes.

Following is a sampling of the justifications for full disclosure of income. It is drawn from the cultural ambiance of modern America, an ambiance that could be described as wholesome:

- The absence of a need to cheat to remain competitive in a well-managed business.
- The climate of disapproval of cheating sustained by the news media.
- The climate of disapproval of cheating sustained by the vast majority of producers of books, plays, movies, and radio and television programs.
- The realization that modest incomes gain little from cheating while large incomes do not require it (a point taught to the author by his father).
- The illegality of cheating.
- The threat of serious penalties if caught.
- The ascendancy of secular morality based on principles of reason and humanity.
- The ascendancy of secular meaning to life based on principles of reason and humanity, and the orientation and spiritual enrichment resulting from it.
- To be morally whole (which is the meaning of integrity).
- To sleep peacefully in the quiet night.

In the author's opinion, the arguments for and against cheating are largely correct and can be amply documented although they are largely subjective. Further, the arguments may be countered and the counters themselves may be countered. The purpose here is to provide the reader with some understanding of the issue so as to be better prepared to deal with it. This preparation is one of the qualifications for ownership. The topic will be discussed further in appropriate sections in the text.

Reasons for Selling a Business. Although the reasons for selling a business are primarily the seller's concern, being able to understand those reasons helps in two ways to qualify a buyer for ownership. It prepares the buyer by removing some of the mystery as to why anyone would sell a viable business, and it warns the buyer to avoid as much as possible the conditions which cause people to sell. As shown below, the reasons may be either business or personal.

Business Reasons for Selling	Personal Reasons for Selling
1. Undercapitalization	1. Retirement
2. Poor sales	2. Burnout
3. Poor profits	3. Health
4. Declining industry	4. Divorce
5. New competition	5. Relocation
6. Technological change	6. Other interest
7. New federal regulations	7. Death of spouse
8. Expansion to new quarters	8. Dislike
9. Synergistic merger	9. Family problem
10. Relocation near customers	10. Marriage
11. Lost lease	11. Long hours
12. And so forth	12. And so forth

Business reasons may be divided into three groups: distress-oriented (reasons 1-7), success- or profit-oriented (reasons 8–10), and other (reason 11). Some reasons may mask others: burnout as an excuse for poor sales is one example; citing divorce when new competitors have moved into the neighborhood is another. Nevertheless, sometimes good businesses come onto the market for genuinely personal reasons and sometimes distressed businesses can be turned around. Thus, a buyer's caution is always warranted but it should be exercised with an open mind. Needless to say, a well-qualified buyer with the skills and character traits extolled earlier in the chapter will be best able to cull the market.

Cautious buyers should look closely at these reasons to be sure that none would adversely apply to them at present or in the foreseeable near future.

Absentee Ownership. Buyers frequently ask about absentee ownership. While such ownership can be successful, it is considerably more difficult than active ownership on the premises. There are several reasons: employees have a greater tendency to steal when the owner is absent, especially when the absence is something they can count on, and that same tendency holds true for suppliers and customers. With respect to standards of productivity, quality of goods and services, and customer relations, employees feel less conscientious about them if an owner is not present to offer guidance and approval and to show concern by his or her mere presence. Employee morale suffers in absentee ownership so turnover increases, especially among well-qualified, ambitious workers who seek recognition and wholesome surroundings and who, by virtue of their above-average ability, are usually welcomed and even lured by competitors. And customers like the security, personal warmth, and better-maintained premises afforded by the owner's presence. Despite these problems, successful absentee ownership is possible if the business is well designed and/or the owner is exceptionally well qualified. Two actual examples will illustrate the point.

> **Example 1.7** A neighborhood tavern is staffed by two bartenders who are hired through the bartenders' union and who are paid union wages. The tavern is open daily from seven in the morning until midnight. The owner makes two visits a day, one in midmorning just to look things over and to say hello to the customers (who give him a noticeably warm greeting) and the bartenders, and one in the evening to look again and to pick up the cash. The owner does all the ordering of inventory and supplies from his second business, a small restaurant about a mile distant where he works full time. When asked how he minimizes theft and keeps order, he replies that the tavern was the first business he owned and that he worked it full time for two years until he took over the restaurant. Having worked it full time, he knows almost ex-

actly what the sales should be in the mornings, afternoons, and evenings, and what they should be by the week, by the month, and by the season of the year. He also knows the personality, the character, and the nuances of his business in most situations. When he walks into his tavern, he knows in an instant by the number of customers and the looks on their faces if things are not well and when he walks into the storeroom he knows in an instant by how high the beer cases are stacked, both empty and full, if sales are not right. Further, the union assures certain minimum standards of performance by its bartenders and it will always send a replacement if one of the bartenders should be ill.

Notice that this is a good arrangement for everybody. The customers are happy—even though they would prefer the owner to be present—because the tavern is professionally staffed, it is always open on time, and it is a good place to socialize. The bartenders are happy because they have steady employment with some security. The union is happy because of the prominence of its role in making this a successful business and also because it has a plum to hand out to a good worker. And the owner is happy because he makes a good profit with few aggravations.

Example 1.8 A coin-operated laundry is located in a city neighborhood where an owner reasonably could be fearful of vandalism. The laundry is open seven days per week from eight in the morning until eight in the evening. There is always an attendant at the laundry and the owner has at least three or four attendants to take turns and to fill in for each other when necessary. Qualifications to be an attendant are that they must be retired or physically handicapped, they must be courteous, and they must reside within a block or two of the laundry. They each have keys to open the doors in the morning and lock them at night but only the owner has keys to the equipment.

They attendants must keep the premises and the equipment clean; they must call the owner if equipment fails or if other problems arise; and they must maintain order. In return, they may take drop-off laundry and set their own prices and, after putting coins into the machines to wash and dry the clothes, they may keep what is left over.

Notice again that everyone is happy but in this case the design is elegant. The attendants make money while adding purpose to their lives and while lifting their status in the community. The customers wash their clothes where the premises are clean and safe, where the equipment is in good repair, and where they can socialize if they want to. The neighborhood benefits from the renewed ambiance which any well-managed business provides. And best of all, the owner enjoys enhanced sales and profits with no fear of vandalism during the day because of the appreciative attendants and customers who treat the store as their own nor during the night, partly because of the iron bars on the windows and doors but also partly because the appreciation of the attendants and customers and their friends and neighbors is continued around the clock. Now notice that the laundry owner's skills were not much different than those required to run almost any laundry whether absentee or not. He mainly kept the equipment in good repair and made sure that it was always attended. What made his absentee business work well was the good design.

The tavern owner had a good design too but in addition, he knew the business so well that he could turn his back on the cash and still know whether there was any significant theft. Thus, these two businesses fit the pattern of most small absentee-owned businesses. They require any combination of good design and much better-than-average management skills to be successful. Further notice the warm greeting the tavern owner received. This is the greeting of customers who not only are happy but who think highly of the owner. Such greetings imply that the owner has been good to his customers and has always treated them right. They further imply that any misconduct observed by the customers would be brought to the owner's attention.

Partnership. A partnership, as explained in Chapter 2, is a joint venture of two or more legal entities such as two persons, two corporations, or one of each. In this context, however, discussion is limited to the human factors whether a corporation is involved or not.

Partnerships, in general, are trickier to enter into than other business relationships because they require both prospective partners (assuming only two) to possess keen insight into the choice of the other. Thus, there are two opportunities for a mistake which otherwise would not be present. If the reason for the partnership is to obtain sufficient capital to purchase the business, a mistake is easy to prevent simply by counting the money. If the reason is for each to provide one or more management skills lacking in the other, a mistake is more likely. The probability of such a mistake may be minimized by each preparing, in workmanlike manner and with an attitude respectful of the other, a written description of skills for the other's edification. Even if both have the skills the other is counting on, if one dies or becomes disabled, the other would be left with a problem. Thus, in this one respect by itself, a partnership is twice as risky as a sole proprietorship.

Note that a twin-engine airplane is to a single-engine airplane what a partnership is to a sole proprietorship. If the airplane can fly on one engine, the risk of a crash due to engine failure is cut in half. If it cannot fly on one engine, the risk is doubled.

Regardless of the underlying reason for the partnership, emotional problems always threaten to wreck the alliance. Such problems usually involve equality—or the perception thereof—of title, rank, workload, or type of work. Some would describe this as a question of fairness while others would call it vanity. In one actual case, two relatives formed a corporation to buy a business, each putting up the same amount of cash, and agreed to take turns being president during alternate years. One of them, during the period of his vice presidency, when the question of title came up on two separate occasions in the normal course of business, described his rank with lowered head, then nodded up and added, "but I'll be president soon."

The obvious question of ability to trust always must be dealt with, as must the question of the trustworthiness of the partner. Bowing to the realities of an imperfect world, each partner's becoming bonded would tend to minimize the risk.

Other human factors dealing with ability to get along with each other or to tolerate each other would have to be considered. Such factors would include how one dresses, one's propensity to lose one's patience or temper, how one talks to customers, whether one plans to cheat on taxes or to cheat the suppliers or the customers, whether one plans to deal in quality vs. quantity, whether one is willing to clean the toilets, and so forth.

It is obvious from the above considerations that the qualifications to enter a partnership are more complex than they are to work alone. There is also added risk to the venture without even considering one's liability for the other's debts. It is probably advisable to have a written agreement even if the partners are the best of friends or blood relatives. In all cases, a lawyer's counsel should be sought and each partner should have his or her own lawyer.

Based on the author's observations of spouses playing mixed doubles tennis, a husband and wife thinking of going into business together should think twice about it. Placing a happy marriage into a new situation may reveal heretofore-undiscovered shortcomings which may be found intolerable. The possible results are a failed business and a broken marriage (not to mention being wiped out in straight sets).

There is one style of partnership which minimizes the risks though still requiring stringent qualifications. It was described to the author in 1982 by the late Bert Steppig (1945–1985) who was known in the St. Louis area for his ability to set up partnerships which flourish. Steppig described his usual arrangement thus: he always is on the lookout for someone who is able to manage the business but who lacks the cash to buy, and he also is always on the lookout for a small business for sale, particularly in his specialty which was retailing, especially groceries. When he is able to match a business with a qualified partner, he arranges bank financing. The partner pays no money down but both he and his partner sign the note, making the partner feel responsible to the bank. The partner gets a fair salary for managing. Whatever is left after all expenses are paid is split evenly between Steppig and his partner. Steppig's role is absentee partner and advisor. Otherwise, the partner has complete charge of operating the business. Steppig never touches the cash unless an emergency requires him to. Otherwise never. His accountant does the bookkeeping and the tax returns. Steppig strives to convey a feeling of trust in the partner in order to evoke high morale and mutual trust. He avoids any type of business he is not familiar with. He has been cheated, but that is part of the game. Most of his partners, however, have been honest, though partly, he thinks, out of fear and respect. If a business gets into trouble, he offers advice. In case of insolvable dispute, Steppig sets a price and offers to either buy his partner's half or sell his own half. Out of 29 stores, 28 were making money and one was marginal.

From this description, it appears that Steppig's design of his partnerships eliminated several of the usually inherent problems. He had enough talent to compensate for an overestimate of a partner's ability. There were never any problems of equality or vanity because he was always clearly the superior talent. Moreover, Steppig's absence from the business minimized any personality conflicts. It also eliminated any question of who performs menial tasks or who's responsible for missing cash. Although Steppig did not say so, he probably incorporated each business individually with himself as president.

Buying a Business vs. Starting a Business. A basic question most prospective buyers ask is whether it is easier to start a business or to buy one. In general, it takes more experience and more talent to start a business because of the possible fundamental mistakes for which there are no easy remedies. For example, the site selected for a retail liquor store usually should be on the same side of the street as the evening rush-hour traffic. That enables drivers on their way home from work to make an easy right turn into the lot to buy their cold six-packs of beer, and an easy right turn out. If a business is started instead of bought, all or nearly all of these fundamental decisions must be made correctly or the business either will fail or will yield disappointing income. If a business is bought instead of started, the buyer has some assurance, through the test of time, that the fundamental decisions have been made correctly by a predecessor or that some way has been found to offset the mistakes. On the other hand, buying a business has dangers and problems of its own and these too can lead to failure. Comparing some of the tasks required to start a business or to buy one will help a would-be entrepreneur to decide which course he or she is better qualified for.

Start a Business	Buy a Business
Imagine concept	Find a business
Study demographics	Get the facts
Estimate sales and expenses	Appraise
Design operation	Negotiate price and terms
Select site	Get financing
Lease premises	Choose lawyer and accountant
Lay out floor plan	Prepare purchase contract
Do leasehold improvements	Sign lease and contract
Shop for equipment	Begin operations
Hire employees	
Advertise for customers	
Begin operations	

Note that these lists are simplified to emphasize the comparison between buying and starting a business and therefore should not be taken as complete guides for implementing either course. Also, they are merely to illustrate the idea of the comparison and should not be taken to apply to any and all types of businesses. Nevertheless they point to some of the comparative dangers and problems of starting a business vs. buying one. To decide which course to follow, one has to determine not only which group of tasks one is better prepared to handle, but also how many weeks, months, or years it will take to begin operations. Then the cost of buying can be compared to the cost of starting, taking into account not only the out-of-pocket costs but also the income denied during the time leading to the start of operations vs. the income denied while developing a clientele.

One idea for getting into business that is a kind of compromise between starting and buying is to find the site of a failed or abandoned business and lease the real estate, equipment, and fixtures. The obvious question of why the previous business failed should be looked into but the mere fact that a failure or even a half dozen failures occurred at the site in question should not by itself be grounds for rejection. There are many reasons for business failure but site selection, though important and sometimes critical, is not usually involved. Usually it is poor management.

The advantages and cost savings of taking over a failed site are especially attractive to any business requiring heavy investments in leasehold improvements. (Leasehold improvements are those made to the real estate by a tenant; see page 28.) Examples of costly leasehold improvements for a manufacturing operation which sometimes can be taken over at little or no cost by a new tenant are high-voltage, high-amperage, and three-phase electrical service and circuits; in-floor conduits for electricity, gas, air, water, or telephone; overhead cranes for heavy lifting; and doors large enough to drive a truck through. Examples of similar possibilities for leasehold cost savings for a restaurant operation are exhaust hood and ancillary items such as fire-suppressors and replacement air; plumbing, gas, and electrical work for the kitchen; and carpeting and other decorative items for the dining area (although these may compromise the decor). Other businesses offering the possibility of great cost savings when leasehold improvements already exist are coin-operated laundries, bowling alleys, cocktail lounges, skating rinks, and so on. Even though these are only small businesses, the cost of leasehold improvements can easily run into six figures.

The large possible savings from leasing a failed or abandoned site notwithstanding, their more important significance is that without them a would-be owner might not be able to afford the type of business of his or her choice. In addition, under the strain of heavy mortgage payments, these savings could represent the difference between failure and survival.

A Final Note on Qualifications for Ownership. This chapter is intended as an objective and analytical approach to determining one's qualifications to own and manage a business. A more subjective list was compiled one day when one of the author's prospective buyers, not exactly sure of himself, asked for a brief description of what it takes to run a business. This list of character traits is very subjective but the author stands by it and offers it for whatever it may be worth to the reader:

1. Honest
2. Fair
3. Self-motivated
4. Happy from within
5. Responsible
6. Energetic
7. Independent
8. Realistically confident
9. Willing to risk
10. Tough when down.

QUESTIONS FOR DISCUSSION
Chapter 1—Qualifications for Ownership

1. Why are compromises often necessary to qualify for ownership?
2. When might compromises weaken the quality of management, and when not?
3. Why is experience in the trade often more important than formal training?
4. True or false: Owning a business provides financial independence, autonomy, and self-determination of ethical standards? Why or why not?
5. With respect to Maslow's Hierarchy of human needs, what's the best way to rise to the top, to be all that you can be?
6. If the pursuit of happiness is the meaning of life, what is the role of cheating on taxes?
7. The business in Real-life Example 1.8 is an inner city, coin-operated laundry with iron bars on the windows and doors to prevent vandalism. Why does the author describe the design of that business as elegant?
8. How is a dual partnership like a twin-engine airplane?

9. How was Bert Steppig so successful at setting up partnerships that work?

10. Is it more difficult to start a business or to buy one?

11. Is it more difficult to absentee manage a business or to manage full time on premises?

12. Considering that this chapter is about qualifications for ownership, does it not strike you as odd that there is hardly a mention of the funds to purchase? What's going on here? Hint: did Bert Steppig worry about funds when choosing his partners?

13. The chapter ends with ten character traits the author thinks are helpful in running a business. Are those traits of equal importance? Would you add or subtract from the list?

CHAPTER 2

Business Terms and Concepts

This chapter explains the terms and concepts used in this book. Most of the explanations are basic but some are slightly elaborate. Although this chapter is a kind of glossary, it is not presented in alphabetical order. Instead, it is in a loosely logical sequence so that the material appearing early in the chapter supports the material appearing later in the chapter. In a technical sort of way, the chapter is a primer to describe the world of business.

An alphabetized list of the terms and concepts appearing in this chapter is included in the index under the heading of "Business Terms and Concepts."

Because the chapter is basic, experienced readers may prefer to pass it by to save time. Such readers should at least skim the chapter while slowing down to peruse new or interesting items. There is probably something in this chapter for everybody. The explanation of illiquidity (page 52) is required reading for everyone, even those most experienced. The explanations of depreciation expense (page 45) and confidant (page 54) also are strongly recommended.

The reader is cautioned that these explanations are not intended to be thorough or exact. They are intended merely to be of sufficient scope and depth for general understanding of the buy-sell transaction. One should always consult with a lawyer and an accountant before making any commitments.

Land, Real Estate, and Real Property. Despite their commonly being used in a loose and casual manner, the terms land, real estate, and real property, have precise technical meanings which are helpful to know. Land is the surface of the earth including the ground below (extended to the center of the earth), and the space above (extended to infinity). Land includes things permanently attached by nature, such as trees and water.

Real estate is land, as defined above, plus man-made improvements such as buildings, pavements, fences, and sewers.

Real property is either land or real estate plus all the legal rights of ownership, such as the right to possess it, control it, sell it, lease it, improve it, and mine it.

Land and such improvements as a house usually bought and sold in the marketplace almost always include the legal rights of ownership. Such properties are properly referred to as real property, not real estate. In practice, however, almost everybody including real estate agents, lawyers, and accountants, generally uses the term "real estate" when what they really mean is real property, and they do this both in speech and in writing. In this book, the term "real estate" will be used in the casual sense unless otherwise specified. Such casual use is harmless as long as the casualness is understood.

Personal Property. Personal property is defined as anything which is not real estate. (Technically, as explained above, personal property is anything which is not real property.) Examples of personal property are a car, clothing, a dog or other pet, a bank account, a United States Savings Bond, a business telephone number, and a piece of furniture not permanently attached to the real estate. Most equipment items associated with a business are considered personal property, including machine tools, computers, telephones, and even such attached items as the triple sink in a restaurant or the large boiler in a laundry. Items essential to making the premises generally functional and livable, such as the washbasin in the rest room and the furnace for heating the building, are usually considered part of the real estate. Some equipment items fall between real estate and personal property depending partly on how they are used and partly, and probably more importantly, on how they are described in writing by the principals in a transaction. Examples of such borderline items are a chandelier, a central air conditioner in a warehouse, a hooked-up mobile home on blocks, or an auxiliary diesel-electric generator in a factory.

Leasehold Improvement. A leasehold improvement is any improvement made to the real estate by a tenant. The tenant generally is the owner of the improvement until the premises are vacated, at which time the improvement becomes the property of the landlord unless removed by the tenant. Leasehold improvements in general have little value if removed from the premises. Examples of leasehold improvements are wallpaper, wall-to-wall carpeting, a privacy fence, a structural support for heavy equipment, and a light fixture.

Legal Entity. Something the existence of which is either recognized or established by the law and which is capable of conducting business.

The Structure of a Business. Under the law, every business has a form or structure defined by law and operating under legal regulations corresponding to that structure. Basically, there are three types of business structures and these are known as sole proprietorship, corporation, and partnership. These structures are described below along with some of their advantages and disadvantages.

Sole Proprietorship. A sole proprietorship is a legal entity consisting of one person (whether married or single) engaged in some form of enterprise. The ease of getting started is the main advantage of operating as a sole proprietor. There are no registrations or fees required and no forms to fill out. Certain municipal licenses may be required which would apply to corporations and partnerships as well. The main disadvantage is that sole proprietors are personally liable for all the losses, debts, and liabilities of the business, in contrast to corporations which have limited liability for their owners though not for the corporations themselves. Other disadvantages are that the ownership of a sole proprietorship cannot be shared nor can it easily be transferred to another owner without a contract.

Corporation. A corporation is a legal entity authorized by and registered with the state. A corporation can conduct business just as a sole proprietorship conducts business, however, it must be operated by one or more persons. The main advantage of a corporation to a small business owner is that personal liability of the owner is limited to the amount invested in the corporation. However, since small corporations are subject to the statistical reality of comparatively high failure rates, they usually are required by their lenders and creditors to be secured by the personal liability of a guarantor, usually the principal owner. Despite this erosion of their limited liability, corporate owners are otherwise protected from unforeseen devastating liabilities of the corporation, such as those caused by large-scale accidents, business losses, and lawsuits. Corporate owners, however, are not necessarily protected from the damages resulting from civil wrongs they may commit as employees of the corporation. Recent trends have further eroded the limited liability described above and legal counsel is recommended.

Ownership in a corporation is documented by certificates known as stock certificates or, for short, stock. The use of stock certificates to document ownership has two advantages important to publicly traded corporations such as those listed on stock exchanges but is usually not important to small, privately owned corporations. When a corporation is sold, the stock is simply signed over to the buyer, making transference of ownership an easy matter. Also, use of certificates allows ownership to be divided into as many parts as desired, making multiple ownership an easy matter. There are various kinds of stock, the most common of which is known simply as common stock. Other kinds of stock are preferred, convertible preferred, voting stock, and so on. Since common stock is the only kind issued by most small business corporations, the other kinds are not covered in this book.

Corporations registered in the state of Missouri are required to file the following information with the Secretary of State: names and residence addresses of directors and officers, name and address of registered agent (whose function is to receive legal notices, correspondence, and the like in behalf of the corporation), and the address of the principal place of business or headquarters. If the corporation operates under a fictitious name, that name also must be registered, although separately. In Missouri, all of this information is in the public realm and may be obtained by writing to the Secretary of State in Jefferson City and enclosing a check for $10.00 for each corporation named.

There are four types of corporations, including general (for-profit), not-for-profit, professional, and other. The general business corporation is the most common. Federal corporate tax laws (subchapter S) allow corporation owners to choose to treat corporate profits as personal income although this choice usually should be made with the advice of an accountant.

Partnership. A partnership is the joining of two or more individuals and/or corporations under a partnership agreement. A partnership is not a legal entity, merely an organization in which the partners act together. One main advantage of a partnership is its ease of formation. A carefully written agreement between the partners is usually advisable even if not legally required. Another advantage is the pooling of the skills, aptitudes, and resources of the partners. Still another advantage is that there are no taxes on partnerships; this allows the profits to flow directly to the partners as in a proprietorship. One disadvantage of partnerships is the possible unlimited liability of each partner for the acts of any of the partners. Another disadvantage is the risk of overvaluing the talent of one's partner, and another disadvantage is the doubled risks of death and disability as described in Chapter 1.

The Concept of a Business. A business is any organization set up to provide goods or services for a profit. A business consists of as much or as little as is necessary to function as such, including equipment, inventory, work in progress, personnel, licenses, the name, structure (proprietorship, etc.), real estate (either leased or owned), customers or customer lists, financing (either debt or equity as explained below), contracts (either written or verbal), telephone number, fax number, web site, written plans or procedures, patents, copyrights, and so on.

Earnings, Profit, and Income. These terms are virtual synonyms, describing the value gained in a transaction or how much remains in a business after expenses have been deducted from sales or revenues. The exact meanings of these terms may vary slightly according to the context.

Operational Earnings. These are earnings produced by the business itself. Excluded are earnings not normally a part of the business, such as interest from cash parked in the corporate savings account or from such non-recurring events as the sale of unneeded equipment.

Internal Revenue Service (IRS). The IRS is the federal agency which administers the tax code devised by the United States Congress.

Small Business Administration (SBA). The SBA is a federally-chartered, non-profit organization created for the sole purpose of encouraging the ownership and operation of small businesses. The SBA is perhaps best known for its financial assistance in the purchase and expansion of small businesses.

Buyer and Seller. A buyer is one who buys and a seller is one who sells. A buyer or a seller may be any legal entity, such as a proprietorship or a corporation.

Principal and Agent. A principal is any legal entity, such as a person or a corporation, with a primary stake in a transaction or in an ownership. For example, the buyer of a small business is a principal in the transaction, as is the seller. An agent is any legal entity who represents another legal entity in a transaction.

Broker and Salesperson. A broker is an agent with the special assignment of matching two legal entities for their mutual benefit. For example, a broker representing the seller of a business will seek a buyer for that business. In this example, the broker is the seller's agent and both the seller and buyer are principals.

The real estate industry has two kinds of agents, brokers and salespersons. Both act as agents but a salesperson is a subordinate and must be supervised by a broker. Generally speaking, the distinction between a broker and a salesperson is important in the real estate industry but not in the buying and selling of a business.

Bank, Savings and Loan Association, Finance Company, and Credit Union. A bank is a for-profit establishment for the custody, loan, exchange, or issue of money, for the extension of credit, and for other financial services. A savings and loan association is like a bank in some respects, including the lending of money, but operates under different federal and state guidelines. A finance company also is similar to a bank but specializes in lending money. A credit union is also similar to a bank but is non-profit and may or may not deal with businesses.

The term "bank" can be used generically when referring to lending institutions in general, as it usually is in this book.

Prime Rate. The prime rate is the rate of interest banks charge when lending to favored, most-viable corporate borrowers such as many of those listed on the New York Stock Exchange. Banks sometimes charge as much as two or two and a half percent above prime when financing the purchase of a small business.

Closing. Closing refers to the final event in a purchase and sale transaction during which the seller receives payment, the buyer receives title to the property, all of the incidentals are completed, and the transaction is thereby closed. Although closing usually occurs within a time frame of about two hours, circumstances sometimes require several days or even several weeks to conclude. See Chapter 12, Part 1 for details.

Job Shop. A job shop is a manufacturer which primarily has no product line of its own but which sells goods designed by other companies. The goods are usually ordered from the manufacturer in specified quantities. When a job shop completes one job, it must look for another job, hence the name. Since job shops must continually bid competitively against other job shops just to remain in business, the accuracy of their cost estimates is critical to their success.

Contract. A contract is any agreement between legal entities wherein one party provides something of value, such as money or goods or services, in exchange for something of value from the other party. The heart of a contract is the meeting of the minds, the mutual, clear understanding as to what is being agreed to. A contract may be written or verbal and in either case is legally binding. A verbal contract is easier to make but harder to prove in court and more subject to misunderstanding. Certain verbal contracts, long-term real estate leases, for example, are prohibited by law. Since a contract is an agreement, the term "agreement" is often used interchangeably for reasons of pleasantness and, sometimes, for subtle tactics.

Escrow and Earnest Deposit. Occasionally it is useful for reasons of security, when a contract is being fulfilled, for an agent who is not a party to the contract to hold in protective custody some of the valuables being exchanged. Such valuables are said to be held in escrow. A typical example of escrow is money held for the buyer of a business by the broker which is delivered to the seller when the seller turns the business over to the buyer.

The money held in escrow in the above example is typically for the purpose of showing the buyer's sincerity. This money is known as earnest money or earnest deposit. While evidence of the buyer's sincerity is sometimes useful, a common reason for an earnest deposit is simply that it is a custom. In the author's opinion, the custom should be questioned and discontinued except as appropriate to the circumstances. Sometimes there are circumstances justifying an earnest deposit by the seller, a buyer giving a non-revocable notice of resignation to his or her employer, for example.

Standard Industrial Code (SIC). The SIC is a federal government designation for labeling all industries and their components by standardized numbers for the purpose of a uniform system of identification and description. The system is described in the reference department of almost any public library. That system, however, was replaced in 1997 by the NAICS described below.

North American Industry Classification System (NAICS). The NAICS has re-placed the SIC. Federal government agencies that collect establishment-based statistics are now required to use NAICS instead of SIC. The codes have been cross-referenced. A description of the NAICS is on its website: www.NAICS.com.

Hidden Earnings, Unrecorded Earnings, and Skim. As used in this book, hid-den earnings are those recorded in the books and records of the business but disguised to look like expenses. The disguise may be legitimate, such as the tax-deductible expenses for attendance at a trade show, or it may be illegiti-mate, such as the personal, non-deductible automotive expenses charged to a corporate credit card.

Unrecorded earnings, if any, are those not recorded in the official books and records of the business. Because they are unrecorded, they are always il-legitimate. Sometimes they are unofficially and separately recorded in which case they are still illegitimate and may be referred to as a second set of books. Unrecorded earnings are often, but not always, in the form of cash.

Skim is a synonym for unrecorded earnings. The name probably derives from the practice of some owners of cash-service businesses who, instead of ringing up all payments for goods and services on the cash register or re-cording them in some other manner, skim some of them right off the store counter directly into their pockets. However, since hidden earnings with il-legitimate disguises have the same effect of cheating on taxes as skim, they also may be referred to as skim. Note that if skimming is done by the owner of the business, the purpose is to cheat on taxes. If done by an employee without the owner's approval, the purpose is to cheat the owner as well as to cheat on taxes.

The practice of skimming, to one degree or another, is probably wide-spread. The author guesses that perhaps 75% of business owners skim delib-erately in substantial amounts while most others skim incidentally in smaller amounts. See Chapter 6 for details on estimating the skim preparatory to appraising.

Turnaround. A turnaround is a business suffering from severely declining sales, profits, or other malaise requiring skilled management to restore viability. Use of the term "turnaround" implies that the problem is solvable but by no means guarantees it.

Eminent Domain. Eminent domain is the absolute right of the government to acquire property for public use or benefit, albeit at a fair price. For example, a street-widening project on a major thoroughfare may require razing the commercial shops on one or both sides of the street. The real estate and businesses to be razed would be bought by the city government or by a private firm empowered by the government under the right of eminent domain.

Zoning Laws. Zoning laws are determined, usually by city or county governments, in order to regulate the use of real estate. The purpose is to assure the safety and comfort of the citizenry as well as the smooth flow of commerce. Typical designations are residential, commercial, and industrial zones. Zoning is like eminent domain in that it is virtually absolute although variances sometimes are allowed. Thus, the buyer of a small business must find assurance that the business is located in a proper zone.

Grandfather Clause. A grandfather clause is a clause modifying a law, statute, rule, regulation, or the like so that the change made by that law will be set aside in cases where long-established individuals of an earlier generation (such as a grandfather) would otherwise be unfairly harmed by it. For example, a new zoning law changing an industrial zone to a commercial or residential zone may include a grandfather clause allowing any companies engaged in manufacturing on the date that the law is passed to continue manufacturing until the ownership is transferred or until some specified future date, whichever occurs first.

Fictitious Name. A business is allowed under the law to operate using a name other than its real name as long as the fictitious name is registered with the state. Fictitious names usually are chosen to enhance or shorten the company's name or to more accurately portray the company's image. Examples are Acme Widget Corporation, which might do business as Widget Wonder, and Thomas W. Jones, a sole proprietor, who might do business as Tom's Retail Supplies. When formal reports such as tax returns and corporate registrations are prepared, the actual name is usually followed by the fictitious name but separated by the expression "doing business as" or, for short, "dba" or "d/b/a." Example: Acme Widget Corporation dba Widget Wonder.

Bargaining Chips. During negotiation of the price and terms, the parties usually make concessions in exchange for concessions. Thus, concessions are like the chips in a poker game where, being something of value but limited in number, they are spent very carefully in order to get the most out of them.

Accountant and Certified Public Accountant (CPA). In the state of Missouri, any individual may legally operate an accounting firm and advertise himself or herself as an accountant without having to pass a test or acquire a license. However, the state will administer a voluntary test to determine if an accountant is sufficiently qualified to be awarded certification. Thus, the St. Louis *Yellow Pages* lists two main categories of accountants, "accountants-certified public" (also known as CPAs) and "accountants servs." Since CPAs are eligible for certain jobs for which non-CPAs are ineligible, such as conducting a public audit, it is probable that CPAs are generally better qualified than non-certified accountants although noteworthy exceptions do exist.

Audit. An audit is a scrupulous examination, usually formal or official, of books, data, and records to verify their substance and verity. With respect to the financial reports of a company, an audit, especially if conducted by a CPA, will cover the receipts, invoices, employee payroll records, bank statements, cash-register tapes, shop records, billings, and virtually anything else necessary in the auditor's judgment to verify that the revenues, expenses, and earnings reported by the company are accurate and true. If an audit has a public or legal purpose, it may be conducted only by a CPA.

Compilation. A compilation is an unaudited organizing of raw data, such as check stubs and bank statements, into a formal report usually consisting of at least a balance sheet and income statement (explained below). The financial statements of most small businesses are compilations. Generally, compilations are accepted by buyers at face value but with the seller's warranty written into the purchase-and-sale agreement that the data are true and accurate.

Lawyer, Attorney, and Attorney at Law. A lawyer is a person who has a law degree and who has passed the state bar examination. An attorney is anyone who is legally appointed to act for another, but notice that an attorney is not necessarily a lawyer, even if they are commonly thought of as synonymous. An attorney at law, however, is not only a lawyer but, strictly speaking, a lawyer with a client. An attorney at law, in other words, is a lawyer who makes a practice of representing others in various legal activities.

Client and Customer. The terms, client and customer, both pertain to the purchase of goods or services. In some cases they are virtually synonymous but in other cases they have important differences. For example, someone hiring a professional person such as an accountant or lawyer is referred to as a client while someone purchasing goods at a department store is referred to as a customer. Generally, a client is more protected than a customer. For example, a person who lists a property for sale with a broker is the broker's client who commands the broker's allegiance, while the person who buys the property is the broker's customer who commands only the broker's honesty and ethical dealing.

Asset and Liability. In business accounting (see below), an asset is anything which adds documented value to the business while a liability is anything which subtracts documented value from the business. Examples of assets are cash on hand, cash in the bank, accounts receivable, raw materials owned, shop equipment owned, office equipment owned, real estate owned, indebtedness to the business, prepaid expenses, and work in progress. Examples of liabilities are indebtedness by the business, payroll accrued, taxes accrued, accounts payable, other payables, and leases. See the below section on book value for further clarification.

Equity. Equity is ownership of property or the cash value of ownership, especially the cash value in excess of any debts or liens against a property. In another sense of the term, equity can refer to the book value of a company, in which case the equity still refers to ownership but, as explained below, the book value of ownership usually is not equal to the cash value.

Some financial statements use the term "equity" to refer to liabilities as well as to ownership because the creditors to whom a business is liable have a claim against the business's assets just as the owners do. In this book, equity refers only to ownership.

A common example of equity is found in the ownership of residential real estate. A home is bought at a price of $100,000 with a down payment of $20,000, leaving a balance on the mortgage of $80,000. The equity at this point is $20,000. After a number of years of monthly mortgage payments, the mortgage balance is reduced to $70,000. The owner's equity now is $30,000. If the appraised value of the home has increased, say, to $105,000, then the equity is $35,000.

Book Value. The book value of a company is equal to the total recorded value of the assets less the total recorded value of the liabilities. The book value, in other words, is the equity or the recorded value of the ownership. Since the recorded value of assets is rarely changed to reflect the market value and since depreciation expense is usually not equal to actual depreciation (as explained below), the book value of a company usually differs from the actual value and often by a substantial amount. In the above example of equity in the owner's home, the book value after the several years of mortgage payments was $30,000, but, after adjustment to reflect the market value of the assets, the book value was $35,000.

Stock Sale vs. Asset Sale. When an incorporated business is sold, the buyer and seller must agree on whether to transfer ownership of the corporation itself or to transfer only the assets owned by the corporation. Most sales of small businesses are asset sales for two reasons: first, and usually more important, if the corporation were sold, any latent liability (for example, a customer injured on the premises six months earlier who had not yet filed a law suit) would follow the corporation to the new owner, thus throwing a kind of legal cloud over the buyer's purchase. Lawyers can word the contract so that the seller indemnifies the buyer should such liability arise and, depending on other factors (mentioned below), this approach is sometimes advisable. Usually, however, small business sales are asset sales to provide maximum (but not absolute) assurance of the clean and simple legal status of the buyer. Second, if the corporation's assets have been fully or almost fully depreciated, the buyer will lose the tax advantage of depreciation expense. Since an asset sale allows the buyer to begin a new depreciation schedule with the resultant tax deferrals, the buyer's accountant will usually concur with the buyer's lawyer on the advisability of an asset sale. Both buyers and sellers should seek advice from their accountants and their lawyers.

In some cases, certain factors may favor the sale of corporate stock, often to the mutual benefit of both buyer and seller. For example, customer contracts may be in the corporate name and not easily transferable to the buyer. A stock sale in such a case may bring a better price for the seller while getting the buyer off to a better start than he or she (or it, if incorporated) might otherwise get. Other situations involving close corporate ties also may favor a stock sale over an asset sale. Examples are regulatory approvals in the corporate name such as those from the Environmental Protection Agency, an employee pension plan, a grandfather clause, patent rights, or a low unemployment-insurance tax rate. In some cases, corporate liabilities, especially if they are large in proportion to assets, may serve as financing already in place for the buyer. In an extreme case, the buyer might acquire a large (by small business standards) corporation with a small cash payment although the buyer would probably have a turnaround to deal with. With several of these factors in effect, the situation may be fairly complex. In any case, the advice of both an accountant and a lawyer should be sought. Until advised otherwise, however, it is best to plan on the purchase and sale of assets.

Generally, an asset sale will include all of the assets necessary to operate the business but will exclude cash on hand (except, possibly, an agreed amount to be left in a cash register for change), cash in the bank, securities, and other items not germane to the business.

Equity Financing and Debt Financing. Most businesses require some financing to start or to expand. If, for example, the business receives money from a bank or an investor under the condition that the money be repaid, the business incurs debt and therefore is said to be debt-financed. If the business receives money from an investor with the condition that the investor becomes a part owner of the business, the business is said to be equity-financed. Frequently, a business is both equity-financed and debt-financed. In such cases, the debt-financing is superior to the equity-financing in the sense that in case of bankruptcy, the law requires that lenders be paid before owners. The same idea may be expressed by saying that equity-financing is subordinate to debt-financing.

Debt Service. Debt financing typically is paid in monthly installments of principal and interest. Such payments are referred to as the debt service. The exact amounts of such monthly payments can be looked up in booklets with such titles as "Interest Amortization Tables," "Monthly Mortgage Payments," and the like.

Note that these payments are usually designed to be constant from month to month. Thus the percentage of each monthly payment dedicated to payment of interest will decline from month to month as the principal is paid off, while the percentage of each payment dedicated to principal will increase.

Lien, Recorder, and UCC Form. When a debt is incurred, notification is filed with a public recorder, typically a department in the county and/or state government. The notification includes the names of the lender and the borrower, the amount of the debt, and the collateral used to secure the debt. Such filing is known as a lien on the collateral. Ownership of the collateral cannot be transferred until any liens are removed. The standard form used to file a lien is called Uniform Commercial Code-Financing Statement, and it is known as a UCC form.

Note that the terms of commercial leases also are filed with the recorder. Such memoranda include the length of the lease, options to renew, and options to purchase.

All of this information is available to the public.

Capital. Anything of value intended for investment, or the investment itself. Capital may include goods, whether tangible or intangible, and cash.

Capitalization of Earnings. An important method of appraising an income-producing asset or business, so named because it converts the earnings of what is being appraised into the amount of capital which would be required to purchase it.

Capital Gain and Capital Loss. Due to a variety of causes, the value of a property may increase or decrease whether or not the property itself undergoes change. For example, a piece of income-producing real estate such as an office building may gain in value because a shortage of office space may allow the landlord to increase the rent, because construction costs are rising due to labor costs, or because speculators are bidding up the prices. A business may gain in value because the management has increased worker productivity, because material costs have been lowered through volume purchases, or because strong marketing efforts have profitably increased sales. An increase in value is called a capital gain while a decrease in value is called a capital loss. For purposes of accounting and payment of taxes, such gains and losses are usually not recognized until a property is sold. For purposes of appraising, current values are generally recognized and reported, especially for the purchase or sale of a property.

Buying and Selling in Distress. There are a number of possible causes to put a business owner into distress. The sudden death of a spouse who was active in the business, a serious health problem whether physical such as a heart attack or emotional such as loss of enthusiasm (ennui), a prolonged business downturn, a family problem unrelated to the business but pressuring the owner to sell, or any combination of the above may cause an owner to feel that he or she can no longer manage the business and that a quick sale is therefore necessary. In such a position, most owners, if they decide to sell, will be motivated to lower the price to hasten the sale. Buyers too may function under distress though probably not as often or as seriously. Examples are the buyer who has quit his or her job to spend full time looking for a business, newly arrived immigrants with limited cash who are desperate to get started, and former owners who have been displaced by eminent domain and who need restarting to earn a living. In such situations, most buyers will be motivated to raise the price.

Variations of Value. A standard dictionary may offer several definitions of the word "value" including "a fair return . . . in goods, services, or money," "monetary worth," "relative worth," and so on. In this book, value will usually refer to monetary worth, especially when speaking of appraised value, unless otherwise indicated by the context.

The monetary worth of an item may vary according to the conditions under which the item is appraised or sold. These variations in value are many (perhaps infinite) but three variations in particular are most noteworthy. They are, in typically descending order, replacement value, fair market value, and auction value. Replacement value is the cost of an identical item if purchased new. Fair market value (FMV) is the value agreed to by a buyer and seller when both are well informed and economically motivated and when neither is in distress. (Note that this definition of FMV is consistent with IRS Revenue Ruling 59–60. See page 266.) Auction value is the price that an item would bring at a professionally managed public auction. These values are gross values. For example, if an item were sold at auction for $1,000 and the auctioneer's fee were ten percent, equal to $100, the auction value or gross value would be $1,000 while the net value to the seller would be only $900.

Liquidation value is almost synonymous with auction value. Liquidation means converting an asset into cash but with a connotation of distress and that the liquidation must be done quickly, as for example at an auction.

The above descriptive terms (replacement value, etc.) apply most often to personal property although they sometimes apply to real estate. These terms are not precise. In fact, they probably are most useful when thought of as relative to one another with replacement value the highest and auction value the lowest. In rare cases their relativity can go askew as, for example, when a new item is sold at a retail clearance at 40% off, while a used but otherwise identical item is sold near replacement value at an auction attended by excited bidders. Other conditions may affect these values. For example, if the owner of a machine shop sells a lathe which is no longer needed to another shop owner who does need it, the agreed price aptly would be described as fair market value. However, in such a case the buyer would usually pay for transportation, mounting, and electrical hookup, with the result that the buyer's total cost would exceed the fair market value. Again, these terms are relative, not absolute.

All values are subject to the usual forces of the market place such as recession, recovery, supply, and demand, not to mention such intangible forces as the negotiating skills of the individual buyers and sellers.

Note that one of the myths of appraising a business is that the value of the business is directly related to the value of the equipment. Although there is a small truth to that statement, it is usually far more accurate and far more revealing to state the reverse, that the value of the equipment is directly related to the value of the business. This seemingly convoluted relationship becomes clear when realizing that the whole idea of owning a business, financially speaking, is to make a profit, and that the bigger the profit, regardless of the equipment owned, the more valuable the business. But the more valuable the business, the more valuable the equipment. Thus, the owner of a prosperous business will pay full replacement value for a piece of equipment if necessary to keep production going, while the owner of a depressed business will be reluctant to pay five cents on the dollar for a bargain at an auction. This idea is developed more fully in Part 3 of Chapter 7 in the section titled "Invalid Zones of Appraising."

Fiscal Year. In some industries, the tax laws allow businesses to operate, report, and pay taxes for yearlong periods differing from calendar years but corresponding with industry practices, seasonal factors, or other factors. Such an accounting period is called a fiscal year. Fiscal years are widely used and cause no significant problems.

Depreciation. When physical assets such as a piece of equipment or a building are owned for a period of time, they generally undergo depreciation of value due to any combination of three causes: physical wear or deterioration, functional obsolescence, and locational obsolescence. Physical wear is self-explanatory. Functional obsolescence occurs when the asset in question is no longer current with the state of the art or when no longer desirable for reasons of style or fashion or other impairments. Examples are manually operated machine tools which largely, though not entirely, have been made obsolete by computerized machine tools; conventional pizza ovens which largely have been outmoded by high-capacity conveyor-belt ovens; and multi-story factories which have been outmoded by more efficient one-story factories. Locational obsolescence applies only to real estate and occurs when the location itself becomes less useful. Examples are a plant affected adversely by a demographic shift such as a flight to the suburbs or by a change in zoning. Since the tax laws allow depreciation expense to apply only to the improvements to land and never to the land itself, locational depreciation is applied only to improvements even though the land itself may suffer actual loss of value. (Such loss to the value of land would be treated as a capital loss at the time of sale.)

Depreciation Expense. Since depreciation is expensive no matter what the cause, a portion of the estimated depreciation may be included with the other expenses on the income statement (explained below). This expense is called depreciation expense. Depreciation expense is unique in that it usually involves neither cash outlay nor new indebtedness during the time period for which it is reported on the income statement and tax return. The cash outlay or indebtedness will have been made on the date the item was bought and will have been accounted for as an asset rather than as an expense.

Since depreciable assets by definition have a life of at least a few years, the tax laws require that the cost of the asset be spread over its estimated life. Thus, for example, the $1,000 cost of an asset with an estimated life of five years might be charged on the income statement at $200 per year for five years. Since the asset was paid for when it was bought, the $200 annual expenses would be bookkeeping entries for accounting purposes, not actual cash outlays. Thus depreciation expense is often wrongly considered as merely an allowable means of lowering taxes and not as a true expense. Like many wrong concepts, this one has a grain of truth to it. To explain, first realize that depreciation expense is real expense which must be paid for with real cash or real indebtedness. If a business buys a new machine which gradually wears out, the business will have paid cash or incurred debt to buy it and will pay cash again or incur debt again to either replace it or overhaul it. For this reason depreciation expense is real expense even though it is not incurred as a cash outlay in the same year that it is charged (except fractionally, perhaps, in the first year of ownership).

However, there is another confusion factor. The tax laws often allow businesses to record depreciation expense at an accelerated rate. Thus, in the earlier years in the life of an asset, the depreciation expense recorded may be (and usually is) greater than actual while in the later years of depreciation the expense recorded may be (and usually is) less than actual. Thus, when analyzing an income statement to determine the true income and, thereby, the appraised value of the business, the depreciation expense should be adjusted downward in the earlier years of depreciation but upward in the later years (a point often neglected by careless or incompetent appraisers or authors). In cases where the equipment has been fully depreciated for accounting purposes, no depreciation expense will be shown on the income statement. To portray a true picture of the income in those cases, an adjusting entry for depreciation expense or for the expense of repair or overhaul must be added to the income statement (another point often neglected by careless or incompetent appraisers or authors).

Amortization and Amortization Expense. Amortization expense is like depreciation expense in one way but different in another. It is a bookkeeping entry, usually with no cash outlay in the year charged, to provide gradual allowance of a one-time payment over a period of years, but it is used only for non-tangible assets such as a patent or a contract right. For example, if a business pays $1,000 for a patent and the tax laws allow ten years to amortize such payments, the business may show an amortization expense of $100 per year for the next ten years on its income statement and tax return.

Cash Flow. Cash flow is the amount of cash generated by a business after all expenses have been paid. Cash flow is equal to profit plus depreciation expense plus amortization expense. It may be expressed, like profit, either as pre-tax or as after-tax. Note that the cash flow to the owner of the business is reduced by any debt service being paid. Nevertheless, cash flow is usually referred to without deducting the debt service.

Goodwill. When referring to interpersonal relationships, goodwill speaks of amiability and trust. When used as an accounting term, goodwill is the equity value of intangible assets.

Typically, the earnings of a profitable, healthy business are the primary basis for appraising the value of the business. Also typically, the value of the earnings will exceed the value of the tangible assets. That excess—the difference between the value of the earnings and the value of the equipment and fixtures—is what constitutes the value of the intangible assets.

Goodwill was once not allowed by the IRS to be amortized but, as this book goes to press, it is.

The Purpose and Method of Accounting. The purpose of accounting is to provide a means to account for the finances of a business in an orderly fashion and to provide answers to most of the questions which may arise regarding those finances. Thus, accounting will track and record all the revenues, expenses, taxes, loans, profits, distributions, deposits, withdrawals, and so forth for a business. The method of accounting is to document every sale that is made, every debt that is incurred, every expense and every tax that is accrued, every bank deposit or withdrawal that is made, and every change in the value of the ownership that occurs. This documentation, primarily, may be made by setting aside a page in a book, or other niche such as a column on a page, for each type of transaction which might occur in the business. Thus there may be a page designated to record each sale, another to record each bank deposit or withdrawal, one for each materials purchase or sale, another for each employee's accrued wage or payment, and so on. Each page or each niche, and the type of data recorded on that page or niche, is referred to as an account.

Every transaction which occurs in a business has two or more effects. If a bill is paid, the cash is decreased but the indebtedness also is decreased. Thus, the transaction of paying a bill must be recorded twice to account for it accurately and thoroughly. In other words, a double entry must be made. As another example of double-entry accounting, if raw materials are bought, the cash is decreased to pay for the materials but the inventory is increased by the same cost of those materials and, again, the transaction must be recorded twice, once in the cash account and once in the inventory account. Sometimes a transaction may require a triple entry. For example, if a profitable sale is made, three things happen: The cash is increased, the inventory is decreased but only by the cost of the material sold, and the equity or the value of the ownership is increased by the amount of the profit (which, in this simple example, equals the difference between the material cost and the price for which the material was sold). This method, now almost universally employed throughout the world by businesses both large and small (and which was already being used by Italian merchants in the fifteenth century) is called the double-entry system even though sometimes three or more entries are required to properly account for a transaction.

In the double-entry system, all transactions are recorded twice or thrice as just described and all entries can be summarized into three groups called assets, liabilities, and equities. The sum of the assets will always equal the sum of the liabilities plus the sum of the equities. In other words, the assets will always be in balance with the liabilities plus equities. A very simple example will explain how transactions are recorded as double or triple entries and how they all are grouped as assets, liabilities, and equities. Suppose that Tom, a college student, decides to earn some cash by selling school supplies to his fellow students. He makes the following transactions:

Transaction 1. Tom mentally commits ten dollars in his wallet to the purchase of pencils. At the instant that Tom makes that commitment, he has gone into a business which is structured as a sole proprietorship and he has entered $10 into the cash account of his business (even though no physical shift of funds was made) and he also has entered $10 into his equity account even if he does not realize it.

Transaction 2. Tom buys pencils at a wholesale cost of $10. His inventory account has increased by $10 and his cash account has decreased by $10.

Transaction 3. Tom sells $7 worth (at cost) of pencils to his fellow students for a total of $14. His cash account has increased by $14, his inventory has decreased by $7, and his equity account has increased by the $7 profit he made on his sales.

Transaction 4. Cheered by his success and hoping to build his business, Tom borrows $10 from his parents in case he should decide to expand his inventory. His cash account has increased $10 and his debts account has increased $10. Before venturing further, Tom asks his roommate, an accounting major, to advise him as to exactly where he stands from an accounting point of view.

Transaction 5 and 6. Tom's roommate prepares the financial data including the balance sheet shown in Figure 2.1 and the income statement shown in Figure 2.2 and informs Tom that he now owes his roommate $2 for professional services performed. The performance of those services, including the verbal billing, constitutes transaction 5 which increases liabilities (accounts payable) by $2 and decreases equity by $2. Tom's roommate also informs him that since his business is showing a profit, an allowance has been made for $1 in taxes accrued. The recognition and entering of the accrued taxes constitutes transaction 6 which increases liabilities by $1 and decreases equity by $1. (Note that, technically speaking, a proprietorship would not show taxes accrued while a corporation would. The accrual is shown, however, for demonstration of method.)

Figure 2.1 A Balance Sheet

THOMAS W. JONES, SOLE PROPRIETOR
dba TOM'S RETAIL SUPPLIES
BALANCE SHEET AT THE END OF BUSINESS
MARCH 20, 2001

Assets

Cash	$24
Inventory at cost	3
Total Assets	$27

Liabilities

Accounts payable	$2
Taxes accrued	1
Debts	10
Total Liabilities	$13

Equity

Capital investment	$10
Retained earnings	4
Total Equity	$14
Total Liabilities plus Equity	$27

Figure 2.2 An Income Statement

THOMAS W. JONES, SOLE PROPRIETOR
dba TOM'S RETAIL SUPPLIES
INCOME STATEMENT FOR TWO-DAY PERIOD

ENDING MARCH 20, 2001

Sales		$14
Cost of goods sold		
Beginning inventory	$0	
Purchases	10	
Closing inventory	3	
		7
Gross profit		$7
Expenses		
Professional services	$2	
Total expenses		2
Pre-tax income		$5
Allowance for income tax		1
After-tax income		$4

It may come as a surprise to learn that the above brief explanation of accounting covers roughly a third or more of all the concepts that accountants employ in their work. It also covers about all that anyone needs to know to buy or sell a business. This does not mean that accounting is easy. It means that the substance and challenge of accounting are in the variety and complexity of applications much more than in the concepts. For the purpose of buying and selling a business, the application of concepts is fairly simple. Add seven or eight zeros to the sales for Tom's Retail Supplies, a corresponding number of zeros to the other figures, and some additional expenses, assets and liabilities, and one is looking at the financial statements of a Fortune 500 company.

Liquidity and Illiquidity. When dealing with investments of any kind, a prospective buyer must ask if the investment could be turned quickly into an amount of cash close to its fair market value should the need ever arise. This quality of an investment to be convertible quickly into cash is known as liquidity. Examples of liquid investments are stocks and bonds listed on an exchange; certificates of deposit (their penalty clauses notwithstanding); gold and silver coins; traded commodities including their futures; passbook savings accounts; and U. S. Treasury bonds. Each of the above may be converted into cash at or near its fair market value within a few days. In contrast, investments in real estate and small businesses tend to be illiquid although the degree of illiquidity may depend on any of several factors related to the economy and to the individual item for sale. Note the following examples:

Generally Less Illiquid	Generally More Illiquid
• Residential real estate	• Commercial real estate
• Distributors	• Job shops
• Manufacturing companies with established product lines	• Most small businesses
• Retail dry cleaners	

There are at least nine reasons that small businesses are illiquid and it is imperative that buyers and sellers understand these reasons. First, the demand for most small businesses is small. The result is that it often requires a year or even two or three years to find an able and willing buyer.

Second, the personal nature of the matchup between the buyer and the business being sold is an opportunity for dissimilarity. Such businesses as restaurants, beauty salons, bars, coin-operated laundries with attendants, convenience stores, gift shops, job shops, and so on are personalized in a myriad of ways, often without the owners realizing it. The wide variety of personality factors making these businesses hard to sell is not superficial or cosmetic but, on the contrary, is substantial and not easy to change. For example, note the wide variety of types of clienteles that a retail business might especially cater to: older clienteles vs. younger; upper class vs. middle or lower; fashion-wise vs. homespun; liberal or trendy vs. conservative or staid; spenders vs. thrifty; tourists vs. locals; service-oriented vs. price-oriented; business vs. consumer; daytime vs. evening; and so on. Each prospective buyer has his or her own preference for the type of clientele to serve and if the business for sale does not cater to that clientele, the buyer probably is not interested. To take another example, in the machine shop trade a wide variety of work types exists: large machinings requiring nine-foot-diameter work tables and ten-ton overhead cranes vs. medium-size machinings vs. small; precision vs. rough vs. anything in between; simple vs. complex; high quantity vs. low quantity; steel vs. aluminum or brass; flight-worthy vs. non-flight-worthy; ordinary metals vs. exotic; harmless metals vs. toxic; stamping vs. milling; full service including heat treating, three types of welding, and various design services vs. machining only; and so on. As in the retail trade, if the seller's type of work or clientele does not match the buyer's preference or experience, there probably is no sale. Since each attempted matchup is statistically improbable, it may require many attempts, and months or years before attaining success.

Third, a business for sale must be checked out thoroughly to provide enough confidence for the buyer to commit his or her wealth and dedicate his or her career. Checking out a business quickly can be accomplished in some cases but generally the process is time-consuming, often taking a month or two or longer.

Fourth, the stakes are so high for both buyer and seller that a deliberate pace is appropriate.

Fifth, when bank financing is involved, about two months or more may be added to the schedule. First, a loan application package must be prepared and submitted. Then the bank needs time to check out both the business and the buyer and to evaluate the entire situation including how the loan may or may not fit into the bank's portfolio. If the loan application is rejected at one bank, the process will be repeated, perhaps several times.

Sixth, if the seller has been failing to record his true income, a more skillful buyer is required to agree with the seller's price, a more skillful pre-parer of the loan application package is required to bring the hidden or un-recorded earnings out of hiding without calling attention to what is going on, and a more skillful bank is required to approve the financing, all three requirements tending to slow the rate of progress.

Seventh, since lawyers and accountants usually are involved, the sched-ule may be delayed depending on their work loads and whether they are on vacation or sick leave, tied up in court, or at the height of the tax season.

Eighth, all parties must set priorities for their time but business sales tend to receive low priorities for a number of reasons. Sellers may give first priority to running their businesses. Banks may give priority to more attrac-tive loan applications or to other matters of importance. Lawyers give prior-ity to court appearances, to emergencies such as clients under arrest, to deals nearing closing, or to matters of greater importance in the lawyer's judgment. Accountants give priority to tax report deadlines, especially from early Janu-ary through the end of April.

Ninth and finally, transactions often are slowed by unforeseen problems: a reluctant, foot-dragging landlord who does not want to lose a good tenant to sublease to an unknown buyer; an arrogant lawyer who refuses to com-promise mundane matters with an opposing lawyer, a problem truly com-pounded when three or more lawyers are involved; a municipal code, catch-ing everybody by surprise, requiring the impending sale of certain businesses to be thrice announced in the minutes of the monthly meetings of the city elders; and so on.

By understanding the reasons for illiquidity, buyers and sellers, and their advisors, should be able to plan more intelligently for their transactions. They should also become more patient. Patience is a prime asset in the pur-chase and sale of a small business.

Discussion of other factors contributing to illiquidity is found in Chap-ter 5 in the section titled "Business Brokers' Fees."

Confidant. A confidant is one to whom problems and secrets are entrusted, especially those which are intimate, dear, or of high importance. There are at least five functions of a confidant. First is to clarify thinking through the process of explaining and being forced thereby to think. Second is to obtain feedback from the confidant with the hope of obtaining additional facts, logic, insights, or, if nothing else, confirmation of one's own ideas. Third is to gain tactical advantage in certain situations by adding intriguing complexity or by having a means of escape when one feels trapped. Such tactical advantage is particularly useful in adversarial situations of high emotion such as negotiations for high stakes. Fourth is for the confider to find relief of emotional burden by means of talking. Fifth is to share for the joy of sharing. These last two functions are not necessarily the least.

Objective and Subjective. Something is objective which is independent of the mind and therefore impersonal. Something is subjective which is dependent on the mind, or on one's point of view, and therefore personal. For example, the statement that the prime rate, as listed in today's Wall Street Journal, is 8%, is a statement of objective truth because the fact stated is independent of the mind. The statement that 8% is a high rate is a statement of subjective truth because the fact stated is dependant on the observer's personal opinion or point of view.

Provisional Truth. Provisional truth is truth, or the perception thereof, which will serve for the time being but which is subject to change with the discovery of additional facts or insights. Expressed in another way, provisional truth is truth which is not absolute or final.

Truth generally should be thought of as provisional until hard evidence proves the contrary. Thus, the provisionality of truth is the underlying basis for diligence in fact-finding. That is why fact-finding, as in Chapter 6 of this book, is often referred to by business purchasers as "due diligence." Such purchasers recognize that as each new fact or insight into a business for sale is discovered, the perceived value of the business is liable to change.

The quality of provisionality is particularly in force when the truth being sought is subjective. Then truth is as changeable as are human viewpoints in their diversity.

Fact-finding, therefore, is a mode of truth, albeit provisional truth. Since negotiating, in a sense, is a continuation of fact-finding, negotiating is also a mode of truth, but still provisional.

(The author, incidentally, thinks that the only absolute truth is the truth that the universe exists. However, he sometimes pinches himself just to be sure.)

QUESTIONS FOR DISCUSSION
Chapter 2—Basic Terms and Concepts

1. True or false: personal property is defined as anything which is not real estate?

2. How does the legal liability of a proprietor differ from that of a stockholder?

3. Can ordinary citizens influence the activities of the Internal Revenue Service? Hint: Who makes the rules?

4. Why must small businesses usually pay a rate of interest higher than the interest paid by businesses listed on the New York Stock Exchange?

5. Why is cost estimating a critical skill in a job shop?

6. Why is a written contract usually better than a verbal contract? When might it not be better?

7. Who should make an earnest deposit, the buyer, the seller, neither, or both?

8. Answer true or false to the following two statements: a) Skimming of revenues is immoral because it is illegal. b) Skimming is quite moral because of societal acceptance of it (an estimated 75% of owners do it systematically in substantial amounts).

9. How is a zoning law like a grandfather clause?

10. Must a compilation be audited? If so, who should do it?

11. If an owner lists his business for sale with a broker, and if he also

hires an attorney at law for legal advice, whose client is the owner, the broker's or the lawyer's?

12. Is the book value of a business equal to the equity? Can book value simultaneously be two different dollar amounts?

13. Do a client's lawyer and accountant usually agree on an asset sale vs. a sale of stock?

14. True or false: A situation of distress always encourages a decrease in sale price.

15. Why do the three kinds of property values compare to each other relatively rather than absolutely?

16. A myth of appraising is that the value of the business depends largely on the value of the equipment. Why is this generally not true? On the other hand, when might it be true?

17. Another myth of appraising is that depreciation expense, almost always being a non-cash expense, is not a real expense. Why is that not true?

18. True or false: Accelerated depreciation expense is real expense?

19. Why is accounting necessary?

20. Explain, in just one or two sentences, the basic idea of double-entry accounting.

21. Why does the author explain illiquidity in such detail as he does?

22. Would you enter an important transaction, like buying and selling a business, without the aid and comfort of a confidant? State why or why not.

23. Is provisional truth objective truth or subjective truth? Please email your answer to the author. He still hasn't made up his mind.

CHAPTER 3

The Buyer's Search for a Seller

Once a buyer has determined the type of business that he or she might be qualified to own, and once a seller has determined that it is time to begin looking for a qualified buyer, they have a similar problem to solve, the match-up, although they must approach it from opposite directions. This chapter deals with the buyer's search for the right seller and Chapter 4 will deal with the seller's search for the right buyer. Business brokers also play a role in the matching of buyers and sellers and they will be covered in Chapter 5.

Buyers and sellers should read both Chapters 3 and 4 so they will gain appreciation of the others' problems and thereby enhance the cooperative spirit needed for the matchup to be successful. Accountants and lawyers also should read both chapters so they will better understand the amount of effort and emotional capital that some of their clients have invested. Then they can offer advice which is more cooperative and less adversarial than the advice which is frequently offered.

This chapter is divided into two parts: Developing Leads to Businesses for Sale and Making First Contact with the Owner. Note that a person referred to as an owner early in the chapter may be referred to as a seller later in the chapter, thus denoting an owner's change in status as the deal progresses.

PART 1:
DEVELOPING LEADS TO BUSINESSES FOR SALE

There is a variety of sources from which a buyer may find leads to the right business for sale. If the buyer will regard each of those sources, and the leads garnered from them, as improbable, he or she will be emotionally prepared for the inevitable disappointments to follow. If the buyer will also count each failed lead as the successful elimination of a wrong answer, a positive attitude should prevail to keep the search alive. As in most numbers games, the greater the number of attempts, the greater the chances for success. Hence, a positive attitude is a buyer's best friend. That attitude will be more important than any of the sources described in this book.

The buyer should keep in mind that the market is vast, that the right business for sale is out there somewhere, hidden perhaps in some unobtrusive market nook or cranny, waiting to be found. It is the buyer's primary duty to himself to go out there and get it.

The *Yellow Pages*. There are at least two ways to use the *Yellow Pages* to develop leads. One is for the buyer to turn to the classification for the selected trade such as dry cleaners, machine shops, and so on, and then to list all the businesses within the desired geographical limits. Such limits may include a part of the city selected for business opportunities, closeness to the buyer's residence, or any other reason that makes sense. This approach to developing leads is simple and direct and needs no elaboration. All that's left to do is to contact the owners as covered below.

The other way to use the *Yellow Pages* is helpful if businesses in the buyer's industry are spread through many classifications instead of being limited to only one classification. Then the *Yellow Pages* index may be used to locate all the classifications which might produce leads.

For example, a prospective buyer seeking any one of several types of chemical manufacturers turns to the alphabetical index starting with the letter A. There he finds a category to pique his interest, "abrasives," referenced to page 2 of the directory. Turning to page 2, he finds several companies listed. Most of those companies probably are of no interest for either of two reasons: 1) they are non-manufacturers such as suppliers and finishing shops or 2) they manufacture abrasives only as a sideline too small to hold the buyer's interest. In cases where the listing fails to identify the company as a manufacturer, a call to whoever picks up the telephone should provide the answer. The process is then repeated for the next relevant classification (which, in the St. Louis directory, happens to be "absorbent products"). The process continues through the remainder of letter A and the rest of the alphabet. At this point, the buyer will have compiled a list of leads numbering perhaps 50, 100, or more.

Next, that list should be culled to eliminate companies that are too large for the buyer's capabilities or too small for the buyer's interest. After culling the list, the number of remaining companies may seem disappointingly small. Further, only about 15 to 25 percent of them will have owners ready to retire or to sell for other reasons. Considering that family, friends, and favored employees have the inside track towards acquisition of desirable companies, the list will seem even smaller. But all is not lost. Some owners are childless, other owners have children who may prefer careers of their own or may simply be unqualified, and for a variety of reasons, other insiders may be ineligible or uninterested. Again, a positive attitude is the buyer's best friend towards finding the right business.

The Public Library. The task of searching for a business to buy is mostly unrewarding. The boredom and drudgery, the uncertainty of success, the inherent frustration in the process, and the long patience and persistence required to see the job through all take an emotional toll on the would-be buyer. A stop along the way promising intelligent, knowledgeable service offered with the cheerful spontaneity and quiet pride of a true public servant constitutes a welcome relief. It also offers a boost to a person's vision of success.

After compiling a list of leads gleaned from the *Yellow Pages* and from other sources, a buyer will want to know the name of the owner or president, the company's products and services, its annual sales, its number of employees, and anything else that possibly could be useful in culling the leads or contacting the owner. The reference section of the public library can usually supply answers to most or all of these questions. It may also supply alternate sources for leads either unavailable from the *Yellow Pages* or inadvertently overlooked. The reference books fall into the categories of national, state, and local (city and/or county). The national books are compiled by such august authorities as Standard and Poor, Moody, Dun & Bradstreet, and others. The national books may or may not list businesses small enough for each buyer's needs, but that is for the buyer to determine. The state and local books may be compiled by regional or local companies. The companies will be organized in a variety of ways, such as by size, by North American Industry Classification System (NAICS), by zip code, and so on. These books tend to be updated annually and libraries almost always have the latest editions. In cities large enough to have branch libraries, the headquarters library may be the only one to have a complete set of the books needed for the entire search. However, the branches probably have at least enough of the books needed to get started. One need only explain to the reference librarian the purpose of the search; the librarian will then name which books are needed and point to the stacks where they will be found or, time permitting, will accompany the searcher directly to the stacks and then point to the books. The books usually include instructions on how best to use them but should the searcher have problems, the librarians always stand ready to answer questions.

It is best not to expect the information in the reference books to be completely accurate or always current. Sometimes the compilers of these books make errors of inaccuracy or omission and the business owners themselves may sometimes feel less than enthusiastic in giving information which possibly could be used by their competitors. A conscientious buyer, therefore, may wish to cross-check sources, at least for leads which look especially interesting.

When companies located in the *Yellow Pages* prove to be subsidiaries of larger companies, they are not necessarily eliminated as possible leads. Large- and medium-size corporations sometimes sell subsidiaries or even individual plants which no longer fit their long-term plans. It is entirely proper to write to the chairman of the board to inquire of such prospects, especially if a specific subsidiary or plant has been targeted. In fact, if a specific subsidiary or plant has been targeted, it would be unwise to write to anyone but the chairman since subordinates might not know of the chairman's plans and, if they do, they might feel so threatened as to scuttle the deal. If interested, the chairman will likely authorize a subordinate to reply thus giving that subordinate, probably a vice president or manager who is not threatened, the clout necessary to pursue a deal.

Illustration 3.1

"...and if you have questions, you just let us know."

Newspaper Classified Advertising. Newspaper advertisements offer more hope than justified by the improbabilities of matchups but enough actual success to merit being religiously followed. Probably most important are those newspapers with circulations in six or seven figures serving an entire metropolitan area. The advertisements offering businesses for sale are probably classified as "Opportunities," or "Business Opportunities" and can usually be found by looking in the newspaper's classified index. The basic idea is for buyers to read the advertisements, circle or mark with a red pen those which look interesting, and follow up as directed by the advertisement with a telephone call or a letter.

The following tips are based on experience with the *St. Louis Post-Dispatch* but they probably will apply to most other newspapers.

The Business Opportunities advertisements are divided mostly according to the type of business for sale but other categories are offered as well. Following are some of the possible categories: "Amusement Businesses," "Bars/Lounges," "Brokers' Business Opportunities," "Business Financing," "Dealerships," "Direct Sales," "Distributors," "Franchises," "General Businesses," "Hotels/Motels," "Investment Businesses," "Miscellaneous," "Restaurants," "Retail Businesses," "Service Businesses," "Vending Machines," "Wholesale," "Money Wanted," and "Partners Wanted."

To be thorough, it is generally advisable to peruse all the categories except those which specifically exclude the type of business being sought. For example, if a cleaner is sought, the searcher should look under any category in which a cleaner possibly could appear such as "Brokers' Business Opportunities," "General Businesses," "Service Businesses," "Investments," and "Partners Wanted." There are at least two reasons that such easy-to-define businesses as cleaners may be advertised under any one of several categories. First, a specific category may not be offered by the newspaper. And second, the newspaper employees, though intelligent and helpful, are not always asked where an advertisement would best be placed.

Brokers' advertisements may appear under any category but are almost always identified by the name of the broker.

Some advertisements will stand out because of their size and the amount of information given and may suggest thereby a seriousness or legitimacy which makes them seem more attractive to follow up. Frequently, however, such advertisements are written by people who know neither how to write an advertisement nor how to sell a business. A simple two- or three-line advertisement describing nothing more than the type of business and the gross sales is as legitimate and as likely to lead to a purchase as a detailed advertisement ten lines long. Small advertisements should therefore be taken as seriously as large ones.

Business opportunities advertisements appear all seven days of the week but the Sunday edition is by far the most extensive, probably because it has the largest circulation. It probably would be most efficient for buyers to scour only the Sunday edition but a thorough prospective buyer may wish to follow the daily advertisements as well.

Unfortunately, advertisements from national companies looking for local representatives are mixed with the advertisements for local businesses for sale. The mix rather sullies the page, increases the tedium, and probably tempts more than a few buyers away from what should be the main path to their goal. Such advertisements perhaps should be segregated. In any case, since setting up local representatives does not constitute selling a franchise, such transactions are not regulated by the government as are sales of franchises. Extra caution is therefore advisable for buyers making inquiries. Usually these companies have toll-free telephone numbers and are therefore easy to identify. Some of them, however, may use local numbers transferred to their home cities without the buyer knowing what is happening.

Another possible source in St. Louis is the *St. Louis Business Journal*, a weekly newspaper dedicated to the local business community and which has counterparts in other American cities. The *Business Journal* has not yet caught on as a communication link between St. Louis buyers and sellers but it is worth checking for the occasional advertisements not appearing in other media.

Neighborhood newspapers may contain occasional advertisements for businesses for sale in their neighborhoods and are probably worth checking as appropriate for a buyer's individual needs. One should not expect to find much though. The same is true for newspapers serving the legal community. That is not their purpose. Nevertheless, these papers may be worth checking just for the sake of thoroughness and it should be relatively easy to do so while at the public library.

For a source with an aura of legitimacy, *The Wall Street Journal* is hard to beat even if it has its limitations. Businesses for sale are found in a section called "Personal Journal," under the heading of "The Mart." The businesses for sale are at various prices including some as low as the five-figure range but, because so many of the advertisements are of regional or national interest, it may be difficult to locate in the right city or county. Nevertheless, desirable businesses are continually offered and worth the searcher's diligence. Thursday editions offer the greatest number of businesses for sale but other days may also be checked.

Trade Magazines. Trade magazines by themselves are probably not much more likely to lead to the right business for sale than other sources but they do expand the overall possibilities for success. They therefore should be explored as any other source is explored simply for the sake of thoroughness.

Business opportunities in a trade magazine exude seriousness and legitimacy partly from the context and partly from the inference that the seller is high on the trade and dedicated to it. Nevertheless, these businesses will not be likely to fall into the city or county convenient to the buyer, thus reducing the odds for success. One can only try to do the best possible under the circumstances.

Trade Organizations. Trade organizations in general are formed to promote the business and fraternal interests of the trades people. Although introducing buyers to sellers probably is not in most of their agendas, a courteously written letter from a buyer probably would be warmly received with the result that it might be posted on a bulletin board, circulated among the members, noted in a newsletter, or announced at a meeting. In any case, writing such a letter requires only a small effort with the possibility of a big return. Telephoning an inquiry probably would not be as well received because of the reduced appearance of seriousness. Telephoning as a follow-up to writing, however, may be useful. In the St. Louis *Yellow Pages*, trade organizations have a category of their own and are listed under "Business & Trade Organizations." If a prospective buyer suspects that a trade organization exists but is unable to find the listing, asking a few owners in the trade, especially of the larger companies, might work.

Suppliers. Since suppliers are middlemen in the marketing chain, they lack the primacy of function and the visibility to the public which normally might broaden their image in the business community. They therefore are easy to overlook as a possible source of leads for a business to buy. Buyers should not underestimate their usefulness, however, because suppliers often have a sharper eye for where their customers are going than the customers themselves and they often are familiar with the local market for businesses being sold in their trade. Note the following two examples:

Example 3.1 A buyer who has had no luck finding a package liquor store for sale decides, in desperation, to call on a liquor supply house in hopes of finding a lead. One of the liquor salesmen says that there are no stores presently on the market but that one will be forthcoming in the next six months or so. He then adds the intriguing comment that the owner doesn't know it yet. The buyer asks the salesman how he can know if the owner doesn't know and the salesman explains that the store no longer is kept up the way it used to be, the owner looks old and tired, and sales have been steadily falling. The writing is on the wall and something is going to happen.

Example 3.2 A very attractive, nicely located, and well-maintained package liquor store grossing in the high six figures is for sale at a price of $225,000 plus inventory, real estate excluded. A prospective buyer hires a consultant who appraises the store at $80,000 plus inventory. The buyer is incredulous that such a nice looking store with that high a gross in a nice location could sell at such a low price, especially considering that the owner had hired an accountant to appraise the value. The consultant then refers to a reference book which suggests that, based on comparative data related to gross sales, a price of about $300,000 plus inventory would be reasonable, thus making the seller's price look attractive (and perhaps explaining how the accountant appraised the value). The consultant, however, notes that his own appraisal is based on profits, not sales, and he therefore sticks with $80,000. The buyer, still incredulous (but respectfully so), then gets hold of a veteran liquor salesman and asks his advice. The salesman knows all about the store and states that it will go for about $50,000 plus inventory based on current local market values. (The wide divergence of values is explained in Example 7.1 where 3.2 is revisited.)

Since sales people are usually out calling on customers, a telephone call to the receptionist inquiring when they are most likely to be in the office probably is the easiest way to track them down. Writing is not recommended because the sales people can not reasonably be expected to write back or even to call. Talking to the sales manager also might prove helpful.

Bank Trust Departments. Bank trust departments serve the public by handling investments or assets for their customers and by providing a variety of services. A typical situation is for the bank to be in charge of a deceased's estate which includes a business. The trust department will have the job of disposing of the business and will therefore be happy to cooperate with prospective buyers. An obvious drawback is that such a business in trust may have lost its employees and customers and may have to be restarted, assuming that restarting is feasible. Such a drawback should be reflected in the price and may prove to be a bargain for a buyer who is well qualified. The best approach is to call the banks in the order listed in the *Yellow Pages* and ask for the trust department. Sometimes the trust officer will provide basic data over the telephone and mail the detailed backup to the prospect. Also, the bank officer may suggest that the caller send a letter briefly describing the business being sought. The letter then will be put on file and referred to as businesses become available for sale.

Accountants. Since accountants are privy to the financial details of businesses, the owners tend to use their accountants as confidants. Thus an accountant may be the first to know if and when a business will be coming on the market. It is certain that an accountant would need the owner's permission to reveal that a business might be for sale. Also, the owner might wish to know more about the buyer before granting that permission. The buyer, therefore, should be happy to answer any questions the accountant might have.

It is hard to say what is the best way to contact an accountant for this purpose. One approach would be for the buyer to call and, instead of asking outright if the accountant knows of any businesses for sale, suggest that if the accountant might know of any for sale, especially in the buyer's trade, the buyer would be happy to write to the accountant describing his or her qualifications. Such gracefulness of approach can sometimes make a difference. Another approach is to write first and follow with a telephone call. Still another is to make a cold call, in which case the buyer should be dressed in appropriate business attire. If the cold call seems to go well, it might be followed with a letter. It is best to contact accountants only in the time period between the middle of May and the middle of December.

Commercial Real Estate Firms. Sometimes one or more of the agents at a commercial real estate firm happen to know when one of its tenants may be looking for a buyer and these agents may be permitted to say so if asked. Some of them will say so even if not expressly permitted. This procedure is not easy to implement, however. First, commercial firms must be separated from residential firms. In St. Louis, the separation is easy because it is done by the *Yellow Pages* and that may be the case in other cities. Separating firms by the location of their tenants, however, is impossible because a firm's tenants may be spread around the city. Telephone canvassing may be tried but that would require smoothness and adroitness of technique to get over and around the minor obstacles and variety of situations which are almost sure to be encountered. Also, many individuals happening to answer the telephone might have trouble understanding the request simply because it is unusual.

The best approach, therefore, albeit the most time-consuming, is to personally visit the commercial real estate offices in hopes of catching the right party in the office. When considering the amount of work, the seemingly low odds, the unusualness of the approach, the quizzical looks which may be encountered, and the emotional drain on the searcher, there is an apparent good case to bypass this approach and move on to something else. Still, this approach may be worth trying because thoroughness and persistence always increase the chances for success. Moreover, the very unusualness of the approach may evoke a favorable and cooperative response in some individuals who, even if they do not have any leads among their own tenants to share, may be able to refer the searcher to someone who does. The author knows of one case where a buyer with exceptional perseverance found an exceptionally nice business using this approach.

The Internet. In the author's experience, the Internet is not yet an important avenue for matching buyers and sellers. Nevertheless, visiting the Internet is so easy for those who are on line that there is no reason not to check what's going on from time to time. Even those who are not on line can visit the public library to browse the internet. Librarians are wonderfully enthusiastic about introducing their patrons to the internet. The International Business Brokers Association maintains a web site with businesses listed for sale, as do some individual business brokers. The *St. Louis Post-Dispatch* maintains a web site where its advertisers can repeat their newspaper ads for an additional small fee. Perhaps trade organizations and trade magazines also offer web sites with businesses for sale. In any case, the Internet is still very much in a state of development and therefore worth checking from time just to stay abreast of progress. But one word of caution: regulatory controls, if and when they exist, exist only within a state. The Internet is an interstate affair (as well as international) and, with respect to the small business marketplace, it is unregulated. One should therefore always seek legal counsel locally from one's own lawyer before making a commitment on the Internet.

The Secretary of State. One shortcoming of the sources described above is that it can be difficult to learn the owner's name, particularly for those leads drawn from the *Yellow Pages*. The library reference books can pose problems too, especially those covering the smaller local businesses, because the books frequently provide the name of a manager or agent instead of the owner. Since it is always more effective to approach the owner directly and by name, an extra effort to determine the name is worthwhile. One approach is simply to call the business and ask whoever answers for the owner's name and correct mailing address for the purpose of corresponding. This approach can work and sometimes does, especially for those who are comfortable using the telephone and who have some aptitude for it. For others, writing to the Secretary of State can help although possibly with limitations. In Missouri, for example, the names of a corporation's officers, directors, and registered agent are available to the public but not the names of the stockholders, although it is usually a safe bet that the directors and stockholders are the same. Also, there is no public record for sole proprietorships or partnerships unless they do business under a fictitious name. Still, since there is a strong possibility that the business is incorporated, a letter to the Secretary of State may be warranted. Figure 3.1 shows a model letter of inquiry for this purpose.

PART 2:
MAKING FIRST CONTACT WITH THE OWNER

Whether only a few leads have been collected or as many as 25 or 30 or more, a point will be reached when the buyer will feel that it is time to begin contacting the business owners. This part of the chapter will describe how to make these contacts by telephone, by letter, and by personal visit.

The Telephone Call. The telephone call has the advantage of immediacy in initiating the process of contacting the owner and near immediacy in determining the owner's interest. Compared to a letter, the telephone has another advantage if the owner's name can not be determined because a letter addressed to "owner" carries the risk of being discarded as junk mail. Still another advantage—this one compared to a personal visit—is due to a certain inherent privacy of the telephone whereas the visit has the possible awkwardness of the buyer's being forced to talk to the owner in the presence of employees, customers, or suppliers. On the other hand, the telephone call has the disadvantage of diminishing the prospective buyer's image as seen by the owner in terms of seriousness or legitimacy and the further disadvantage

Figure 3.1 Request for Corporate Search by Secretary of State

HONIGMANN, INC.
1932 GREENGLEN DRIVE
ST. LOUIS, MISSOURI 63122-5229
(314) 822-4602

April 29, 2001

Rebecca McDowell Cook, Secretary of State
Truman Building, 8th Floor
Jefferson City, Missouri 65102

RE: Corporate Search of Widget Wonder
123 Business Boulevard
St. Louis, Missouri 63000

Dear Ms. Cook:

Enclosed please find our check for $10.00. Please send us a report showing correct name of corporation, name and address of registered agent, names and addresses of directors and officers together with status. If Widget Wonder is not incorporated, would you please check the fictitious name filing for us and advise if so listed.

We very much appreciate your service.

Yours very truly,

Ernest J. Honigmann, President (signed)

enclosure

of possibly catching the owner while busy, distracted, or not in the best frame of mind. It may also find an owner who is an immigrant with limited facility of spoken language. The judicious buyer, therefore, must weigh these advantages and disadvantages carefully before making the approach. Sometimes the best approach will be unclear and hard to decide on. When that happens the buyer must make a choice and get on with it.

One situation where using the telephone may be a good approach is when correspondence may seem not to match a typical owner's capability (or, for that matter, the buyer's). Examples of such businesses would occur where the owners are less likely to be well educated, such as small grocery stores, cleaners, coin laundries, and so on. On the other hand, the art of diplomacy begins with enhancing a person's image, thus the attractive and well-written letter gains favor by playing to an owner's presumed sophistication.

When making the telephone call, there are important guidelines to follow:

1. Calls should be timed to fit the owner's schedule. For instance, calling a restaurant between meals or a manufacturing shop at the end of a shift.
2. Immediate self-identification by caller.
3. Immediate statement of intended recipient's name.
4. Absolutely no phony conversation.
5. Statement of qualification for ownership.
6. Statement of purpose.
7. Brevity.

Following are two illustrations, the wrong way and the right way, of how a prospective buyer, Betty Williams, might try to make telephone contact with the owner, Jack Owens, of the Elm Street Cleaners.

WRONG

(Telephone rings.)

Answerer: Elm Street Cleaners.

Williams: May I speak to Mr. Owens, please?

Answerer: This is Owens.

Williams: Mr. Owens, how are you today?

RIGHT

(Telephone rings.)

Answerer: Elm Street Cleaners.

Williams: This is Betty Williams. May I speak to Mr. Owens, please?

Answerer: This is Owens.

Williams: Mr. Owens, I'm presently employed in the retail cleaners business and I'm trying to find a business of my own. Would you know of any that might be available?

As simple and as direct as this illustration may seem, there are several directions the conversation may take from this point on. Owens may be confused or startled by the directness of the approach and may ask Williams to say again why she is calling, or Owens may understand instantly and ask for more information before committing himself. Owens may be busy and ask Williams to call back or he may ask for her number and promise to return her call. In any case, Owens will take charge of the conversation as soon as he understands the purpose of the call and Williams should allow Owens to take charge because the relationship at this point is one of the owner as provider with the prospective buyer as supplicant. Later, as buyer and owner gradually realize that they each would like to have what the other has to offer, and as the owner's status gradually becomes that of the seller, the relationship will become one of equals working towards a common goal, the mutually beneficial transfer of ownership.

If someone besides the owner answers the telephone, several possible situations may develop. If the answerer asks the purpose of wanting to speak to Owens, Williams may reply that it is a personal call. If pressed further, Williams either may reiterate that it is a personal matter or volunteer that it involves personal investments but that she can't say more without speaking to Mr. Owens. If the owner's spouse comes to the telephone, the spouse is probably the co-owner and must be assumed as such, in which case Williams should state her qualifications and purpose to the spouse. If the owner is not in, Williams may ask when is the best time to call or she may leave her name and number. The former is better because it leaves her in control and eliminates, at least temporarily, the awkwardness and deflation of having to repeat a call to someone who has forgotten or refused to return her call. If she is given no best time to call, she should say that she will try again later. Other situations may develop which are not covered here, in which case the buyer will have to improvise.

An unannounced caller who immediately identifies himself or herself, immediately states his or her qualifications, and then comes directly to the point will almost always be treated with courtesy and respect. An occasional owner's curtness may be caused by having a lot of work to do.

The Letter. Contacting an owner by a letter has several advantages. A letter documents the identity of the prospective buyer, thus offering some assurance that the owner will not be dealing with a competitor, a snoop, or an agent of the IRS. A letter can be opened, read, thought about, and replied to at the owner's convenience. If the letter is prepared in workmanlike manner as explained below, it will connote a seriousness which most people will respect even when not interested in the proposal. Since the letter may be revised and reworked as much as necessary to make it perfect or nearly so, it may cast the buyer in his or her best light. A disadvantage of the letter is that it may be maliciously intercepted or innocently lost before reaching the owner or it may be discarded by the owner if perceived as junk mail. Another disadvantage is that the owner may fail to take the initiative to respond because of overwork, illness, fatigue, confusion of alternatives, some other problem, or any combination thereof. The disadvantages of the letter, however, can mostly be overcome by a follow-up telephone call about a week or ten days after the mailing.

Figure 3.2 presents a model letter of inquiry. Standard word-processing techniques allow such form letters to be sent in substantial quantities with minimal effort and cost. However, since computerized letters have become so common that they are easy to disregard, the letter's appearance should stand out.

Figure 3.2 Letter of Inquiry to a Prospective Seller

ELIZABETH R. WILLIAMS
19322 ELM TREE LANE
ST. LOUIS, MISSOURI 63122
(314) 020-4602

April 17, 2001

John Brown, President
Brown Chemical Company
1000 Elm Industrial Drive
St. Louis, Missouri 63100

Dear Mr. Brown:

I have been employed with a chemical manufacturer for a number of years, including the last five as a plant manager. Now my technical and financial capabilities have grown to where I believe I am qualified to become an owner.

I have no reason to think that you wish to receive an offer and I am writing only on the random chance that you might be interested or that you might know someone who could be.

If you have no interest at present but could be planning to retire or semi-retire in a few years, I would consider working as an employee if I could look forward to eventual ownership.

If my proposal could interest you in the least, I would be grateful if you would call or write.

Sincerely,

(signed) Elizabeth R. Williams

The letterhead can be prepared at home using standard word processing and a quality printer, preferably a laser printer because its printing is resistant to moisture. If a printing company is hired to prepare a letterhead, steel engraving is not necessary, but high-quality offset printing is. Raised-letter printing should not be used because it is thought by some to seem presumptuous and cheap. The color of the ink should be black. The letterhead design should be simple and straightforward, just as shown in Figure 3.2 with no logo, border, or other affectations. The buyer's residential address is adequate and probably necessary. If the buyer has a facsimile machine, that number may be added beneath the telephone number. An e-mail address may also be added. The stationery should be brilliant white, 8.5" x 11" with number 10 business envelopes, 24-pound weight paper with 100% cotton content preferred (Cranes Crest, for example) but 20-pound weight with 25% cotton content is acceptable. Deviations from these admittedly narrow specifications may be effective if in consonance with the style of the industry, but the buyer would have to be very self-assured in making such a choice and still would needlessly risk sending letters giving the wrong signal.

If the buyer does not feel capable of handling the typing or computer chores, there are secretarial services listed in the *Yellow Pages* which do a professional job at a reasonable cost.

Although compromises of the above specifications are not recommended, one might consider a letter printed by hand. Hand lettering may lack the authority of a professional-looking letter but it would have the advantage of standing almost no chance of being mistaken for junk mail. A hand-written letter might also be suitable if the writing is attractive and legible.

The above specifications may seem demanding but they are designed to grab an owner's attention in a high-stakes gambit. It does not matter if some of the owners receiving these letters do not know the difference between a letter which is well crafted and one which is not, or if some who do know the difference don't care. What does matter is that an owner who has just the right business to sell be attracted to the letter, open it, read it, and act on it. The loss of that one opportunity could diminish the buyer's career for the remainder of his or her life. That dismal possibility should be enough to inspire a prospective buyer's best effort.

The Figure 3.2 letter mentions the possibility of employment leading to eventual ownership. Such an arrangement probably should include an exclusive option to buy the business at a pre-agreed price. The price might have to be conditional on future sales and/or profits. The benefits of such an offer accrue to both parties. The buyer gets an ample period of training, an inside view of the business, virtually eliminating the normal risks and unknowns of buying, and a smooth transition for customer relations. Additionally, these three advantages will be viewed very favorably by the bank which is asked to finance the purchase, an advantage to the seller as well as to the buyer. The seller gets his life in order well in advance of actual retirement with a well-trained successor. That successor would assure better than average success for repayment of seller financing, if required, and for sustaining the seller's reputation and pride. The arrangement would also help to protect the interests of loyal employees and customers.

Before such an agreement becomes binding, a trial period of six months or so would provide both parties ample opportunity to observe each other. Such an agreement could have tailor-made variations. One variation could have the buyer taking ownership shortly after the trial period with the seller contractually retained for a few years as an employee or consultant, perhaps with a gradually diminishing workload. Another variation might have the buyer working as an employee for several years with gradually increasing shares of stock until majority ownership is gained. As always, legal counsel would be necessary for both parties. Again, the opportunities to buy the type of business being sought may be few and the probability of success low, but the prospective seller receiving a warm letter of inquiry with an enticing prospect for the twilight of his or her career would have to give that prospect more than a passing thought.

The Unannounced Personal Visit (The Cold Call). The unannounced personal visit has the advantage of providing the opportunity for a prospective buyer to sell himself or herself to the owner. Such advantage is obviously of greater benefit to individuals blessed with at least a semblance of charm. However, even those less gifted can do well if they follow some basic guidelines of presentation and courtesy. Another advantage of the personal visit is the ability to see the business, or at least a part of it, with one's own eyes. Still another is that prospective buyers with enough experience to have developed an intuitive sense of things can begin the processes of fact-finding and appraising. (The nature and value of intuition are explained in Chapter 6.) Another advantage still is that the owner has the chance to size up the caller and to ask questions. Finally, the personal visit connotes seriousness of purpose.

One disadvantage of the cold call is the difficulty and awkwardness of announcing the purpose of the call to anyone but the owner. Another disadvantage is that the timing of the call may turn out to be poor because of the owner's workload, mental state, absence, or other difficulty. Still another is the amount of time and effort required to make all the visits. And another still is that the cold call is somewhat demeaning, or at least it can feel that way.

After weighing the advantages and disadvantages, it can be genuinely difficult to decide which approach is the more desirable. In general, the author likes to send letters followed by telephone calls, but has also used both unannounced telephone calls and unannounced personal visits for making first contacts and has found them to be effective. The personal visit is perhaps best avoided when making first contact with businesses likely to have no truly private areas, such as retail dry cleaners, taverns, and donut shops.

No matter the approach, the buyer's mood and self-assurance play no small role in the success of it. If the prospective buyer is in much less than high spirits, first contacts may best be postponed to another day or time.

The guidelines for an unannounced personal visit are similar to but broader than those for an unannounced telephone call:

1. A route logically planned to minimize travel time.
2. Visits timed to fit the owner's schedule. For instance, visiting a restaurant between meals or a manufacturing shop at the end of a shift.

3. Appropriate dress, usually consisting of standard conservative business attire.

4. Immediate self-introduction of the buyer when greeted by a receptionist, employee, or owner.

5. Immediate statement of wish to see the owner while referring, if possible, to the owner by name.

6. Absolutely no phony conversation.

7. No pretense of being anything other than self. Wearing a necktie is an acceptable violation of this guideline.

8. Strong attempt to meet owner in private.

9. Brief statement of buyer's qualifications prior to statement of purpose.

Following is an illustration of the right way to make a cold call on the owner of a company, such as Brown Chemical Company, which is likely to have a private place to meet with the owner.

(Buyer enters door marked "Offices," "Entrance," "Visitors," "Brown Chemical Company," or the like and walks into visitors' area, then stops to look and see what to do next. Employee sees buyer and approaches.)

Employee: Can I help you?

Williams: I'm Betty Williams. I wonder if I could see Mr. Brown.

Employee: Is he expecting you?

Williams: No, Mr. Brown doesn't know me.

Employee: What would you like to see him about?

Williams: It's a personal matter.

Employee: I see. Wait here and I'll see if he's busy.

The reception by the employee is fairly typical and average in terms of politeness and friendliness. The approach by Williams is correctly done. Her statement that Brown does not know her precludes her being viewed as pretentious and is properly humbling. As was the case with the unannounced telephone call, the unannounced visit may take any of several directions. The buyer may be told that Brown is busy and that she can try again later and take her chances. She may ask for an appointment but she may or may not get one. If she is lucky, the employee will suggest a good time for her to try again or, if not, she is within her rights to ask when is a good time. A slightly awkward situation develops if Brown sends a subordinate to ask Williams what she wants. She can only say that it is personal and that she can only discuss it with Mr. Brown. The subordinate may persist by saying that he or she handles Brown's personal affairs, in which case Williams may say that it involves personal investments. If the subordinate still persists, Williams may state her purpose or she may retreat gracefully while saying, perhaps, that she will telephone or write. If she states her purpose, she can do so tactfully by saying that she has no reason to think that Brown might know of a chemical company looking for a buyer but that she is just taking a random chance that he might.

A more awkward situation develops if the owner himself steps out of his office to meet her in the reception area within earshot of any employees and asks what it is that she wants to see him about. She can ask to see him in private but if he says he has no secrets to hide she is still responsible to be discreet even though the owner is not being cooperative. Then, in quiet voice, she may say that she has many years' experience in the chemical manufacturing business, with the last five years as a plant manager, and she would like some day to become an owner. She wonders if Mr. Brown could offer any advice. If the owner says no—even if it is said firmly—it is permissible for the buyer to repeat her proposal although she must do it while exiting, as shown in the following illustration:

Owner: I'm really not interested and I'm sure I don't know any one who might be.

Williams: I honestly know how to run a manufacturing plant but if you're sure you're not interested, I'll be on my way.

Owner: I'm quite sure. Thanks for calling.

Williams: Thanks for your time. Would it be all right if I call you a year or so from now?

Note that the underlying reason for repeating one's proposal when exiting is to allow for the natural human tendency to say no and to then give the person a chance to change his or her mind. (The author, by using this ploy, once made a sale to a prospect who had given him a no that was both firm and absolute.) This psychological ploy can be carried a step further if the prospective buyer has a calling card to hand to the owner while exiting. Then, after several months or even a year or two, the owner will have another chance to change his or her mind and to contact the buyer, assuming that the owner saved the card. The card should bear no logo, motto, embellishment, or other distraction; it should give only the buyer's name, address, telephone number, and e-mail address; and it should be on quality white stock with quality offset printing in black ink.

Throughout this awkward and somewhat demeaning experience of making a cold call, the buyer must appear self-confident but not cocky, yet subordinate but not inferior.

At this point in the book, the reader should have begun to sense a growing awareness of the psychological importance of being well qualified to own and operate a business. A baseball player was once asked how he knew when he had become truly proficient at his position. He replied that he knew he had arrived when he began wishing in tight situations that the ball would be hit to him.

Other situations not covered here are bound to develop, but the above illustrations should provide the general idea of how to make the cold call, with reliance on improvisation to fill in the rest. In every search of this type there is inevitably, if one makes enough cold calls, a degrading incident or two where one is treated rudely or where opportunities are blown. These are part of the game and must be accepted as such. The proper tactic when treated rudely is to brush it off and retreat to the next call, but no matter what the circumstances, one must always be courteous.

In any case, once the owner understands the visitor's purpose, the owner will take charge of the situation and say yes, no, or maybe. The buyer's course of action from that point on will be obvious.

Building the Relationship with the Owner. Normally, the owner should begin by testing the buyer's qualifications with such questions as which companies the buyer has worked for, what kind of experience or training he or she has had, and how much cash or cash equivalent is available to get started. The buyer should cooperate fully so as to build the seller's confidence in the buyer's capability to take over the business. If the seller fails to ask these questions, the buyer should volunteer at least some of the answers but should ease into them by first asking if the seller would like to know something about the buyer's background. When the seller starts to feel comfortable with the buyer, the flow of information will gradually increase with little prompting. Attaining that level of comfort may take two or three meetings.

There are other matters for prospective buyers to consider when beginning the relationship but, except for the item below, these are covered, albeit more from the seller's viewpoint, in Chapter 4.

As a final note in this chapter, there is one type of seller whom the author views with delight but whom others may view differently. It is the seller who is so proud of the business and its heritage that he or she will insist on taking the buyer through a long tour more oriented on nostalgia than on business. Thus the buyer may be shown or told about such items as what appears to be a ramshackle corrugated storage shed but which actually is the original shop where the business was started 75 years ago by the seller's grandfather and which has some original tools still hanging on the walls; an extension to the original structure erected five years later with real brick walls, a loading ramp, and an indoor toilet; what year the first employee was hired; what year the company went from proprietorship to corporation (back in the thirties); what it did to support the national effort in World War II (it made army hats, mess kits, bomb casings, or whatever); what year the grandfather died; an alcove where the seller's father used to take naps during the day or sleep all night when snowed in; an album full of pictures (most of them ancient) of everybody and everything ever connected to the business; a scrapbook of newspaper clippings (also mostly ancient); other pictures, articles, and mementos on the office wall; and so on. The buyer should realize that the seller is doing much more than sharing something dear. He is satisfying a psychological imperative. If the buyer wishes the relationship with the seller to get off to a good start, he or she must go along with the showing which is liable to last 45 minutes but seem like an hour and a half, even if perceived as a waste of time, and feign interest, even if viewed as a bore. There is an upside, however, even for those who don't view such a tour with delight: someday, if they are lucky, the buyer and his or her progeny may have a story of their own to tell.

QUESTIONS FOR DISCUSSION
Chapter 3—The Buyer's Search for a Seller

1. Why should sellers read this chapter as well as buyers?
2. Thomas Edison considered each failed experimental filament for his light bulb as a success. How would his mindset be helpful for buyers searching for the right business?
3. Why is information about businesses contained in reference books not entirely trustworthy?
4. Why are lengthy newspaper advertisements no more serious than three-line ads?
5. Consider that there are almost a dozen sources of leads to a business to buy described in this chapter. Should a buyer

consider resigning his or her job to have enough time to pursue a dream business? Which is more important, the cost of pursuit or the reward of success?

6. Making first contact with an owner can be a demeaning experience. Is it worth it?

7. The author asserts the psychological importance of being well qualified for ownership. Why is that important?

8. In light of Chapter 3, why does the author consider Chapter 1 the most important chapter in the entire book?

CHAPTER 4
The Seller's Search for a Buyer

This chapter has four parts dealing with the main concerns of a business owner thinking about selling: Preparing To Market the Business; Developing Leads to Buyers; Deciding Which Leads To Pursue; and Greeting the Buyers. Woven into the text for the first of these concerns are discussions of some of the more important emotional factors mentioned in this book. These factors should be noted not just by sellers but by anyone connected to the transaction, so that a seller's feelings, needs, and behavior can be better understood and dealt with.

Brokers may play an important role in the seller's search for a buyer but they are covered in Chapter 5.

PART 1:
PREPARING TO MARKET THE BUSINESS

When preparing to sell a business, there are seven main areas to consider. Although suggestions are offered for making these decisions, each owner has to weigh these suggestions in the context of his or her individual circumstances and then make his or her own decision. Some of these decisions will be difficult; talking them over with a confidant is therefore strongly recommended.

Improving the Profits. The logic of improving the profits is obviously to sell the business at a higher price, but it should also encourage the banker who is asked to finance the purchase to view the loan more favorably.

Although there may be various approaches for building sales and profits such as increasing advertising, doing more sales calls, submitting more bids, or expanding store hours, there also may be various hindrances such as a slowing economy, growing competition, a shortage of skilled labor, or, for an owner nearing retirement, ebbing energy. When any of these hindrances come into play and a business owner is discouraged by them from attempting to boost profits, discussing with a confidant may help to find a course of action. If the confidant is a consultant with expertise in the industry, chances for success will improve markedly.

Another approach to boosting profits is to look for a buyer, with exceptional energy and talent for growing the business, to be brought into the business as an employee, and with whom the owner can negotiate a mutually beneficial deal. Since banks prefer to finance buyers who have demonstrated their ability to manage the business being bought or who have at least worked in it, the prospects for a bank loan are enhanced, a benefit for both seller and buyer.

Some owners may prefer not to hire a prospective buyer as an employee for fear of disrupting existing employees or for the more rational fear of divulging trade secrets or giving away a customer list. For such owners, the hiring of a talented, non-buyer employee to help manage, to make sales calls, or to do whatever is necessary to boost profits may have strong appeal. This course of action, however, requires consummate skill by the owner to hire someone who will perform well enough to justify the exceptional salary which will have to be paid and the exceptional trust and latitude which may have to be granted. If the new hire falls far short of expectations, profits will decline and things will become worse instead of better. More than one owner has regretted making the attempt.

Another hindrance to boosting profits is lack of motivation. If such lack is due to absence of necessity—as may be the case when the children are raised, the house is paid for, and there is little or no business indebtedness—a better sale price may not be worth the effort. Then a business owner's best course of action may be simply to sell the business at its current profit level for the best price attainable under the circumstances and then to concentrate on enjoying life. That is not a bad course of action and may even be thought of as commendable, especially if family members will be helped to enjoy their lives too.

If the lack of motivation to boost profits is emotional in nature and marked by weariness and dissatisfaction (such an emotional state is known as ennui or perhaps more commonly as burnout), discussing with a confidant may help. If the owner mentions the weariness and dissatisfaction to the confidant, a solution becomes more probable since the confidant will have more understanding of the problem and the owner and confidant together may overcome any stigma which might be present in the owner's mind. The solution may include professional counseling with a social worker, a psychologist, or a psychiatrist. Some emotional problems are relatively difficult to solve and some are relatively easy, but in either case, the simple acknowledgment of the problem coupled with the desire to improve and a request for help constitutes half the solution. In light of the autocracy typical of business owners, acknowledgement can be the more difficult half of the solution. It is important to recognize that emotional problems can happen to anyone, literally anyone, no matter how successful or emotionally healthy the individual may seem to be. The business owner in Example 4.1 below is a case in point.

An owner who has been cheating on taxes may face a moment of truth. If the cheating is decreased or eliminated in order to increase the recorded profits, a story must be fabricated to justify the suddenness of the increase to the bank which finances the purchase and perhaps to the IRS if its suspicions are aroused to the point of making an inquiry. If the cheating is continued, the owner must explain to the buyer, in a room shrouded with privacy, where the profits are or the owner must simply hope that the buyer will be sophisticated enough to realize what is happening without having it explained. If the owner informs the buyer, he or she must do so at the risk that, if the deal goes awry for whatever reason, there may result an unfriendly person at large with the power to make trouble. The alternative is to accept a disappointing price for the sale of the business.

An approach to improving the profits not recommended is to begin forgoing some of the perquisites of ownership. This idea is one of the myths that plague the small business market place. It was proposed by a syndicated columnist writing in a business publication. The problem with this approach is that it is predicated on a buyer who is not intelligent enough to understand the perquisites and their value. Such a buyer probably would not be qualified to own and operate the business. An intelligent buyer will find the perquisites and their value during fact-finding as shown in Chapter 6 (see Owner's Revelations in Part 2), or during negotiating as shown in Chapter 8 (see Part 3). A more difficult problem is to convey the value to the bank being asked to finance but this too can be handled as shown in Chapter 9 (see Part 5).

Getting a Medical Checkup. Another aspect of preparing for the sale is a regularly-scheduled medical checkup. The idea is to catch health problems in their early stages when they best can be treated, but also to assure an early start on selling the business if the owner's health so dictates. The reader is reminded that most small businesses are relatively illiquid, requiring perhaps several years to sell.

Dealing with Children Who Disdain Taking Over the Business. Some owners hope that children who previously disdained taking over their parents' business may find a change of heart. Here is as deep and searing a desire as an owner can have. The answer is that the children probably will not change nor should they be expected to or even hoped to. Owners need to allow that children are not replicas of their parents but unique individuals with personalities and preferences of their own. If, through love or at least resolute fondness of the work they will be doing, they are not motivated to take over the business, then no matter how talented they may be, they are not qualified for ownership. Once the children have said that they are not interested, an owner should proceed with his or her plans almost as if the children did not exist. To delay is to risk being too late in looking for a buyer, as illustrated in Example 4.1.

Deciding When to Start Looking for a Buyer. To determine when to start, the owner must first decide if he or she would like to set up the kind of employer-employee relationship between buyer and seller explained in the previous chapter and repeated above. If so, the owner should start looking at least four or five years before planning on going into complete retirement. That would allow roughly two or three years to find a buyer and another two or three years for an employer-employee relationship. If the owner prefers an outright sale with no employment relationship of any kind, the search for the buyer may be delayed in accordance with the seller's timetable for retirement and the degree of liquidity or illiquidity of the business. A prospective seller should bear in mind the tremendous role that luck plays in finding the right buyer and that finding that buyer may take anywhere from four weeks to four years or more. Also, it is better to find a buyer too early than it is to start looking too late. If the former, the buyer can be offered employment with eventual ownership or, at worst, can be asked to come back in a year or two. If the latter, the business will be sold at a distress price or, at worst, will be shut down and sold piece by piece at auction, and probably at well less than half its otherwise value. Moreover, starting too late to look for a buyer can itself cause distress as well as cost the owner a severe financial penalty, especially if things do not go as hoped or expected, as illustrated in the following example:

Example 4.1 An owner has been in business for 31 years, has been thinking for a few years of retiring, but has done nothing about it. Now, at age 66, he is ready to retire to spend more time with family and friends, to travel, and to relax. His business has sales in seven figures, it has always been profitable, its future looks good, and so he expects to get a good price. He lists the business, exclusive of real estate, for sale at $800,000 with a real estate broker who quickly brings a contract for full list price subject to appraisal. The owner is elated at the price and at the prospect of looking forward to his retirement. He also is gratified at the quickness of results which is understandable since he has been a results-oriented person all of his life and has long enjoyed the own-

er's power of autocracy to command such results. The owner and
the buyer share the fee for an appraiser who prices the business at
$736,000, which both parties then agree to. The bank, however,
denies a loan and the buyer backs away. The owner is let down and
let down hard, both at the suddenness of the reversal and at losing
the buyer. Now slightly soured on brokers but not knowing what
else to do, he reluctantly hires a business broker who appraises
the business at $550,000. The low appraisal dejects the owner
further and he respectfully tells the broker so. With the help of
good luck, the broker quickly finds a qualified buyer, thus giving
the owner's spirits a lift. The buyer, however, correctly insists on
a thorough fact-finding of the business; she takes three months
to do it, and then comes up with her own appraisal at $525,000.
The buyer, motivated to buy the business and persuaded by the
broker's appraisal, offers $550,000 but the owner, confused by
the divergent appraisals, still relishing the $800,000 previous of-
fer, and unable to truly understand what's going on, counters at
$650,000. The buyer holds firm at $550,000 and an impasse results. Two and a half weeks go by and no one relents. Finally they
compromise at $550,000 plus royalties on certain potential future
sales which the owner had set up but never exploited.

Now begins the grind of ironing out the contractual details;
obtaining financing; additional fact-finding to prepare the buyer
for takeover; lining up insurance; arranging municipal inspections, licenses, permits, utilities, and so on. A target closing date
ten weeks away is set. A month goes by, then the closing date is
slipped two weeks by the buyer who needs more time to arrange
financing. One day, out of the blue, the owner confides to the
broker that he is tired, that he is too old for all of this back and
forth, that he doesn't need the hard work and the aggravation
any more, that he can't take it any more, and that if the deal does
not wrap up soon, he will shut down the business, sell the equipment, and bring it all to a close. The owner's disciplined tone, his

sincere expression, and the complete honesty and cooperation he has given the broker as well as the buyer convince the broker that the owner is neither bluffing nor venting his feelings and that he means exactly what he says. The broker cautions the owner that such a move could result in having to auction the equipment at a loss in sale price of $500,000 but the owner replies that he no longer enjoys going to work, that he has run out of patience, and that he needs peace of mind more than he needs the money, a statement which is literally true since the owner's net worth, exclusive of the business, is ample.

It is instructive to note that the owner in this example was as straight, as honest, and as decent as anyone could be. He was active in the community, well-liked and respected among outsiders and employees alike, positive-thinking, cheerful, assertive while soft-spoken, financially independent, and emotionally stable. Yet, he was almost crushed by the experience. It is true that starting too late to look for a buyer—he had wanted his only child to take over—was only a part of the reason for his affliction. The unqualified buyer brought by the first broker, the errant $736,000 appraisal (explained in Example 11.4), the owner's lack of understanding or preparation for the process of selling, and his helplessness in dealing with things beyond his control after so many years of autocracy, also contributed to his bent spirit. Still, the point remains that selling a business is not like selling a house, that it can be and often is a long, drawn-out affair with the ups and downs of a roller coaster taxing everyone's patience and nerves, and that the best way to sell is to allow more time than can be reasonably imagined necessary. (The sale, incidentally, did close; the seller is enjoying his retirement; he is collecting royalties; the buyer is enjoying his new business, profits and all; and some day the seller's child will realize a full inheritance.)

Further explaining the above owner's loss of equanimity is that when owners begin to contemplate the sale of their businesses, they have decisions to make and prospects to consider which are so copious and so stressful that they make up a plague of the mind. How much will I get for my business?

How much will I lose to taxes? How much of the sale price will I have to finance? Will I receive my payments on time? Might I have to foreclose and, if so, would I have to come back out of retirement? Will I have enough to retire on in reasonable comfort? Or, if I am not retiring, will I have enough cash for my new venture? Will my new business succeed? Will my health hold up? Will my buyer be fair to my employees and customers who have been so loyal and so important to my success? Will I still see my old business associates and will I still maintain those friendships? Will I enjoy my retirement or will I grow old with boredom? Will I live long enough to enjoy the fruits of my lifelong labors? And last but not least, how can I enjoy anything as I mark, one by one, the deaths of my contemporaries?

Now realizing the myriad concerns that can bother an owner's mind and recalling all that weighs on a buyer's mind (such as the financial risks of buying a business, making bank payments for the business as well as for the buyer's house, and so on), and further realizing that the buyer's and owner's emotions play on each other, it becomes easier to understand how everyone's emotions during a purchase-and-sale transaction can rise to previously unknown heights—and depths. Thus the wise owner preparing for the sale of a business recognizes the importance of emotions in both buyer and seller and, by simply recognizing them, becomes better able to keep them under control. The wise owner also allows plenty of time for the sale and, when feeling stressed, talks things out with a confidant.

Deciding When to Notify the Employees. As though there were not already enough thoughts and decisions to drive an owner to distraction, here is another: How soon should I tell my employees that I'm thinking of selling? Or should I not say anything until I close the sale? If Logic were king, owners would share this information with their employees just to unburden themselves of the gnawing concern when they already have more on their minds than they comfortably can deal with. Instead, owners generally avoid the issue with explanations like the following: "They don't need to know that yet;" "I'll tell them when the time is right;" or "They're not dumb; they can figure it out for themselves." Such statements obviously are inconsistent with owners' expressed concerns for the well-being of their employees, concerns which the author views as sincere. It is therefore speculated that a variety of feelings and fears combine to cause the owners' irrational reticence and that some of these are fear of hurting the employees; fear that some of them, especially key employees, will look for new jobs for fear of losing the jobs they have; inability to be assertive in what is perceived as an awkward and unpleasant task;

Illustration 4.1

"But Dad, that's not what I want to do with my life."

reluctance to face the finality of the end of a lifestyle; fear of the unknown; and confusion caused by all that is on their minds. Adding to the confusion is one of the more prevalent myths of the small business marketplace that if a sale is being contemplated, customers will defect; so will employees and suppliers, and competitors will find a way to take advantage of the news.

Adding to the complexity is that telling the employees of a contemplated sale is a matter of kindness and gentility, and perhaps a moral issue, because to deny such information is to strip the employees of their dignity. Putting that issue aside, however, when employees are told as far as possible in advance of the contemplated sale date, say, one or two years, several advantages accrue.

A climate of trust is established, thus inspiring sustained productivity including minimal absenteeism and theft. Letting the employees know that their skills as individuals and as a team are the difference between a viable business and an empty shell and that a new owner will need these skills even more than the present owner, will add feelings of security to the climate of trust.

Informing the employees well in advance of the sale allows time for them to mentally adapt. A long lead-time also increases the chance for a defecting employee, if any, to do so with ample time for the owner to find and train a replacement.

The seller, by disclosing to all parties concerned, is relieved of maintaining a secret which, as closing approaches, becomes increasingly difficult to keep. Moreover, the owner who shares this information is much more likely to find cooperation and support at an emotionally trying time in life, a time when an owner can use all the support he can get.

Telling the employees simplifies showings to prospective buyers by allowing showings during working hours, if convenient, and without the burden and indignity of deceit.

When employees are brought into the selling process by being asked to help explain things to the buyer, they become graced with enhanced status and dignity and are much more likely, when the sale closes, to roll out a psychological red carpet for the buyer, a point worth considering on its own merits but especially noteworthy for the seller who finances the purchase.

The employees almost always discover the truth despite determined efforts to deprive them of it. Discovery occurs in a variety of ways: a slip of the owner's tongue; a careless or innocent leak by a buyer or broker; and necessary dealings with licensing agencies, outside accountants, and others which cannot easily be hidden or explained and which sometimes can be downright obtrusive. Finally, the intuitive faculties of the employees, especially the older ones with keener sensitivities, may easily recognize such clues as "insurance inspections," frequent visits by unexplained strangers, letters marked "personal and confidential," the expressions on people's faces, and so on.

Unless the seller can specifically identify a probable danger such as, say, customer defections to a competitor with perceived greater permanence in an industry where such permanence is critical, full disclosure to all parties concerned is likely to provide the easier, smoother course to closing the sale of a small business. It is also likely to promote lasting feelings of good will.

The following two examples illustrate how difficult it is to hide the fact of the sale, and example 4.2 also illustrates some of the hurt and anger that can result.

Example 4.2 The purchase and sale of a restaurant has been locked in place by the agreement on price and terms, the approved bank financing, and a signed contract with just a few weeks to go before closing. The broker reiterates an earlier suggestion to the seller that he inform the employees of the impending sale. The seller replies that he will introduce the buyer to the employees after the sale actually closes, not before, and that that is the way it will be.

Since a change in tenancy requires the municipal building inspector to approve the premises before issuing an occupancy permit, the buyer makes the required arrangements. The inspector dutifully mails a notice of scheduled inspection to the buyer but uses the restaurant's address. The letter is opened by the office manager (opening the mail is one of her duties) who is shocked and angered to see the contents and to realize that her years of loyalty and scrupulous honesty (she handled much of the cash) have been rewarded by the planning of such a major event while keeping her in the dark. She shows the inspection notice to the kitchen manager who happens to be in the office and he utters an exclamatory phrase followed by an announcement to the office manager that he will resign on the spot (a threat, however, which he fails to carry out). When confronted, the seller states that he had intended to inform them but had not yet gotten to it, a true statement which is interpreted correctly as a lie. The purchase and sale does close but in an ambiance of employee bitterness and confusion.

Fortunately, the buyer had been informed of the general status by the broker and he had enough sensitivity and common sense to placate the employees by meeting with each one of them individually and assuring them of the security of their jobs with no cuts in pay. The business is now thriving and everyone is happy.

Example 4.3 A broker with a restaurant for sale is describing it to a prospective buyer in the buyer's home. Unbeknown to anyone, part of the conversation is overheard by the buyer's daughter who later that day tells her girl friend who happens to be a waitress at another restaurant. That night there is an after-hours party attended by a number of workers in the restaurant trade. The next evening the owner is told by two of his waitresses that there is a rumor going around that their restaurant is for sale and that everybody seems to know about it except the people who work there. Fortunately, the owner had a few months earlier told two of his senior employees, his maitre d' who had been with him for twelve years and the head cook who had been with him for 17 years, that he was beginning to think about retiring and that he would keep them and the other employees informed if anything developed. He calls the cook over to verify his statement and then he informs the three of them that he still plans to sell, that he will keep everybody informed if anything significant is about to happen, but that nothing is in the works at present nor is it likely to be in the near future. This owner eventually does sell and everything goes smoothly. (Incidentally, the buyer's first act of ownership was to remove his jacket and his necktie, roll up his sleeves, walk into the kitchen, ask the dishwasher to teach him how to use the chemical dishwasher, and start washing dishes, thus making an instant hit with the employees. This restaurant has sales in seven figures which means that there were almost 50 employees to make a hit with as well as lots of dishes to wash.)

Deciding Whether to Conduct the Sale in Confidence. The question of whether to conduct the sale in confidence troubles many sellers. They have great antipathy to disclosing the fact of the sale to suppliers, customers, competitors, and, as already noted, employees. They seem to fear that suppliers may cut off credit for fear of the seller's skipping out without paying, that customers may desert to invest their loyalties in businesses with seemingly greater permanence, that competitors somehow may lure customers from them, and that employees may seek security in other jobs for fear of being laid off. These fears are justified partly because they are a natural product of the human imagination and partly because they have a certain plausibility. Further, there are probably actual cases where these fears have come true with dire results. From the author's experience, however, such fears are rarely actualized and they are therefore more imagined than real. Moreover, if the sale is to be kept in confidence, the employees will have to be denied access to the fact, a difficult task as demonstrated above, and one which is hardly worthy. Therefore, with the possible exception of businesses limited by very special circumstances, owners who disclose their intentions to sell at about the same time they begin their search for a buyer probably will enjoy smoother transactions than those who do not. The disclosure need not be formal or rigorous; in fact, just the opposite. A casual mention during ordinary conversation is all that it takes. To illustrate, an owner might be chatting with a supplier as follows:

Supplier: Did you hear about Gateway Widget? That company just got bought out by a New York conglomerate.

Owner: That's not bad. I don't think I'd mind if someone
           bought me out.

Supplier: You're not serious.

Owner: I'm not ready yet but give me another year or
           two and I could be interested.

Nothing more need be said by the owner. The supplier will probably mention the owner's comment to his colleagues and perhaps to other tradespeople and the word will begin to spread. Note the owner's use of a buffer, "I'm not ready yet but . . ." This phrase softens the announcement and removes any immediacy while in no way disguising or equivocating the owner's intent. Thus the owner is forthright and honest while setting his or her own pace. In other words, the owner is still in control and still riding the crest of autocracy. Before such disclosure is made to anyone outside the company, however, it should first be made to the employees, especially to such key employees as a foreman or an office manager. The same sort of buffer demonstrated above can be used with the employees. but one thing should be different. The disclosure still can be casual but it should be deliberate, not offhanded, to maintain the dignity of both the owner and the employees. For example, the owner might disclose to the foreman as follows:

(Owner walks up to his foreman in the shop.)

Owner: Jim, when you have a minute, could you see
        me in my office?

(Later, in owner's office)
Owner: Jim, I just wanted to let you know that one of these
        days—I haven't decided just when—but one of these
        days I probably will start thinking of looking for a

buyer for the business. I don't know if this comes as a surprise to you but I just felt that since you've been with me for eight years and always done a good job, you have a right to know where the company's headed. As I said, I haven't decided just when, in fact, the actual sale probably would be two or three years away, maybe more. But one of these days I'll have to start looking and I didn't want you to find out from anyone but me. Just in case you're worried about keeping your job, you won't have a problem. Good foremen are not easy to come by and a new owner will need you even more than I do. He'll have a lot to learn and he'll probably have to build the sales so he can pay for the business. Your job will be safe and, in fact, a new owner, probably about 20 years younger than me, will make the place grow and make your job even safer. I'm also going to tell Sue [office manager]; I don't want her to worry either. Actually, all your jobs are safe. If I didn't have good employees, I wouldn't have anything to sell and a buyer wouldn't have anything to buy.

Jim: What if the new guy brings his own people?

Owner: That won't happen because one of the best assets that a buyer gets is the team of employees with just the right training and just the right mix of skills to make the business successful. If the new owner has his own people, he doesn't need to buy a business; he can start his own. One other thing, Jim, if you don't mind talking to the prospects who come in to look at the business, that'll give you the chance to look them over and you can tell me what you think. I guess that's all I had to say. Any time you want to know where things stand, just let me know. Same for all the employees, in fact, it's O.K. to pass the word around but just don't make a big deal out of it because it'll be a while before anything even begins to happen and when it does I'll let you know.

This owner did everything right. He came out in the open with his plan to sell. He broke it first to his most important employee signaling that employee's continuing importance. He used a buffer so that no one will panic. He gave a straight answer and a correct answer to Jim's question about job security. He brought Jim into the selection process, elevating Jim's status. He said it was all right to tell the other employees thus signaling that he has nothing to hide from anyone. And he fortified his openness and his trust by inviting Jim to let him know any time Jim (or, by implication, any one else) had questions. If these employees do not stand up for the owner with their loyalty and trust; if they do not defend him against aspersions or critical reflections of any kind raised by fearful suppliers, creditors, or customers; if they do not give their all to welcome a prospective buyer and to make everything go smoothly, then nobody ever will. This owner still can not look forward to an easy sale; smooth dealings are not naturally inherent in the purchase-and-sale process and they probably never will be. But what this owner can look forward to is a peace of mind that he has been straightforward with everyone. The resulting clearness of mind will help him focus on the real substance of a transaction: finding a buyer, showing the buyer what he has to offer, negotiating the deal, and then cooperating with the buyer in every way possible to close the sale while knowing that he can count on his employees for full support.

Determining an Offering Price. The final requirement of preparing to sell a business is to conduct an appraisal. The appraisal is necessary for the seller to have a reasonable price to hold out to prospective buyers. Although appraising is covered in detail in Chapter 7, there are five mistakes commonly made which are worth noting as a preliminary warning.

First, it is a mistake to appraise by using a rule of thumb. Rules of thumb are useful but they can be terribly misleading when used improperly. They should be used only by those who understand their basis and limitations. Generally this means that they should be used only by professional appraisers who know what they are doing.

Second, it is wrong to count the owner's salary as part of the earnings of the business. The obvious result is to overvalue the business.

Third, it is wrong to count non-operational income, such as interest earned on cash parked in the company account, as earnings generated by the business. Again, the obvious result is to overvalue the business.

Fourth, it is mistaken and misleading to quote an offering price without including the underlying conditions. Examples of such conditions are whether the sale is of assets or corporate stock and whether such assets as real estate and surplus equipment are included in the price.

Fifth, it is a mistake to request a lawyer or accountant who lacks special training or experience to appraise a business. As will be noted in later chapters, the seriousness of this mistake is not so much in the wrongness of the value (although that is serious enough) as it is in the authoritative finality with which such appraisals are often stated. The problem is simply that a finality of tone tends to kill the deal.

When all of the preparations noted above are in place, the owner is ready to begin looking for buyers.

PART 2:
DEVELOPING LEADS TO BUYERS

The basic approach for a seller developing leads to buyers is to use the same avenues of communication used by the buyers, but from the opposite direction. The sources to be discussed are in the same order as those discussed for the buyers in Chapter 3. For brevity, the source information offered below does not stand alone. Instead, it is supplementary to the information provided in Chapter 3. After discussion of the sources, guidelines are offered for contacting prospective buyers, whether by telephone, mail, or personal visit.

The *Yellow Pages*. There are two types of prospective buyers which a seller may look for in the *Yellow Pages*: owners in the same trade who may want an additional location and owners in a complementary trade, such as the plumbing contractor in Example 1.6, who may want to broaden their services or product line. Depending on the trade, either type may be a likely source. Advantages and disadvantages of each are discussed below.

The Public Library. A visit to the public library should be as pleasurable for a prospective seller as for a prospective buyer with one important difference: going to the library requires some extra effort and initiative. Prospective buyers tend to be charged by the excitement and energy of comparative youth looking to the future while prospective sellers tend to languish in the sedateness of age looking to the past. Further, going to the library to do research may be alien to the normal routine of buyers and sellers alike except that sellers will generally have had longer lifetimes to become fixed in their ways, especially if they have waited too long to sell. On the other hand, people seem to treat older citizens with more courtesy and respect than younger ones, offsetting some of the disadvantages of age. In any case, sellers may refer to the same books used by buyers to determine the names of owners in their trade or in complimentary trades, and to find such information as size of company, products, and services, which might help to target possible buyers.

If the seller prefers not to do this work, perhaps a librarian can be hired to do the research or perhaps a college English major. Also, there may be a *Yellow Pages* classification for Library Research.

Newspaper Classified Advertising. Some obvious advantages of newspaper advertising are that the process of selling may begin with almost instantaneous facility, a large audience may be reached, and the cost is relatively low. Perhaps the best advantage is that anyone responding to an advertisement is probably motivated. The only disadvantage is the occasional snoop or curiosity-seeker who responds. Using an address to reply to rather than a telephone number should minimize the problem if the seller does not feel comfortable dealing with it. The seller might also order an additional but unlisted telephone line for the sole purpose of placing that number in the advertisement.

Recalling from Chapter 1 that nothing is more important in the purchase and sale of a business or more timely to consider at the outset than the qualifications of the buyer, the information in the advertisement should help the buyer decide his or her ability to own. In fact, the advertisement should be strictly limited to that information. Thus the two pieces of information which should most appear in the advertisement are the type of business offered for sale and the gross sales or revenues. The importance of the type is obvious. The importance of the gross sales is that, for a knowledgeable buyer, it roughly describes the business in a nutshell. For example, gross sales of $500,000 in a manufacturing shop would imply about six or seven employees with a certain mix of skills and a certain mix of machinery; the same sales in a cafeteria would imply about ten or eleven employees with a certain mix of skills and so on; while the same sales in a sit-down restaurant might imply about 16 or 17 employees with still another mix of skills, and so on.

Generally, an advertisement written to occupy the minimum space requirement by the newspaper is adequate and any advertisement larger than the minimum by more than a line or two is probably wasteful. The *St. Louis Post-Dispatch* has a three-line minimum which is often enough space to convey the information needed by a buyer for an initial screening and contact. That minimal information is the type of business for sale, the gross sales, and the seller's telephone number or mailing address. A mention of the general location is also helpful when there are a large number of businesses in the trade as there are, for example, in the restaurant trade.

Some information is usually best omitted from an advertisement for various reasons: the offering price usually should be omitted because it is too dependent on other conditions such as whether real estate and other property are included in the sale. Down payment usually should be omitted because that term means one thing to a seller but something entirely different to a financing bank and it would therefore be confusing to a buyer. The seller's intent to finance or not to finance almost always should be omitted partly because financing is a nebulous matter in the early stages of a buy-sell transaction, but more importantly because financing almost always should be discussed and settled only during the negotiation and not before. Some items of information are mostly irrelevant for initial communication and much of it even in the final analysis. Such information should therefore not appear in the advertisement. Examples are "completely remodeled," "good location," "recession-proof," "steady trade," "new equipment," "illness forces sale," "price reduced," "owner retiring," and "must see."

Inclusion of brief hints of the character of the business can be useful to minimize incoming telephone calls. For example, a manufacturer specializing in punching operations or a beauty salon exclusively using blow-drys probably should say so in the advertisement. Exclamation points should not be used because they tend to cheapen the message and insult the buyer.

Figure 4.1 offers examples of advertisements suitable for a local newspaper as they might appear under typical classified headings:

Figure 4.1 Newspaper Classified Advertisements

8540 GENERAL BUS. OPP.	**8333 MFG. BUS. OPP.**
Hair salon, gross $180,000, 6 sta., NW County 820-1000	Sheet metal job shop, steel, Gross $800K, 510-2000
Travel Agency, gross $1.4 million, W County, PO Box 2377, St. Louis MO 63170	Custom wood shop, Sales $800,000 980-2222

8570 RESTAURANT BUS. OPP.
Short order, sales $600,000 North City, 840-7000
Gourmet lunch & dinner Sales $1 million plus, 220-4000

As this book goes to press, these advertisements cost about $24 per line in the Sunday edition with a three-line minimum. Advertisements need not be run more often than every third or fourth Sunday because serious prospective buyers will continue perusing the advertisements week after week. Residential telephone numbers generally should be used to minimize disturbances on the job. A telephone answering machine may be useful to allow the owner to return calls at his or her convenience or to assure privacy by hooking to an unlisted number. A mailing address can be used if the telephone is not convenient. It has the advantage of helping to confirm the inquirer's identity and it can be used to assure privacy by means of a Post Office Box or newspaper box.

Advertising in *The Wall Street Journal* is more expensive because of the greater circulation and the larger minimum linage, but the advertisements are easier to write because of the extra lineage. To fill up the extra lines, truly useful information such as "established 1972," "10% growth last 3 years," "potential national market," "established product line," and "patented product," may be offered.

Trade Magazines. The same guidelines for writing newspaper classified advertisements will apply to writing trade magazine advertisements. There probably will be few if any advertisements for business offerings and the paucity will provide a hint of the market activity. Nevertheless, their markets can produce purchases and sales. The key, as usual, is timing.

Trade Organizations. Depending on the activities and procedures of the individual organization, a prospective seller can use word of mouth, a notice on a bulletin board, and/or an announcement at a meeting to advertise the offering. More dignified and probably most effective would be a formal notification in the form of a letter from the prospective seller to the trade organization. The letter should be brief and should include little more than would appear in a newspaper advertisement.

Suppliers. As evidenced in Examples 3.1 and 3.2, suppliers are usually willing to mention the availability of a business for sale to the right party. The briefest sort of mention should suffice.

Bank Trust Departments. Although bank trust departments generally do not serve as business brokers in the usual sense, some of them may agree to act as an intermediary by introducing a seller to a qualified buyer if they should happen to find one in the normal course of their other duties. A prospective seller should telephone a bank trust department to determine if it would provide such an introductory service and, if so, for what fee. Then the seller would send a letter to the trust department providing a brief description of the business for sale and acknowledging the fee. Such a fee might be one percent of the sale price, with extra charges for a variety of services. Depending on the caliber of the personnel, the trust department might also provide other services, such as preparing a loan application package, mediating a negotiation, or appraising the business.

Accountants. A prospective seller generally should inform the company's accountant that a prospective buyer would be welcomed. The seller might also contact other accountants, preferably by letter.

Commercial Real Estate Firms. If the prospective seller is leasing the premises from a commercial real estate firm, the firm should be notified just to increase the chances of the right buyer making either a serendipitous or determined discovery. Lining up other real estate firms in a kind of network probably would have a very low probability of payoff simply because the other firms would have no interest in the premises and thus little if any interest in helping out. This thorough approach will not generally be useful but may be worth considering.

The Internet. The Internet as an important avenue for matching buyers and sellers is still in a state of development. Nevertheless, visiting web sites is so easy for those who are on line that advertising a business for sale on a web site may be worthwhile for the sake of thoroughness. Even those who are not on line can visit the public library to browse the Internet. The *St. Louis Post-Dispatch* presently offers to run its newspaper advertisements on its web site for a small additional fee. Other newspapers may do the same. Perhaps trade organizations and trade magazines also offer web sites with businesses for sale. If listing a business for sale with a broker belonging to the International Business Brokers Association (IBBA), the broker may elect to advertise on the IBBA web site. Some brokers have their own web sites for displaying their businesses for sale. Since the Internet is still developing, one should browse it from time to time just to stay abreast of progress. But one word of caution: regulatory controls, if and when they exist, exist only within a state. The Internet is an interstate affair (as well as international) and, with respect to the small business marketplace, it is unregulated. One should therefore always seek legal counsel locally from one's own lawyer before making a commitment on the Internet.

PART 3:
DECIDING WHICH SOURCES TO EXPLORE FOR LEADS

When confronted by the variety of sources for prospective buyers outlined above, a seller can easily be confused or intimidated unless there is a way to decide which of those sources may best be applied to the search for a buyer. Unfortunately, there is no sure method of choosing the best source or sources partly because of the variety in the character of small businesses even in the same trade, partly because of the varying personalities of their owners, and partly because of the innate and somewhat surprising complexity of buy-sell situations in general. However, there are some considerations discussed in the following sections which should help a seller to at least have a sense of direction when deciding how to proceed. These considerations include whether a buyer might be sought in the same trade or in a complimentary trade; whether the business has regional or national interest or just local; and whether a buyer experienced at ownership or one who is inexperienced would be preferable to deal with. Although the decisions which must be made are less difficult than those discussed earlier in this chapter, they can be vexing nevertheless.

Similar or Complementary Businesses as Prospective Buyers. Approaching an owner of a similar business sometimes offers an easy solution to the problem of finding a buyer because some lines of business lend themselves to multiple ownership. A good example is a retail dry cleaning chain where the main store has a retail section in the front and a fully-equipped cleaning plant in the rear. Other stores in the chain serve as customer outlets, staffed by counter persons who tend to be relatively unskilled workers at relatively low pay. The equipment needed at an outlet is minimal and inexpensive and a simple panel truck equipped with clothing racks transports the clothes to and from the cleaning plant and outlets. The attraction of such a setup is the synergism of one well-equipped plant for two or more stores. Even if the seller's business has a full set of equipment which would duplicate the prospective buyer's, the deal could be attractive for several reasons. One is that the value of a business for sale is in the profits made, not in the equipment owned, and duplication of equipment is therefore usually not important. Another reason is that if the profits still can be made using only the buyer's equipment, the seller's equipment can be sold and the proceeds applied to the price of the purchase. Still another reason is that the additional sales will result in a higher profit margin because some expenses, such as legal, accounting, advertising, medical insurance, and some utilities, will remain fixed and because employee productivity at the plant will improve due to the increased volume keeping the employees busy.

The disadvantages from the buyer's point of view are the dilution of management, the usual shortcomings of operating without an owner at a remote site (theft, compromised customer relations, higher employee turnover, etc.), increased difficulty of hiring the right employees to work in the absence of an owner, and so on. Some owners of similar businesses would not welcome these problems but some would, especially the more capable owners who know how to solve these problems.

Other lines of business may benefit from a second location, but for different reasons. For example, manufacturers of products which are bulky, heavy, or fragile might benefit from a second plant a few hundred miles from its own plant to minimize transportation costs. Examples of such products are bulletin boards (especially if they are glass-enclosed) and large metal or concrete castings. The obvious disadvantage would be the need for an exceptionally trustworthy manager for the second plant. The need for a good manager, however, could be a blessing for a business owner who already has someone capable but with no appropriate slot for that person to fill.

Possibilities of buyouts by complementary companies forming synergistic mergers are numerous and are usually driven by increasing sales to the same customers. Examples are the dry cleaner buying a shirt laundry or vice versa; a candy distributor buying a tobacco jobber; a plumbing contractor buying a sewer contractor as in Example 1.6; and a national soft-drink manufacturer buying a national retail pizza chain, which has the added advantage of locking out an arch competitor.

A prospective seller must weigh the advantages and disadvantages from a buyer's viewpoint and decide whether or not there is a reasonable chance of selling to the owner of a similar or complementary business.

National or Regional Prospective Buyers. There are several factors to suggest whether a business for sale may have national or regional interest. Large profits, uncommon goods or services, an independent operation which could fit into a chain, and a candidate for synergism as illustrated above are examples of what might entice a buyer from one state to relocate to another or to assign a trusted manager. Also, some individuals might find personal reasons to make a move. In any case, what is important is to recognize the possibility and to pursue it if it seems reasonable to do so.

Some examples of St. Louis businesses attempted to be sold to regional or national sources illustrate the diversity of responses and the difficulty of success a seller might encounter.

Example 4.4 Four approaches are taken to sell a cash-cow retail store with a documented annual cash flow of $400,000 including the owner's salary. First, it is advertised twice in the Midwest Edition of *The Wall Street Journal* and once in the Asiatic Edition, with only one response. (The response, ironically, is from a St. Louisan who was lured by the broker's St. Louis address shown in the advertisement.)

Second, a national chain headquartered in an eastern state is called; the manager of site development is very cordial and explains that they have learned from experience to follow a fairly rigid formula which requires, among other things, a certain building size and lot size. By sticking to the formula they have enjoyed a high rate of success. The store for sale does not conform to their specifications (parking lot too small) so they will have to pass.

Third, letters are sent to several prominent local retailers and to the 25 largest accounting firms in the St. Louis area. Three retailers reply. One is just snooping; one seems serious but does not follow up; and one (thought by the broker to be the best candidate because of his eminent success as an absentee owner) expresses enthusiastic interest, goes on a showing and meets the seller, then backs away with no explanation except that he doesn't have time to follow up. (It is learned later that he did not care for the seller's personality and he did not trust him.) One accountant sends a note to the broker saying thanks but he doesn't have anyone who could be interested at present, and another telephones saying thanks for the notice and adds that in his opinion the broker has got a tough sale simply because there are not many people walking around who have nearly a million dollars to invest and even if they did, they would be reluctant to put it into something with the high failure rate which characterizes individual retailers.

Fourth and finally, a one-time three-line advertisement in the *St. Louis Post-Dispatch* produces several responses including two buyers already in business and looking for a second location. The first of those two is leaving that evening for a one-week ski vacation but he will call back immediately when he returns. The second visits the store the same day, offers full list price two days later, and ultimately closes the purchase. The buyer, incidentally, is doing well.

Example 4.5 A well-equipped, well-established, and exceptionally profitable machine shop with $2.8 million annual sales is advertised in the Midwest Edition of *The Wall Street Journal*. Several responses are received including one from a technically well-qualified buyer in Indiana who is an owner attempting to expand. This buyer, however, has already bought a second shop; this was to have been his third; he has already over-reached his capacity; and he is forced to back away. Another of the responders is a broker. The others are superficial in their inquiries and do not follow up.

Example 4.6 A retail dry cleaner with annual sales of $1.8 million is advertised in the Midwest Edition of *The Wall Street Journal*. Eight or nine responses include an Ohio broker specializing in dry cleaning companies, a Wisconsin agency wondering if the business could be relocated to that state, and a Californian who had read the Midwest Edition on the airplane.

Dealing with Experienced Owners vs. Inexperienced. There are some important differences between prospective buyers who have been or presently are in business and those who are not in business and never have been. Experienced owners are generally more direct in their questioning, quicker to make up their minds whether or not to make an offer, much more prone to hunt for a bargain, more prone to delete pieces of equipment which they don't want and are not willing to pay for, much more able to start an operation similar to the seller's if the sale price is not right (and therefore able in some cases to become a competitor), and more desirable from a bank's point of view to finance.

Those who have never owned a business are generally slower to decide because they need more time for fact-finding, appraising, and negotiating; much less prone to hunt for a bargain; slower to obtain financing; much more cooperative at every stage of the transaction; more likely to rely heavily on a lawyer or an accountant for advice including appraising; and more often in need of training or at least substantial assistance during the early phase of ownership. Also, their qualifications for ownership are more difficult to evaluate. These differences will manifest themselves from the first time the buyer and seller meet until some time after closing the sale. The net effect is that buyers who are not owners or former owners are generally slower and more taxing to deal with, but financially more rewarding.

PART 4:
GREETING THE BUYERS

Greeting the buyers may occur in either of two situations. One is when being contacted by buyers responding to advertisements and the other is when contacting targeted buyers. The similarities and differences in the two situations and how best to handle them are covered below.

Buyers Contacting the Seller. When responding to a seller's advertisement, a buyer may expect to be given all the information that he or she needs forthwith. Although such expectation is not unreasonable considering that the seller has issued an invitation, it is better for all parties concerned for the relationship to start with the buyer doing the giving to show his or her qualifications for ownership. Once those qualifications have been shown, the relationship between the buyer and seller can start to grow. If those qualifications have not been shown and the buyer and seller continue the relationship, they may both be wasting their time and, what is worse, they may be headed into a relationship dangerous to both. In any case, if the buyer does not offer it, the seller should ask, at the very beginning of the first conversation with a buyer, how much experience that buyer has in the trade. If the buyer appears to have little or no experience, the seller should ask how the buyer proposes to prepare himself or herself to manage the business. If the buyer's answers do not seem satisfactory, the seller may say, very politely, that the business for sale is not an easy one to manage and it probably would require someone with stronger qualifications to succeed.

If the buyer does appear to be well qualified, the seller then should provide a rough idea of the sale price, taking care to mention whether or not real estate is included, whether the price is based on the sale of assets or the sale of stock, and any other important conditions underlying the price. Then the seller may add that no matter who finances the purchase, a cash infusion of anywhere from 20% to 40% of the purchase price probably would be necessary to get started. If the buyer does not recoil, the seller may then ask if the cash for the infusion would be readily available, assuming that they eventually reach agreement on price and terms. During exchange of the above information, the seller should ask any questions which will increase the seller's comfort with respect to the buyer's qualifications, such as what company the buyer worked for, what kind of equipment he or she used, how many years in the trade, whether the buyer knows how to estimate costs (for production bids in a job shop, menu items in a restaurant, or whatever is germane to the business), what special training the buyer has had, and so on.

Although the main purpose of these questions is to determine the buyer's qualifications for ownership, another purpose is to start the relationship and to discover the personal chemistry which might or might not develop between the buyer and seller.

If the buyer is brought by a broker, the seller should not assume that the broker has asked the right questions or understood the answers. Instead, the seller should assume exactly the opposite and determine positively that the buyer is qualified both technically and financially. All of the questioning described above should take place within a few minutes of when the buyer and seller first say hello, whether by telephone or in person although, if in person, some delay may be allowed for polite exchange of pleasantries.

If the buyer proves not to have adequate qualifications, the seller, so as not to spend any more time than necessary, must dismiss the buyer but must do so politely: "I appreciate your interest but I feel sure that, unless there is something I don't understand, this probably is not the right business for you and I think we should bring this meeting to a close." If the buyer does have adequate qualifications, or nearly so, the seller can loosen up and start to provide such details as a tour of the business, balance sheet and income statement, advertising brochure, list of equipment, and more or less whatever the buyer asks for. If the seller has lingering doubts about the buyer's qualifications or suspects that the buyer may be something other than claimed, the seller has the right to provide information in small amounts to stretch out the process, cause the buyer to revisit an extra time or two, and thereby provide the seller more time to get comfortable with the buyer. The seller would not be rude for doing so, considering that there is so much at stake for both parties and also considering that familiarization and fact-finding are as much for the buyer's best interest as for the seller's.

Since the seller probably has never before sold a business, since the buyer probably has never bought one, and since they probably are new to each other, the first meeting may tend to be tentative and exploratory. As the deal progresses, both will rely heavily on intuitive judgment and guessing as to what to do and when to do it. One point on which sellers generally agree is to not provide the buyer with anything which could aid a competitor if the deal fails to close. Examples of such information are customer lists and non-standard manufacturing processes (note that the importance of such information with respect to a competitor may vary from one situation to another). Otherwise, the sale of a business should be thought of as one of those times in life when an owner must forsake privacy to get the job done, while a prospective buyer must partially subordinate himself or herself in deference to the owner's station and in consideration of the owner's loss of privacy. As the deal progresses, the buyer will gradually become less subordinate, the seller will gradually become more comfortable with the loss of privacy, and, if things go well, the spirit of cooperation will take hold and rule the negotiation. There will be brief times, as in all human relationships, when things do not go smoothly. The obvious remedy is to be patient and understanding and let time run its course. There also will be cases where the buyer, though well qualified for the business, does not seem to have good chemistry with the seller. Such cases seem to be infrequent, but when they occur, an intermediary can save the day. Even when things seem to go well, both buyer and seller should have a confidant with whom to talk things over.

One of the more common mistakes made during their early meetings, by buyers and sellers alike, is failing to understand the difference between fact-finding and negotiating or, if understood, failing to act accordingly. This difference will be fully explained in later chapters but for now suffice it to say that fact-finding is the process of acquiring data about the business, the operation of the business, the profits of the business, and so on. Negotiating is attempting to reach agreement on price and terms. What must be understood is that fact-finding has to be completed before negotiating can begin simply because the buyer cannot determine what price and terms to offer until the necessary facts have been found. A typical mistake is for a buyer during an early meeting to ask the seller if the seller will provide financing. Since that question can not be answered unless the seller has the entire offer to look at, it belongs in the negotiation. In fact, if it is important to the buyer, seller financing should be made a part of the buyer's offer regardless of whether the seller has agreed to it. Another typical mistake is for a seller during fact finding to answer the buyer's question about financing with a yes or a no. The seller's correct answer almost always is that seller financing might be considered, once an offer is received, if the overall price and terms are satisfactory.

The Seller Contacting Targeted Buyers. Since a targeted prospective-buyer's qualifications have already been determined or reasonably presumed by virtue of the prospect's ownership of a business, the seller should simply introduce himself and state forthwith that his business is being placed on the market. If the targeted prospect indicates an interest, the seller will have to provide the same information to that prospect as to any other buyer. Whether any of this information might be used by the prospect to gain a competitive edge is left to the seller's judgment.

To make the contact, the seller will telephone, write, or personally visit the prospective buyer. Virtually all of the guidelines for making these contacts offered in Chapter 3 will apply to sellers even though there are important differences in their situations. One difference is that sellers, due to their experience as owners as well as by virtue of their nature, tend to be autocratic and they therefore rebel, to one degree or another, at the thought of reducing themselves to supplicants. Another difference, this one tending to alleviate the first difference, is that sellers have accountants and lawyers whom they can assign to make the contacts for them. Since accountants and lawyers already have the proper stationery plus an aura of legitimacy and importance, they are almost ideal choices for sending letters likely to be opened and read by prospective owner-buyers. The seller can ask the accountant or lawyer either to provide the seller's name and telephone number to the prospective buyer, or the buyer's name and number to the seller. The accountant or lawyer can assure a temporary level of confidentiality, by making generic reference in the letter such as to "a chemical manufacturer," or "a dry cleaner," without revealing the name of the company, the owner, or any telltale clues. An example of such a letter is shown in Figure 4.2.

Figure 4.2 A Letter in Confidence from the Seller's Accountant

JONES & JONES, P.C.
CERTIFIED PUBLIC ACCOUNTANTS
12199 NORTH KIRKWOOD ROAD
ST. LOUIS, MISSOURI 63122
(314) 000-6400

April 24, 2001

John Brown, President
Brown Chemical Company
1000 Elm Industrial Drive
St. Louis, Missouri 63000

Dear Mr. Brown:

We have been asked by one of our clients, a chemical manufacturing company, to inform several firms in the industry that our client would welcome a prospective purchaser.

The firms we are contacting were chosen by our client as likely to realize substantial synergism if one of them were to acquire the company.

If you could have an interest, please call me for discussion. If, for the time being, you wish to pursue your interest in confidence, you have my promise that your name will not be provided to my client without your permission. As an alternative, your accountant could call me and we could explore the mutual benefit of the purchase and sale, at least superficially, while protecting each party's confidentiality.

You have my personal assurance that my client's offering is genuine and reasonable.

Yours very truly,

(signed) John P. Jones, CPA

Note that in the Figure 4.2 letter there is no mention of sales, profits or specific product line (such as coatings, adhesives, etc.) which could give away the company's identity to a sharp tradesperson. Although such closed dealing is not in consonance with the general recommendations of this book, it demonstrates how a buyer can be sought while a sensitive seller remains temporarily anonymous. The lures for the buyer are the synergism; the probability that the seller, also a tradesperson, knows what he or she is doing; and the accountant's authentication of the offering.

The accountant or lawyer also could make telephone calls or personal visits, as could the seller. However, there are problems with these approaches. As illustrated in Chapter 3, telephoning or visiting can be demeaning and, considering that accountants and lawyers are no more known for their ability to suppress their egos than are entrepreneurs, mailing letters is the more comfortable and therefore the more likely approach to be effective. Moreover, telephoning and personal visiting are time-consuming, either drawing the seller away from managing the business or running up the accountant's or lawyer's bill. In some cases, a broker might be hired to do the work but problems would still exist. A broker's letterhead and text would be viewed by some owners as junk mail partly because of the stationery, partly because of the less-than-letter quality of the appearance, and partly because it is from a broker. Moreover, some brokers exhibit an understanding of English grammar and spelling which falls short of professional standards. A broker might be hired by the hour to telephone or personally visit targeted buyers, but their fees, even if less than an accountant's or a lawyer's, would still be sizeable. On the other hand, brokers are well experienced at these activities and therefore might be more effective than accountants or lawyers.

QUESTIONS FOR DISCUSSION
Chapter 4—The Seller's Search for a Buyer

1. Why should buyers read this chapter as well as sellers?

2. Why should buyers realize that a retiring owner's profits may be well short of potential?

3. Regular medical checkups are advisable for older people in general, but why especially for business owners?

4. When owners want to sell or bequeath their businesses to their children, should those children qualify for ownership as described in Chapter 1?

5. One of the questions for discussion at the end of Chapter 2 asked why illiquidity was described in such detail. How does the answer to that question relate to a) when to start looking for a buyer, b) when to notify the employees, and c) whether to conduct the sale in confidence?

6. Are employees graced with human dignity? Do they have feelings? What are your clues?

7. Why should a seller not bother to write a lengthy newspaper advertisement to attract a buyer?

8. Expressed in one short sentence, what is the underlying basis of the sources of leads to buyers?

9. Assume that you have a specific type of retail business for sale such as a dry cleaner, a pharmacy, or a sporting goods store. Compare the advantages and disadvantages of selling to a similar or complimentary business.

10. How might a national chain be interested in buying an independently owned business?

11. Would you rather sell to someone who's never owned a business or to someone who has?

12. Define fact-finding. Define negotiating.

CHAPTER 5

Business Brokers

The basic role of business brokers is to match up buyers and sellers of businesses, much as real estate brokers match up buyers and sellers of real estate. This chapter describes the brokers' role in detail and includes information on their services, their competency, their qualifications, their ethics, their fees, and how best to use them. The chapter is divided into two parts: What Business Brokers Do and Other Aspects of Business Brokers.

PART 1:
WHAT BUSINESS BROKERS DO

Business brokers' services cover a spectrum of activity in line with matching up their buyers and sellers. Exactly which services get provided and to what degree they get provided depends on the circumstances, the seller's needs, the buyer's needs, and the broker's capabilities.

The fourteen services discussed below are virtually all that are needed by buyers and sellers to meet their goals. It should be clear that most brokers provide only some of these services and that the services they do provide may not include those which are most critical, such as appraising and negotiating. Thus buyers and sellers sometimes are left to their own devices to solve their own problems.

Some brokers will perform all fourteen services if lured by a large enough commission on the sale. This may be especially true if the broker, sure of his or her own competency, wishes to obviate the risk of an incompetent performing these services and ruining the deal, thus losing the broker's commission. Services requiring considerable time and effort as well as considerable expertise, such as appraising and preparing a loan application package, may be offered only for an extra fee. The brokers most likely to provide a full range of services may be those willing to work for an hourly fee or requiring a non-refundable retainer up front.

Note that much of the work done by brokers is for the direct benefit of buyers even though sellers usually pay the fee. Arranging bank financing is one example, although, to be sure, the seller also benefits. Note also that one of the most important services performed by brokers working for a commission is seldom mentioned because it is passive rather than active. That service is to accept the risk that if the sale does not close, the broker does not get paid. That service is covered in the second part of the chapter in the discussion of brokers' fees.

Search for Sellers of Businesses. Most brokers follow a conventional approach to brokering by searching for owners willing to sell, listing their businesses for sale, and then searching for matching buyers. These searches for sellers may be conducted passively by a *Yellow Pages* listing or more actively by newspaper advertising, by canvassing on the telephone and through the mail, or by making personal visits. These brokers usually collect a commission from the seller when the sale is closed. A small minority of brokers also search for sellers but instead of trying to obtain listings, they merely keep a record of available businesses and then try to find buyers willing to pay for the match-up. Many brokers will work either for the seller or the buyer, whichever is willing to pay the fee. In any case, brokers relieve both buyers and sellers of the time, the effort, and the drudgery of making a match. This relief is possibly the brokers' most valuable service, a point further discussed below as part of the explanation of their fees.

List Businesses for Sale. If an owner who is willing to sell is also willing to pay a broker's fee, the owner and the broker may enter into a listing agreement making the broker the owner's agent and authorizing the broker to conduct selling activities on the owner's behalf. Such agreements are usually in writing on a pre-printed form. The terms of listing agreements may vary from one brokerage to another in accordance with the experience and the concerns of the individual brokerage or in terms of the experience and concerns of the lawyer preparing the agreement.

There are basically four types of listings: exclusive, non-exclusive, exclusive-agency, and single-buyer. An exclusive listing is probably most common. It gives the broker the exclusive right to sell the business and assures the broker of a fee or commission regardless of who finds the buyer. If, for example, an owner sells the business to someone in the owner's immediate family, with or without the broker's help, the broker is entitled to the fee called for in the listing agreement. Sometimes an owner may wish to exclude certain prospective buyers from the listing agreement, especially buyers for whom a possible matchup already exists. Examples of such exclusions are members of the owner's family and past prospective buyers who still may be contemplating purchase. Such exclusions should always be specifically identified by name and in writing on the listing agreement.

An example of an exclusive listing agreement is shown in Figure 5.1. Note that the list of 21 services attached to the listing agreement is greater in number than the 14 services mentioned in this chapter. The greater number is merely an elaboration of the services here mentioned. Note also that the blank spaces have been filled in to exemplify use of the form. Italics have been used to simulate signatures and the broker's handwriting.

Figure 5.1 Exclusive Listing Agreement (Page 1 of 2)

EXCLUSIVE LISTING AGREEMENT

March 3. 2001
Date

The undersigned owner hereby authorizes Honigmann, Inc., hereinafter referred to as Broker, to endeavor to find a buyer for the below-described business and hereby appoints Broker its agent with the exclusive right to sell said business for _One hundred eighty thousand dollars*_ _($180,000.00)_ or for any other price and terms to which owner shall agree. *Real estate not included._

ABC Corporation

14988 Business Boulevard

St. Louis, Missouri 63100

This agreement shall apply to the sale of the above-named business to any buyer found by Broker or by anyone else during the 12-month term of this agreement if said sale closes within 24 months after termination of this agreement.

Broker's commission shall be ten percent (10%) of the purchase price or six thousand dollars ($6,000), whichever is greater, and shall be payable in full by cashier's check at closing. Said commission shall be paid whether real estate is sold, leased, or lease-optioned, and whether sale is of stock or assets.

If a sale agreement is entered into and the buyer defaults, any earnest money shall be divided equally between owner and Broker.

If legal action is required to settle a difference between owner and Broker, reasonable legal expenses including attorney's fees of the prevailing party shall be paid by the other party.

Allowing that the need for each itemized service of a Broker is subject to a variety of circumstances, Broker's services are described, more or less, by the attached "Description of Services."

This is a binding agreement which binds and inures to the benefit of the parties, their successors, heirs, and assigns.

By _J. Q. Seller_
    Owner

    2548 Elm Grove Lane

    St. Louis, Missouri 63198

    _314-000-0999_

By _E. J. Honigmann_
    Broker Honigmann, Inc.

    1932 Greenglen Drive

    St. Louis, Missouri 63122

    _314-822-4602_

Figure 5.1 Exclusive Listing Agreement (Page 2 of 2)

DESCRIPTION OF SERVICES

1. Collect and analyze financial and other data.
2. Appraise the company to confirm reasonableness of offering price.
3. Advertise and search for buyers.
4. Prepare answers to buyers' questions.
5. Maintain confidentiality. (Note 2.)
6. Entertain buyers.
7. Write letter of intent for buyer. (Broker provides format; buyer dictates terms.)
8. Mediate the negotiation.
9. Prepare the contract and lease.
10. Prepare the bank-loan application package.
11. Respond to interrogatories from bank, SBA, and local development company.
12. Assist buyer in applications for permits.
13. Assist buyer in applications for insurance.
14. Mediate conflicts, if any, between buyer and seller.
15. Provide and receive guidance to and from attorneys and accountants.
16. Hold funds in escrow.
17. Prepare a closing statement.
18. Arrange and attend the closing.
19. Perform various post-closing services.
20. Coordinate all of the above including the whole transaction.
21. Maintain files for future reference.

NOTES:

1. Although the broker works for the seller's best interest, the overriding spirit of the typical purchase-and-sale transaction is spontaneous cooperation between buyer and seller in recognition of a mutually beneficial end.

2. Confidentiality can be maintained up to a point. That a company is being marketed eventually becomes evident. Informing employees of the owner's plans well in advance of closing is therefore recommended.

3. Broker practices full disclosure to the buyer.

Note the phrase saying that the commission is payable " . . . whether real estate is sold, leased, or lease-optioned." The listing is for the business but it may include the real estate if both are owned by the same corporation but probably not if owned by the same individual. If separately owned or if owned by the same individual, the real estate probably should be placed on the market in a separate listing. The purpose of the above phrase is to assure that the commission for the sale of the business is due no matter how the real estate is handled. But also note that the broker will usually collect an additional commission based on the total rent on the first term of the lease or, if not leased, on the sale price. Sometimes, depending probably as much on the owner's ability to negotiate as on anything else, the broker may collect a commission on the rent under the buyer's first term of the lease, the rent on any lease options that get exercised, and/or on the exercised option to sell.

A non-exclusive listing differs from an exclusive listing in that the broker earns a fee only if the buyer is produced by the broker. Such listings may appeal to owners who feel intimidated by an exclusive agreement or who have prospective buyers in mind for whom matchup services would not be needed. An owner trying to speed the sale of his or her business may legally sign non-exclusive listings with two or more brokers. Such practice is generally not recommended. In fact, it is rather unethical without some sort of special procedure. The problem is that the eventual buyer may legally and ethically visit two or more brokers who by coincidence have the same non-exclusive listing thus creating confusion and controversy as to which broker deserves to be paid. Moreover, a broker's effectiveness in making the sale is partly dependent on the owner's cooperation in explaining the workings of the business to the broker, a difficult task to begin with and all the more difficult with multiple brokers. An example of a non-exclusive listing agreement is shown in Figure 5.2 (less the list of services, which is the same as in Figure 5.1).

Figure 5.2 Non-Exclusive Listing Agreement (Page 1 of 2)

NON-EXCLUSIVE LISTING AGREEMENT

March 3, 2001
Date

The undersigned owner hereby authorizes Honigmann, Inc., hereinafter referred to as Broker, to endeavor to find a buyer for the below-described business and hereby appoints Broker its agent to sell said business for *One hundred eighty thousand dollars* ($180,000.00)* or for any other price and terms to which owner shall agree. **Real estate not included.*

ABC Corporation

14988 Business Boulevard

St. Louis, Missouri 63100

This agreement shall apply to the sale of the above-mentioned business to any buyer found by Broker during the 12-month term of this agreement if said sale closes within 24 months after termination of this agreement.

Broker's commission shall be ten percent (10%) of the purchase price or six thousand dollars ($6,000), whichever is greater, and shall be payable in full by cashier's check at closing. Said commission shall be paid whether real estate is sold, leased, or lease-optioned, and whether sale is of stock or assets.

If a sale agreement is entered into and the buyer defaults, any earnest money shall be divided equally between owner and Broker.

If legal action is required to settle a difference between owner and Broker, reasonable legal expenses including attorney's fees of the prevailing party shall be paid by the other party.

Allowing that the need for each itemized service of a Broker is subject to a variety of circumstances, Broker's services are described, more or less, by the attached "Description of Services."

This is a binding agreement which binds and inures to the benefit of the parties, their successors, heirs, and assigns.

By *J. Q. Seller*	By *E. J. Honigmann*
Owner	Broker Honigmann, Inc.
2548 Elm Grove Lane	*1932 Greenglen Drive*
St. Louis, Missouri 63198	*St. Louis, Missouri 63122*
314-000-0999	*314-822-4602*

A kind of compromise between the exclusive and non-exclusive listing may be found with an exclusive-agency listing. Such a listing allows the owner to sell the business but also restricts the owner to listing with only one broker. An exclusive-agency listing may be created by adding the following sentence to a non-exclusive listing agreement: Owner agrees to list for sale with no other brokers during the term of this agreement.

A single-buyer listing agreement, sometimes referred to as a specific-engagement agreement, may be preferred by owners who feel intimidated by listings in general, or by brokers who have targeted a business for a specific buyer but who do not wish to carry the listing as a continued obligation to serve the owner. Owners who feel intimidated by listings should consider that simply telling the broker to bring the owner a buyer and that then the owner will sign a listing for that buyer, minimizes the broker's effectiveness. The problem is that without written authorization to conduct selling activities, the broker is limited in carrying out those activities, partly through fear of lawsuit from an owner with whom the verbal agreement might cause misunderstanding, and partly because the lack of written agreement denotes lack of motivation in the owner in which case the broker and the buyer may be wasting their time. Further, in some states it may be illegal for a broker to conduct selling activities without a written authorization from the owner.

One disadvantage to the owner who insists on a single-buyer listing is that the broker may require a higher commission. The reason is that with listings covering more than one buyer, the broker's vested efforts to list, fact-find, appraise, and so forth, may be applied to several buyers, giving the broker repeated chances to make the sale and earn a commission. With the single-buyer listing, the broker has only one chance.

An example of a single-buyer (specific-engagement) listing agreement is shown in Figure 5.3.

Figure 5.3 Specific-Engagement Agreement (Page 1 of 2)

SPECIFIC-ENGAGEMENT AGREEMENT

March 3, 2001
Date

The undersigned owner hereby authorizes Honigmann, Inc., hereinafter referred to as Broker, to conduct selling activities for the below-named business but only to the below-named buyer for *One hundred eighty thousand dollars* ($180,000.00)* or for any other price and terms to which owner shall agree. **Real estate not included.*

Business's name and address: _ABC Corporation, 14988 Business Boulevard_
St. Louis, Missouri 63100

Buyer's name and address: _J. Q. Buyer, 123 Shady Lane Avenue_
St. Louis, Missouri 63189

Broker's commission shall be twelve percent (12%) of the purchase price of the business or $10,000, whichever is greater, and shall be payable in full by cashier's check at closing if said closing is within two years of above date.

For purposes of this agreement, the total purchase price shall be defined as all consideration received by the owner including, but not limited to, cash, notes, or other property received; liabilities which are assumed by the buyer or subject to which the business is sold under either an asset sale or sale of corporate stock; amounts or property paid in return for lease or rental of seller's property in excess of the fair market value; and amounts or property paid in return for employment of owner, his representatives, or other employees.

Owner agrees that all representations pertaining to the above-named business shall be true and accurate to owner's best knowledge, and owner shall indemnify and hold Broker harmless from any claims made by any party relying upon said representations.

If legal action is required to settle a difference between owner and Broker, reasonable legal expenses including attorney's fees of the prevailing party shall be paid by the other party.

Allowing that the need for each itemized service of a Broker is subject to a variety of circumstances, Broker's services are described, more or less, by the attached "Description of Services."

This is a binding agreement which binds and inures to the benefit of the parties, their successors, heirs, and assigns.

By _J. Q. Seller_
Owner

2548 Elm Grove Lane

St. Louis, Missouri 63198

_314-000-0999_

By _E. J. Honigmann_
Broker Honigmann, Inc.

1932 Greenglen Drive

St. Louis, Missouri 63122

_314-822-4602_

There are two paragraphs in the Figure 5.3 listing agreement which do not appear in the listing agreements in Figures 5.1 and 5.2. One defines the purchase price and the other indemnifies the broker. Perhaps these paragraphs should be included in all listing agreements to protect the broker. Whether they are necessary or not depends on how comfortable the broker feels with the owner and on how comfortable the broker's lawyer feels. The advantage of omitting them is to simplify the agreement, making it less intimidating to the owner. In any case, these paragraphs are harmless to owners who are honest in their dealings.

The primary term of a listing to sell a business usually should be about one year. A primary term of one year seems excessive compared to the three-month and six-month terms typical for residential real estate but it is justified by the illiquidity of most small businesses. The agreement should also state that if the sale is made within a secondary term of, say, two years after the primary term has expired, but only to a buyer procured during the primary term, the broker shall collect a fee. The secondary term, also known as a security term, protects the broker in cases of unavoidable delays but also in cases of unethical sellers who would use dilatory tactics to nullify a commission. When an owner lists with a new broker upon expiration of the primary term of a listing with a previous broker, the owner must be careful to exclude in writing any prospective buyers still in their secondary terms with the previous broker. To minimize chances for confusion on this point, a list of any buyers procured by the broker whose primary term has expired should be furnished to the owner within a day or two of expiration, if not earlier.

In the author's opinion, a price at which the business is to be offered should always be written into the listing agreement. Such price is referred to as the listing price but may also be called the asking price or offering price. It is the price the broker presents to prospective buyers. It should be changed only in writing with the owner's and broker's signatures or in negotiation with a buyer. Some brokers, however, prefer not to state a price in the listing agreement; they simply solicit offers.

Some brokers appraise a business before listing it to determine if the owner's price is reasonable. These brokers may decline the listing if they feel that the owner's price is too high, or they may ask the owner to lower the price to conform at least roughly to the appraisal. Since many brokers are not competent enough to appraise and since most owners also are not competent to appraise, not even their own businesses, owners generally should hire an independent appraiser. Since even experienced appraisers have varying degrees of competency and since it is hard to tell the competent from the incompetent (their degrees, licenses, and certifications notwithstanding), appraisers should be chosen with the utmost care. The appraisal is critical because if the appraised price is too high, buyers are discouraged from looking seriously at the business, and the business, illiquid to begin with, is made more illiquid and practically unsellable. Listing prices that are too high eventually come down, but until they do, everyone's time is wasted. If an appraisal is too low, the owner is deprived of part of the value.

A possible solution to the problem of finding a competent appraiser is to assign the owner's accountant to the task with instructions to rigidly follow the procedures detailed in Chapter 7 on appraising. This solution is dicey, however, because accountants generally have little or no training as appraisers. They therefore tend to struggle with the process. Another solution is to hire a nationally recognized group like the Institute of Business Appraisers (800-299-4120) or the American Society of Appraisers (703-478-2228). See Chapter 7 for more discussion on appraising.

A clause stating that the winning party in a lawsuit shall have its legal expenses paid by the other party offers protection to both the owner and the broker by discouraging unfair or malicious practices not likely to stand up in court. Such clauses also have the remarkable effect of keeping honest people honest. They are particularly welcomed by brokers since their fees often pose enticing targets to less-than-scrupulous owners, and their lawyers, who use the threat of drawn-out litigation to extort their brokers into reduced fees. See Example 5.3 below.

Search for Buyers. Conventional brokers usually obtain listings for businesses for sale before searching for buyers. Their searches may employ any of the avenues of communication covered in Chapters 3 and 4. These avenues include the *Yellow Pages*, the public library, newspaper classified advertising, trade magazines, trade organizations, suppliers, bank trust departments, accountants, commercial real estate firms, and the Internet. Most brokers also have a backlog of prospective buyers.

Qualify Prospective Buyers. When a buyer responds to a broker's advertisement for a business for sale, the broker will probably be unwilling to offer much information until the buyer's experience and financial capability have been shown to qualify the buyer for ownership. If a broker has any listing other than an exclusive one, a prospective buyer probably will be required to sign an agreement promising to make any offers for the business only through the broker. The broker needs such an agreement with the buyer to help validate his or her claim for a fee from the seller and to discourage the buyer from trying to skirt the broker. Such an agreement will probably include a promise by the buyer not to disclose any facts of the business being offered to anyone but the buyer's advisors, such as the lawyer and accountant. Such non-disclosure agreements are usually described by brokers as necessary to protect the confidence of the seller. However, the brokers themselves receive protection by minimizing the chances of other buyers dealing directly with the owners and depriving the brokers of their commissions. Although there are arguments against attempting to conduct sales in secrecy (as explained in Chapter 4), buyers should nevertheless respect any requirements for non-disclosure. An example of a non-disclosure agreement is shown in Figure 5.4. Note that the name of the business should not be added to the agreement until the buyer has signed it.

One should not assume that brokers necessarily are talented at qualifying buyers. One should assume exactly the opposite. Brokers often do not understand the businesses they have for sale. Examples are offered in the section below. Owners therefore should check to their own satisfaction the credentials of any buyers brought by a broker.

Figure 5.4 Non-Disclosure Agreement

NON-DISCLOSURE AGREEMENT

Date_____

The undersigned prospective buyer understands the confidential nature of all information provided by Broker and the owner regarding the below-named business, and agrees to treat said information in the strictest confidence. The use of this information is exclusively for consideration by the buyer for the purchase of the business.

The undersigned buyer understands that information provided by Broker is the representation of the seller, and that Broker therefore does not certify or warrant the validity or accuracy of said information.

The undersigned agrees to submit all contracts to purchase the below-mentioned business through the Broker for a period of three years from the date of this agreement.

The undersigned understands that the Broker's commission is paid in full by the seller. In the event, however, that the below-named business is purchased by the undersigned or his or her agent in violation of this agreement, the undersigned will be held responsible to pay the Broker ten percent (10%) of the offering price listed below or $10,000, whichever is greater.

Business name and address _____

_____

Offering price _____

Buyer's name and address _____

_____

Buyer's signature_____   Broker's signature_____

Help Buyers Fact-Find. One of the main duties for all buyers is to find all of the relevant facts. Some brokers will offer their help, but there are at least three problems with relying on a broker's help for this activity. First, most brokers work for the seller's best interest, not the buyer's, and they are obligated only to refrain from passing false or misleading information or from withholding known defects. Thus, their help may be relied on but only with due caution. In some states, such as Missouri, if a real estate agent is working for the seller's best interest, the buyer must be so informed both verbally and in writing early in the relationship and well before an offer is placed. If an agent is working for the buyer's best interest, the seller must be likewise informed. Whether these and other real estate regulations apply to businesses for sale is not well defined (at least not in Missouri) although there seems to be a national trend in that direction. Samples of such agency disclosures are shown in Figure 5.5. Note that the buyer's broker is permitted to share the commission paid by the seller.

When the author lists a business for sale, he usually prepares a fairly detailed description of the business that may run three or four pages long. He covers all pertinent aspects of the business. He starts with a rough draft and submits it to the owner for corrections. After two or three drafts run past the owner, the description is completed. This procedure offers several benefits:

- Involving the owner in the preparation assures accuracy.
- It helps protect the broker from errors and omissions.
- It gives the buyer a good start in understanding the business.
- By mailing a copy to the prospective buyer, it minimizes the broker's effort to explain the business, and it minimizes his time on the telephone.
- By providing the same description to each prospective buyer, it assures equal opportunity to purchase, a noteworthy point in case of an exceptionally attractive and exceptionally sought-after plum of a business.
- The description can be included in the loan application to the bank.
- Provided to the lawyers and accountants, it eases their learning and minimizes their fees.
- It introduces the buyer's insurance agent to the business.

Figure 5.5 Agency Disclosures to Buyer and to Seller

AGENCY DISCLOSURE TO BUYER

The undersigned prospective buyer(s) acknowledge that the broker, Honigmann, Inc., has previously informed them verbally that it is working in behalf of the seller, that its commission is paid by the seller, and that any information given to the broker by the prospective buyer(s) may be disclosed to the seller.

Buyer _____   Date _____

Buyer _____   Date _____

Buyer _____   Date _____

AGENCY DISCLOSURE TO SELLER

The undersigned prospective seller of the following described business _____ _____, and the undersigned seller's agent acknowledge that the broker, Honigmann, Inc., is the agent for the following named prospective buyer(s) _____ _____. Seller and seller's agent further acknowledge that the broker is working for the buyer's best interest; that the broker's commission, 45% of the listing agent's commission, will be paid either directly or indirectly by the seller; and that the broker has previously made verbal disclosure to the seller's agent.

Seller _____   Date _____

Seller's agent _____   Date _____

Broker _____   Date _____

The second problem with relying on a broker to help a buyer fact-find is that if the broker's fee is a commission payable only upon closing the sale of the business, the broker has an obvious conflict of interest. Some brokers retain their objectivity and integrity while helping the buyer, but such brokers are hard to identify. Any broker's help should therefore be accepted with caution.

The third problem with relying on a broker to help fact-find is that brokers generally have not yet established reputations for sagacity or the general ability to collect, analyze, and evaluate the facts pertinent to buying a business. Sometimes they show a glaring lack of knowledge basic to the businesses they are attempting to sell and sometimes they simply lack common sense. Note the following two examples:

Example 5.1 A machine shop with annual revenues of well over $2 million is listed for sale with a business broker. The name of the shop includes the words "tool and die;" as in Acme Tool and Die, Inc. The name, however, is a misnomer explained by the company's history. The company was started 45 years earlier by the seller's father, a tool and die maker. Due to customer requests combined with greater profitability, the company gradually took more orders for production parts and fewer orders for tools and dies until finally eliminating tools and dies altogether. The broker, not realizing the difference and judging by the company's name, then advertises the shop as a tool and die manufacturer. When would-be buyers inquire as to whether the shop does any production work, the broker, now with a dimly vague idea of what's happening while trying to be accommodating in an effort to make a sale, says that the shop may do some production work but that it is mostly a tool and die shop. When buyers quiz the broker further on what the shop actually does, the broker replies that it is best to go on a showing and see for themselves what the company does and to talk to the seller in person. The result is that buyers who might be qualified to manage the shop tend to feel that it would be a waste of time to inspect a shop described as tool and die—especially if it takes 20 minutes to drive to the broker's office, ten minutes to wait around and sign a non-disclosure agreement, and another 45 minutes to drive to the shop—while buyers actually wanting a tool and die shop do go on showings and waste their time as well as the seller's. Even worse, buyers looking for light manufacturing companies with established product lines (such buyers happen to be both aggressive and numerous) and not realizing that this is a job shop with no product line, are also taken on showings further wasting everybody's time. Worse still, the broker's many and frequent showings raise questions in the employees' minds as to what exactly is going on and the seller (who was hiding the sale from the employees), sensing his employees' apprehensiveness, becomes apprehensive himself and hard to deal with.

Example 5.2 A well-established dry cleaner with annual sales well into six figures is listed for sale with a business broker. Due to federal requirements concerning worker safety and the environment, new equipment will eventually have to be installed, at a cost of about $100,000. This new equipment cost, when added to the listed price of the cleaner and which price the seller is holding firm, appears to make the total price too high. The company therefore sits unsold for over a year even though the seller is strongly motivated and even though such a company could well be managed by buyers from a variety of backgrounds, making it less illiquid than the average business for sale. Eventually a buyer comes along who, like buyers before him, concludes that the total price is too high but also who, having good acumen and the intuition of many years experience, senses that this is a good company for sale and that there is more to the story than meets the eye. The buyer then hires a consultant to appraise the business. The consultant also concludes that the total price appears to be too high but asks whether the new equipment will result in significant reduction of operating expenses and, if so, how much. The buyer asks the broker and learns that the broker not only does not know the answer but never thought to ask the question and that the seller knows that some savings are possible but, not having the figures, said nothing to the broker. The buyer, now realizing that he may be on to something, digs further and finds that the sales representative for the new equipment is delighted to answer the question with written documentation showing more operating savings than anyone would have imagined, making the total price reasonably attractive.

For buyers and sellers alike it is discouraging that such cases are not uncommon. More discouraging is that the broker in each case was well established, with years of experience. The rule, therefore, for buyers accepting help from brokers is to accept all the information and advice which is offered but to rely on their own understanding of the industry and on their own abilities in evaluating the facts.

Appraise Businesses. Appraising a business is an exceptionally difficult task. The challenges in appraising are to know which financial and other data are relevant, to know where to find the necessary data and how to extract them, and to know what to do with them once obtained. Appraising is a science of straightforward procedures, as will be demonstrated in Chapter 7, but it is also an art of intuitive probing and judging, as demonstrated by the buyer and the consultant in Example 5.2 above.

Realizing the difficulties and challenges of appraising, it is evident that most brokers are not likely to be good appraisers and that any advice they offer should be viewed with caution. For example, an appraisal tool sometimes offered by businesses brokers is that a small business is worth the value of the assets plus one year's profit. This formula is a rule of thumb which may be useful when the assumptions and limitations underlying the formula are properly understood. Those assumptions and limitations are seldom mentioned, however, nullifying the usefulness of the formula and making it downright risky to use.

One of the dangers of listing a business for sale with a broker is that many brokers, perhaps most, will list the business at any price requested by the owner, and with no real attempt to appraise or even to find the right order of magnitude. For example, in one actual case a broker was asked by the owner to list a restaurant at "$80,000 to $100,000," real estate not included. The restaurant was nicely equipped and well kept but earned only $7,000 pre-tax per year after all expenses were paid, including the owner's reasonable salary. The owner's CPA was present to document the income, and the owner made it clear that she was not skimming. In addition, the restaurant had virtually no opportunity for growth. The broker then had the unpleasant duty to inform the owner that she could realistically expect no more than $20,000 to $25,000 and that it might take a year or two, or more, to find the right buyer. The broker advised her to get a second opinion from another broker and to please let him know what she decided to do. A week later, she informed him that she had listed elsewhere at $100,000. Such listings, sadly, are a waste of everyone's time since nobody will pay more than about three times earnings, and even if somebody were willing to pay more, no bank would finance the deal.

Note that the equipment in the above example might have cost anywhere from $60,000 to $100,000 including installation, depending on whether it was new or used when purchased. Thus, the rule of thumb stated in the paragraph above would have priced this restaurant out of the market. This owner's best course probably was to contact equipment dealers and sell to the highest bidder. Then, at least, she could end the frustration and get on with her life.

Help Principals Negotiate Price and Terms. There are several kinds of help from which buyers and sellers can benefit from the broker's participation in a negotiation. Among these are planning the negotiation, preparing a written offer, using a third-party intermediary, talking things over with a confidant, and planning a counter-offer. Since negotiations are critical not only to determining price and terms but also to making or breaking the deal, principals are generally advised to seek competent help. Business brokers can be helpful but—depending on their level of skill—their help is often limited to one area, serving as intermediaries to receive and deliver offers and counter-offers from and to their principals. Their sole service as a third-party intermediary, however, can be extremely useful or even critical to the success of the deal for these reasons: intermediaries keep the principals apart at a time when emotions are at their peak, precluding such potentially deal-breaking incidents as untoward glances and uttered expletives. Intermediaries provide emotional release because the principals will speak their minds (foul language, foul thoughts, and all) to intermediaries with stark directness. Intermediaries, in other words, bear the brunt of the abuse but do so easily because they are not the objects of it. Brokers, because of their experience as intermediaries as well as their third-party status, thus provide a service which can be very valuable and sometimes even necessary to close the deal. Some idea of the value of an intermediary will be provided in Chapter 8 (particularly Example 8.3).

Prepare Purchase-and-Sale Agreements on Preprinted Forms. Depending on the quality of the pre-printed forms, a broker's preparation of the purchase-and-sale agreement has several advantages. A pre-printed form is faster and cheaper than an agreement tailored by a lawyer for a specific transaction. It also has the advantage of having been carefully thought out before being printed, hopefully by a lawyer experienced in business marketing. It is probably free from errors or omissions. In particular, a well-designed pre-printed form will include at least the common contingencies (such as for obtaining financing, licenses, insurance, etc.), the common warranties (such as non-compete, truth and accuracy of information, etc.), and common general provisions (such as the agreement surviving the closing, binding on heirs, etc.). A well-designed agreement also will have the ring of fairness both to buyer and to seller.

Any pre-printed form should be reviewed by the buyer's lawyer and by the seller's lawyer as a routine matter of due caution, such review accruing another advantage: The form serves as a kind of basic check list for the reviewing lawyers thus allowing those lawyers to concentrate on the particulars of the transaction instead of having to spend time on the basics.

An example of a pre-printed purchase-and-sale agreement is shown in Appendix A. Note that in contrast to traditional practice in the real estate industry, no earnest deposit is requested from the buyer. In the author's opinion, earnest deposits usually serve no purpose. They persist mainly because of tradition. If the buyer is required to make an earnest deposit, perhaps the seller should make one too so that if either defaults, the other may be compensated. The point was driven home in an actual case by a buyer who planned to quit his job upon the seller's signing the contract and who, if the seller were to default, would not have been allowed to return to his job. Later in the transaction, especially after financing has been arranged, an earnest deposit by the buyer can make sense because then the seller will take major steps towards vacating the business.

Help Arrange Bank Financing. There are two kinds of financing help a broker may be able to offer: referrals to banks or other lending institutions believed to welcome small business purchase loans, and preparation of a loan application package. Most brokers have some idea of where to apply for loans but many of them are incapable of package preparation. The former service is useful but may be of minor value because 30 to 45 minutes of calling lending institutions listed in the *Yellow Pages* should provide ample leads, as noted in Chapter 9. The latter service can be critical because a well-prepared loan application can win a bank's approval in a borderline case while a poorly prepared application can cause rejection in a deserving case. Preparation of a thoroughly prepared package can require up to two weeks or more of full-time effort to complete, depending on how complete is the information made available to the preparer. If the broker charges a fee for preparation, the fee probably is justified, but the buyer should review a sample of the broker's work before agreeing to the fee. The buyer also should review the completed package just to understand what is happening in the transaction.

Coach Principals and Help Solve Problems. By virtue of their experience, brokers become knowledgeable about a variety of such practical matters as obtaining licenses and permits, and assigning chronological priorities to tasks. Sometimes they may also recommend such professional assistants as accountants, lawyers, insurance agents, building inspectors, appraisers, and others, although such referrals, it should be recognized, are as likely to be helpful as the broker is likely to be competent. Therefore the general rule in buying and selling a business, as in all other lines of endeavor, is the following: when relying on the advice of others, the more important the matter or the less qualified the advisor, the more necessary the caution.

Provide Escrow Services. Probably the most common type of escrow service provided by a broker is the holding of a buyer's earnest money while a transaction proceeds towards closing. Typically the earnest money will be in the form of a check made payable to the broker. The broker deposits the check into a brokerage account reserved for the holding of earnest deposits. If the business broker also is a licensed real estate broker, the escrow account may be registered with the state real estate commission, as are all such accounts in Missouri. However, whether escrow deposits for business purchases must be treated the same as for real estate purchases is open to question due to the void of business marketing regulation. Moreover, as noted above in the section on the purchase-and-sale agreement, the need for an earnest deposit is questionable. In any case, it is probably wise to consult with a lawyer before depositing funds with a business broker.

There is another kind of escrow service which is useful when nearing the closing of a purchase and sale and when the transaction is marked by distrust between buyer and seller, or simply when due caution is recommended by either or both lawyers to be in everybody's best interest. Typically, the broker will hold in escrow a cashier's check and promissory note payable to the seller and a bill of sale made out to the buyer. The broker will be instructed to deliver the escrow items only upon completion of a specified event, such as the buyer's acquiring a license or the seller's repairing a piece of equipment. An escrow agreement signed by the buyer, seller, and escrow agent (broker) will specify what is to be delivered to the escrow agent and by whom; what the agent is to distribute, when it is to be distributed, and to whom; under what conditions the agreement should be altered and exactly how it should be altered; how the agreement will be terminated; liability of the escrow agent; and other terms and covenants as required by the lawyers. The broker always should be protected by being acknowledged as serving only in a clerical role and should be held liable only for gross carelessness or willful misconduct. Such protection is necessary no matter what the amount held in escrow but is of particular importance when the funds run into five, six, or seven figures. An example of such protective definition of the broker's liability is shown in Figure 5.6.

Figure 5.6 Protective Definition of Broker-Escrow Agent's Liability

LIABILITY OF THE ESCROW AGENT

The duties of the Escrow Agent are only such as are herein specifically provided, being purely administrative in nature, and he shall incur no liability whatsoever except for willful misconduct or gross negligence. Other than the obligations of Escrow Agent as set forth above, Escrow Agent shall have no other obligations, rights or duties with reference to this Escrow Agreement, and Buyer and Seller jointly and severally hereby agree to indemnify Escrow Agent against all loss, costs, damage or expense arising out of his performance as Escrow Agent hereunder, so long as Escrow Agent shall in good faith carry out his duties as herein set forth. Escrow Agent shall be under no responsibility in respect of the Escrow Funds other than to safeguard the same and to follow the instructions herein. Escrow Agent may consult with counsel and shall be fully protected in any action taken in good faith, in accordance with the advice of counsel. Escrow Agent shall have no responsibility for the genuineness or validity of any document, signature or item deposited with him, and may act in accordance with any duly given instructions or assent.

Arrange and Attend Closings. Depending on the size of the transaction, the complexity, and whether good will prevails between buyer and seller, one or both lawyers may attend and manage the closing. The broker, however, will usually set the time and place for the closing after obtaining inputs from the relevant parties. The broker usually will also prepare the closing statement which itemizes what is owed by the buyer and by the seller to each other along with the net amount. Additional information on the closing appears in Part 1 of Chapter 12.

Lead and Coordinate All of the Above. Again depending on the size of the transaction, the complexity, and whether good will prevails, leadership and coordination may be provided by the broker or by one of the lawyers or accountants. If the broker's leadership takes hold, it usually is partly because he or she is involved from the start and partly by force of personality. Such leadership by a broker may occur even on large complex deals. The broker-leader will coach the seller and the buyer on what to do and when to do it; feed information to the various parties such as the accountants, lawyers, insurance agents, banker, licensing agencies, and so on; and gently remind laggard performers of their responsibilities and schedules. An experienced and sharp broker occasionally will even coach the lawyers. If one of the lawyers takes charge, the broker-leader will defer but will stay alert to the needs of the deal.

Maintain Files for Future Reference. A file should contain virtually all the documentation from the start of the transaction to the finish such as the following: Listing agreement; agency agreement; names, addresses, and telephone numbers of all involved parties; buyer's resume, financial statement, and supporting data; seller's financial data and company description; business and real estate appraisals; record of offers and counter-offers; loan application package and related data; all correspondence from and to broker; broker's notes and/or log; and complete set of closing documents. When a transaction is marked by ill will or skullduggery, a wise broker may keep a special log tracing the pertinent sayings and incidents for possible court evidence.

PART 2:
OTHER ASPECTS OF BUSINESS BROKERS

The first part of this chapter described what business brokers do. This part of the chapter covers various other aspects of business brokers including their fees, their limited cooperation with one another, and their optimum use by sellers and by buyers.

Business Brokers' Fees. A fairly typical commission on the sale of a small business is ten to twelve percent of the sale price with a minimum of $6,000. Using ten percent, for example, an $80,000 sale would pay a commission of $8,000 while a $35,000 sale would pay $6,000. When sale prices are much above $300,000, some brokers scale down their commission rates. For example, on a $700,000 sale a broker might charge 10% of the first $300,000 and only 6% of the balance for a total commission of $54,000. On sales well over a million dollars, the so-called Lehman formula seems to have won acceptance by sellers in general. A commission based on that formula is 5% of the first million dollars, 4% of the second million, 3% of the third, 2% of the fourth, and 1% of the balance. Thus a $2.4 million sale would pay the broker $50,000 on the first million, $40,000 on the second, and $12,000 on the $400,000 balance for a total of $102,000.

Commissions are always applied to the total value of the sale as opposed to a specified price. For example, if corporate stock is sold at a price of $1,000 for a company with a book value of $1,000, but said company has liabilities of $199,000 which transfer with the sale, the total value of the sale is $200,000. A ten percent commission therefore would be $20,000. Thus is explained the meaning of the paragraph in the Figure 5.3 listing agreement beginning with the words: "For purposes of this agreement . . . ." That paragraph, it should be noted, is sometimes omitted by the broker because such tight wording can frighten away a skittish, prospective seller and because it is generally understood that an assumed debt is a form of payment, as are the other considerations in that paragraph. (The paragraph was written by a lawyer who, as lawyers are wont to do, was protecting his client from any conceivable danger.)

The commission for the sale of a business is calculated the same way as the commission for the sale of real estate. If, for example, a business sells for $200,000, a ten percent commission correctly calculated would equal .10 x $200,000 = $20,000, and the seller would net $180,000. A common error is to start with the amount that the seller expects to receive and then to apply the percentage of the commission which, in this case, would incorrectly equal $18,000. The correct way to calculate the commission starting with the seller's net price is to work backwards. First, find the gross price by dividing the net price by 100% less the 10% commission:

$$\text{Gross price} \; = \; \$180,000 \; \div \; (100\% - 10\%) \; = \; \$200,000$$

Then apply the 10% commission to the gross price to get the $20,000 commission.

Whether speaking of the $6,000 fee on the $35,000 sale mentioned above, the $102,000 fee on the $2.4 million sale, or any other fees, whether higher or lower or anywhere in between, these fees may be viewed not only as large but also as excessive. Such perceived excessiveness helps to explain why some sellers refuse to list with brokers and why some buyers, fearing that the fee will be passed along to them, refuse to patronize them. This perceived excessiveness may also explain why clients and customers sometimes attempt to cheat their brokers out of part or all of their fees (although avarice and depravity also help to explain.) The question therefore arises as to whether the brokers' fees are fair and reasonable or whether they are excessive. Putting aside the question of competency, if the full range of brokers' services can be brought to light, perhaps the question of excessive fees can be resolved. A brief marketing analysis will help to answer the question.

In college marketing classes, students are taught to analyze marketing by breaking it into eight basic functions:

- Buying
- Selling
- Storing
- Grading
- Transporting
- Financing
- Disseminating information
- Risking

In a classic illustration of the usefulness of marketing analysis, middlemen—the often-maligned distributors who receive goods from manufacturers and sell them to retailers at prices often viewed as excessively marked up for having done little or nothing useful—are seen to serve the market by providing warehouses (storing) and by sorting the goods (grading). Since storing and grading are necessary to bring goods to the marketplace, the middlemen are now seen to justify their markups. (The importance of middlemen as separate entities has of course declined with the rise of the superstore.)

The questions now are whether brokers do anything useful to justify their fees and whether, like middlemen, they perform services not easily seen or appreciated. Actually, brokers perform six of the eight functions listed above, the exceptions being storing and transporting. Obvious examples are the advertising of a business for sale, which is part of the selling function; qualifying buyers, fact-finding, and appraising, which are part of the grading function; arranging bank loans, which is part of the financing function, and so on. All very good, but the function which is not obvious and which escapes almost everyone's notice because it is so passive is risking. Risking, in fact, usually constitutes the costliest part of the broker's performance and it justifies the largest part of the broker's fee. That is not only because so many of the transactions fail to close, bringing no pay for the broker's work, but that so many fail to close for reasons beyond the broker's control.

Following are some of the reasons that transactions fail to close. Note that these reasons are mostly, though not entirely, beyond the broker's control:

- Misunderstandings of any kind whatsoever as to any aspect of the deal, including misunderstandings of earnings, sales, sales potential, reliability of customers, industry trends, and so on, and by any of the parties to the transaction, including the principals, their lawyers and accountants, the bank loan officer, the landlord, the insurance agent, and so on. A common cause of misunderstanding is innocent though nevertheless exaggerated claims of the seller.
- Personality differences causing buyer or seller to back away. The broker in Example 5.4 below, in two separate instances, lost a

prospective buyer who, after meeting the seller in person, related to the broker his distrust of the seller and thereupon declared no further interest.

- Legal difficulties such as incipient lawsuits or the threat thereof. Such threat may be more perceived than real.
- Fact-finding uncovering reduced earnings or earnings potential or uncovering any other kind of problem unknown by the seller but repelling the buyer. Such instances are common.
- Remorse of buyer or seller.
- Changes in plans by buyer or seller.
- Illness or family problems of sufficient severity to break the deal.
- The basic illiquidity of small businesses causing discouragingly protracted efforts to sell.

The above list of common problems which can break a deal is only a start. The actual list is endless, covering everything under the sun including marital disputes, reluctant landlords denying subleases for fear of losing good tenants, and even such improbabilities as a policeman with a vendetta who blocks a tavern-buyer's application for a liquor license by arresting the buyer on a set-up technicality.

When the author lists a business for sale, he usually offers his client the option of paying an hourly fee which, almost always, will amount to substantially less than the standard commission, the only catch being that the hourly fee is payable even if the sale fails to close. An owner's typical response is, I won't pay for performance that I don't get. What an owner never says, however, is that it is acceptable for the broker to work for payment that the broker doesn't get.

Brokers are not alone in dealing with risk. With every crop they plant, farmers face a variety of risks, such as the risk of unsure growing conditions at home, unsure growing conditions in other countries affecting world prices, growing conditions for competing crops, political factors such as subsidies both at home and abroad, and general economic conditions. Farmers, however, can unload at least some of their risks in the futures market. Brokers have no choice but to accept their risks. Therefore, they need to be paid for performing the necessary marketing function of risking.

In one actual case, the broker worked half time on one transaction for the better part of the year. If he closed the sale he would get $90,000 less expenses and less double the social security tax. If he failed to close he would get nothing, but would still have bills to pay, for living expenses as well as for business, which would drain his savings, and he had no other sales materializing in that year. The transaction was nip and tuck, one day looking good and the next day looking bad. Sometimes he would wake up at three in the morning wondering if he were sane to stay in this business. He refuses to state whether he closed the sale or not. He doesn't want to talk about it. As one might guess, business-brokering has a high rate of turnover.

Some brokers require a non-refundable retainer to list a business for sale. Advantages to the broker are less risk of unpaid work and a steadier flow of income. Advantages to the seller are a lower percentage on the commission and—assuming that the broker is competent and is willing to do the work—an appraisal of the seller's business.

In addition to the normal, necessary risk of a transaction failing to close, there is the ever-present risk of being cheated:

Example 5.3 A small manufacturing company is listed for sale at $530,000 with a 10% broker's commission. A prospective buyer has excellent technical qualifications but modest financial resources (a net worth of $120,000 with about $70,000 available for a down payment). The buyer considers trying to negotiate a lower price but decides to offer full list price because he knows he will need the owner's cooperation and also because he feels that the price is fair. The broker is impressed by the buyer's wisdom and his sense of fairness. The owner accepts the $530,000 offer.

Financing will be difficult partly because of the buyer's modest means, but, more importantly, because the owner and his accountant have used all sorts of tricks to hide most of the earnings to minimize taxes. The broker prepares a full-scale loan application package carefully crafted to discreetly bring the earnings out of hiding and also carefully crafted to exploit the considerable potential available to a young and energetic new owner. (The seller, at retirement age, is turning away work because he is tired and he does not need the money.) The buyer reviews the package and expresses enthusiasm over the quality of it. He then tells the broker that heretofore he had viewed brokers as a shallow lot but that he has just changed his thinking. The broker and the buyer then begin working as a team and they submit the package to one bank after another while suffering one rejection after another. Finally a bank accepts on condition of obtaining SBA type 504 financing. (SBA 504 is explained in Chapter 9.)

Now comes the struggle of working through the approval process. The Local Development Company (an LDC is a quasi-political group closely involved in all Type 504 financing) turns down the application without comment. Not knowing what else to do, the broker refers the buyer to a very successful lawyer whom the broker previously has worked with and been impressed by. The lawyer, with a single telephone call to an LDC board member (who is a fellow member at the lawyer's country club), learns that the machine tools pledged as collateral were deemed to be highly depreciable and therefore unsuitable for a 15-year loan. The package is then resubmitted along with an explanation that these tools can and do have long lives with the aid of periodic refurbishing. The LDC responds with a list of questions, several of which probe into the nature of the hidden, and mostly illegitimate, earnings. The broker carefully crafts a responsive letter (which is like walking on eggs) and submits it to the buyer who signs and submits it to the LDC. The loan then is conditionally approved by the LDC pending approval by the SBA. The SBA rejects but submits a list of its own probing questions. The broker again crafts the replies for the buyer's signature and submittal to the SBA, and total approval of financing is finally won.

At this point, more than seven months have elapsed since the broker's first showing to the buyer. From the time that the buyer expressed admiration for the loan application package and realized the broker's quality, the two have worked closely together, communicating almost daily by phone or in person and they have developed a relationship wherein the buyer has shared some of his intimate thoughts and feelings about how this business will affect his life. The buyer's father is a university chancellor and his brothers are physicians with lucrative practices. The buyer up until now has been the low person in the family in terms of prestige but all that will change with the acquisition of this business. The buyer tells the broker that he is grateful for all the broker has done to make this dream possible. He takes the broker to lunch where they exult in having obtained the financing which virtually assures that the sale will close. All that remains to be done is for the lawyers to work out the details of the contract with the bank, the LDC, the SBA, the landlord, and each other.

The lawyers now are in charge of everything and the broker has little to do except wait for closing. A month passes without the broker's hearing from anyone so he calls the buyer to check on progress. The buyer is diffident but, on coaxing, allows that the contract is complete. Upon further questioning the buyer agrees to bring a copy to the broker but only after three days pass. The buyer stops by the broker's home, hands the contract to him at his doorstep, and takes a few steps back. Then the buyer states that there is nothing that the broker can do to prevent the closing. The broker notes that the contract has no provision for the broker's fee but the buyer says that the fee is not his problem, and there the conversation ends.

The broker hires a lawyer and provides copies of the listing agreement and the buyer's non-disclosure statement promising not to skirt the broker. The broker's lawyer calls the buyer's and seller's lawyers, then reports to the broker that the seller will agree to pay only $44,000 instead of the $53,000 he is liable for. But I've got a signed contract with both the seller and the buyer, protests the broker to his lawyer. The lawyer agrees that a lawsuit would result in a full $53,000 award since the broker has a cut-and-dried case. He also points out that the buyer, the seller, and both of their lawyers are in collusion to cheat and he recommends that the broker accept the reduced commission because it would take two years to reach a trial court and that the broker would lose the use of the money during that time, not to mention the legal fees. The broker agrees with the lawyer's recommendation, the sale closes (after a total of nine months), and he collects $44,000. Later, the broker confides to a colleague that what hurt the most was not the loss of $9,000. What hurt the most was that he thought he had made a friend.

In Example 5.3, the broker lost only a minor part (17%) of his commission. In Example 5.4, the seller had a bigger share in mind.

Example 5.4 A very lucrative business (actually, the place is a gold mine) is put up for sale for $950,000 with a broker who has a non-exclusive listing. The broker and seller agree on a $50,000 commission. The broker advertises and canvasses for a year before finding a well-qualified buyer who, after fact-finding and negotiating, agrees to the full list price. The broker then prepares a full-scale loan application package and finds a bank willing to lend $600,000 conditioned on an SBA guarantee of most of the loan. The SBA, however, agrees to guarantee only $320,000, thus killing the loan. (Helping to kill the loan is that the bank is being reorganized and can't seem to do anything right.) Several other banks are approached by the broker until finally one agrees to lend $400,000 with no SBA participation. The buyer will pay $320,000 down and the seller will accept a promissory note for

$230,000, for a total of $950,000.

Now about four months have passed since the broker found the buyer. Another six weeks should be sufficient to close the sale since the contract has already been prepared by the broker on a pre-printed form and the broker can use a commercial pre-printed form to prepare the lease. Progress, however, is slow, with the seller emphasizing minute details and insisting on some exorbitant terms which finally are grudgingly resolved to the point where the contract is ready to be signed. Nobody can understand why the seller has been acting this way, thus the buyer's patience has become strained, almost to the breaking point, and so has the broker's. (Although patience with idiosynritic and even irrational behavior is a primary and necessary asset of a good broker, this seller has pushed the broker to the point of exasperation.)

Finally, the broker takes the contract, signed by the buyer, to the seller for his signature and hears the following story: Another buyer has made an offer almost matching the broker's offer but which is better for the seller because no broker's fee is involved. The seller adds that, since he is a fair person and wants to see the broker rewarded for his efforts, he is willing to pay a $16,000 commission. The seller admits to the broker that the lower commission is probably disappointing but that it is still a large paycheck considering the small amount of work that the broker has done. The broker replies that the agreed commission is $50,000, that he has kept his part of the agreement, and that he therefore deserves the full commission. (The broker actually has invested major time and effort and some expense, not the small effort claimed by the seller, but deliberately does not mention it because it is not relevant.) After a brief discussion of what constitutes fairness, the seller says that he is very sorry to see the broker and his buyer lose all that they had worked for but that the new offer is too good not to accept. The broker and the seller then say goodbye. (All of the conversation is reserved and polite, as well it should be.)

Now the broker performs his loathsome duty of telling the buyer that the deal is dead and explaining why. The next day the seller surprises the broker with a call to say that he has thought it over and, as a matter of fairness, he wants the broker and his buyer to close the sale after all and he will increase the broker's commission to $18,000. The broker declines while restating the agreed $50,000. After more haggling by the seller in favor of what he considers to be a fair fee countered by the broker's continued insistence on keeping the agreement, the seller agrees to pay the full commission. (The broker thinks to himself that fairness is not the issue and that the seller has been caught bluffing. He does not mention it, however, partly because it is speculation and partly because it is not relevant.) Then the broker informs the buyer that the deal has come alive again but the buyer, having spent considerable time and effort, having run out of patience, and having become disgusted with the whole affair, states that he is no longer interested.

Examples 5.3 and 5.4, unfortunately, are not rare occurrences. The perceived excessiveness of fee coupled with the low esteem in which brokers often are regarded justifies in many minds the cheating they inflict and is part of the reason that brokers' fees are as large as they are.

In addition to performing six of the eight marketing functions, there are other reasons underlying the fees charged by brokers. Buying and selling a business, even a small one, is high-stakes dealing that requires competent performance. The high stakes are not just the money involved and the need to remain solvent. They are the equally high stakes of life style, direction of career, family relationships, and personal happiness, all at the high end of Maslow's hierarchy.

Larger commissions for larger sales are justified because of the increased responsibility of the broker even though the increase in work is not necessarily in the same proportion. Larger commissions on larger sales are also justified for the presumably more polished personalities of brokers working on such sales and by the resulting increased pleasure of the relationships enjoyed by the principals. Though no certification or licensing may be required for business brokers to show that they are capable of handling the responsibility, they nevertheless may have bachelor's or master's degrees, certification as accountants, licensing as lawyers, special training, or solid business experience qualifying at least some of them for what they do.

There is also the cash value of the broker's service. The broker, with luck, can save time for both buyers and sellers in reaching their goals. A buyer earning $50,000 per year, for example, may be avoiding brokers because of their fees. If the broker can find the right business with earnings, say, of $80,000 per year not counting the buildup in equity and can do so a year or two sooner than the buyer could through his or her own efforts, the income differential may more than offset the fee. If an owner finds himself or herself burned out and ready for retirement, hiring a broker can mean the difference between selling a viable business at or near appraised value and selling a depressed or closed business at auction for a fraction of appraised value, a point well evidenced in Example 4.1 where the seller came close to tossing away half a million dollars.

The possibility also exists that a business listed with a broker may be the only business reasonably suitable for a certain buyer which will appear on the market within, say, a five-year time frame. As a practical matter, therefore, it represents a once-in-a-lifetime opportunity for that buyer. In such a case, the broker's fee would be of minor concern and virtually irrelevant.

The question arises as to who actually pays the broker's fee, the buyer or the seller. One possible answer is that the buyer pays because the seller just adds the fee to the price. That answer is not viable, however, because adding the fee to fair market value will set the price too high to attract buyers and, more importantly, to qualify for bank financing. A more plausible answer is that the seller pays because the business will sell only for what can be negotiated and financed.

Actually, the ultimate payer tends to be indeterminate, with the effect that the buyer and seller more or less share the fee. One reason is that the value of most small businesses is not absolutely fixed but falls within a range of reasonable values reflecting diverse human judgments (as explained in Chapters 7 and 8) in which the broker's fee becomes somewhat obscured. Also, effective negotiation may yield savings or gains considerably larger than the broker's fee, thus further obscuring the fee while reducing the importance of it, especially for the party more effective at negotiating. Of course, the party assisted by a broker skilled at negotiating has a reasonable chance of offsetting the fee, and then some.

In summary, the fees charged by brokers at least come close to being reasonable considering the totality of their services, the risks they take, the benefits they provide, and the considerable stakes of both buyers and sellers in terms of personal happiness. Many brokers feel that their fees are not high enough for all the work they do and for all the risk they take. In any case, the broker's fee is the same as the lawyer's fee or the accountant's fee in this respect: it is the cost of doing business, and that's how it should be thought of.

A comparison of the sale of residential real estate vs. the sale of small businesses will throw additional light on the services provided by brokers and on the fees they charge. See Figure 5.7 at the end of the chapter.

Cooperation Among Business Brokers. If a broker with a business listed for sale is approached by another broker with a buyer who could be interested in that business, the listing broker may or may not be willing to cooperate with the buyer's broker. Thus, a partial unwillingness to cooperate characterizes and blemishes the profession of business brokering. From the viewpoint of buyers and sellers, there are advantages and disadvantages to the situation. One advantage involves the complexity of small business sales in general. When a business is for sale, the workings of the business must be explained first by the owner to the broker and then by the broker to the prospective buyer. Introducing another broker to the flow of information tends to distort and obscure the description of the business, especially considering that less competent brokers sometimes lack clear understanding of what they have for sale. Moreover, the listing broker presumably has been shown the premises and the operation of the business by the owner, gaining an important mental graphic and an intuitive grasp which is not easily communicated to a second broker. Another advantage of brokers not cooperating is that if confidentiality is important, the fact of the business being for sale is released to fewer people. (As noted in Chapter 4, however, the advantage of confidentiality itself is questionable.)

One disadvantage of brokers failing to cooperate is that buyers are forced to work harder to contact more brokers to thoroughly explore the market. Another disadvantage is that the broker's refusal to cooperate occasionally may lose a sale for an owner wanting to sell, a particularly hurtful loss for an owner in distress or for one really needing to retire.

Brokers, of course, have their own viewpoint on the advantages and disadvantages of unwillingness to cooperate. A broker may work hard to find a good business for sale and harder still in applying his or her special expertise to discover and analyze data preparatory to appraising the business. Such brokers may feel their work is not amply rewarded if forced to share a commission with another broker who does little more than fill out a purchase-and-sale agreement on a pre-printed form. Such a listing broker may also feel that a truly motivated buyer will read the classified advertisements and will make the necessary telephone calls to contact all the brokers, reducing the need for shared listings. On the other hand, a conscientious broker always works for the client's best interest and receives satisfaction from such service, not to mention possible referrals from happy sellers to other owners.

Some listing brokers, perhaps most, will pay a referral fee to a broker who sends the ultimate buyer. The referral fee usually is ten or 15 percent of the commission. Some brokers refuse to pay a referral fee, apparently feeling that they can sell the business without any help. The author usually feels this way, though not always. The author also is usually content to hand off a listing without receiving a referral fee when he finds himself unable or unwilling to handle the sale.

The mixed evaluation of the broker's failure to cooperate suggests that owners and brokers handle individual situations on their individual merits. The author, in general, feels comfortable with independent brokerages but tries to keep an open mind.

Optimum Use of Brokers by Sellers. There are three basic approaches to selling a business. The first is for the owner to handle all of the selling activity alone. The second is for an owner to hire a broker by the hour. The third is for the owner to list with a broker and pay a commission. Choosing between the approaches would depend on the owner's self-confidence, skill level, available time and energy, and whether the owner would enjoy doing the work. Obviously, the least expensive approach is for the owner to conduct his or her own selling activities, assuming that the owner knows what to do and how to do it. With this book in hand, an intelligent owner could succeed, especially if the owner were to hire an experienced intermediary during the negotiation. Most brokers would serve well as intermediaries, even those of lesser talent.

Hiring a broker by the hour is probably less expensive than paying a commission. The problem is that it is not easy to choose a broker who is both honest and competent, making the second approach difficult.

To help decide between the three approaches, an owner may first discuss with a confidant to develop some feeling of the owner's own comfort level and to hear some feedback from the confidant. An owner might then discuss these approaches with a broker to gain further insight into the owner's own comfort level with these approaches and to determine the broker's interest, if any, and whether the owner senses a good rapport with the broker. At this point, which approach to use would begin to become clear. The broker should propose what the commission would be on the sale of the business or what the hourly fee would be along with an estimate of total hourly charges. Any estimate of total hourly charges would be very approximate due to the unpredictability of most purchase-and-sale transactions. At this point, the owner could tell the broker that he or she wishes to think it over and, in the meantime, could repeat the process, for purposes of comparison and greater insight, with a second broker and perhaps even a third. Shopping brokers is perfectly ethical.

To determine which brokers to approach, brokers may be divided into two groups according to the price range of the businesses they sell. With some arbitrariness, the dividing line is around $500,000. Brokers who handle businesses in ranges both above and below the dividing line probably should be thought of as more suited to the lower range, although exceptions do exist. Some idea of a broker's range may be found by consulting the newspaper classified advertisements under Business Opportunities or simply by calling

Illustration 5.1

A relationship with no risk, i.e., no risk for the human.

and asking. After finding a few names of brokers dealing in the owner's price range, some feeling for the broker's competency and personal rapport may be found by asking colleagues for their experiences and by calling the brokers and following up with personal visits to those seeming to have rapport over the telephone. This procedure for choosing a broker is not guaranteed to find the best available. An unethical incompetent may have impressed a previous client through some stroke of good luck or through smooth talk. A competent artisan may have encountered bad luck in one case and, for lack of glibness, may have sounded like a bumpkin in others. An owner therefore should request to see some written work done by the broker, such as a letter to a bank officer requesting a loan, a letter canvassing for clients, a loan application package, or an appraisal. A loan application package or an appraisal, if the owner has the capability to understand them, will offer more substantial clues to a broker's competency. Neatness, organization, spelling, grammar, logic, and such writing qualities as clarity and tone are the qualities to look for as clues to a broker's (or anyone else's) competency.

Assuming that high ethical standards suggest high overall competence, one should also watch for clues to a broker's ethics. In one actual case, a St. Louis broker canvassing business owners sent a letter promising to charge the buyer for the broker's services while at the same time getting the best possible price for the seller. That broker's lack of integrity attested to his paucity of talent. More commonly, business brokers who hold real estate licenses, as most of them do, will sometimes advertise their services while stating "We are fully licensed." That statement would be true but also misleading since Missouri does not license business brokers. Such brokers ask for and deserve the contempt which some principals hold out to brokers. Sadly, such duplicity is not rare in the profession.

Brokers' fees are sometimes negotiable and it is perfectly ethical for an owner to shop for a lower fee. If an owner has a business for sale which is less illiquid than most small businesses, the listing of that business will be more desirable from a broker's point of view and the fee therefore more negotiable. The competency of the broker, however, is always more important than the fee for any number of reasons including likelihood of a quicker sale, likelihood of any sale, a better price and terms, smoother dealings for all parties concerned, and bank financing vs. owner financing. Sometimes a broker's competency can pay off in an unexpected way such as in the following example:

Example 5.5 A broker has listed a business for sale with the owner agreeing to a commission of $44,000 regardless of the sale price. To prepare a selling plan and for better all-around understanding of the business he is trying to sell, the broker studies the business from several aspects, including clientele, history of company, employee salaries, product line, and competition. In line with these studies, the broker visits a major competitor and learns that the competitor's price list closely approximates his client's list but for one difference: the competitor, unbeknown to the broker's client, adds a surcharge. If the surcharge were added to his client's prices, it would increase revenues by $60,000 per year with no additional cost of material, labor, or overhead and, probably, no loss of customers since the price would still meet or beat the competitor's. Since it is the owner's policy to set his prices by what the competition charges, he follows the broker's advice to add the surcharge. The extra $60,000 annual income is a windfall which helps to persuade the buyer to pay the full offering price and which further helps to convince the bank loan officer that there is sufficient cash flow to pay the bank loan. The sale closes about seven months later meaning that the owner realizes enough additional income that year to cover about two thirds of the broker's fee. As a bonus to the whole transaction, the buyer will continue to reap the surcharges indefinitely.

Optimum Use of Brokers by Buyers. The main contribution that the broker makes to the buyer—at least at the beginning of the relationship—is to discover businesses for sale, reducing the buyer's time and effort to do that work, and also reducing the loss of enthusiasm caused by failures and rejections. The broker also discovers businesses that the buyer might never find through the buyer's own efforts. Moreover, if the buyer is not sure of the type of business being sought (a common dilemma for buyers), the broker will make suggestions. But here due caution is required: not all brokers are good judges of buyers' qualifications. There is danger, therefore, of a buyer's wasting time pursuing an unsuitable business.

Most brokers, but not all, will be listed in the *Yellow Pages*. Whether a broker is listed or not has no bearing on the quality of performance, nor does whether or not the broker has a commercial office. (The author, for example, is not listed and his office is in his residence. He also works out of and enjoys such makeshift offices as coffee shops and motel dining rooms where food and drink are always handy, and where good service is the rule and always rewarded with a good tip.)

Some brokers will advertise in the Business Opportunities section of the newspaper's classified advertisements. Since brokers generally must be careful to hold any information they have about their sellers in confidence, buyers usually will not receive much information over the telephone. Instead, they may have to travel to the broker's office and sign a statement promising confidentiality of information and also promising to protect the broker's commission on any businesses introduced to the buyer by the broker.

A key problem for the buyer is to determine during a telephone conversation whether the broker has anything of interest to show the buyer. It is a problem for three reasons. First because of the aforementioned confidentiality, second because many brokers lack competence to understand what they have for sale (one reason some of them do not know how to qualify a buyer), and third because many buyers, due to their inexperience at buying a business, do not know how to ask questions, how to appraise a business, or how to screen their prospects. The twofold result is, on the one hand, missed opportunities and, on the other hand, wasted time spent chasing opportunities which never existed. Example 5.1 illustrated the problem and, partly, so did Example 5.2.

To contact a broker, whether responding to an advertisement or simply canvassing for businesses for sale, a buyer should begin by calling on the telephone and stating the purpose of the call. If it seems reasonably certain that the broker has no listings of any special interest, the buyer can proceed to the next broker. If the broker does appear to have something of even slight interest, the buyer should make an appointment to visit the broker in the broker's office. Having reached the office, the buyer will probably be asked to sign a non-disclosure statement. Then the broker will relax and become more giving of information. How the buyer should evaluate the information and handle the situation from this point on will become more apparent in later chapters.

Since business brokers tend not to cooperate with one another as do real estate agents—nor do they enjoy the advantages of multiple listing services as do real estate brokers—the buyer will have to go from broker to broker to learn what is available for sale. It is perfectly ethical to do so.

The buyer's telephone call to the broker may be received by an answering machine with an outgoing message requesting name and telephone number. Such a reception should not carry a stigma suggesting that the broker will be of questionable service. It more likely signifies the need to reduce overhead and increase efficiency. If several days pass with no return call, the buyer should call again. If still no reply, the buyer should let a week or two pass before trying again. Granted that to be so patient one must allow the benefit of a doubt as to whether the broker is working twelve hours a day on a closing or is otherwise legitimately indisposed (which may be the case) or is simply not very conscientious about returning calls (which also may be the case). The game plan is to ignore such annoyances and remain focused on the goal, to find the right business for sale.

The reader will notice that in Chapters 10 and 11, the author holds lawyers and accountants to much higher standards of telephone courtesy than he does brokers. First, the standards described in the paragraph above are at the very beginning of any relationship between broker and buyer or between broker and seller. At that point in time, no deal is threatened to be killed for the simple reason that the relationship is just getting started. Once a deal gets started, however, the broker should be held to the same standards as anyone else. What's more, from the buyer's viewpoint prior to the beginning of any transaction, the first priority is to discover if the broker has the right business for sale; it is not to worry about the broker's lack of courtesy. But from the viewpoint of the seller looking for the right broker to list with, the broker can and should be held to high standards of courtesy. There is no reason not to.

Most brokers list with the seller and work for the seller's best interest.

In some states, if real estate is involved, such a relationship must be declared by the broker early enough in the transaction for the buyer to have ample warning. If the broker does not declare the relationship, the buyer should ask about it.

If the broker does work for the seller, the buyer may feel cautious about disclosing his or her financial qualifications for fear of jeopardizing the buyer's negotiating position. Generally, a buyer gains no tactical advantage by concealing his finances. In fact, strong financial qualification increases the buyer's attractiveness to the seller. Therefore, if the broker asks for it, a rough indication of the buyer's ability to make a cash down payment should be provided so that the broker can fulfill his or her duty to the seller to qualify the buyer. This rough indication may consist of a statement to the effect that the buyer will do what is necessary to raise the cash and that the amount will depend on the circumstances of the business, although if the buyer does not mind giving a specific figure or range, it will increase the broker's comfort level. It is also acceptable, if the broker asks for it, to provide the broker with some indication of the buyer's net worth although, for reasons of privacy, the buyer may prefer to reveal only that portion of the net worth commensurate with the price of the business being bought or may simply state that he or she has means which are ample to the situation. (The reader is reminded that, in virtually all cases, the buyer's ability to manage the business is by far the qualification which counts most. Besides, based on the author's experience, money tends to follow talent.) The buyer may indicate the price range of the business being sought but such range should be liberal enough to allow the broker to mention possibilities which might initially seem beyond the buyer's capability but which could fall within it when the full story becomes known. The earlier Example 5.2 of the dry cleaner showed one way in which this can happen.

Some brokers specialize in working for the buyer, usually for an hourly fee which may be sweetened with a share of the earnings of whatever business is bought. Such brokers are likely to offer full services, including the extensive financial analysis necessary to appraise the business. The quality of such services is usually open to question and the buyer therefore may prefer to have such analysis done by his or her own consultant. Such an arrangement would probably have to be negotiated with the broker and, in fact, the broker possibly would not agree because of the diminished total fee. In any case, the service which is key to such brokers' success is finding the right business for the buyer. Since sizeable hourly fees totaling $10,000 to $20,000 or more are possible, the buyer should have some indication of the broker's rate of success at culminating matchups. The price of businesses sold by the hourly-fee brokers probably ranges upward from the high six figures so as to justify the extensive effort and cost expended in searching for sellers.

Most brokers, even when paid by the seller, offer to provide the buyer with a variety of services sometimes including appraising and seeking financing. Since the competency of brokers is questionable, the buyer who relies on these services is gambling with high stakes. The problem finds little relief from hiring outside consultants because those who are qualified to conduct small business appraisals and write loan application packages are not easy to find, not even among accountants and lawyers. The buyer who hired an outside consultant in Example 5.2 was lucky enough to find the right party and he was sharp enough to know the difference. That buyer, however, had better-than-average acumen. Most buyers are not so blessed, but some advice along these lines will be offered in later chapters.

Occasionally, ethical problems arise. The general rule is to assume that everybody has high ethical standards but to be prepared for those who do not. Another general rule is to not take too seriously such public statements of ethics as plaques hung on office walls and institutional ethical guidelines. Such ethical statements are too easy to ignore considering that they are seldom written by the same people who display them.

Some brokers may try various ruses to lure buyers into their offices, to lure them to go on showings, or to otherwise lure them to do business. The following example illustrates the problem:

> **Example 5.6** A broker calls a buyer with whom he has previously worked to inform the buyer that he has a new listing of a restaurant for sale that sounds about what the buyer has been

looking for, and at the right price. The restaurant is described as an ethnic restaurant with annual sales about $375,000, well established for a number of years, reasonable rent in a nice neighborhood, good clientele including lawyers, business people, and professional athletes, and the price is only $150,000. The buyer drives to the broker's office, signs the nondisclosure agreement, and walks with the broker downstairs to the parking lot to go on a showing. As they climb into the broker's car, the broker informs the buyer that in addition to all of the basic assets for sale, the seller is also willing to pass along the recipes for an additional amount of only $150,000. The buyer then asks if that means that the total price of the restaurant is $300,000. The broker replies that oh no, the price of the restaurant is only $150,000, but that the seller is willing to give up the recipes for an additional amount. The buyer then tells the broker what he thinks of the deal and goes home.

Although this example is offered to illustrate the ethical standards of some brokers, it also illustrates the incompetence which blemishes the profession. Whether the broker was sincere (and therefore not unethical) or not, he failed to have enough common sense to realize that the customers at a restaurant are there to enjoy the food as well as the other amenities such as ambiance, good service, and so on, and that if the character of the food is changed, the customers are very liable not to return. What was basically offered for sale was the restaurant equipment without the business. At $150,000, the price was too high. Moreover, this broker seemed to hold the same mistaken notion held by many business brokers, especially by those who formerly sold real estate, that taking buyers on showings, the more the better, is the quickest and most effective way to sell a business. This broker's background is not known, but the broker in Example 5.1 who took so many buyers through the "tool and die" shop is a former real estate agent.

Despite levels of competence and ethics which appear to be less than the highest, it is advisable for buyers to resign themselves to deal with business brokers simply on the chance that the brokers, despite themselves, may have the very business for sale that the buyer is looking for. Most situations, even if unpleasant, can be handled with a mixture of the buyer's own common sense and some low-keyed skepticism, the application of which will become increasingly clear in subsequent chapters.

This section on the buyer's use of a broker to find the right business for sale may have raised more questions than it answered. Those unanswered questions will be taken care of as the reader proceeds through the book. The main point here was to show how brokers, despite limitations, can be helpful in finding the right business for sale.

Figure 5.7 (page 1 of 2)

WHY THE COMMISSION FOR THE SALE OF A SMALL BUSINESS
IS GREATER THAN FOR THE SALE OF A HOME

A typical business-sale commission is about ten to twelve percent of the price. A typical home-sale commission is only about six to seven percent. The reason is that businesses are more difficult to sell than homes. Following are outlined some of the difficulties.

Type of Effort	Home for Sale	Small Business for Sale
Publicity	Sign on front lawn; description in multi-list.	No sign because sellers want secrecy. No multi-list; only loose cooperation between some brokers.
Effort required to sell	Sign is effective because buyers can look in neighborhood and see house, then look in multi-list for number of bedrooms, etc.	Sign (if allowed) only partly effective because it fails to tell important details such as stated earnings and hidden earnings. Finding hidden earnings is usually a major effort.
Appraising	House is easy to appraise. Professional appraiser will do a good job for $300. Bank will accept appraisal.	Business appraisal is difficult and time-consuming. May cost several thousand dollars but few people are capable of doing. Bank will not accept appraisal unless in the form of cash flow projections.
Financing	Almost all banks willing to finance residential real estate.	Banks are reluctant to finance purchases of small businesses, especially restaurants, bars, beauty salons, retail businesses in general.
	No loan application required except financial statement and appraisal.	Extensive loan application often required providing history of business, state of industry, description of competitors, financial plan, manufacturing plan if applicable, background of buyer, and supporting data.
	House makes excellent collateral for loan. Insurance can protect against fire and other hazards.	Business usually is poor collateral for loan because buyer may mismanage and deplete value. No insurance can protect from this hazard.
Matchup between buyer and seller	Relatively easy; almost any house can be lived in. main challenge is to find one in preferred neighborhood.	Extremely difficult; small businesses are very personalized (much more so than houses), buyers sometimes look for years before finding right match. Personalization results in illiquidity of most small businesses.

Figure 5.7 (page 2 of 2)

Regulation of industry	Highly regulated. Laws well established and deeply rooted in history. Real estate agents must be licensed in most states. Regulation promotes smooth transaction, most everything is cut and dried.	No regulation in Missouri and, probably, in most other states. No licensing of brokers in Missouri and, probably, in most other states. Lack of regulation sometimes causes rough dealings; some cheating including on brokers' commissions.
	Regulation has brought everything out into the open.	The field is arcane. Even lawyers and accountants grope for right procedures.
Complexity	House sale requires few documents: listing agreement; description of house showing number of bedrooms, bathrooms, lot size, etc.; sale contract; loan application; appraisal; inquiries to filing agencies regarding liens and debts; inspection reports for building and termites; closing statement; warranty deed; and mortgage.	Business sale requires many documents: listing agreement; registration of fictitious name; contract; directors' and shareholders' authorizations to sell, to buy, and/or to lease; bulk sales affidavit; inquiries to filing agencies regarding liens and debts; bill of sale of personal property; list of equipment; UCC Form to notify filing officers of buyer's debt to seller; memorandum of lease to filing officers; personal guarantee of buyers and/or lessees as individuals if corporation defaults; agreement to transfer telephone number; occupancy permit; commercial lease; bank letter of credit to secure state sales tax license; various bank documents if bank financed.
Lawyers	Usually no lawyers unless special problems occur.	Imperative for all parties to have lawyers including buyer, seller, and, depending on various factors, bank, SBA, insurer, lessor, and title company.
Accountants	Minimal effort required, if any.	Effort to determine corporation vs. proprietorship, set up books and fiscal year, allocate sale price, etc.
Broker's risk of reduced commission or no commission	Some risk but relatively small.	Substantial risk due to illiquidity of small businesses, and due to principals and their lawyers cheating the broker.

QUESTIONS FOR DISCUSSION
Chapter 5—Business Brokers

1. What are the benefits of listing a business for sale for the following business people: a) business owners? b) buyers? and c) commercial loan officers?

2. Why is a non-exclusive listing agreement rather unethical? Why would it tend to be ineffective?

3. In contractual dealings, what is a good way to keep honest people honest?

4. Why is it hard to determine a listing price? How would you do it?

5. Thinking of them as a group, do the four listing agreements described in this chapter convey a sense of reasonableness and fairness to all parties concerned? Could you improve these agreements and, if so, how?

6. The author expresses contempt for some of his fellow business brokers. Is he just slamming the competition, or do his views have merit? How would you improve the industry?

7. Brokers have been accused of tending toward greed because they make their fees a percentage of the sale price, the higher the price, the higher the fee. a) Is the accusation fair? b) How might the issue be resolved? And c) would a broker ever urge his seller client to lower the price? Hint: What is ten percent of zero?

8. What are the eight marketing functions, and how do they affect the broker's fee?

9. Recall how the brokers were cheated in Real-Life Examples 5.3 and 5.4. Considering that the majority of business owners (a guesstimated 75%) are cheating on taxes and that the brokers know whom they are dealing with, do the brokers have a legitimate complaint about being cheated?

10. Who, in actuality, pays the broker's fee?

11. If a listing broker refuses to cooperate with brokers representing buyers, should that be considered as a sign of greed?

12. Consider that the author is a business broker (or at least he was until he fell into publishing). Where do you think he sees himself in Maslow's Hierarchy? Where do you see him?

CHAPTER 6

Fact-Finding

Once the buyer has met the owner and established his or her qualifications for ownership, the buyer must begin finding all of the relevant facts about the business to prepare for appraising, negotiating, and financing. This chapter describes the process of fact-finding. It is divided into three parts: Introduction, Financial Facts, and Non-Financial Facts.

PART 1:
INTRODUCTION

Introduction to Acme Widget Corporation. Most of the references and examples in this chapter and throughout the book deal with real businesses such as restaurants, dry cleaners, and machine shops. However, a fictitious company, Acme Widget Corporation, is hereby introduced and will be followed in subsequent chapters to bring out the interrelationship of fact-finding, appraising, negotiating, and financing.

The work done by Acme Widget and its financial data and other details make it a kind of composite of small businesses. Following are some data on the company: the assets of Acme Widget are offered for sale at a price of $300,000, real estate excluded. The company is a manufacturer, wholesaler, and retailer of widgets. The net profit before taxes shown on the most recent income statement is $2,504. The owner states the value of the equipment to have been appraised recently at $75,000 fair market value in place; liquidation value around $20,000; it was purchased new at $90,000; and replacement with new equipment would cost about $100,000. Further discussion on Acme Widget will be offered later in the chapter.

Introduction to Fact-Finding. The facts to be discovered will fall into two somewhat indistinct groups, financial facts and non-financial facts, and they will be collected more or less simultaneously as the situation permits and as guided by the owner. Although this chapter is more for the edification of the buyer than the owner (since the buyer has much more to learn), an owner will also benefit by being brought to realize how hard the buyer has to work to appraise the company and to prepare a reasonable offer. An owner will further benefit by preparing to do his or her own appraisal to determine a marketable price, and to prepare for negotiating with a buyer.

While collecting these facts, a prospective buyer should continually look for problems or shortcomings in the business as currently managed by the present owner which the buyer would be capable of correcting. If correctable problems are found which would translate into greater profits, the buyer would then appraise and negotiate based on present profits and realize a sort of windfall when ownership is transferred and corrections are made.

The buyer should also try to determine whether the business is dependent on personal traits or talents peculiar to the present owner which could not be duplicated or effectively replaced by the buyer. If so, the buyer would be in the unenviable position of taking over a business almost guaranteed to lose sales and profits with the loss of the owner.

As previously stressed, the purchase and sale of a business is an emotional high point in the lives of most principals. When a buyer starts to ask questions of an owner, the owner's loss of privacy is exacerbated by the owner's emotional state. Buyers therefore have to sense the owner's readiness to be asked certain questions, especially those delving into secrets shared only with a trusted employee, the accountant, a confidant, or perhaps no one at all. One way to sense the owner's readiness is to introduce the beginning of questioning with a buffer such as "I've got all sorts of questions about the equipment, the employees, and how to get from the profit shown on the income statement to your selling price but I don't know exactly where to begin." Such phrasing asks the question without pressuring the owner and may help to endear the buyer. If employees or other persons are present, no mention should be made of financial and other matters pertinent to the sale, including the sale itself, unless the owner so indicates. With these caveats in mind, the balance of this chapter is presented with little further consideration of the owner's sensitivity so as to concentrate on finding the facts and understanding them.

PART 2:
FINANCIAL FACTS

The primary tool for appraising a business is the statement of income and expenses or, for short, the income statement. It is primary partly because it provides a more comprehensive picture of the profits being made than any other document and partly because making a profit is the primary financial purpose of owning a business. The income statement of a small business by itself, however, usually fails to provide a complete or accurate picture. The reasons are several. Owners and their accountants use a variety of tricks to minimize the stated income in order to minimize taxes. Normal variations in sales or in any of the expenses can cause an income statement for a given year to be misleading. So can aberrations. Moreover, trends of one kind or another cannot be detected by looking only at a single year's statement. For these reasons, a number of facts, documents, and procedures must be combined to develop a reasonably accurate picture of a business's ability to make money. It should be clear that the discussions below probably cover virtually all of the fact-finding necessary for most small business appraisals, but that additional important facts may be brought out and perhaps should be in accordance with an individual buyer's knowledge and insight.

Income Statements. The best way to get started on the income statement is to round all the figures to the nearest thousand dollars, omitting the zeros as shown in Figure 6.1. The idea is to minimize the number of digits which have to be studied, worked with, and math-checked. Minimizing the digits makes the page less intimidating, far easier to work with, and far less error prone. The small inaccuracies introduced by rounding are negligible, especially considering that the purpose of these data is to estimate the future, a task of notorious imprecision. Note that the income from the corporate investment ($6,107) is not rounded because that income is not due to operations of the business and will therefore not be part of the appraisal.

Also note that rounding all figures to the nearest thousand dollars is not just for the mathematically challenged. The author himself always rounds these data before beginning an appraisal. What's more, he does it by hand to assure dwelling on and understanding each figure on the page. (He likes to do it on a sheet of accounting paper to take advantage of the lines and columns already in place.)

Another procedure for easier understanding of the income statement is to copy the figures, if available, from at least the three most recent complete years into adjacent columns, as shown in Figure 6.2. The juxtaposition of figures tends to make trends, similarities, and irregularities stand out, and it provides a good starting point for sitting down with the owner in private to hear his or her revelations as to what is going on in the company.

Also shown in Figure 6.2 is a column of hidden earnings which is explained below.

Figure 6.1 Rounding to the Nearest Thousand Dollars

ACME WIDGET CORPORATION
STATEMENT OF INCOME AND EXPENSES

	As shown on income statement	Rounded with zeros omitted
Sales	$414,907	$415
Expenses		
Advertising	8,412	8
Automotive	9,219	9
Depreciation	15,190	15
Insurance	13,789	14
Legal and accounting	6,500	6
Maintenance and repair	4,714	5
Miscellaneous	342	0
Office supplies	8,501	9
Raw materials	45,609	46
Rent	27,260	27
Taxes and licenses	21,333	21
Telephone	2,770	3
Utilities	8,043	8
Wages		
Owner	31,956	32
Other employees	208,765	209
Total expenses	$412,403	$412
Subtotal pre-tax profit	$ 2,504	$ 3
Other income		
Interest on corporate investment	$ 6,107	N/A
Total pre-tax profit	$ 8,611	N/A

Figure 6.2 Juxtaposition of Data and Hidden Earnings

ACME WIDGET CORPORATION THREE-YEAR SUMMARY
OF INCOME AND EXPENSES (000 omitted)

	1998	1999	2000	*Hidden Earnings*
Sales	$405	$412	$415	
Expenses				
Advertising	3	3	8	*5*
Automotive	7	8	9	*6*
Depreciation	18	16	15	*6*
Insurance	16	13	14	*5*
Legal & accounting	5	5	6	*1*
Maintenance & repair	4	5	5	
Miscellaneous	0	0	0	
Office supplies	8	8	9	
Raw materials	45	45	46	*6*
Rent	27	27	27	
Taxes & licenses	20	21	21	*1*
Telephone	3	3	3	
Utilities	8	8	8	
Wages				
Owner	31	34	32	
Other employees	206	211	209	*16*
Total expenses	$401	$407	$412	
Pre-tax net profit	$4	$5	$3	*$46*

Owner's Revelations. After the buyer has studied the income statements and any other data supplied by the owner and assuming that the buyer and owner are establishing rapport with each other, a point will be reached where the buyer needs to sit down with the owner in private and determine the necessary facts to make these data truly meaningful. The meeting described below between a business owner and a prospective buyer, though fictional, is a kind of compilation of some actual cases, but not the general case.

A buyer is looking at Acme Widget Corporation. The buyer thinks to himself that a $300,000 asking price for a business showing pre-tax operational earnings of only $3,000 seems absurd. The buyer also notes, however, that the company has an aura of prosperity about it and that except for the seemingly low earnings, it appears to be attractive. The buyer therefore decides that the owner should be given a chance to explain why the company is worth $300,000. Thus, a meeting after hours is arranged.

The buyer, though never having owned a business, knows the widget industry (which is the main reason the owner is willing to meet with the buyer) and expects that the owner will pull some earnings out of hiding. The buyer brings along a sheet like the one in Figure 6.2 with a special column to itemize any earnings which have been hidden to minimize taxes. (Italics are used to simulate the buyer's handwritten figures in the Hidden Earnings column.) The buyer, sensitive to the emotional needs of the owner, knows how to ask questions or, as the occasion demands, how to gently probe.

The advertising expense shows an increase from $3,000 in 1998 and 1999 to $8,000 in 2000. Did that increase help to boost sales? The owner answers that the increased advertising had nothing to do with sales. Acme Widget relies solely on *Yellow Pages* advertising since other media have proved ineffective in the widget industry. The $5,000 increase went entirely into radio advertising but was bought through a public relations firm just started by the owner's brother-in-law. The expenditure was made under pressure from the owner's spouse. The buyer, now realizing that the $5,000 is not a true expense but discretionary income, enters that amount as hidden earnings as shown in Figure 6.2. The buyer also thinks to himself that this is a strange and costly way to keep peace in the household but that since the radio advertising was actually delivered, it is a legitimate expense in the eyes of the IRS. (Such seemingly wasteful expenditures as this one are occasionally found in the world of small business. They are a part of the game.)

The buyer asks whether automotive expense is in line considering that some wholesale customers pick up their widgets at the company facilities and that raw materials are usually delivered by the suppliers. The owner allows that there is a company credit card for the sole purpose of servicing the pick-up truck but that there are three cars in the family (owner's, spouse's, and one teenager's) and that the company credit card sees a lot of use to pay for gas, oil changes, and repairs. The justification is that any one of the three cars may be used on occasion to run a business-related errand. The owner estimates personal and family automotive expenses at $3,000 or $4,000 annually, then reconsiders and ups it to $6,000. The buyer enters that amount under hidden earnings as shown in Figure 6.2. The buyer also makes a mental note that these expenses seem to represent an exaggerated interpretation of the tax code that would not survive an audit but that probably would not be considered fraudulent. The buyer further notes mentally that since there appears to be no fraud, the owner would probably suffer no more than minor penalties if caught by the IRS despite the obvious misinterpretation of the code.

The buyer notes that depreciation expense for the last three years totals $49,000. Comparing it to the cost when new of $90,000, he wonders if the equipment must have a short life to be more than half depreciated in only three years. The owner replies that the actual expected life is ten years, but that their CPA is taking full advantage of accelerated depreciation as allowed by IRS rules. The buyer then divides the $90,000 cost-when-new by the ten-year life expectancy to get an actual depreciation of $9,000 per year, then enters $6,000 ($15,000 − $9,000) into the column for hidden earnings.

The owner explains the variations in insurance expense from one year to the next as nothing more than the result of changing insurance companies and interrupted payment schedules. The $14,000 shown for 2000 is accurate and reflects the ongoing needs of the company. The owner also states that about $5,000 is for personal and family insurance. The buyer enters that amount under hidden earnings.

No questions are raised regarding office supplies but the owner volunteers that the amount shown is about right since any pens, pencils, stationery, and postage stamps taken by the family for personal use probably do not amount to more than $40 or $50 per year. Well, maybe $75 or $100.

The buyer wonders if the legal and accounting expenses don't seem a bit high for this size of operation. The owner says that normally the accountant's charge of about $3,000 per year is Acme's only professional expense. Three years ago, however, they hired a lawyer to explore obtaining a license to manufacture a unique widget which was invented and patented by another company. Some ongoing legal problems have arisen costing about $2,000 per year. In year 2000, the owner continues, the same lawyer took care of some family problems which cost about $1,000 but which were included in the lawyer's bill to Acme. The buyer asks if there is a written company policy regarding employee benefits and whether legal services are included. The owner responds that no written policy exists but notes that no auditor would ever catch the admittedly questionable charge because the lawyer made no mention of it in his statement to the company. The buyer enters the $1,000 figure under hidden earnings while making a mental note not only that charging the company for personal expenses is probably illegal but that, if so, the lawyer is a party to the fraud.

The buyer, having written several cost proposals for his employer, observes that raw material seems about 10% high for the level of sales experienced at Acme. The owner replies that they have found a way to store wealth without being taxed on it and describes the following scheme: Acme is on a job-order system whereby each batch of widgets made is assigned a separate job order, and all direct expenses for each batch including materials and labor are charged to the job. By estimating generous scrap allowances (translation: by purposely charging more materials than are needed), each job is completed with raw materials left over. The leftover materials go into the storage bin but since they already have been charged as an expense, there is no record (no official record, anyway) that these leftover materials exist.

Several advantages are realized. Since these excess materials are charged as an expense, they reduce earnings and taxes. While they sit in the storage bin, they gain in value due to inflation but obviously no tax has to be paid on the gain. Though no material shortages have occurred recently, if any ever do, Acme Widget will be prepared. If, for the record, earnings ever need to be improved—say, for the purpose of looking good when borrowing money from a bank—the materials in the bin can be used on upcoming job orders, reducing the expenses charged and boosting earnings. Finally, if ever a little quick cash might come in handy, selling those materials to other users will provide it and nobody will ever know the difference. Moreover, if those other users happen to be smaller companies not eligible for the wholesale price breaks that Acme gets, some nice profits can be made. The owner volunteers that about $6,000 worth of raw materials at cost went into the storage bin this year. The owner adds that the $6,000 does not include any profits made by selling the materials to smaller companies. The buyer notes to himself that the overbuy of materials, conceptually speaking, is skimming in the same way that a retailer placing cash into his pocket without ringing it up on the cash register is skimming. The buyer also notes that profits made by selling the overbought materials constitute profits on the skim, imbuing the scheme with a wry elegance seldom found with humble merchants dealing in cash. The buyer, however, regardless of what his feelings toward such illicit schemes may or may not be, reasons that silence is the wisest course and offers no comment other than nodding to acknowledge that the scheme is understood.

Moving quickly to the next items on the income statement, the buyer notes that the rent, maintenance and repair, taxes and licenses, telephone, and utilities expenses all seem to be reasonable and orderly. The owner affirms that they are.

The buyer asks if wages might be improved a bit. The owner replies that their three teenage children draw a total of about $16,000 per year ostensibly for cleaning the office and running errands but for actually very little that's useful. The buyer makes no mention that useless employment of family members for tax avoidance is probably illegal but enters the $16,000 figure into the column for hidden earnings and notes that those earnings now total $45,000. The buyer reviews his figures and notices that if the payroll decreases by $16,000, the payroll taxes (mostly for social security) should also decrease. He enters $1,000 in the hidden earnings column for taxes and licenses and changes the total to $46,000.

A moment of silence ensues. Then the buyer, with halting voice, says that he would like to ask a question and that he asks this question only in the spirit of thoroughness with no personal implications intended. The buyer realizes that business owners and their accountants strive to put down all the expenses they can think of in order to minimize taxes. The $46,000 in hidden earnings, however, raises the question in his mind of whether there are any hidden expenses. The owner compliments the buyer on his insight and replies that no, there are no hidden expenses in his business but that he knows exactly what the buyer means. The owner's accountant, for example, is very active in his political party and he doubts, therefore, that it is any coincidence that his accountant receives a piece of the municipal auditing assignments each year. Although his accountant has never said anything, the owner speculates that his accountant probably pays for those auditing jobs in one way or another, such as cash contributions to the party or below-scale accounting services either to the party or to the political bosses in power. The owner adds that one of his colleagues—who, he has to admit, produces a fine widget—pays off the purchasing agents for two of his best customers. Some of these costs probably would be accounted for as entertainment expenses but most of it, he speculates, would, for obvious reasons, never show on the books. Then the owner repeats that he does not engage in any of these sorts of activities. He abhors the thought of having to pay a purchasing agent to get business. It is against his principles.

The buyer has no more questions to ask and so the buyer and owner chat about the widget industry, where it is going, and how bright the future is for a young person contemplating ownership. The owner is impressed with the buyer's knowledge of the industry, his preparation for their meeting, and his tact at asking questions. They chat for a while longer. The conversation is warm and friendly. The owner feels comfortable with the buyer. At an opportune moment, the owner refers to the extra money to be made in the business. The buyer feels comfortable too but, still in the role of a supplicant, merely raises his eyebrows at the mention of extra money. The owner continues by noting that many retail customers wander into the store on Saturday afternoons even though the store officially closes at noon. The purchases made after hours are not always rung on the cash register and even if they are, the tapes are discarded. The buyer is emboldened by the owner's directness and asks whether an IRS audit would reveal lack of accountability for the widgets sold after hours. The owner replies that holiday sales, special discounts, clearance sales, and markdowns for shopworn and damaged widgets are not just for purposes of inventory clearance, meeting the competition, or building a customer base although, to be sure, those are important benefits. Equally important is to obviate reliable audits, the idea being that whatever cannot be otherwise accounted for is explained by the various and frequent price reductions that nobody can realistically keep track of.

The buyer thinks for a moment, then remarks that the owner has just provided a new perspective on price-cutting and that now the buyer understands why, when customers at the local tavern are high at happy hour on two drinks for the price of one, the tavern owner is even higher on loss of accountability. The owner nods in agreement and observes a generality that the fuzz on a pricing system almost always creates an opportunity for making some extra money.

The buyer and owner agree that there is nothing more to discuss at this time and the meeting is adjourned. On his way home, it begins to sink in on the buyer that now he has become an accessory to the fact. He will have to think about that.

Note that the meeting and owner's revelations described above are not typical but nevertheless approximately represent the exchange of information which may occur at a private meeting between buyer and owner. What is fairly typical is that cheating on taxes in the world of business is occurring in one form or another, including, in addition to the devices shown in the above example, such schemes as a manufacturer using shop labor to build his home (even on defense contracts subject to government audit); paying workers in cash, either partly or wholly, to avoid social security and unemployment taxes, but also to offset any revenues that are being skimmed so as not to arouse suspicion of the IRS; paying suppliers partly in cash while the suppliers in turn omit the cash-paid supplies from their invoices, destroying accountability for both the business owner and the supplier (a cooperative system aptly described as two-tiered or vertical cheating); tavern owners purchasing their liquor at retail stores; retailers cheating customers by making "mistakes" at the checkout counter; and so on.

The cheating itself is usually not described so starkly or so honestly as to refer to it explicitly as cheating. Instead, a host of pet names and innocent-sounding phrases is employed such as "my golf money," "household funds for the spouse," "pocket change," "spending money," "special bonus," and so forth. The cuteness or triteness of the term can belie the amount. One manufacturer, when asked how much his pocket change might amount to in a year, replied around $60,000. Interestingly, some owners are too boastful to hide behind euphemisms. One restaurateur with a high-profit-margin menu enjoyed telling the first buyer brought to him by the broker that he skims $350,000 a year. (The broker's cost analysis roughly corroborated the owner's boast.)

Some owners defer to secrecy and silence rather than mention any untoward activities. Such secrecy may be absolute and accompanied by such words as "what you see is what you get," a non-informative disclosure referring to the financial data and tangible assets, or it may be suggestive when expressed by such words as "whether there are any other profits to be made in this business or not I would rather not comment on." If the buyer is brought by a broker, the owner may disclose his schemes only to the buyer during which meeting the broker may be told to wait in another room, or the owner may level with the broker but refuse to divulge anything to the buyer, the idea presumably being that information from the broker to the buyer is hearsay for which the owner could not reasonably be held accountable.

Some company accountants may be a party to or may even have initiated such schemes. Other accountants are so clean that they will refuse to work for a company in which cheating occurs if they discover it. If they do not explicitly discover it, they will probably continue to work for the company though they may suspect it.

A kind of irony or double standard may accompany the cheating. Some business owners will cheat on taxes in every way possible if they think they can get away with it, but these same owners would never cheat a customer, a supplier, an employee, or any individual out of a penny. For other owners, cheating is a way of life.

Since cheating for some owners is a way of life, a buyer must be alert to the possibility of being misled to pay a higher price through exaggerations of the money being made. A buyer's best safeguard is to be well qualified to own and manage the business being bought. Strong qualifications provide two lines of defense. First is the thorough understanding of the business which helps to see through misinformation. Second is the ability, once the busi-

Illustration 6.1

"The fuzz on a pricing system. That's where you make your golf money."

ness is owned and the deceit discovered, to overcome the resultant cash-flow problem by smart application of hard work and long hours. The buyers of the coin-operated laundry in Example 6.4 below were misled into paying too high a price (the seller had lied about the sales) but still managed to make a salary and a capital gain through smart management and hard work.

Another line of defense against being lied to or misled is found in the maxim that human beings tend to see others in their own image. Happy people, for example, tend to see others as happy while the bitter tend to see others as bitter. The same holds true for the honest and the dishonest. Thus a business owner who seems trusting is probably trustable while one who seems guarded probably needs to be guarded against. But the clues themselves can mislead. The cheat may trust a person on minor matters to set that person up for a kill. Or the person who seems extravagant in protecting himself may have been a cheat's victim. In any case, unless the person being dealt with is known for his or her probity, the plan is always to use sound business procedures. Tried and true business procedures include putting everything important into writing; obtaining bank financing as opposed to seller financing even though it means a lot more work and a higher rate of interest; hiring both a lawyer and an accountant even when they don't seem to be needed and even when they seem to cost too much; refusing to take short cuts during fact-finding such as not bothering to check on a person's references and not taking the time to check the zoning laws or the environmental implications; and so on.

It should be clear that some business owners are strictly and totally honest and proud of it, and that some of them who are doing well even make conscious efforts to disburse some of their earnings once they have attained financial stability. They do so out of genuine altruism or deep appreciation of how good the business and the community have been to them. Such disbursements may be to charitable organizations but they may also take the form of larger-than-needed purchases from community businesses and organizations such as neighborhood newspapers for advertising, local gardeners for landscaping, service companies for maintenance, and so on. These owners also may reward employees with above-scale year-end bonuses, with benefits above the industry standard, and/or with continuous pay the employees can count on even when work is slow (the latter being fairly common in businesses which need to hold onto their skilled employees). These disbursements are not always easy to identify as expenses which are unnecessary—like the year 2000 advertising expense in Figure 6.2—and must be sought out to form an accurate picture of the earnings. Thus, owners who bury such disbursements in their expenses pose the same problems for buyers needing to discover the hidden earnings as do owners who cheat on taxes.

It is apparent from the above descriptions that business owners as a group are extremely variable in the management of their affairs. A buyer therefore should be prepared for anything

Contingent or Undisclosed Liabilities. Sometimes liabilities of a company will not show on the books. Examples are maintenance or repair of equipment for which the owner has not yet been billed; supplies and raw materials delivered on credit; a contract for future goods or services; employees' accrued vacations, sick leave, or bonuses; and a promissory note or royalty agreement to be paid if attaining a specified level of sales. The buyer should ask the owner if any such liabilities exist. The buyer's lawyer should include an indemnity clause in the purchase and sale agreement but should also check the state and county recorders' offices for any outstanding liens. Some states have bulk sales laws requiring sellers to notify creditors of an impending sale of a business. Such laws seem to offer protection to both the creditors and the buyer but the buyer still needs to have a lawyer's assistance to be assured of being protected. If the buyer's lawyer, for example, senses some danger and if the seller is providing any of the financing, the lawyer may add a clause to the purchase and sale agreement allowing the buyer to withhold payments to the seller in case of unforeseen liabilities. The buyer's lawyer may also request that the seller obtain certification from the state that taxes have been paid. These types of protection are prudent and perhaps necessary even if the sale is of assets rather than stock. Although an asset sale, in theory, frees the buyer of the corporation's liabilities, if the business being bought holds itself out to the community as a continuation of the business previously owned by the seller's corporation, the law may hold the buyer responsible for a seller's liability. Again, a lawyer's advice is very much in order.

Depreciation Schedule. A depreciation schedule is a document usually prepared by the company accountant listing all the depreciable assets of the business, the original cost of each asset, and the amount of depreciation of each asset for each year during the life of the asset. Following is an abbreviated example of entries on a depreciation schedule.

Item	Cost	Date Bought	Expected Life	Depreciation Expense 1998	1999	2000
Drill press	$1,200	7/1/98	12 yrs.	$50	$100	$100
Wood desk	$400	4/1/98	10 yrs.	$30	$40	$40

If the drill press and wood desk were the only equipment owned by the company, the total cost of the equipment shown on the balance sheet would be $1,600. On December 31, 1998, the accumulated depreciation would be $80 and the book value of the equipment shown on the balance sheet for that date would be $1,600 less $80, or $1,520. On December 31, 1999, these figures would be $220 and $1,380, respectively. And so on. The depreciation expense shown on the income statement for 1998 would be $80, for 1999 it would be $140, and so on.

The depreciation schedule is necessary to verify the depreciation expense shown on the income statement and to break it into its components. That allows the depreciation charged by the accountant to be compared with the depreciation expense actually occurring, thus revealing the hidden earnings, if any.

When attempting to analyze a depreciation schedule, most persons probably should get help from an accountant.

Insurance Statement. Insurance expense for a business usually covers all the property owned in the operation of the business, including real estate, personal property (equipment, inventory, etc.), and money. The risks covered usually are comprehensive loss of, or damage to property; loss of income if the business is forced to close because of fire or other causes; liability for personal injury, property damage or other such claims; and worker's compensation. The buyer must be sure that the kinds of property and the kinds of risk covered are adequate to the needs of the business and to the buyer's capacity for self-insurance. Attention should be paid to the deductible; the coinsurance; and the degree of comprehensiveness such as the inclusion or exclusion of earthquake damage, whether theft of cash is covered off premises as well as on premises, and so on. Since insurance is a broad and complicated field, expert advice from a lawyer or an exceptionally capable insurance agent is very much in order. If the present insurance does not seem adequate, the buyer will have to allow for higher insurance cost when he or she assumes ownership.

Lease. In addition to the basic monthly rent, a lease may call for other charges to the tenant. These charges may be conditioned on certain events which may or may not affect the present owner of the business but which may occur in the future. Examples are an increase in property tax which is passed on to the tenant or an increase in common maintenance or advertising costs shared by the tenants in a mall. Some leases have rents based on sales, usually sales above a certain level below which a minimum rent is in force. Charges may be made for trash collection, snow removal, security guards, and so on and some accountants assign such charges to accounts other than rent, making those charges hard to detect. Last, but not least, the lease may contain a schedule of periodic increases. For all of the above reasons, reading the lease as compared to examining the income statement is sometimes the best way to determine both the actual rent paid by the present owner and the rent likely to be paid by the buyer. Some leases, however, are 50 pages or more in length and fairly complex, in which case assistance from an accountant or lawyer may be necessary. In many cases and perhaps in most, a new lease with new rents and other charges will have to be negotiated with the landlord.

Check Stubs or Check Register. Sometimes there will be an expense shown on the income statement which may seem high or low but for which the owner has no sure explanation. The only way to determine the exact nature of such an expense is to refer to the check stubs or to the check register. A check register is a document which itemizes the information usually shown on the check stubs but which offers more room for explaining the expense being paid or for explaining any other purpose of the check. By reviewing the check stubs or register and itemizing the expenses which seem to contribute to a questionable expense shown on the income statement, a breakdown of that expense may be obtained, thus explaining that expense. However, if whoever wrote the checks failed to adequately explain the purpose of each check by so noting on the stubs or register, no explanation will be found. This situation is most likely to occur when check writing has been performed by someone not trained in the rigors and benefits of accounting, possibly the owner or a family member. If the accountant who compiled the income statement was very conscientious, as those who are certified usually are, he or she will have contacted the owner and clarified any questionable checks. If the accountant was not so conscientious, he may simply have guessed at what the check was for, locking the problem into place if the guess was not accurate. To solve the problem, someone who understands the situation must sit down with the owner or whoever wrote the checks and determine, check stub by check stub, what the checks were for. Then the expenses can be assigned to the proper accounts.

If the person assigned to the task is lucky, the accountant who compiled the income statement will have noted an account number on each stub. Then some of the guesswork is removed and the task reduced to one of itemizing on a sheet of paper the stubs with the appropriate account numbers. If the person assigned to the task is not lucky, the check stubs will have to be compared one at a time to the accountant's ledger (see below), a truly painstaking job. Unless the buyer has the time and the motivation to do the job—not to mention the aptitude for working with numbers—the job should be done by an accountant or a very reliable bookkeeper. If possible, the task should not be handed to an accountant during tax season, January through May, because of the heavy workload.

Accountant's Ledger. The ledger is a kind of work sheet used by accountants to assign the payments noted on check stubs or register to the proper accounts. For example, if a check for $100 has been written to pay for advertising, a double entry will be made on the ledger, one to add $100 to the advertising expense account and one to subtract $100 from the checking account. For convenience, each account may be assigned a number. For example, account number 101 is for food sales, 102 for liquor sales, 201 for accounting expense, 202 for advertising expense, and so on. Then the ledger entries can be grouped by account number to compile the income statement and balance sheet.

Sales by Month. In some industries, particularly those with retail sales, a monthly breakdown of the sales for at least two or three years will show if there are any seasonal variations or economic trends. Knowing the seasonal variations is obviously useful for planning cash flow, for ordering supplies, for staffing, and so on. More important from a buyer's perspective is that a sudden downtrend in sales—say, in the most recent one or two months—may be the early signal of a broader downturn for the company being bought, for the industry, or even for the economy. Such a downtrend may not have become apparent in the complete-year sales, as shown, for example, on the juxtaposed income statements in Figure 6.2. If a downtrend should seem to be developing and if the owner can offer no explanation, the buyer may wish to wait another month or two to follow the development before making any commitment. The buyer may also use a downtrend as a bargaining point in the negotiation. Likewise, an uptrend may be a bargaining point for the owner.

Some business owners request their accountants to prepare an income statement at the end of each month or at the end of each quarter. The most recent monthly or quarterly statements, if available, might also be looked at to find any newly developing trend in expenses as well as in sales. However, such interim statements of expenses tend to be incomplete or subject to distortions due to normal variances in short-term payment schedules; they therefore tend to be of limited usefulness.

Sales by Product Line. A breakdown of annual sales by product line can show whether the business offered for sale is what it is purported to be and can also suggest whether there is a healthy product mix, particularly from a buyer's perspective. An exaggerated case was in Example 5.1 where such a breakdown would have shown the so-described tool and die manufacturer to have zero sales of tools and dies. A less blatant case and the kind of danger which disproportionate sales can suggest are described in Example 6.1.

Example 6.1 An independent neighborhood grocery store is offered for sale. The store seems fairly typical with the usual variety of goods on the shelves and in the bins except that meat accounts for 55% of sales, a fact which the owner not only does not hide but which he seems proud of, especially since he works behind the meat counter. The annual sales are $900,000 and are verified by tax returns and by canceled checks for retail sales tax. The buyer has strong experience, having owned and prospered in a similar store for ten years before losing it to a rehabilitation project and eminent domain. The buyer is deliberate in his fact-finding and takes time to look at each of the product lines and how they are managed and takes three or four weeks to observe the overall operation. He drops into the store at different times on different days just to get a sense of the sales activity and a general sense of what goes on in the store. Finally, the buyer makes an offer, the offer is accepted, the papers are drawn up by the lawyers, and the deal is closed. On the first day of the new ownership sales turn down sharply. They continue down until they level off after three weeks at about 60% of what they had been under the former owner. The buyer tries to rebuild sales through advertising but to no avail. He is losing money and, only nine months after purchase, closes the doors. The buyer and the broker discuss the calamity but neither can offer an explanation as to what happened. The buyer thinks that the former owner must have played some kind of a trick but can not imagine what it could have been.

One day about two years later, the broker has lunch with the store manager of one of the national chains (such as K-Mart, Target, etc.) and relates the above story. The manager expresses surprise that someone with ten years in the business fell into such a trap. Meat customers, he explains, are notoriously loyal to their butchers and the sudden loss of sales at the former owner's departure could have been predicted. The manager adds that what had been offered for sale was not a grocery store with strong meat sales, but a meat market with related grocery sales. If the store had been so described, the buyer might have seen the problem. (On the other hand, he might not have seen the problem, and no one will ever know.)

The obvious lesson from this example is that when sales break down into any kind of disproportional mix, no commitment to purchase should be made until an explanation is found. If necessary, a consultant should be hired. If one consultant fails to provide a reasonable explanation, another should be sought until the explanation is found.

Sales-Tax Canceled Checks. In Missouri and, probably, in other states taxing retail sales, the retailer must mail a form each month declaring the sales for that month along with a check for the tax on those sales. The amount of sales can be calculated by dividing the amount on the check by the tax rate. If, for example, the amount on the check is $6,211.53 and the tax rate is 5.25%, the sales would be calculated as follows:

$$\text{Sales} = \text{dollar amount of tax} \div \text{tax rate}$$

$$= \$6,211.53 \div .0525$$

$$= \$118,315$$

The form accompanying the check could be used to verify the sales except that it is too easy to falsify or to confuse a discarded draft for the final form.

Suppliers' Invoices. There will be situations where the owner has probably been skimming but is either unable or unwilling to show evidence of the true sales. If the suppliers have shown on their invoices the amounts or quantities delivered as well as their charges, the sales and gross profits can be estimated from those invoices.

In the Chapter 2 example of Tom's Retail Sales, if Tom's sales of $14 were not known, they could be calculated from the inventory, markup, and invoice. In real life, however, the situation is not nearly so simple. Allowances have to be made for breakage, scrap, and fluctuations in retail prices due to clearance sales and sales promotions. Depending on the nature of the business, additional complexity would be added if there were a variety of goods with differing markups and if there were additional charges for labor. In other words, the tangle of complexity making it difficult for a buyer to analyze the finances is exacerbated by the same loss of accountability designed to frustrate the IRS. Still, it is possible for a buyer, probably with the help of a patient owner, to estimate at least approximately the sales and gross profits from the invoices.

Body Count by Stakeout. If an owner declares a certain sales amount on the income statement and if the amount is repeated on the tax return, there probably is little reason to doubt the verity of those sales. However, there are times when for a variety of reasons a buyer may wish for additional verification. The price being paid for the business may (and almost always does) constitute a major commitment thus motivating the buyer to seek maximum assurance of the verity of numbers. There may be reason to suspect that the owner is omitting some sales from his or her tax return and the suspected omission may be especially large. Or there may be a simple emotional need for the buyer to have further assurance. In any case, a stakeout is not a perfect answer but, depending on the type of business, it can go a long way towards verifying the actual sales or at least building confidence.

A stakeout is a positioning outside a place of business to observe whatever clues may be present to help determine the nature and viability of the business. Of particular concern is a body count of customers entering the premises. For some businesses such as manufacturing or contracting, the stakeout would be of little use since most customers would order by mail or telephone or through a sales representative. For some other businesses, the stakeout would be of limited use because there would be no way to tell the size of the customers' purchases. For example, at a shoe store there would be no way for someone outside to determine if a customer bought shoes for $80 or slippers for $20. Even for the shoe store, however, if a body count of the customers seen exiting with packages would be multiplied by an estimated average sale, with allowances for returns and exchanges, that would provide a rough verification.

A stakeout at a restaurant would probably work about as well as for any business. That's because the comparatively small variation in amount spent from one customer to the next would allow a fairly accurate estimate of the average amount per customer, especially if the stakeout would be made by a buyer who has developed a sense of sales through solid experience in the business.

The stakeout is performed by the buyer finding an inconspicuous means to loiter near the premises. The ideal is to be seated in a legally parked car on the street some distance from the entrance but close enough to see and count the customers. The date should be recorded along with the times for beginning and ending the stakeout and the number of persons seen entering. Multiplying the number of persons entering the place of business by the estimated dollars spent per person would give the estimated sales for the period observed. The stakeout should last as many hours and be repeated as many times as time and conditions permit. The stakeout especially should be conducted during the busiest hours, as suggested by the owner, although the slow hours should also be checked to gain a more complete sense of the activity. The estimated weekly or monthly sales is completed by extrapolating the collected data.

Balance Sheets. The usefulness of the balance sheet in appraising a business being sold depends mostly on whether the sale is of corporate stock or of assets. If of stock, the buyer will receive all the assets and all the liabilities shown on the balance sheet less any of those assets or liabilities specifically excluded from the sale. If the sale is of assets, the liabilities shown on the balance sheet would, by definition, be excluded from the sale. In most asset sales, such assets as cash, accounts receivable, certificates of deposit, and others not germane to the operation of the business would also be excluded.

Some liabilities, however, could be included in an asset sale to help finance the purchase or to facilitate the deal.

In a sale of stock, the balance sheet can yield strong clues as to the financial health and the value of the company. Examples of such clues are whether the total current assets are comfortably greater than the total current liabilities and how closely the book value of the company (total assets less total liabilities) compares to the purchase price. A clue useful for either stock or asset sales is whether the equipment is fully or almost fully depreciated, suggesting the need for imminent replacement. However, there are several reasons that such clues should not be relied on to any large degree in appraising the company unless the buyer is closely assisted by an accountant and a lawyer. Small businesses tend to reflect the owner's personality, the owner's needs, and the owner's peculiarities simply because the owner is making virtually all decisions of any importance. Small business balance sheets therefore cannot always be judged by conventional standards. For example, the equipment may be owned by the owner himself or herself, not by the owner's corporation. Such personal ownership of equipment has the advantage of converting what otherwise would be income taxable to the corporation to rental income taxable to the owner, but it makes the balance sheet look weak for lack of assets. In another example, the corporation may be endangered by some form of latent liability not shown on the balance sheet. In still another example, the balance sheet may include assets which for one reason or another cannot be sold or transferred outside the corporation. Examples of unsellable assets are government approval of the corporation's procedures for the manufacture of possibly polluting chemicals, and a corporate licensing agreement to manufacture another company's patented product.

Equipment List. An equipment list is simply a list of all the personal property included in the sale. The equipment list has several important purposes: it identifies personal property as distinct from real estate. (A chandelier, a room air conditioner, and an auxiliary diesel-electric generator are examples of equipment which sometimes need such distinction.) The list segregates business-owned personal property from vendor-owned property such as a candy vending machine. The equipment list is obviously necessary to conduct and substantiate an appraisal of equipment. The list documents for purposes of insurance. It provides the accountant with a list of depreciable items. And it satisfies certain legal needs such as being attached to the bill of sale to transfer ownership, being attached to a declaration of personal property for tax purposes, being recorded for public notice of any liens against it, and so on.

Such lists are usually prepared by the seller, by the broker or, for a fee, by the appraiser. To make the list most useful, the equipment should be grouped in a meaningful way. In a restaurant, for example, the equipment would be listed by room such as kitchen, prep room, north dining room, east dining room, waitress station, foyer, exterior, and so on. For a machine shop, the equipment would be grouped by type, such as milling machines, lathes, drill presses, office equipment, automotive equipment, and so on. Whenever possible but especially for larger-value items, the manufacturer's name, model number, and serial number should be included. Small items may be grouped into lots such as one lot of pots and pans for a restaurant or one lot of hand tools for a machine shop. Figure 6.3 is a sample list of equipment. It is excerpted from an actual restaurant list ten pages in length.

Aside from appraising, there are two important questions to be asked by the buyer: is the equipment sufficient to carry on the operations producing the current sales and profits? If so, the buyer can continue with no purchases of additional equipment until required by growth in sales. If not, the buyer may have to purchase additional equipment at a cost over and above the price of the business. Is there excess equipment which might be excluded from the sale or sold after the sale by the buyer? If so, the effective price being paid for the business may be lowered by the value of the excess equipment.

Figure 6.3 Sample List of Equipment

LIST OF EQUIPMENT

Abbreviations:
D	Depth	No.	Number
Dia.	Diameter	SN	Serial Number
H	Height	SS	Stainless Steel
L	Length	W	Width
MN	Model Number		

Vendor-owned Equipment
The cigarette machine, coffee-making equipment including coffee servers and the SS work stand holding the coffee equipment, the iced-tea dispenser, wine-dispensing system, and the ice-storage bin in the bar are vendor-owned.

Kitchen
1   SS wire 5-shelf assembly on wheels,
     29.5"W x 24"D x 79.5"H
1   Hobart mixer, MN D-300, SN 1905439
1   Puffer Hubbard Challenger refrigerator,
     MN SAE 23, SN C397060 ST #3
1   Exhaust hood, 21'L
1   Southbend 12-burner gas stove
1   U.S. Range gas grill, 36"W x 28.5"D x 40"H
     with rear-mounted double shelf, additional 16"H

Basement
1   Norris walk-in cooler, inside dimensions:
     66.5"W x 66"D x 84"H, MN WID-4, SN 430901
1   Wood 3-shelf assembly, 96"W x 24"D x 92.5"H
1   Lot Miscellaneous smaller shelves, stands, ladders, hoses, dolly, etc.
     Southwest Dining Room
4   Dining tables for two, steel pedestal, Formica top, 2' x 2.5'
10 Dining tables for four, steel pedestal, Formica top, 3' x 3'

1   Dining table for four with 7" hinged extension leaves
    on two sides, 3' x 3' before extending

56 Dining chairs, rattan, cushioned and upholstered

1   Original oil painting, 11.5" x 15.5", double-framed

4   Prints, 11" x 16", matted and framed in glass

1   Planter, wall-mounted, cast iron, 36"H x 18"W,
    with spray of about 100 artificial flowers

Waitress Station by Manager's Office

1   Custom-made work stand with two 2-shelf bays below,
    wood with Formica top, 60.7"W x 24"D x 40"H

1   Tannetics, Inc. Beverage Air SS top-loading
    refrigerator, 49.3"W x 27"D x 33"H

Exterior

4   Outdoor signs

Equipment Appraisal. The value of used equipment is subject to all the vagaries of the market place. Such vagaries include economic recession or growth, fashion and fad, shortage, glut, technological change, regional differences, and so on. Equipment appraisals therefore tend to be very subjective. It is important for both buyers and sellers to realize the subjective nature of appraisals, because without such realization, their confidence can be easily shaken by the differences of opinion which almost inevitably arise. It is also important to realize that subjective differences usually pose no problem partly because the value of a business depends far more on the profits to be made than on the value of the assets and partly because the main purpose of the equipment appraisal usually is to provide documentation to a lending bank which accepts the equipment as collateral.

Equipment appraisals usually can be conducted competently by most dealers in used equipment. The dealer will appraise the fair market value, which is what the dealer would sell the equipment for to a buyer. Generally, the dealer may be willing to buy the equipment at about half of fair market value. Note that if the dealer conducts the appraisal at the shop or business site, the dealer will probably qualify the appraisal with the words "in place." That means that the dealer did the appraisal where the equipment is located but it also means that changing the location may change the value of the equipment (which condition is not unlike that for an appraisal of residential real estate). Note also that if the business is in distress, the equipment is very liable not to remain "in place" and, therefore, that the value of it is liable to diminish.

In the case where a business losing money is sold for the value of the equipment, the skill of the appraiser may be of greater importance than usual. Then extra care may be in order when choosing the appraiser. Several opinions of appraisers' reputations should be sought from bank loan officers, business owners in the same industry, bankruptcy lawyers, tax assessors, and so on. When a business is losing money, however, the seller may be in distress and forced into a quick sale below appraised value just to cut the losses and perhaps to end the agony.

Additional insights are provided in Chapter 7 in the section titled "Invalid Zones of Appraising."

Notes to the Accountant's Financial Data. When preparing the income statement, balance sheet, and whatever other data may appear in the company's year-end report, the accountant may include a set of notes to clarify, expand, or otherwise make these data more useful. The notes may be technical in nature and innocuous or they may include such critical information as conditional liabilities of the company, questionable data from which the financial statements were compiled, a negative comment on the general health and future of the corporation, or some other matter of compelling interest. These notes therefore should be thought of as integral to the financial statements and requisite to the buyer's being properly informed. If the seller or the seller's accountant should withhold these notes partially or wholly for any reason whatsoever, the buyer should interpret such action as clear warning that something is amiss and that caution is much in order, as in Example 11.2.

Real Estate Appraisal. If the real estate is being bought along with the business, the real estate appraisal provides the seller, the buyer, and the lending bank with documented evidence that the price is fair and reasonable. If the real estate is being leased instead of bought, the appraisal provides documented evidence of market rent. If the appraisal is done by an exceptionally skilled appraiser, it provides possible alternative uses for the property, which may be helpful if the business fails to prosper as planned or even if it does prosper. If well prepared, the appraisal may also provide a look into the future by noting expansion plans of local authorities, demographic trends, and so on which may be helpful to the buyer's planning. The author holds the opinion (partly empirical but mostly intuitive) that real estate appraisers who are members of the Appraisal Institute are a cut above most other appraisers and, if they charge a higher fee (which is not necessarily the case), are probably worth it for the extra insight they may offer into the value and usefulness of the property.

PART 3:
NON-FINANCIAL FACTS

As mentioned at the beginning of the chapter, the income statement along with the other financial facts provide the primary information for appraising a business. The non-financial facts, therefore, constitute a secondary level of information but with the potential of primacy under certain conditions. Because of this potential primacy, the non-financial facts are as important as the financial and merit the same deliberate effort to unearth and to analyze. The types of non-financial facts discussed below cover virtually all that are necessary for most small business appraisals along with the procedures for obtaining these facts. It should be clear, however, that additional important facts may be and should be sought in accordance with the business being looked at and the individual buyer's experience and insight. The well-qualified buyer, in fact, by virtue of his or her training and experience probably will find ways beyond the limits of this book to discover all the facts necessary to appraise the business.

Tour Through the Store or Shop. Business owners usually like to give a prospective buyer a tour of the premises as soon as the buyer's qualifications have been at least approximately established. Other owners prefer to wait until the time is right, probably when they begin to feel comfortable with the buyer. In any case, the tour is important regardless of the timing so the buyer can be sure that the business being looked at is one which the buyer will be capable of owning and managing. The tour will also help the buyer discover if he or she will love the work or at least feel resolutely fond of it and whether the ambiance will be compatible with the buyer's sensitivity. During the tour, the buyer can also start looking for problems to solve or improvements to make, especially those likely to increase the profits, making the business more valuable to the buyer than to the owner.

Observations of the Buyer as a Customer. Viewing as a customer means actually being a customer, if feasible given the nature of the business, but doing so incognito or unannounced in order to discover things which a tour with the owner might never find. The buyer can learn first hand how customers are being treated, whether the premises are routinely clean and orderly, whether the prices are reasonable and whether they represent good value given the overall quality of the goods and services, whether any warranties or other terms of customer purchase are reasonable and clear, and so on. Thus, the buyer can begin to know whether or not improvements can be made. Following is an example not only of the type of shortcomings along with their improvements which can be discovered by a buyer acting as a customer but also, surprisingly, the large number and variety of shortcomings which may be present even in a popular and profitable business:

> **Example 6.2** A restaurant with annual revenues over $700,000 is for sale. The owner is about 40 years old and not ready to retire. His reason for selling is that he has learned the hard way that owning and operating a restaurant is a full-time job (to say

the least). Also, he has other interests. He realizes that he has not done a good job managing but he usually has been profitable, though barely so, because some of his menu items are well prepared and attractive to carry-out customers and because his site is well situated for the tourist trade. The buyer and the broker have lunch there incognito on two occasions. Afterwards, they compile the following list of problems and improvements that the buyer would make were he the owner:

- Clean salt and pepper shakers daily; some are filthy.
- Replace most or all of the salt and pepper shakers; they are metal and most are battered from use.
- Initiate use of paper place mats with the menu printed thereon. Reasons are for improved looks, for sanitation, for comfort where no tablecloths are used, and to always present the customer with a clean, fresh menu.
- Discard the present tablecloths; they are unsightly. Either replace them or use bare tables with place mats. If bare tables are decided on, apply plastic coats to table tops for looks, comfort, and sanitation.
- Instruct waitresses and bus people always to replace covers on cake trays for sanitation and to prevent drying out. Also move cake trays away from cash register where trays, especially when uncovered, are exposed to customer flow.
- Train waitresses to inspect tableware for unclean or bent pieces.
- General decor needs much improvement. Put fresh paint on walls and hang attractive, properly framed pictures in dining areas. Prints of Degas, Renoir, and other impressionists would be especially suitable for present customer base and architecture.
- Clean cobwebs from ceiling.
- Remove storage crates from dining area. Very unsightly.

- Carpeting appears not to have been shampooed in years. Clean or replace.
- Replace artificial potted plants with real plants, at least near windows where they will get good light. Artificial plants are not bad looking but real plants add freshness, both real and perceived, and are always a sensual delight. They also add to the owner's and restaurant's image of integrity.
- Exterior needs cosmetic improvement badly. A coat of paint would do wonders.
- Mount blow-up of carryout menu on wall near cash register where customers can see for themselves and cashier will not always have to look up prices, especially when inquiries are by telephone.
- Replace head waitress who devises waitress schedules and functions as an acting manager. Her sleeping with the owner makes unwholesome ambiance for employees which, in turn, is picked up by customers. (Owner was candid about relationship with waitress and aware, at least partially, of resulting problem with employees.)
- Retrain (or replace, if necessary) waitresses who seem to feel they are doing customers a favor when they show customers to their tables and wait on them.
- Put more meat on sandwiches. At $8.50 each, customers deserve more.

Although this example was unusual for the large number of problems observed—especially considering that the restaurant was profitable—it still illustrates the value of acting as a customer and how much can be learned from it. The buyer and the broker both felt that correction of the problems would without question result in a sizeable boost of sales, a point well-evidenced by the fact that neither would have eaten there a second time had they not been required to by their responsibilities.

Patronizing the business while the owner is away may also uncover lackadaisical, disorderly, or otherwise improper behavior by employees, customers, or suppliers. If the owner is absent from the premises on a regular schedule, the buyer acting as a customer may even discover brazen thievery by employees, customers, or suppliers, as Example 6.3 below will illustrate. Whatever the case, routine misbehavior (whether in a small business or in a Fortune 500 company) may not always begin at the top, but that usually is where the solution is. The problem is correctable if the buyer recognizes it and determines to do something about it when he or she becomes the owner.

Example 6.3 A small grocery store with annual revenues around $600,000 is for sale. The business was established three years ago, at which time all new equipment was installed. The store is attractive and the rent is reasonable. The store is located near a sizeable retirement home which offers kitchen privileges to the residents. Because the store is small, it is unable to get price breaks at the wholesale level and must therefore charge the high prices typical of convenience stores. Since the store has a more-or-less captive clientele, the prices are accepted by the customers. Despite the sales which have to be considered very good for a small store and despite the ample markups on the goods, the store has lost money from the beginning. The owner has always been absentee but, for the last two years, he has had a family member (his cousin) manage.

A prospective buyer makes several trips to the store to buy groceries while observing what goes on. He feigns a humble demeanor and a mild infirmity, blending into the scene though he is younger by 25 years than the average customer. He observes the following scheme that some customers are using to steal goods: there is a ledge which is built into the wall near the exit and just beyond the sight line of the cashier. Customers discreetly place goods on the ledge while making their rounds through the store. Then they check out at the cash register and pick up the goods on their way out. The manager is usually at the cash register and could easily put a stop to the stealing if he were alert and watchful. The manager, however, has a perfunctory attitude and seems not to care about anything. On his third or fourth shopping trip, the buyer notices the manager handing a case of can goods to someone at the door, accepting cash in return, then failing to ring it up on the cash register. In addition to this type of theft, the buyer speculates that given the manager's thoughtless performance and apparent dishonesty, he is also either in collusion with one or more suppliers to cheat the owner or he is simply failing to monitor deliveries, providing what is tantamount to an invitation for the suppliers to steal. The buyer has no doubt that he can eliminate the customers' stealing, either by relocating the cash register or installing a mirror to monitor the provident ledge, but he makes an offer which is extremely remote from the seller's offering price, neither party is willing to compromise, and the deal dies before it even gets started. (Example 6.3 is revisited in Example 7.2 to show why the deal died.)

Following is an example showing not only the problems which can be observed and the improvements to be made but also the results which can occur when fact-finding, planning, and execution of improvements are all done well:

Example 6.4 A coin-operated laundry in depressed condition is for sale. The store occupies 3,000 square feet and has 46 washers, 19 dryers, and two dry cleaning machines, most of which are in various states of disrepair and most of which are scratched and unsightly. The general appearance of the store is one of neglect and the employees are under-trained and uninvolved. The buyers (a man-and-woman partnership) realize that by improving the entire operation, they can increase the sales and then sell the store at a profit. The buyers pay $85,000 for the store using $45,000 of their own money and borrowing the balance. Then they go to work.

They make the following improvements to the store and equipment:

- Repair washers and dryers where possible.
- Buy new equipment where necessary.
- Touch up or paint the equipment for cosmetic improvement. In some cases, they replace front panels of washers.
- Correct faulty installation of boiler which does not meet city code.
- Add energy-saving devices to dryers.
- Scrub dirty walls clean.
- Add a furnace to provide heat in winter.
- Repair the air conditioner to cool the store in summer.
- Paint inside the store and outside as necessary.
- Add 10 or 15 live potted plants, some very large, to freshen up the place.
- Make the overall appearance look attractive and prosperous.

Next the buyers upgrade the employees as follows:

- They train employees to clean the washers and dryers on a regular schedule and to immediately tend to any individual washers which have been soiled.
- Train employees to pick up soap cartons, empty trash, and sweep and mop the floor on a regular schedule. Also to immediately tend to any spills.
- Train employees to greet customers and to offer assistance.
- Fire any employees who do not meet rigorous

standards of quality work and friendly customer relations. They hire and train 22 new employees to get four who meet their standards.

The buyers expand their services:

- They add mending and alterations. (The seamstress becomes a business booster by telling her friends and neighbors.)
- Add shirt laundering.
- Add suede and leather cleaning.
- They add rug cleaning, sleeping bag cleaning, etc. (The dry cleaning business nearby now takes its rugs to their laundry because of superior cleaning at attractive prices.)

The buyers market their improved laundry services as follows:

- They give out coupon bonus cards so customers can get free washes.
- They deliver 6,000 flyers with coupons for free washes throughout the neighborhood.
- They get the supermarket located in a nearby shopping center to share space on flyers and to split the cost. (The tie-in with the supermarket, a prominent chain store, also gives the laundry additional recognition and credibility.)
- They get customers to fill out marketing questionnaires (Sample question: Would you use our laundry more if we were open 24 hours a day?) by holding drawings for free baskets of groceries. Winners are given gift certificates for use at the supermarket.

Six months after taking over the store, the customers are complimenting the owners on the appearance and all-around quality, and the sales have increased from $850 per week to $1,800 per week. After 18 months of ownership they sell the store. At this point the sales are $2,500 per week. During their 18 months of ownership, the buyers work only part time and draw regular salaries. They sell the store for $115,000. Their capital gain, after deducting $10,000 for capital improvements, is $20,000 or 24% of their purchase price.

Owner's Revelations. As suggested above in the discussion of financial facts, the owner's revelations may deal with anything that comes to mind but a good place to begin is with the history of the company. The value of the history is manifold. It provides a perspective in terms of evolution and time and it satisfies a curiosity. It tells why the current line of goods and services came into being and why others were discontinued. It tells of competitors who failed and of those who are still in the business. It tells of financing, profit margins, production tools, employee problems, and sales promotions. The past suggests the future. Perhaps most important, it helps to discover why the company is successful, possibly in ways which would not be found other than to hear the owner tell his or her story. Some examples will illustrate the point:

> **Example 6.5** A machine shop routinely has been putting a polished finish on all of its machined steel parts for some years whether or not such a finish is required by the engineering drawing (it rarely is) and at no extra cost to the customer. The owner explains that everyone, literally everyone, notices the polished finish and reacts with pleasant surprise. As the shop during its beginning years continued month after month and year after year to ship all its parts with polished finishes, customers grew to expect them and they also began to associate them with extra quality even though such finishes, though attractive, had no practical use and even though some of the parts were ultimately buried in assemblies where no one could see them. Because of the attention its bright finishes drew and because of their association with qual-

ity in general as well as with the actual quality and good service delivered by this shop, the shop eventually came to be thought of whenever emergency needs ruled out competitive bidding. Thus the shop acquired an elevated status resulting in extra sales at lucrative profits. The owner warns, however, that the silent boasting of the polished finish will incur a customer's sarcasm if the parts are not delivered on time and especially if not within drawing tolerances. The buyer who takes over that shop gets a plum of sorts but has also been given fair warning to maintain standards.

Example 6.6 The owner of a pancake restaurant tells of a customer who once mentioned that this restaurant is the only pancake restaurant he ever dined at which consistently, in fact always, offered syrup dispensers which were absolutely clean and never sticky from prior use. The customer also noted that the kitchen must clean these dispensers every day, perhaps more than once. Then the owner informed the customer that the dispensers in his restaurant are cleaned after every use, which means several times per day, that they always have been cleaned after every use, and that they always will be as long as he continues to be the owner. Again, fair warning has been given to maintain standards.

One set of questions which is an imperative for every buyer to ask concerns what work the owner does, why he or she does it, the hours spent doing it, and whether any of that work could be delegated. Note the following example:

Example 6.7 After being given a tour of an exceptionally successful retail dry cleaning store, the owner invites the prospective buyer into his office for a chat. The buyer remarks that the employees seem to be doing everything that needs to be done, from receiving the articles at the service counter to bagging and tagging them to be ready for pickup. The buyer asks if the owner does anything besides managing the business. The owner replies that he personally inspects every article that leaves the store and that no article is bagged without his approval. The owner adds that he rejects and recycles any article which is not cleaned and pressed to his satisfaction or which failure (such as a spot which truly is impossible to remove) cannot be explained by his employees. The buyer notes that at their level of sales, in seven figures, there are hundreds of articles to inspect every day requiring several hours per day to inspect. The owner replies that if the buyer plans to let an employee do the inspecting instead of himself, he is getting into the wrong business.

By learning exactly what the owner does and the importance of it, the buyer may discover whether he or she has the same ability and energy level as the owner and whether the buyer will be happy expending all the time and energy required to manage successfully. On the other hand, the buyer may discover ways to lighten the load which the present owner has not realized or the buyer may bring a higher energy level than possessed by the present owner, a common situation when the owner is retiring. The buyer also needs to know what each employee does and whether any of the employees possess irreplaceable skills. If so, the buyer would need to know if temporary employees or consultants could be hired on an hourly basis until another skilled employee could be found. (A possible source of temporary employees is retirees. They seem to enjoy an occasional call out of retirement as a chance to revisit an occupation they loved, to once more be useful, and to augment their social security and pension payments.)

Once the meeting of buyer and owner is underway, any and all questions and doubts should be raised. Generally the non-financial facts of a business require less sensitivity than the financial; questioning and probing can be more direct.

Comments of Nearby Merchants and Business People. Sometimes, if one is lucky, all sorts of useful information will be found, ranging from large-scale plans of the city government to backed-up neighborhood sewers. The best way to obtain this information is for the buyer simply to walk into a place of business, be it a retail store, a contractor, a manufacturer, or any other, and introduce himself or herself as a prospective business owner in the community who is trying to find a sense of the business climate and learn whatever advice might be available before making a commitment. If first contact is made with an employee, an attempt should be made to talk to the owner although sometimes employees offer good information. Some owners will not have time or will not take time while others will be willing to talk but will have little to say. The buyer should therefore contact several owners if necessary to obtain information or, in the case where something important has been discovered, verification from at least one other source. If the buyer is willing to tell what business he or she might be getting into and give specific details such as when and where (but without violating the confidence of the owner or the broker and without suffering from any resultant tactical disadvantage), such forthrightness may prompt the contacts to be just as forthright with the buyer. As usual, brevity is helpful as is the avoidance of phony conversation such as "How are you today?"

Comments of Suppliers. Although the information and advice sought from suppliers will differ from that sought from the nearby business people—it will be more industry-oriented and less community-oriented—the approach is basically the same with only minor differences. It may be more informative to talk to the sales people, since they have such broad contacts, than to the owner or president, and it may be better to telephone in advance just to learn the best time to find the sales people in the office.

Comments of Owners of Similar Businesses. The approach to owners of businesses similar to the one being bought should consist of the buyer's introduction of himself or herself as someone who is thinking of buying a similar business and who is wondering if the owner or proprietor might have any advice to offer. Again, the ticket to success comprises forthrightness, brevity, and the avoidance of phony conversation, and again, honoring the seller's and broker's confidence is required as is the avoidance of tactical disadvantage. One other possible benefit from calling on the owner of a similar business: it could be the start of a beautiful friendship.

Zoning Laws, Eminent Domain, and Other Political Aspects. Although zoning laws and eminent domain are conceptually different, their similar involvements in politics and the basic right of a citizen to do business suggest strongly that they be thought of and dealt with together. The buyer who discovers after making a commitment that a zoning restriction or eminent domain will devastate his or her business probably has no recourse, although a very excellent lawyer possibly could find a way to mitigate the damage. Following is an example of how easy it can be to overlook a problem and of the damage which can result:

> **Example 6.8** A buyer has prospered so well in his first 18 months after taking ownership of a manufacturing company that he decides to expand his business by starting a complementary product line which will require an additional 5,000 square feet of factory space. His present plant is used to capacity but the building on the lot immediately next door is vacant and suitable for his operation. Also, that building is only 20 feet from his present building which will allow his foreman to cover both buildings with no loss of travel time. The owner obtains a five-year lease on the building, orders $200,000 worth of new equipment, and contracts out the installation of electrical conduits, compressed air lines, special lighting, and other additions necessary for the operation. Most of the work has been completed and most of the new equipment delivered and set into place when he is approached by an official from the local municipality who wants to know what he is doing. He tells the official of his plans but is then told that the zoning laws prohibit manufacturing in the newly leased building. The owner explains that his existing plant and the building right next to it are in the same zone so surely the official must be

mistaken. The official agrees that they are in the same zone. That zone, however, was changed from industrial to commercial some years ago but a grandfather clause allows manufacturing to go on indefinitely as long as it is continuous. Manufacturing in the newly leased building was discontinued when the previous tenant vacated. It therefore will not be allowed to restart. The owner hires a very sharp lawyer who verifies the official's information and who also verifies that nothing can be done about it.

Now the owner has to decide between forgetting his plans for expansion, disposing of the new equipment at 50 cents on the dollar or less, and accepting the loss, or of leasing a less convenient site. Since prospective orders for his new product line realistically appear abundant, he pays the landlord of the restricted building to void the lease, leases another shop about ten miles from his present shop, reinstalls the electrical conduits and so forth, transports the new equipment, hires employees, and begins operations. Sales are as good as he had expected but now his foreman loses one to two hours per day traveling between the two plants and has to work overtime to compensate, incurring new expense to the owner. Problems needing immediate solutions in one plant go untended while the foreman is at the other plant, idling both equipment and workers and further adding to operating expense on the established line as well as on the new line. Schedules begin to suffer and additional overtime at additional expense is required for timely deliveries. Bugs in the new product line begin to emerge but are unsolvable except through trial and error because of the owner's and foreman's inexperience in the new line. Customers begin discovering the bugs, goods are being returned for rework, and expenses are out of control. Now the owner and foreman are under stress, employee morale is down, and two longtime employees find jobs elsewhere. A new foreman is hired for the new shop, allowing the existing foreman to return to full time in the original shop and bringing that shop partly back to normal. But the new foreman proves unable to eliminate the manufacturing bugs in the new product line and is fired after seven months on the job, his wages during that time adding to the company's losses and the continuing customer complaints adding to the company's woes.

Although the devastation in the above example (the company went from extreme prosperity to bankruptcy) was due as much to poor management as to zoning problems (the poor management, incidentally, was partly due to the owner's being unqualified to handle the new product line and partly the hubris which kept him from exercising due caution), the point remains that zoning and other political aspects must be checked before making a commitment to buy. To minimize the chances not only for problems of zoning and eminent domain but for other political problems such as residency requirements for ownership and/or licensing, restrictions or intricate procedures required for transference of ownership, and so on, the buyer and the seller should visit city hall in the proposed municipality and find the right individuals for guidance. As an extra precaution, the buyer should seek legal counsel with respect to county, state, and federal laws. Further, because of the increasing complexity and array of environmental codes, a scientist or engineer specializing in these codes should also be consulted if there is the slightest reason to think there may be a problem. For example, an environmentally safe business such as a grocery store or an accounting firm may be situated on property once used as a gas station which dumped used oil into the ground and which eventually will require cleanup. The buyer of such a business will find great relief and protection for little cost by consulting with an environmental specialist. As usual, the specialist should be chosen with due care, especially since reports of erroneous environmental audits are not unheard of.

Longevity of the Business and the Industry. Generally speaking, the longer a business has been established, the greater its chances of remaining established. The obvious logic is that the business, in proportion to its years in business, has demonstrated its acceptance in the community along with its profitability. It has also demonstrated its ability to overcome whatever shortcomings or problems it may have had to deal with. Long success, on the other hand, never rules out such problems as new competitors, demographic shifts, owner mismanagement, and so on. Long success is merely a point in favor of continued survival, not a guarantee.

The same logic applies to an industry. The longer established, the more probable its survival. A popular general rule is that any industry established less than ten years cannot yet be considered as established and will therefore pose dangers either to the industry itself or to businesses within the industry. The increasing rapidness of all sorts of change in the modern world, however, suggests that the ten-year rule, while still a useful guide, is more open to question than it used to be. In technologically oriented industries such as personal computers, facsimile machines, television sets, telephones, and the internet, being established ten years or more may even signal a ripeness for obsolescence.

Even low-technology industries that would seem immune to obsolescence pose dangers to owners of small businesses, especially while the industries are still new. When coin-operated laundries proliferated in the 1950s, the concept then seemed sound and indeed was sound as time has proved, and the industry probably will flourish for years to come. Yet, individual store owners in the 1950s and 1960s experienced high failure rates due to any combination of problems such as frequency of equipment breakdown, difficulty and expense of equipment repair, poorly chosen location, over-saturation of industry, and all the problems of absentee ownership including customer insecurity, overflowing washers, vandalism, dirty stores, and unreliable hours. The stores which survive today have the benefit of the industry's years of experience in dealing with those problems and probably have a low failure rate as a result.

Bankers' Insights. Whether a buyer needs bank financing or not, a consultation with an experienced bank commercial loan officer sometimes can reveal unforeseen problems. In fact, borrowing money from a bank, even if not needed, will provide the benefits of bank involvement at relatively low cost.

Bankers are good at assessing a buyer's qualifications for ownership, the viability of a business, the cash flow likely to result when the buyer takes over, and the overall probable success of the venture. For example, the owner of the manufacturing company in Example 6.8 paid for the new equipment and setup out of profits. Had he sought bank financing for just a part of the cost of his new venture, say for $100,000, he might have been warned that his inexperience in the new product line posed possible trouble. Since bankers tend to be fairly thorough in documenting their loans, the owner might even have been required to show an occupancy permit for his newly leased premises before receiving the loan, thus exposing the zoning problem. It is also true that bankers are not infallible and that their advice therefore should be accepted with due caution in making decisions. The important point is that commercial loan officers are very good at assessing new business startups and transfers of ownership and their advice sometimes can mean the difference between failure and success.

Observations of the Buyer as an Employee. If a buyer is well qualified to become an owner, starting as an employee with an option to buy will usually be unnecessary insofar as fact-finding is concerned simply because that is the meaning of being qualified. In some cases, however, the buyer may have strong credentials but lack direct experience in a narrow line specialized in by the business being bought. This would be similar to the situation of the owner starting a new product line in Example 6.8. The close inside look provided by a short stint as an employee, say two or three months, should offer a clear indication of whether the buyer is properly matched to the business. It would also raise the confidence level of the bank, the seller, and anyone else helping to finance the purchase. On the other hand, the seller could reasonably object if the buyer-employee would gain access to a coveted secret such as a customer list, a proprietary formula, or a manufacturing technique. The seller also might object on the simple ground (which the author tends not to agree with) that a buyer-employee would be upsetting to the other employees. Still, the buyer as a temporary employee is an idea which may be desirable in some situations.

Another case where a stint as an employee would be useful and even necessary for a different reason would be if the company's sales and profits are too low to support the purchase but the company is otherwise sound. Then the buyer could work to build sales and, if successful, could exercise his or her option to buy. A longer stint probably would be required, say six months to a year, and the buyer and owner would have to agree on whether the buyer would be on a straight salary, a commission based on sales to new customers, or on a salary plus commission. The contingent price would probably reflect the value of the business at the beginning of the buyer's stint. That would allow the buyer to receive most of the benefits of the increased sales. Otherwise, the buyer probably would not be interested. The option to buy would have to have a time limit to allow the owner to seek other prospects if the one in hand delayed too long. All of these terms of agreement would have to be expressed in writing and both parties would require a lawyer.

Intuitive Insights. To call upon intuition, especially in the process of something so objective as fact-finding, may seem less than entirely rational. However, the presence of intuition is a fact, as is the usefulness of it by some individuals. The following explanation may help the reader determine the usefulness of one's own intuition.

As human beings gain experience in life (which is to say as they grow old), the knowledge they accumulate becomes stored. Some knowledge is easy to recall, precisely define, and put to use, such as names of people and places, titles of books and reports, dates, mathematical constants, concrete facts of various kinds, and so forth. Some knowledge is not easy to recall, precisely define, and put to use such as how one might feel in a certain human relationship, a pattern of thought or a pattern of activity, one's body language or facial expression, the spirit or mood of the time, vocal inflections and their situational variances, the interrelationship of such knowledge, and so on. Still other knowledge may be a mixture of the two. Exactly how the brain stores and processes this variety of knowledge may be a mystery. Nevertheless, this knowledge can be thought of as occupying a complex matrix in the brain where all the bits of knowledge are interconnected to form a meaningful organic whole.

One result of this coordination of accumulated knowledge is human intuition. Intuition brings to the conscious mind an intelligent reaction to whatever is being observed or realized, even if those observations and realizations are subliminal. For example, the employees in a business office where all employees are treated by the president on down with thoughtfulness and respect will almost automatically respond with high morale, self-dignity, and job satisfaction even when the work load is heavy and deadlines are imminent. The person with a well-developed intuition who steps into that office for the first time will sense in five seconds or less that something is right, that something is very right. Intuition processes the information picked up by the senses and compares it to the information stored in the matrix of the mind. The information picked up and processed might include the eye contact and the look of purposefulness given by the receptionist, the tempo of computer keyboards, the way the workers' bodies are positioned while seated at their desks, the pace and stride of people walking and the erectness of their shoulders, the quality and pitch of their voices, the cared-for appearance of the physical plant, and so on. There are probably other bits of information picked up by the senses and processed by the intuition which may or may not be identifiable. That indefiniteness constitutes at least part of the mystery of how intuition works. But mystery or not, intuition does work and individuals learn that it works by gradually realizing as they become older and more experienced that they are able to feel whether a situation is right, healthy, or prosperous or whether it is something gone awry. What buyers, sellers, and anyone else involved in the transfer of ownership can rely on, to the degree that their individual intuitive faculties are developed, is that the feelings and perceptions which occur seemingly out of the blue are bona fide facts to be weighed with all of the other facts in making their judgments and decisions. Needless to say, due caution is in order because intuitive facts, like other facts, can be misleading. But the point remains that intuition often corroborates the facts already found and sometimes it is the only fact telling the truth.

In cases where the observable facts and intuition seem not to agree, it is difficult to say whether the facts should overrule the intuition, or vice versa.

What can be said, however, is that when they do not agree, caution is the rule. Then the key is to keep digging for more information until facts and intuition fall into line. A case where intuition pointed to something right while the concrete facts pointed to something wrong was in Example 5.2 where the buyer, sensing that the dry cleaning business he was looking at had more promise than shown by the given data, continued his fact-finding until his facts and his intuition were in alignment. In another case, Example 4.4, a prospective buyer backed away because of his intuitive dislike of the owner. The buyer's intuition proved to be correct: the seller's bad faith eventually became clear when an annual bonus expected by the employees but not shown on the books cost the ultimate buyer around $10,000. (The buyer who backed away probably made a mistake of another kind in that, being exceptionally well qualified, he had enough expertise to make the purchase without being cheated. The cash-cow store could have been his. Moreover, to avoid or minimize the displeasure of dealing with someone suspected of being a cheat, he could have used an intermediary which, in this example, was easily available in the form of the broker.)

Owner's List of Defects. It is reasonable to ask the owner to furnish a list of known defects of any equipment, raw materials, real estate, or other tangible assets to be included in the sale. It is also reasonable to request a written list of other possible problems, either known or suspected, which could seriously affect the operation or the stability of the company. Examples of such possible problems are a rumor which has reached a gourmet restaurateur through one of his waiters that his kitchen manager is considering jumping to a larger restaurant for more money; and a warning to a job shop owner from a friendly purchasing agent employed by the owner's best customer that the customer is threatened with loss of one of its best customers. If an owner does have important information which is not likely to be made public for several months, he or she may choose to withhold it because the owner's foreknowledge would be hard to prove. On the other hand, there is no harm in the buyer's asking. If the owner has no such information to reveal, a written statement to that effect would be in order. It would also be in order for an owner voluntarily to disclose any unfavorable turns of events threatening to occur and to do so before being asked by a buyer. Such openness would go a long way towards establishing credibility and improving the owner's chances of making the sale.

Advantages vs. Disadvantages. When the buyer has completed his or her fact-finding, itemizing the advantages and disadvantages into two lists for comparison usually will help place the facts into a clearer perspective. Also, the act of itemization itself prompts a good review of the facts and may suggest new questions for the owner. Figure 6.4 shows how such a paper might look for the Acme Widget Corporation:

Figure 6.4 Advantages and Disadvantages to Buyer

ACME WIDGET CORPORATION ADVANTAGES AND DISADVANTAGES

Plus	Minus
• Well established, 28 years in business.	• Forty-minute drive to work.
• Low employee turnover.	• Company is well managed, little room for improvement.
• Always profitable if hidden earnings included.	• Personal relationships of present owner account for 3% of sales.
• Sales growth possible if owner makes sales calls.	• No place to expand the building.
• Widget industry has good future well represented by small manufacturers.	
• Present plant and equipment will support about 25% of growth in sales.	

QUESTIONS FOR DISCUSSION
Chapter 6—Fact-Finding

1. Acme's buyer used a buffer and other tactical devices when delving into the owner's secrets. a) Give three reasons why. b) Do you feel he did a good job?

2. Give three reasons why Acme's buyer rounded the figures on the statements of income and expenses to the nearest thousand dollars while also eliminating the last three zeros. And why did he do it by hand?

3. Why did Acme's buyer juxtapose three consecutive years of income and expenses?

4. Why was Acme's owner willing to sit down with the buyer and reveal so many of his secrets? Hint: What is Chapter 1 all about?

5. This chapter lists so many areas to search for facts that one might wonder if the list is exaggerated or atypical. What do you think and, if you were a buyer, what would you do?

6. Discuss intuitive insight with several others. Do you know anyone who has it? Some experienced entrepreneurs can step through the door of a business in their trade and know in an instant what the annual sales are. Or they can step into almost any business and know instantly if it is well managed. How will you know when you acquire it?

7. Were you surprised by the variety and depth of cheating that's going on? Does the discussion of "An Arguable Reason for Buying a Business" in Chapter 1 now make more sense and seem more relevant? Do you still want to own a business?

CHAPTER 7

Appraising

Although this chapter is the only one in the book entitled "Appraising," the topic of appraising actually began in the previous chapter. Finding the facts is both the core and the substance of any good method of appraising, and finding the facts and doing a good job at it fulfills the larger and more difficult part of the appraisal. All that remains is to use the facts to appraise the business.

As the explanations below reveal, appraising is rife with subjectivity. That is what makes appraising an art as well as a science and it is also what makes it controversial. The element of subjectivity cannot be eliminated (a truism for almost everything in life). It can be minimized, however, by recognizing that it exists and by declaring one's valuations provisionally, that is, with less than absolute conviction pending the discovery of new evidence and insights. Provisionality when appraising (as when seeking truth in general) is useful because it provides the opportunity for one to refine one's judgments or to correct one's mistakes. It also nurtures good human relations and is usually necessary in the process of negotiating.

This chapter has four parts: Introduction, Capitalization of Earnings, Cash-Flow Projections, and Other Aspects of Appraising.

PART 1:
INTRODUCTION

Approaches to Appraising. There are three basic approaches to business appraising: earnings, assets, and market comparisons. (Although not within the scope of this book, these approaches might be modified for tax, estate, legal, insurance, or other purposes. However, appraisals for estate, insurance, and other legal matters should be prepared by professional appraisers to safeguard against possible legal ramifications.)

The earnings approach is the one most important for appraising small businesses for the purpose of buying and selling. Using that approach, there are two methods of appraising: capitalization of earnings and preparation of cash-flow projections. These two methods are the main focus of this chapter.

The assets approach is also useful but mostly when the value of the earnings is less than the value of the assets or when the earnings are in a downward trend with a doubtful future. Then the value of the assets becomes significant, particularly the liquidation value. This scenario is discussed in Part 4 of the chapter in the section titled "Invalid Zones of Appraising." (Asset values in general are discussed in Chapter 2, page 43 in the section titled "Variations of Value.")

The assets approach may also be used to estimate the adjusted book value of a corporation (see page 39 in Chapter 2 for definitions of book value and adjusted book value).

The market comparisons approach is to compare the subject business with businesses recently sold of similar location, type, and size. The idea is to adjust the actual sale prices and terms to align with the subject. This is an important approach commonly used in real estate appraisals. It is also used for types of businesses such as franchises with a high degree of commonality. This approach, however, does not apply well to small businesses in general because of their dissimilarity to one another and also because the data needed to make market comparisons—actual sale prices and terms—are not usually a matter of public record. The market approach, therefore, is not very useful to small business appraising and is not covered in this book. (See the section titled "Liquidity and Illiquidity" in Chapter 2, page 52 for details on dis-similarity.)

Stock Sale vs. Asset Sale. Whenever an incorporated business is placed on the market, a decision must be made as to whether to sell the corporate stock or the assets. For most small businesses, the buyer's accountant and lawyer will both advise a purchase of assets, and in virtually all such cases the seller's advisors will agree.

Still, there are special cases where a corporate owner will advisedly sell the stock rather than the assets. (See the section titled "Stock Sale vs. Asset Sale" in Chapter 2, page 39.) In those cases, the approaches to appraising mentioned above apply to stock sales just as they do to asset sales, but with this exception: when two or more owners are involved, new rules and strategies come in to play. For example, discounts to appraised value must be applied for ownership of less than fifty percent of the stock and, in some cases, for reasons of marketability. In those and other special cases, buyers and sellers are advised to seek the advice of well-trained professionals like those in the Institute of Business Appraisers (800-299-4120) or the American Society of Appraisers, (703-478-2228). (The author is not a member of either group although his friend and brokering colleague, Bud Howe, is an active member of the IBA.)

Sales of corporate stock are briefly discussed in Part 4 of this chapter.

PART 2:
CAPITALIZATION OF EARNINGS

The Basic Formula. The basic idea of capitalization is to determine the earnings of a business and then to estimate the fair market value of those earnings or, more correctly, the fair market value of the business producing those earnings. Since the fair market value is the estimated amount of capital that will have to be paid for a business (even if the capital is borrowed), this method of appraising is known as capitalization of earnings or, for short, capitalization. Note that capitalization is based on the general premise that the value of a business is directly proportional to the earnings. That premise generally prevails despite various modifications.

The capitalization method is expressed in the following formula:

$$\text{fair market value} = \text{earnings of business} \div \text{assumed rate of earning}$$

where the fair market value (FMV) is the price a buyer and seller agree to when both are well informed, economically motivated, and not in distress; the earnings are the pre-tax operational earnings as shown on the statement of income and expenses but adjusted to reflect actual revenues and actual business expenses; and the rate of earning is the assumed or expected percent return on the capital invested.

Note that for appraisal purposes, business expenses do not include interest on money borrowed to purchase the business or to improve it even though such interest is tax deductible. Such interest is not a true operational expense. Also note that operational earnings usually exclude the following: any income not germane to the business such as interest earned on cash parked in a corporate savings account; non-recurring gains or losses such as a capital gain on the sale of equipment; and the owner's reasonable salary and benefits.

Following is an example of how the above formula is applied. If the operational earnings of a business are $40,000 per year and if the assumed rate of earning is 25% on the capital invested, the appraised value of that business is:

$$\text{FMV} = \text{earnings} \div \text{rate}$$

$$= \$40,000 \div .25$$

$$= \$160,000$$

The basic idea of capitalization is actually as simple as shown above. However, a variety of complications enters the appraising process and these are explained, more or less, in the following sections dealing with development of earnings and development of the rate of earning. Much of the explanation is centered on a continuation of the example of the Acme Widget Corporation. Emphasis is placed on the buyer's viewpoint because the buyer has much more uncertainty to deal with than the seller. Note, however, that the seller, by being exposed to the buyer's problems, will become more understanding of the buyer's needs.

Development of Earnings. Development of the actual earnings of a business is begun by adjusting the income statement to represent what the seller is actually turning over to the buyer. Thus, the sales shown on an adjusted income statement are those estimated to remain after the seller departs. Unrecorded sales, if any, obviously do not appear on the income statement but will be treated separately.

The adjusted expenses include only those necessary to operate the business. Personal expenses are excluded except reasonable medical benefits as allowed by the IRS. (Medical insurance is almost universally thought of as a legitimate adjunct to the owner's salary.) The estimated actual depreciation and amortization expenses replace anything other than actual which might have been charged by the seller's accountant.

The adjusted owner's salary and benefits are whatever are deemed reasonable by the appraiser or necessary by the buyer. Obviously, the buyer—because of a difference in education, training, experience, or perceived self-worth—may have one opinion of what is reasonable or necessary and the seller may have another. As a result of such difference, as well as other differences discussed below, the buyer's and seller's appraisals may be so far apart that it will be difficult for them to reach agreement on price and terms. Solutions to such problems sometimes evolve during the negotiation.

The adjusted operational earnings for Acme Widget Corporation, as shown in Figure 7.1, have been developed by starting with the accountant's compilation of the most recent annual statement of income and expenses (which is identical to the statement in Figure 6.2 except that the insurance expense has been broken into business and personal). The sales have been reduced from $415,000 to $403,000 to reflect the 3% loss which is estimated to occur when the seller departs. Raw materials expense has been reduced $1,000 to reflect the $12,000 loss of sales (and further reduced as indicated below). Expenses have been purged of hidden earnings (the same hidden earnings shown in Figure 6.2) to show only those expenses actually required to operate the business. Expenses thus reduced include advertising, automotive, legal and accounting, raw materials, taxes and licenses, and employees' wages other than owner's. Depreciation has been reduced from what is legally allowed to what actually occurs due to wear and tear. The owner's personal insurance has been decreased to reflect medical insurance the buyer and his family would need were he the owner. And the owner's salary has been increased to what the buyer feels he will need to support himself and his family. As a result of these changes, the earnings have been adjusted from $3,000 to $32,000. Note that no expenses other than raw materials have been reduced in line with the $12,000 reduction in sales. The only expense which possibly could be significantly reduced would be wages but, in real life, small reductions in sales usually are not accompanied by small reductions in personnel.

Another way to establish the earnings of a company is to adjust the income statement for two or more years and then average the pre-tax profits. For example, if Acme Widget's adjusted pre-tax net profit for 1999 had been $27,000, the average for the two most recent years would be $29,500 ($27,000 added to $32,000 and the sum divided by two). Since the sales, expenses, and profits for Acme have been fairly steady for three successive years, such averaging in this case would not be useful. If there should be a fairly sharp change in earnings from one year to the next, either upward or downward, with no apparent explanation, a weighted average is usually advisable.

For example, if the adjusted earnings of Acme Widget had been $19,000, $21,000, and $32,000 for years 1998, 1999, and 2000, respectively, and if the owner had not been able to explain the sharp increase in 2000 thus

Figure 7.1 Development of Adjusted Income Statement

ACME WIDGET CORPORATION STATEMENT OF INCOME AND EXPENSE (000 omitted)

	Compiled by Accountant	Adjusted
Sales	$415	$403
Expenses		
Advertising	8	3
Automotive	9	3
Depreciation	15	9
Insurance		
Business	9	9
Owner's personal	5	3
Legal & accounting	6	5
Maintenance & repair	5	5
Miscellaneous	0	0
Office supplies	9	9
Raw materials	46	39
Rent	27	27
Taxes & licenses	21	20
Telephone	3	3
Utilities	8	8
Wages		
Owner	32	35
Other employees	209	193
Total expenses	$412	$371
Pre-tax net profit	$3	$32

diminishing the buyer's confidence in that increase, a weighted average favoring the more recent figures might show earnings of $26,000 as follows:

1998	$19	x 1	=	$ 19
1999	$21	x 2	=	$ 42
2000	$32	x 3	=	$ 96
		6		$157

weighted average = $157 ÷ 6 = $ 26

As shown above, the more recent the year, the greater the weight given to that year. The greater weight is to allow that current attitudes of customers, the current state of the economy, current technological levels, trends one way or the other in employee productivity, and so forth are more relevant than those of the past. Moreover, a different gradation of weights would be appropriate if the appraiser would so judge. For example, the last three years could be weighted 2, 3, and 4 or 1, 3, and 5, or whatever would make sense under the circumstances. Conceivably, the most recent year might even be given the least weight if, for example, a business had been shut down for part of that year due to an abnormal cause such as a hurricane, a labor strike, or a street paving.

Capitalization of Unrecorded Earnings. Once the most recent adjusted earnings based on recorded data have been determined, the question is how to deal with any undocumented earnings that the seller might allege to have received. In the case of Acme Widget, the seller claims additional income from selling overbought raw materials at a profit and from unrecorded retail sales made after closing hours. Dealing with undocumented earnings always presents a dilemma. The Acme buyer thinks that he might or might not overbuy raw materials if he becomes the owner but he does not plan to spend valuable time peddling those materials to small manufacturers when he could be out making sales calls on prospective new customers. Those profits were relatively small anyway, probably not more than $1,000 or $1,500 per year. Therefore, he will ignore them.

As for the skimmed retail sales after hours, the buyer proceeds through the following thoughts: the first question is whether the unrecorded retail sales truly exist and are not just the seller's ploy to get a higher price. The buyer recalls the meeting when the seller revealed the various schemes for cheating on taxes. The seller's ease and comfort during those revelations left the buyer with the feeling that the seller was telling the truth. In addition, the buyer knows from his years in the industry that material and labor costs shown on Acme's books are disproportionately high compared to the sales (or, in other words, that the sales are low compared to the expenses) and he further knows that the factory layout and operations are efficient and that the seller appears to be a skillful manager. The buyer's observations, in other words, corroborate the seller's claims even if they do not prove them. The buyer, therefore, is ready to believe those claims. But just to be sure and also to get some idea of the amount, he does a stakeout to count the customers leaving the store after hours while carrying packages large enough to hold a widget and estimates the retail skimming at about $600 per week or $30,000 per year. The $30,000 figure at first seems high but when put into the perspective of being only seven percent of the $415,000 sales shown on the books, and the further perspective of the ample loss of accountability described by the seller, that figure seems realistic.

The next step would be to add the $30,000 estimated skim to the $32,000 adjusted recorded earnings for a total of $62,000. But now the dramatic increase in earnings from the $3,000 shown on the income statement to the estimated $62,000, along with the realization that the buyer is expected to pay for those earnings, causes new doubts to arise. He still has only the seller's word that the retail sales after hours are not shown on the books. The $6,000 personal automotive expense also is based only on the seller's word as are the $6,000 worth of over-bought raw materials and the alleged uselessness of the $16,000 payroll for his teenage children and the $5,000 radio advertising. But then he begins to realize, though his doubts are reasonable, that if he allows himself to, he can turn his doubts into fears and talk himself out of ever buying a business. Now coming to grips with the full scope of the situation, he allows that the only sure things in life are taxation and death and that buying a business, just like everything else, entails risk to one degree or another. There is even risk in doing nothing and that is the risk of spending the rest of his life languishing in the bureaucracy of the corporation. He further realizes that his present goal is not to avoid risk but to minimize it, and that all the years he spent with the corporation learning the widget trade and developing his business acumen have qualified him for ownership. Those years of learning, in other words, have built his bridge to the future. Now standing on that bridge and applying those qualifications for ownership to his advantage, he reaffirms his conviction that the seller's material costs are high, that the payroll and automotive expenses are also high, and that radio advertising for widget sales is money down the drain. Here the self-confidence borne of his own abilities takes hold and for the first time in his long hard search of a business to buy, the value of being qualified to own and operate a business sinks deeply into his psyche. Now he is ready to accept the risk. But he will do it his way.

He learned in school that when decisions have to be made based on only partial knowledge of the facts, the way to deal with such uncertainty is to use probability techniques. For example, if a person has $100 to invest but some of the facts are missing or doubtful, it is reasonable to invest only in proportion to one's level of confidence. If one feels, say, 75% sure of the outcome, then one might invest much less than $100, say, only $50 or maybe only $15 or $20. What is important is that the successes in the long run must compensate for the failures in the short run. That is exactly the reasoning of baseball managers who assign left-handed pinch-hitters against right-handed pitchers and of gamblers who calculate the odds before betting on their cards. The pinch-hitter may strike out and the gambler may lose the hand but in the long run, the successes will compensate for the failures as long as the placements of bets are consistent with the percentages of probability. When buying a business, however, it is usually not possible to offset a failure in the short run with compensating successes in the long run because that one failure may cause financial ruin leaving no opportunity for successes. If the buyer is to accept some risk on the estimated earnings of the business, the buyer must also allow some room to recover if the estimate proves to be wrong. Such allowance may rest, to a degree, in the sheer ability of the buyer, through skill and hard work once acquiring the business, to recover from paying too high a price, as demonstrated in Example 6.4. But the buyer also must limit the estimate to an amount the loss of which will not cause failure if wrong.

So reasoning, the buyer thinks to himself what would happen if he would allow the full $30,000 unrecorded earnings to be incorporated into the appraisal and if none of those earnings would come true. He would suffer a loss equal to the capitalized value of those earnings (which, assuming a rate of earning of 25%, would be $120,000). Such loss would be clearly intolerable. Next he wonders what kind of a loss would be tolerable. The answer is hard to estimate because he does not know mathematically how to figure it out. It is also hard to estimate because of the possible harms to his life-style, his family, his solvency, and, last but not least, his sanity. Still, he must face up to the decision: he can not risk everything but he must risk something. So he decides intuitively to go with unrecorded earnings of $10,000. He does not know exactly why that amount but somehow it seems reasonable to him.

Now the buyer is bothered by all of the guessing that he has had to do and so he reviews the situation. The only way to arrive at a better estimate of the unrecorded earnings which allegedly are skimmed at the cash register would be to sit next to the register all day every day for a long enough time to verify exactly what's going on. He heard a story once, perhaps apocryphal, that the IRS conducts such overbearing investigations whenever its suspicions are aroused. Such a detailed check, however, would be impractical both for the amount of time involved and for the commotion it would cause in the store. He still feels confident of his $30,000 estimate, so he will stay with the $10,000 portion of that amount, the capitalized value of which he has decided is tolerable to risk. He will stay with it because he feels comfortable with it and because, for the present, he does not know what else to do. He does know that he will keep an open mind.

Development of the Rate of Earning. In the example at the beginning of the chapter demonstrating the basic idea of the capitalization method, the assumed rate of earning was 25% with the following result: $40,000 ÷ .25 = $160,000. If in the same example the rate of earning had been assumed, say, as 30%, the appraised value would have been $40,000 ÷ .30 = $133,000. Thus, a seemingly small change in the assumed rate of earning can produce a large change in the appraised value. For this reason, the rate of earning has to be carefully assigned. The basic idea in determining the rate of earning, whether for a small business or for any other investment, is that the rate should be in line with the degree of risk. To develop a rate, the earning rates and degrees of risk for alternative investments should be compared to those for the investment in question. The assignment of the rate of earning is up to the appraiser. Once a rate is assigned, one may refine or corroborate it by seeking the advice of someone with experience in the marketplace. However, finding someone competent is not easy. One may also refine the rate of earning by taking into account factors other than risk, as explained below. In any case, the rate finally used in the appraisal, no matter how carefully arrived at, is still somewhat a matter of subjective individual judgment. It is therefore also provisional; in fact, very much so.

One may begin developing a rate of earning by referring to a source such as *The Wall Street Journal* to find the rates of earning on several alternative investments. Rates current at the time of the appraisal, for example, might be 4% on one-year certificates of deposit; from 4% to 6.5% on various Treasury Bills, Notes, and Bonds; and 14% (including 11% capital gains in the past year) on Standard & Poor's 500 Stock Index. A telephone call to a local real estate school informs that real estate investments might earn from 11% to 15% depending on the type, condition, location, degree of risk, and so forth. Since investing in a small business usually entails considerably more risk than investing in any of the above alternatives, an owner should expect a considerably higher return, at least 5% higher than what is paid by any of those alternatives. Since small businesses are of various kinds with various degrees of risk, they have various rates of earning. Some examples are listed below:

Type of Business	Expected Rate of Earning
Manufacturer with established product line	20% to 30%
Retail dry cleaner	20% to 25%
Restaurant	30% to 40%
Mfg. job shop	30% to 40%
Beauty salon	35% to 40%

It should be clear that the capitalization rates shown above are approximate and that they are based primarily on risk. They are also influenced by sundry other factors such as motivation of the buyer and/or the seller; opportunity for growth; value of assets, especially if they can be used as collateral; the buyer's management ability compared to the seller's; interest rates; location in a pleasing neighborhood; the buyer's or the seller's skill at negotiating; state or local licensing laws, especially those limiting the number of businesses in a trade; and pride of ownership.

In practical use, when buyers and sellers are adjusting or negotiating their prices, they usually do not run through the mathematics of changing the rate of earning to calculate a new price or a new offer or counter-offer. They just make the change according to their overall circumstances, including their intuitive feelings, and put it into action. The effect and the reality, however, are to change the rate of earning.

It is useful to note some of the specific risks and other factors influencing the above rates so that even if the business in question differs from the above, one's improved understanding will help to set a fair rate.

Manufacturers with established product lines have lower rates because they are thought, by virtue of those established lines, to have greater safety of sales and earnings. Such manufacturers also tend to have good long-life asset values by virtue of their machine tools which banks usually welcome as collateral. They further offer a type of work and social station adding to a buyer's motivation, especially if the buyer is well educated. And they are comparatively less illiquid, which tends to reduce the risk of a distress sale in case of health or other business or personal problems.

Retail dry cleaners bring lower earning rates because they are comparatively less illiquid and because the trade is relatively easy to learn, both factors increasing their desirability to less educated persons and to immigrants needing to become established quickly. In some minds, they also are perceived (somewhat incorrectly as evidenced in the example of Acme Widget) to offer better-than-average opportunity to cheat on taxes due to their cash receipts.

Restaurants tend to have higher earning rates because they generally require long hours and have a relatively high failure rate. The high failure rate is partly explained by the long hours and partly by the many inconspicuous difficulties of managing a restaurant. Restaurants have high asset costs by virtue of their expensive equipment but the equipment tends to have low resale value because used equipment seems to be in plentiful supply and tends to be unattractive as collateral. Also, restaurants are illiquid, especially if they are very personalized. Finally, banks are reluctant to finance the purchase of restaurants thus partly explaining their illiquidity.

It is instructive to note that McDonald's restaurants are the antithesis of the foregoing description. They have an extremely low failure rate. They do have long hours and difficulties of managing but the managers are so carefully selected and so well trained by the franchisor that these problems are overcome. The problems are also minimized by the franchisor's good restaurant design and good menu design and by the franchisor's support when problems arise. McDonald's restaurants are about as depersonalized as a business can be. They also seem to be the least illiquid that a business can be and most banks probably would be delighted to finance the purchase. In light of these factors, they must have a low rate of earning, possibly about 15%.

Manufacturing job shops usually have expensive machine tools offering good long-term collateral value. They nevertheless have a higher earning rate because they continuously have to bid competitively for new business. (A standing joke in the trade is that the winning bidder is the one who makes the biggest mistake.) Also, they are somewhat personalized and therefore illiquid and they seem to lack the prestige (rightly or wrongly) of manufacturers with established lines.

Beauty salons have high a high earning rate partly because they are personalized and therefore illiquid and partly because they are thought to have a high failure rate (or at least reputedly so). A particular risk of a beauty salon is that if an employee who is an excellent stylist defects to another salon, much or most of his or her clientele may follow.

Note that beauty salons are not the only type of business that may suffer from loss of sales with a defecting employee. The author was surprised once to come across a machine shop where the owner had hired a foreman away from another shop, presumably by offering more money. The foreman had brought with him several of the other shop's customers. The foreman explained his clientele's loyalty to him as being based not only on his skill at handling technical problems but also on always treating every customer, including every employee of every customer, with uncompromising honesty, dignity, and respect. For example, always greeting a truck driver arriving to pick up finished work immediately as soon as the truck pulls up to the dock so the driver is never kept waiting, and always assigning at least one of the shop's workers to help the driver load the truck. The foreman emphasized the importance of meeting schedules, and the greater importance, when a shipment is unavoidably delayed, of immediately informing the customer as soon as the problem arises so that the customer can best prepare for the delay, and of always providing the customer with a thoroughly honest assessment of the situation.

The Appraisal of Acme Widget Corporation. With the above knowledge about the variety of factors which influence earning rates, it should be clear how to estimate a rate. In the case of Acme Widget, the company has an established product line which would put the earning rate in the range of 20% to 30%. Although its product line is not patented, the widget industry itself seems well established and secure. Large manufacturers like GW (General Widgets) and IWG (International Widget & Gizmo) have always threatened to dominate the industry. Such factors as brand loyalty, freshness and quick availability of locally produced products, unique styling, customizing, cachet, and superior service for widgets under warranty have kept the industry fragmented and have assured small manufacturers like Acme continuing niches in the trade. The buyer decides on the basis of his gut feeling that a rate of earning of 25% is reasonable and he makes the following appraisal:

$$\text{fair market value} \ = \ \text{earnings} \ \div \ \text{rate of earning}$$

$$= \ \$(32{,}000 \ + \ 10{,}000) \ \div \ .25$$

$$= \ \$168{,}000$$

The $168,000 figure seems reasonable but the buyer's curiosity takes hold and he repeats the calculation while assuming the full $30,000 estimated illicit retail sales and gets $62,000 ÷ .25 = $248,000. At $248,000, he is still shy of the $300,000 seller's offering price and so he increases the earnings by the $11,000 ($12,000 sales expected to be lost when the seller departs less $1,000 raw materials expense) which the seller still commands and he gets $73,000 ÷ .25 = $292,000. Now he has some inkling of how the seller determined his offering price of $300,000. Then he wonders what would happen if he would assume a higher and safer rate of earning. If he would assume, say, 30%, he would get lower appraisals, $42,000 ÷ .30 = $140,000, $62,000 ÷ .30 = $207,000, and $73,000 ÷ .30 = $243,000. The buyer now realizes that an appraisal can be made to yield almost any price one might desire, within reason, simply by changing such assumptions as the rate of earning, the buyer's salary and/or benefits, the portion of skim to be added to the documented earnings, whether any skim at all should be added, how much of the seller's declarations of personal expenses charged to the corporation should be considered as earnings, and so on. Then he begins to wonder if making an appraisal is really worth the time and effort and if he and the seller will ever be able to agree on price. He also begins to feel discouraged and depressed at all the uncertainties and complications he has encountered which nobody ever warned him about. He manages to find cheer by recalling that he has faced difficult situations before and that he has always found one way or another to deal with them. With self-confidence thus renewed, though still boggled, he decides to take the rest of the day off, seek the pleasant diversion of a movie, and get a good night's sleep.

The fictitious buyer's handling of his appraisal is appropriate and correct and he has done about all he can do up to this point. Note that he is beginning to realize that the large variety of somewhat indefinite factors affecting his appraisal, his doubts about the sales and earnings, the seller's disclosure of cheating, and his questioning of his own abilities to deal with the situation are all a part of the game. Additionally, he has come to realize that an attitude of dogged determination, aided perhaps by sustenance of the spirit, constitutes at least a part of the ticket to success. Now he wonders how or where he might find the remainder of that ticket. Or at least a part of it.

PART 3:
CASH-FLOW PROJECTIONS

The Basic Idea. Cash-flow projections are not a perfect answer to a buyer's plight (probably nothing is) because they do not eliminate all of the inherent estimating and guessing when appraising a business. Still, they offer a comparatively reliable way to determine whether a purchase price is reasonable. They also offer the kind of valuation welcomed by bank commercial loan departments and the SBA.

The basic idea of cash-flow projections is to estimate the sales and itemized expenses over a three-year span after the buyer takes ownership, and then to check if the resulting cash flow (operational earnings plus depreciation expense plus amortization expense) will be enough to cover one and a half to two times the debt service. The reason for substantial excess of cash flow over debt service is to provide a margin of safety to cover miscalculations, recessions, customer defections, major equipment failures, and other unwelcome surprises.

If the cash flow is inadequate to meet the debt service with ample margin of safety, then either the price being paid for the business is too high or there is something amiss with the way the cash-flow projections have been prepared.

Cash-flow projections are also comparatively reliable indicators of the overall reasonableness of the deal. They are reliable because they take into account not only the price being paid for the business but also the down payment, the terms of the loan, the buyer's personal needs such as salary and benefits, acquisition costs such as professional fees (legal, accounting, brokering, appraising, banking, etc.), working capital, and so on. They are also reliable because they do not use such a subjective factor as the capitalization rate, which can introduce such a wide variance in the result. Cash-flow projections apply to virtually any business, no matter what the type, from grocery store to manufacturing company, and no matter what the size, from mom-and-pop to Fortune 500.

If help is needed to prepare these projections, it is usually best to consult with a bank commercial loan officer (not a real estate loan officer), an accountant at one of the large national firms, or someone at the SBA. Although loan officers have varying degrees of competence, they tend to be good at making projections because that is a part of their normal routine and because their success at it is critical to the success of their banks. Other professionals individually may have the necessary skill but they seem to be few in number and they are hard to identify. Even some accountants, probably only in the smaller firms, seem to have problems with projections. Thus, hiring anyone but a banker or someone with proven skill poses a serious risk to an unwary buyer. One other possible source of appraising help exists in a nationally recognized group like the Institute of Business Appraisers (800-299-4120) or the American Society of Appraisers (703-478-2228). (The author is not a member of either group.)

In addition to corroborating the appraisal and the reasonableness of the deal, cash-flow projections have several other purposes. In some cases, as explained below, cash-flow projections constitute the appraisal even if only through trial and error. They help the buyer determine if still interested in the purchase. They are a negotiating tool to help the buyer determine his or her bidding range and to show the seller why his or her price is too high (if it really is too high). They are a negotiating tool to help the seller determine his offering price and to show the buyer why his bid is too low (if it really is too low). Cash-flow projections are almost always necessary when applying for a bank loan and absolutely necessary when applying for SBA participation in a bank loan. Last but not least, cash-flow projections are a good tool for studying the effects of changes in underlying assumptions such as those for equipment purchases, manpower changes, sales efforts, inflation rates, and so on.

Two disadvantages of cash-flow projections are that they require more

Illustration 7.1

Cash flow projections are a sanity check on the price and terms of the purchase and sale. Properly prepared, they show whether the overall deal makes sense. That's why they are so welcome at banks and the SBA.

time to prepare than most other appraisal methods and they require more talent.

Cash-flow projections are prepared in several steps, beginning with the same fact-finding required for capitalization. The remaining steps are explained below and applied to the Acme Widget Corporation. The results are shown in Figure 7.2.

Making Assumptions. Cash-flow projections should be based on conditions and assumptions which will prevail under the buyer's ownership, not the seller's. They should also reflect, as nearly as possible, the buyer's skill at managing the business, not the seller's. Any assumptions affecting sales and expenses under the buyer's ownership should be put into writing; that forces the preparer to think more clearly about what he or she is doing. It also provides a record for future reference, an especially important point if the projections are used to test the effects of various ideas and assumptions. Finally, the written assumptions become part of the substantiation which must be provided to the bank in the loan application package.

Acme's buyer writes the assumptions on which his cash-flow projections will be based. He also notes what the assumptions themselves are based on.

1. Inflation at 3% per year. This assumption is based on the current 3% rate of inflation and the knowledge that the Federal Reserve Board seems committed to maintaining a low rate.
2. The buyer will spend eight hours weekly making sales calls on prospective new customers. From this he will attain real growth in sales of about $20,000 per year. Assumption 2 is not based on any direct sales experience of the buyer (since he has none) but on what he has learned from sales people through the years. The secret to producing new sales is to make sales calls on prospective new customers and to keep making them when discouraged by rejection. His $20,000 figure was estimated with the help of a sales manager friend who also offered the advice that he should always be himself and that even homely, slow-witted people manage to find

acceptance if they just keep on making their sales calls.

3. The first few months of sales growth will be accommodated by present staff, perhaps with some overtime.

4. The present plant and equipment will accommodate growth for at least the first three years.

5. The seller's departure will cost Acme about $12,000 per year in personality-intensive sales.

6. The buyer's contacts will gain Acme about $4,000 per year in personality-intensive sales. Assumption 6 is based on conversations with the buyer's contacts in the trade, several of whom have promised that they will do business with him when he becomes an owner. Since he knows the uncertainty of good intentions (no matter how sincere), his assumed $4,000 sales gain is less than half of what he has been promised.

7. The buyer's management skill will not significantly differ from the seller's. Actually, he hopes to be able to manage more efficiently than the seller but he knows through experience that almost everything in life looks easier than it really is and that assumption 7 therefore is a challenge.

Note that assumptions 3, 4, and 5 are based on the owner's advice but also on the buyer's ability to assess that advice. If assumptions 3 and 4 prove not to have been valid, the responsibility does not rest with the seller. It rests with the buyer who is experienced enough to be able to make such judgments. Assumption 5 regarding the loss of the seller's personality-intensive sales probably should be put into writing by the seller and signed by the seller. Legal advice should be sought to assess final responsibility for assumption 5.

The buyer might also have written the assumption that key employees will remain under his ownership. He didn't because his common sense tells him that people do not give up their jobs lightly and that they will probably give him a try before making any decisions. If any do leave, he has a contact or two which could help fill the vacancies. If the contacts should prove fruit-

Figure 7.2 Development of Cash-Flow Projections

ACME WIDGET CORPORATION CASH-FLOW PROJECTIONS
(000 omitted)

	Adjusted Income Statement	Baseline Sales & Expenses	Projection Factors	Year of New Ownership		
				1	2	3
Sales	$403	$407	1.08	$440	$475	$513
Expenses						
Advertising	3	3	1.03	3	3	3
Automotive	3	4	1.03	4	4	4
Depreciation	9	9	–	9	9	9
Insurance						
Business	9	9	1.05	9	10	10
Owner's personal	3	3	1.03	3	3	3
Legal & accounting	5	5	1.05	5	6	6
Maintenance & repair	5	5	1.05	5	6	6
Miscellaneous	0	0	1.05	0	0	0
Office supplies	9	9	1.05	9	10	10
Raw materials	39	39	1.08	42	45	49
Rent	27	27	1.03	28	29	30
Taxes & licenses	20	20	1.05	21	22	23
Telephone	3	3	1.05	3	3	3
Utilities	8	8	1.05	8	9	9
Wages						
Owner	35	35	1.03	36	37	38
Other employees	193	193	1.05	203	213	223
Total expenses	$371	$372		$388	$409	$426
Pre-tax net profit	$32	$35		$52	$66	$87
Cash flow				$61	$75	$96

less, he would scramble to hire replacements while working long hours.

Baseline Sales and Expenses. Acme's baseline sales under the new owner are developed as follows:

The buyer has purposely not included the $10,000 tolerable amount

Seller's recent year (or average)	$415,000
Seller's personal customers	-12,000
Adjusted sales	403,000
Buyer's contacts	4,000
Baseline sales	$407,000

of the unrecorded income in the baseline sales because when he started to put it on paper, he remembered that the cash-flow projections will likely be submitted to a bank as part of the loan application package. He fears that if repercussions should arise from his calling attention to the seller's cheating on taxes, he might lose his opportunity to buy the business. Besides, he reasons, if he needs to, he can increase his sales-calls gain from $20,000 to $30,000 and no one will know the difference. It does not escape his notice, however, that he now stands, somewhat uncomfortably, at the threshold of deceit.

The baseline expenses in Figure 7.2 are identical to the adjusted expenses in the left hand column (which, in turn, are the same as the adjusted expenses in Figure 7.1) with one exception: automotive expense is increased from $3,000 to $4,000 to allow for the added expense due to the sales calls the buyer will be making. (The buyer could have omitted the left hand column from Figure 7.2 but he felt that its presence helped his continuity of thought and that it might also help the banker's continuity of thought.)

Projection Factors. A projection factor is applied to the baseline sales and to each baseline expense except depreciation to estimate future sales and expenses. The sales factor will account for the increased sales resulting from the sales calls the buyer will be making. The expense factors will account for the increased expenses resulting from the increased sales. All the factors will also account for price inflation.

The factor applied to sales is developed by converting the $20,000 an-
nual increase to a percentage of the baseline sales and adding that percentage
to the baseline projection factor along with the inflation percentage:

$20,000 ÷ $407,000 = 4.9% or .049

		Factor
Baseline		1.00
Sales increase		.049
Inflation		.03
		1.079
	USE	1.08

The factors applied to expenses will differ according to whether the
expense in question is fixed relative to sales, semi-fixed relative to sales, or
directly proportional to sales. Acme's advertising expense, for example, is
considered fixed because it is independent of sales. Raw material expense, on
the other hand, is directly proportional to sales. Rent expense, since it is not
a function of sales, is considered fixed even if it increases each year in accordance with the lease. In the retail industry, however, shopping-center leases
commonly make the rent a percentage of the gross sales. Some expenses such
as utilities are semi-fixed because they are partially affected by sales. Depreciation expense requires no projection factor because it is an allocation of a
past expense, not a projection of a future expense.

Semi-fixed expenses are difficult to assign factors to without studying
the details of each expense. Insurance expense, for example, may be a function of sales for the liability portion, employees' wages for the workmen's-
compensation portion, and value of the assets for the comprehensive-loss portion. Wage expenses are a function of a relatively fixed number of employees
in the office, tool room, and warehouse and of a relatively proportional (to
sales) number of employees on the production line.

For Acme Widget, the buyer estimates that the factor for projecting
expenses proportional to sales will be the same as the 1.08 factor for project-

ing sales. He sets the fixed-expenses factor at 1.03 to project inflation. He estimates the semi-fixed factor as follows:

	Factor
Baseline	1.00
Half of 4.9% sales increase	.024
Inflation	.03
	1.054
USE	1.05

Note that the buyer did not assume simply that all expenses would continue as historical percentages of sales. Rather, his use of factors applied to each individual expense allowed for the economies of scale. Note also that the economies of scale work in reverse, a principle recognized by the buyer when he set up his adjusted sales and expenses by lowering the sales from $415,000 to $403,000 but by purposely not lowering any expenses except raw materials.

If the sales were to change by a large amount, say, up 100% or down 50%, then each of the expenses would have to be carefully reviewed because of the substantial change in the framework of the business.

Projecting Sales, Expenses, and Earnings. Sales and expenses are projected by multiplying the baseline sales and expenses by the appropriate factors and rounding to the nearest thousand dollars. (Rounding errors are insignificant compared to all of the estimating and guessing that is required in appraising.) Making the projections is best explained by the following sample calculations:

Sales

Year 1	$407,000 x 1.08 = $439,560
	USE $440,000
Year 2	$439,560 x 1.08 = $474,725
	USE $475,000
Year 3	$474,725 x 1.08 = $512,703
	USE $513,000

Advertising expense

Year 1	$3,000 x 1.03 = $3,090
	USE $3,000
Year 2	$3,090 x 1.03 = $3,183
	USE $3,000
Year 3	$3,183 x 1.03 = $3,278
	USE $3,000

Insurance expense, business

Year 1	$9,000 x 1.05 = $9,450
	USE $9,000
Year 2	$9,450 x 1.05 = $9,922
	USE $10,000
Year 3	$9,922 x 1.05 = $10,419
	USE $10,000

Estimating the Funds Necessary to Purchase. The funds necessary to purchase a business usually include, to one degree or another, the price agreed to by the buyer and seller, working capital, work in progress, materials inventory, merchandise inventory, lease deposit, and acquisition costs.

Since the purchase price is not yet negotiated, the buyer's $168,000 appraisal will serve as a preliminary estimate. If an appraisal had not been made, any reasonable figure would serve as a preliminary estimate including, for example, the seller's offering price of $300,000. No matter how the estimated price is determined, the cash-flow projections will show whether it is too high and by approximately how much. They will also show whether it is too low. Most sellers do not set their prices too low, however.

Working capital varies widely with the type of business being purchased. For example, a restaurant dealing strictly in cash with no credit cards or other credit (as most cafeterias do) needs little or no working capital because it will produce a positive cash flow beginning on the first day of the buyer's ownership. In contrast, a manufacturing job shop requiring one month to produce and ship a customer's order and another month before receiving payment on that order needs substantial working capital to pay the shop's wages, materials, and other expenses during that two-month period of no income. Working capital for such a shop with sales, say, of $1,200,000 per year might be estimated very roughly and conservatively by taking two-twelfths of the annual sales (to account for the two months' accumulated expenses) to get $200,000. The necessary working capital might be estimated more accurately by itemizing the shop's expenses to determine which expenses require payment as work progresses (like wages and rent), which ones have some lag in the shop's payment date (like gas and electric), and which ones might inherently be deferred for several months (like property taxes and the accountant's year-end fee).

For Acme Widget, the buyer estimates working capital to be one month's worth of the baseline expenses less depreciation:

$$\text{working capital} = (\$372{,}000 - 9{,}000) \div 12$$

$$= \$363{,}000 \div 12$$

$$= \$30{,}250$$

$$\text{USE} \qquad \$30{,}000$$

Work-in-progress (WIP) funds, like working capital, also vary widely with the type of business being bought. For example, retail stores typically have no work in progress since they typically do no manufacturing. Instead, they have substantial merchandise inventories. In contrast, the job shop referred to above may have several jobs in various stages of completion such that the amount of labor and materials at closing will have to be estimated for each job. Usually the buyer's and seller's accountants arrange to complete this estimate on the final day before closing the purchase and sale. For Acme, the buyer estimates the work in progress will be two weeks' worth of non-owner wages plus materials plus a 60% markup for overhead costs such as utilities and rent.

$$\text{WIP wages and material} = 2 \div 52 \times (\$193{,}000 + \$39{,}000)$$
$$= 2 \div 52 \times \$232{,}000$$
$$= \$8{,}923$$

$$\text{overhead expense} = \text{total expense} - \text{employee labor} - \text{materials}$$
$$= \$372{,}000 - 193{,}000 - 39{,}000$$
$$= \$140{,}000$$

$$\text{overhead markup} = \$140{,}000 \div (\$193{,}000 + 39{,}000)$$
$$= 60\%$$

$$\text{WIP overhead} = \$8{,}923 \times .60$$
$$= \$5{,}354$$
$$\text{WIP total} = \$8{,}923 + 5{,}354$$
$$= \$14{,}277$$
$$\text{USE} \quad \$14{,}000$$

To estimate material inventory, the buyer notes that since the seller orders raw material in wholesale lots to get the price breaks and then assigns the cost as required to each job order, it is impossible to tell in advance whether the inventory at closing will be a nearly-full wholesale lot or a nearly-depleted one. Since wholesale lots are about $10,000 each, the buyer estimates $5,000.

Merchandise inventory will consist of completed widgets in the warehouse and in the retail store. Such inventories are hard to estimate in advance because sales often come in spurts while the rate of production tends to be constant throughout the year. (It is well known that widget sales have little, if any, seasonal variation. That's because Santa's elves haven't learned yet how to deal with them.) The buyer roughly estimates the merchandise inventory to equal the work in progress, or $14,000.

The lease deposit is estimated as one month's rent:

$27,000 \div 12 = \$2,250$
        USE $2,000

The buyer talks to a lawyer and an accountant who both agree to a preliminary discussion with no fee, then makes the following educated guesses
at what his acquisition costs might be:

Lawyer's fee		$2,000
Accountant's fee		500
Broker's fee (seller pays)		0
Building inspection and		
occupancy permit		300
Loan application fee		500
Miscellaneous		1,000
	Estimated total	$4,300
	USE	$4,000

The buyer's estimated total funds requirement is as follows:

Purchase price		$168,000
Working capital		30,000
Work in progress		14,000
Materials inventory		5,000
Merchandise inventory		14,000
Lease deposit		2,000
Acquisition costs		4,000
	Estimated total	$237,000
	USE	$237,000

Estimating the Debt Service and the Cash-Flow Ratio. Having made an
estimate of the total funds necessary to buy the business, Acme's buyer determines his debt service by deducting his cash down payment from the total
funds and referring to a book of standard interest amortization tables (also
known as mortgage payment tables) to find his monthly payment.

The amount required for down payment on a business is one of the two or three most commonly asked questions about financing. Depending on the circumstances, the amounts typically range from 20% to 40% of the total funds to purchase although they occasionally run higher or lower. (Details will be presented in Chapter 9.) For most situations, 30% is a reasonable estimate of the down payment. Acme's buyer decides to try 30% partly because it seems reasonable and partly because it is within the range of his ability, though barely.

$$\text{estimated down payment} = \$237,000 \times .30$$
$$= \$71,100$$
$$\text{USE} \qquad \$70,000$$

The preference of $70,000 to $71,000 is simply for the greater roundness of the number at a point where exactitude is irrelevant.

$$\text{estimated amount to finance} = \$237,000 - 70,000$$
$$= \$167,000$$

The debt service depends on the interest rate and the number of years to pay the loan. Interest rates on loans for the purchase of small businesses are usually in the range of 2% above the prime rate. Under very favorable conditions and with some luck, one may discover by shopping from one bank to the next, an interest rate at prime. The term of such loans is usually about five years for most personal property and about 15 years for real estate or, in some cases, machine tools. (The value of real estate is more estimable and much more stable and tangible, thus, its greater acceptance as collateral for a bank loan and for a longer term for the loan.) Assuming a prime rate of 7.5%, Acme's buyer adds 1% and gets 8.5%. For lack of anything better, he assumes a term of five years. (He will later add the 5-year term and the 8.5% interest rate to his list of assumptions.) For a five-year loan at 8.5%, the amortization tables show a monthly payment of $2,051.66 on a loan of $100,000. For a loan of $167,000, the debt service is proportionally higher:

monthly debt service = $2,051.66 x $167,000 ÷ $100,000

= $2,051.66 x 1.67

= $3,426.27

annual debt service = monthly debt service x 12

= $3,426.27 x 12

= $41,115

USE $41,000

Referring to Figure 7.2, the cash flow for year 1 of new ownership is estimated as follows:

Pre-tax profit	$52,000
Depreciation	9,000
Subtotal cash flow	$61,000
Allowable unrecorded earnings	$10,000
Total cash flow	$71,000

Ratio of cash flow to debt service:

Based only on recorded earnings

cash-flow ratio = cash flow ÷ debt service

= $61,000 ÷ $41,000

= 1.49

Based on recorded earnings plus tolerable unrecorded earnings

$$\text{cash-flow ratio} = \$71,000 \div \$41,000$$
$$= 1.73$$

Banks like to see a ratio of cash flow to debt service of around 2.00, but they tend to accept a lower ratio when satisfied about the future of the company, the industry, the economy, the buyer's qualifications, and so on. Sizing up his own situation, the buyer feels that, all things considered, his probability of success at managing Acme is high because Acme is a good company in a stable industry and because he has the right training, experience, and talent. He therefore hopes that the bank will not be too demanding on the ratio of cash flow to debt service. In any case, the ratio of 1.49 seems too low for comfort and the 1.73 figure, though better, is too close to count on, especially since Acme does not have much collateral to back the loan. Moreover, the closeness of these figures shows that the appraisal and cash-flow projections have to be carefully reviewed to check their reasonableness and accuracy. And he still has one other problem which weighs heavily: his projections are based on a purchase price of $168,000 which not only has not been agreed to by the seller but is not even close to the seller's $300,000 offering price.

The buyer reviews his appraisal and finds no mistakes in his arithmetic or in his assumptions. He decides to stay with $168,000 because he still feels comfortable with the tolerable loss of $10,000 unrecorded earnings on which that appraisal is based and because everything is starting to make more sense to him. Equally important, as the pieces of the appraisal puzzle start falling into place, his self-confidence rises and the strong earnings projected in years two and three of his ownership persuade him that he will overcome any problems he encounters. Here he pauses to ask himself once more if he can really build sales by calling on potential customers and, recalling the discussions he has had with various sales personnel, he knows he can, even if he lacks the experience. The trick, he reminds himself, is to get out of the office into the market and to make the calls, to actually make them. That is what brings new sales.

Returning to the problem of the low ratio of cash flow to debt service, he thinks of several possible ways to improve the ratio, including lowering his salary, making a higher down payment, and making seller financing a part of his offer. Lowering his salary will not lower the actual amount of cash available to him and his family. It will merely convert part of the salary into corporate earnings. Increasing the corporate earnings will increase the cash-flow ratio and make his loan application more acceptable to the bank. The bank, of course, will ask if he and his family can live on whatever salary he might declare. He believes that he can get by on about $5,000 less than he has shown on his projections and that if he has to, he can convince the bank. Just for a trial run, he calculates his ratio of cash flow to debt service to reflect a $5,000 conversion of salary into corporate earnings as follows:

Ratio of cash flow to debt service:
> Based only on recorded earnings

$$\text{cash-flow ratio} = \text{cash flow} \div \text{debt service}$$
$$= (\$61,000 + 5,000) \div \$41,000$$
$$= 1.61 \text{ (was 1.49)}$$

Based on recorded earnings plus tolerable unrecorded earnings

$$\text{cash-flow ratio} = (\$71,000 + 5,000) \div \$41,000$$
$$= 1.85 \text{ (was 1.73)}$$

Next, the buyer starts to consider the effect of increasing his down payment but quickly rules it out, at least for the present, because he would have to borrow from family. He does not feel comfortable about that and will do it only as a last resort.

Finally, seller financing would increase the ratio of cash flow to debt service with respect to the bank's portion of the financing but it would not increase the ratio to the overall debt. He therefore rules out seller financing as a means of improving the ratio itself but probably will use it to increase the bank's comfort level with the existing ratio.

Now the cash-flow ratio looks better (with the salary conversion) but he still is faced with the problem of negotiating the price, not to mention the seller financing. He is also rather tired of manipulating numbers but he makes the interesting observation that, having played with the numbers as much as he now has, the whole process seems less arcane and less intimidating than when he started. He is even getting used to the sleaziness of unrecorded earnings. But why not? He recalls how bad and how frightened he felt the first time he was told by his boss to fabricate a report in order to satisfy a contractual obligation. If caught, he could have gone to prison for fraud. He had confided with one of the high middle managers he had developed a close relationship with, someone whom he admired both for his competency and his decency and who also was in on the scheme (involving about 25 workers in all), and he will never forget his words: "Either you play by the company rules or you'll be replaced by someone who will." He had hoped to leave all of this behind—he had also hoped to leave behind the paper work, so much of which caters to human failings—but now he has his doubts. In any case, he does not doubt that he loves the widget trade or that he wants to own his own business. Towards those ends, he will do what is necessary as long as it is not hurtful or unkind.*

*The buyer's statement is paraphrased from Tennessee Williams.

PART 4:
OTHER ASPECTS OF APPRAISING

Although the basic explanations of capitalization and cash-flow projections presented above will serve the needs of most buyers and sellers of small businesses, there are other aspects of those techniques and of appraising in general which will broaden and deepen one's understanding of the whole appraising process. These other aspects are covered in the following sections.

Some Differences Between Large and Small Corporations. There are differences between large corporations and small corporations that are worth noting for the general knowledge to be gained but also for a better understanding of the risk of investing in a small business. Large corporations such as those listed on the New York Stock Exchange are always discussed on an after-tax basis, not on a pre-tax basis. The reason is that large corporations regularly pay substantial income taxes in contrast to small corporations which have greater flexibility in avoiding those taxes. The point is not that large corporations don't use all the legal tricks and schemes possible, as well as many illegal tricks and schemes, to minimize their taxes. They do. The point is only that large corporations and small corporations cannot be judged on exactly the same basis.

Large corporations are described by their yield and their price-to-earnings ratio (PE), not by their rate of earning. Yield is the annual dividends currently paid by a company expressed as a percentage of its price. For example, if AT&T is paying an annual dividend of $1.32 per share of common stock and is selling for $59.25 per share, the yield is $1.32 ÷ $59.25 = 2.2%. The PE ratio is the ratio of the price per share of common stock to the earnings per share. For example, if the after-tax earnings are $2.96 per share, the PE ratio is $59.25 ÷ $2.96 = 20. Note that the PE ratio is the reciprocal of the rate of earning. For AT&T, the rate of earning is 1 ÷ 20 = 5% which compares to the 25% rate of earning assumed for Acme Widget except that Acme's 25% is before income taxes while AT&T's 5% is after income taxes. In reverse, Acme's PE ratio is 1 ÷ .25 = 4 which compares to AT&T's PE ratio of 20.

There are several reasons that large corporations appraise and sell at lower rates of earning (higher PE ratios) than small corporations. Large corporations reinvest proportionally more of their earnings in research, development, and expansion of facilities and markets than small corporations do. In the above example, AT&T's dividend of $1.32 is only 45% of its earnings of $2.96. Large corporations generally have greater reliability of growth in sales and earnings made possible by reinvesting earnings. They have more variety of skills to take full advantage of opportunities for growth and for efficiency. They also have greater reliability of earnings made possible by several tiers of top executives and managers so that if one of them is disabled or dies, the others will provide the management necessary to maintain the sales and earnings. If the owner of a small corporation is disabled or dies, the corporation may have to close its doors in a matter of days. If that happens, the value of the business is greatly diminished and a substantial loss in the capital invested is a virtual certainty. That is partly why bank loans for purchasing small corporations are of such short term; the longer the term of the loan, the greater the probability of disability or death. Another advantage of large corporations is that they have boards of directors empowered to replace chief executives who fail to perform to expectations. Still another advantage is that the quality and talent of large corporation executives and managers is considerably higher, probably, than that of small corporation owners although, to be sure, they must compete against executives and managers of similar high quality and talent. Other advantages of large corporations compared to small corporations could be discussed (such as multi-national potential, greater ability to harness new technology, instant liquidity of listed stocks, and so on) but the point is already made that small corporations have comparatively large risks, which should be understood to properly appraise.

A Proposed Definition of a Small Business. Except for a brief note in the preface, no mention has yet been made in this book of how to define a small business. Although such definitions are usually arbitrary and based on some quantitative factor such as the amount of revenues or the number of employees, a conceptual definition can be useful both for better understanding of the essence of a small business and for purposes of appraising.

A small business is hereby defined as one with only one tier of management, namely, the owner. If a second tier were added in the form of one or more assistant managers with skill equal to or nearly equal to that of the owner, the business would no longer qualify as a small business. That is because having two or more tiers of management is one of the characteristics of businesses which are not thought of as being small.

It is also because two major risks of small businesses disappear or are at least minimized by adding the second tier. Those are the risks to the owner of death and disability, either of which may force the business to shut down and sold with a substantial loss of the capital invested. With a second tier of management, the business would survive. There would be some loss of management skill, but it would survive, preserving most if not all of the capital invested.

Invalid Zones of Appraising. One can begin to picture two invalid zones of appraising by plotting appraisal-datum points on a graph. Starting with the Acme Widget Corporation as an example, one would plot the $42,000 earnings assumed by the buyer along the horizontal axis (the X axis), and, using the 25% capitalization rate, the $168,000 appraised value along the vertical axis (the Y axis). The first datum point would fall where the $42,000 and $168,000 values would intersect when projected into the field of the graph. If several more datum points were plotted using different earnings but with the same 25% capitalization rate, these points would fall in a straight line sloping towards the intersection point of the horizontal and vertical axes. The line thus formed could be used to determine graphically other appraised values for other amounts of earnings. One simply would locate the earnings along the horizontal axis and project upward to the plotted line to get the appraised value. The question arises how far up the line or down the line one might validly use the graph.

Looking first at the upward side of the line, assume that the sales, number of employees, number of customers, and other elements of the business are in a state of growth. It follows that the management duties also would grow and, presumably, so would the earnings. A point eventually would be reached where the owner would be forced by the increased management duties to hire an assistant to manage the company and where the company would produce enough earnings to pay the assistant's salary. Assuming the assistant capable of handling most if not all of the owner's functions, the owner's prolonged absence due to death, disability, or other cause would no longer inevitably result in shutting down the operation. The risk to the capital invested would largely diminish. At that point, however, the business in question would no longer be a small business. It would be a medium-size business or at least a business in the zone between small and medium. If the business now would be placed on the market, then, as a normal consequence of market forces, the buyer's expected rate of return on the capital invested in such a multi-tiered business would have to be reduced to compensate for the reduced risk of invested capital. The new rate would be less than 25%. Thus, the graph described above for appraising various amounts of earnings would become invalid above the point where the second tier of management is added. (How the business with a second tier of management would be appraised is beyond the scope of this book but it surely would appraise with a lower rate of return on investment.)

The downward side of the appraisal graph is more complicated and much more interesting than the upward side. When the Acme Widget Corporation was introduced at the beginning of Chapter 6, the equipment was described as having a fair market value of $75,000, in place, as determined by a competent appraiser, the replacement value was described as $100,000, and the liquidation value as $20,000. If the earnings of Acme Widget were to start declining to a range approaching zero, especially if the decline were steady enough to form a trend, the value appraised by using the capitalization method would become largely invalid *and so would the value of the equipment as appraised by the equipment dealer.* For example, if the earnings were to decline, say, to $9,000, the appraised value using the 25% capitalization rate would be $36,000. But this appraisal contradicts the equipment appraisal at $75,000. Which appraisal is valid?

The answer to this conundrum lies in what is meant by appraised value. Appraised value is fair market value which is the price a buyer and seller would agree to if both were well informed, economically motivated, and not in distress. What is happening is that the conditions underlying the definition of appraised value, particularly motivation and absence of distress, are being eroded. This erosion can best be understood by looking at a case which is fairly common, if not typical:

The seller, nearing retirement, has let the sales decline for several reasons. The seller's home is paid for, the children are raised and started on careers of their own, the seller's energy is not what it was 20 years or even ten years earlier, the seller does not need a lot of money and therefore is not trying to bring new customers to restore sales to former levels, and attrition not only has been, but still is causing the sales to decline. Despite the sales decline, the seller feels no pressure to restore sales because, in addition to the above reasons, the seller still takes a regular salary, the business is still profitable even if barely so, and the sales do not appear to have declined by a worrisome amount. However, what is happening, somewhat inconspicuously, is that as sales decline, even by a seemingly small amount, earnings decline at a faster rate due to the tyranny of fixed expenses such as rent, payroll, advertising, and medical insurance, and due to the semi-tyranny of semi-fixed expenses such as business insurance, legal and accounting, and maintenance and repair. The seller, in other words, does not quite realize the extent to which his business has slipped and does not quite realize that the trend is ongoing.

The seller's situation now is that, though motivated to sell, he no longer enjoys the vitality and economic motivation which once made the business thrive. Now, in the state of decline with earnings approaching zero, he is approaching a state of distress even though the distress may not yet be felt. In short, the conditions underlying what is known as fair market value have deteriorated and are continuing to deteriorate. Therefore, the appraised value no longer qualifies as fair market value. The value of this business is now headed towards liquidation value of the equipment. To confirm this hard-to-accept reality, recall that the equipment was appraised at $75,000 in place. But equipment remains in place only when it is making a profit. When the profit-making ceases, the only way the equipment can remain in place is for the business to be sold to someone capable of making a turnaround, in which case a distress sale or at least a semi-distress sale will have occurred. If a turnaround does not occur, the equipment will not remain in place, and probably will be sold to someone at another location at prices approaching those at an auction.

What commonly happens in such cases is that if the buyer offers the capitalization value of $36,000 for the business, the seller will reject the offer while citing the $75,000 equipment appraisal, and he may do so with a tone of righteous indignation: "The equipment is worth $75,000," the seller will contend, "and it's up to you to make the proper use of it." The buyer will reply that the business with its present earnings of only $9,000 cannot pay for itself at the seller's price and the bank, therefore, will not lend the money necessary to purchase. The buyer will add that if he has to build the sales to a level capable of justifying the $75,000 price, then he would be paying for the fruits of his own labors, something that he is not willing to do.

In an attempt to solve the impasse, the seller will consult with his accountant who, being neither trained nor experienced in these matters, probably will tell him that the equipment appraisal is valid because it was professionally done and that he should stick to his demand for $75,000. Likewise, the buyer will hire a consultant, either a lawyer or an accountant, who, also being neither trained nor experienced in these matters, probably will tell him that a business earning only $9,000 is barely worth $36,000, much less $75,000, and that "the equipment appraisal is probably trumped up, as everyone knows most of them are." With contradictory appraisals fortified by contradictory professional advice and further fortified by the suspicions that the principals now harbor towards each other, the impasse they have reached is probably permanent and the deal is probably dead. One more case of shattered hopes and broken dreams.

This case, as the reader may already have surmised, describes more than an invalid zone of appraising. It also describes the anatomy of a broken deal. It is a woefully common happening in the business marketplace, and one where both sides lose.

The solution is for both parties to recognize that when the earnings of a business approach zero, conventional appraisals lose their validity. The principals should therefore ask themselves how badly they wish to make a deal and whether they are willing to negotiate a compromise. The intelligent, motivated buyer will recognize that if he can turn the business around—and he should not be bidding on it if he does not have that capability—he can do very well while paying more than $36,000. The intelligent, motivated seller will recognize that the buyer is not necessarily a thief in businessman's clothing and that the low earnings in a downward trend cast a cloud over the value of the equipment. They also cast a cloud over the viability of the business. A compromise therefore is very much in order. A compromise that most buyers and sellers could live with might consist of splitting the difference between the two appraised values, settling in the range, say, of $50,000 to $60,000. Another type of compromise might set a firm price, say, $36,000, plus a contingent price, say, a 15 or 20 percent royalty on sales in excess of present levels, such that an additional $39,000 to bring the total price up to $75,000 might be forthcoming. Such an agreement would place a cap on the royalties (as shown at $39,000) and a date, say, five years after closing, past which no further royalties would be paid whether the cap had been reached or not. Such an agreement also would minimize the buyer's risk while assuring the seller of a better price if the business does turn around.

One may speculate on what would have happened if, by chance, the accountant advising the seller had never met the seller and, in normal course, had been hired by the buyer while, likewise, the buyer's accountant, by chance, had been hired by the seller. Would the accountant now paid by the buyer still emphasize the $75,000 equipment appraisal and would the accountant now paid by the seller still laud the $36,000 capitalization appraisal? The author thinks not although he has no documented evidence to hold that opinion. What he does have is a modicum of experience suggesting that advisors who lack training and experience usually don't understand appraising and, what's worse, they usually don't realize that closing the deal is probably more important to their clients than getting the best price.

The clients themselves often don't realize the full importance of closing the deal but could be swayed if their advisors would place things in perspective. Instead, thinking only of price, the advisors suggest their clients take the safest course of action. What is safest, however, may apply more to the professional advisor than to the client. If the buyer's accountant should advise paying $55,000 for a business appraising at $36,000, and if the business should fail causing financial and emotional ruination for the client, could the client sue the accountant for damages, both actual and punitive? Or, if not sued, could the accountant lose the trust and confidence of the client and, possibly, the client's business?

Such questions may be speculative but they take on fearful possibility in a society so litigious as America. In a way, one can hardly not sympathize with the accountant being pressed to offer advice in a field so arcane as the small business marketplace and in a society where malpractice suits are so common. The author even questions himself as to how he would behave were he in the accountant's shoes and asked for advice on something which he is not sure about in an arcane field where exist no licensed or certified advisors to whom one could refer the client. It is not the kind of situation most normal people would ever wish to find themselves in.

In any case, it is clear that two zones of invalid appraisals exist: the upward part of the capitalization graph beginning where a second tier of management is added, and the downward part of the capitalization graph where the earnings approach zero, this lower zone to include the equipment appraisal. Actually, a third zone of invalid appraisals exists in the offices of lawyers and accountants who lack training and experience in these matters, their good intentions notwithstanding. There also may be other invalid zones not yet discovered.

Doing Cash-Flow Projections and Appraisals On a Computer. In general, using a computer for cash-flow projections is inadvisable and even harmful for several reasons. Most small business buyers and sellers probably would not understand the software and thus would lose the biggest value of the projections which is to understand what is going on. Learning the software would take more time than doing the projections by hand. The projection procedures, as described in this chapter, probably would have to be modified to fit the software, or vice versa, thus impeding the computer's primary value which is speed. Besides, the work and the challenge of cash-flow projections is in finding the facts and then organizing them. Doing the arithmetic on a paper spreadsheet with the aid of a pocket calculator is relatively quick and easy. Using a computer is therefore not warranted. The exception may be in the case of a person specializing in acquisitions who does his or her own fact-finding and who has developed the proper software for his own use and who will use it repeatedly, in which case all of the above objections would disappear.

The use of a computer for capitalization or for other appraisal methods is harmful for the same reasons shown above. See Example 11.4 (page 427).

A Good Reference Book on Appraising. The subject of appraising is so broad that it requires book-length treatment to do justice to it. *Valuing Small Businesses and Professional Practices* is highly recommended. It exists in several editions. The first edition was written by Shannon P. Pratt, a well-known authority on business appraising. The third edition is by Pratt, Robert F. Reilly, and Robert P. Schweihs. A fourth edition is available. The coverage of the topic is exhaustive, dealing with virtually any aspect of appraising. The chapter titled "Common Errors" is particularly recommended.

An Appraisal Based on the Cost of a Startup. Sometimes the value of a company is best determined by estimating the cost to start a similar business. For example, a small chemical laboratory using proprietary techniques is made an offer by one of its regular customers, a much larger company with strong engineering and scientific staffs. The owner, who is not ready to retire, knows the capability of the prospective buyer to build and staff its own laboratory and to quickly find a customer base. Since the prospective buyer with all of its clout would become a formidable competitor, its offer to buy, however innocent, might resemble that of an extortionist who makes an offer one can't refuse. It is likely that the prospective buyer has estimated its cost to start a similar business and has done so with the advantage of synergism. Thus its offer to the smaller company probably would not be close to its otherwise true worth. There is probably little that can be done about it except perhaps to seek a lawyer's advice regarding the possibility of legally unfair tactics.

Appraising Corporate Stock. Any of the approaches mentioned in Part 1 of this chapter may be used to appraise a corporation. The earnings approach, which has already been explained in detail, will apply most often, but a brief discussion of arriving at a corporate adjusted book value is in order.

The book value of a corporation is simply the assets minus the liabilities. Since the values of the assets as stated in the corporate books are usually not current with market value, they usually will need to be adjusted (recast).

Assets typically needing adjustment are the real estate, which should be appraised by a licensed real estate appraiser; the accounts receivable, which should be adjusted realistically for doubtful debtors; and the equipment and inventory, which should be discounted for items that are shop-worn, damaged, or obsolete. Accumulated depreciation of equipment should be decreased by 25% to 50% to remove the accelerated portion and/or adjusted for refurbishment and repair.

Liabilities typically do not need adjustment except those which are contingent, in which case the probability of the contingencies becoming actual would have to be taken into account.

Revenue Ruling 59–60. In 1960, the IRS released a document known as Revenue Ruling 59–60 to provide guidelines to appraising corporate stock. (The IRS uses the term, valuing, instead of appraising.) This document is remarkable for its thoroughness, keen insights into the appraising challenge, and correctness, especially since it is still relevant after more than 40 years. Although it is directed at corporate appraising, the guidelines also apply to the asset sales typical of small business. The following few statements from 59–60 exemplify its agreement with the guidelines in this book:

- Often, an appraiser will find wide differences of opinion…. (Section 3.01)
- A sound valuation [includes] the elements of common sense, informed judgment and reasonableness…. (Section 3.01)
- The fair market value…will vary as general economic conditions change…. (Section 3.02)
- The appraiser must exercise his judgment as to the degree of risk… (Section 3.02)
- Valuation … is, in essence, a prophecy as to the future…. (Section 3.03)
- In the final analysis, goodwill is based upon earning capacity. (Section 4.02 f)
- A determination of the proper capitalization rate presents one of the most difficult problems in valuation. (Section 6.) The complete

ruling can be found on line:
www.trugmanvaluation.com/RevRul5960.html

A Critique of an Accountant's Financial Projections. The following critique offers some understanding of the difficulty some accountants seem to have in projecting historical data into the future. The purpose is not to be critical of this accountant or of accountants in general (a defense of the accountant appears below) but to provide a note of caution to be careful about hiring an accountant to do this kind of work. This critique also will provide further explanation of financial projections.

The accountant's client was the buyer of a small manufacturing job shop. The projections were ten pages in length, including the title page and a cover letter, and were submitted in lieu of a loan application package to the bank asked to finance.

The report included projected balance sheets and projected statements of income and retained earnings. Neither the projected balance sheets nor the projected retained earnings are generally required by lending banks or by the SBA. If the bank becomes seriously interested in making the loan, it may or may not request projected balance sheets. Therefore, unless specifically asked for, they are probably superfluous and irrelevant. Projected retained earnings are usually not asked for simply because they serve no purpose. Providing this material (and other superfluous material mentioned below) increased the work for all parties involved, increased the likelihood of the accountant's making a mistake, and made finding such a mistake more difficult and more time consuming. It also delayed getting the loan and increased the accountant's bill.

The projected cash flows were separated from the projected income statements in the format commonly used by accountants. Separating the cash flows from the income statements destroys the perspective and the continuity of the presentation. Moreover, presenting the cash flows in typical accountant's format makes the report esoteric to the average entrepreneur and probably to many bankers. (Notice, in contrast, how easy it is to understand the projections in Figure 7.2, especially the last three columns.) In any case, the standard accountant's format is not generally preferred by bankers and not required by the SBA. The accountant should have contacted his own bank to learn the format. The format required by the SBA and accepted by most banks is similar to the format in Figure 7.2.

The cover letter states "We believe these projected financial statements are compiled in all material respects to give effect to the assumptions described in the paragraph above and to the application of those generally accepted accounting principles which [company name] anticipates will be appropriate in the periods projected." The accountant's effusive and stilted verbiage hint at his failure to understand what he is doing. Moreover, other than starting with the standard format for an income statement, "generally accepted accounting principles" are mostly useless, irrelevant burdens when estimating the future. Particularly irrelevant are amounts stated to the nearest dollar (amounts should be rounded to the nearest thousand with zeros omitted, as in Figure 6.1). Also irrelevant are rules for calculating depreciation and amortization and for estimating taxes (as explained below).

The cover letter states " . . . we do not express an opinion on the reasonableness of the assumptions on which these projections are based, the achievability of the projected results shown, or the probability that actual results may approximate the projected results shown." Although the accountant's disclaimer may seem like a craven hedge, it stands as fair warning to the client and to the lending bank that the accountant's participation is purely mechanical. The disclaimer is therefore appropriate. Still, this accountant completely separated himself from the essence of the matter, which was to determine if the sales and expenses projected were reasonable. A client deserves better than that. The client should have sought help from someone who had experience with such matters, a bank commercial loan officer or one of the larger accounting firms, and the accountant should have so advised the client.

When a buyer goes to a bank with a strong commercial loan department, the banker probably will express an opinion (often bluntly), especially if the bank is hired expressly for that purpose. The exceptions, regrettably, are that some bankers are loath to sound critical and others may have hidden reasons for rejecting the loan. The shortcomings of banks notwithstanding, the chances of obtaining good advice for financial projections are better than when dealing with accountants in small firms or with lawyers.

The accountant combined the assumptions with the notes to make one list. Assumptions should always be clearly identified so they will not be taken as anything other than assumptions. The only way to assure such understanding is to place them into a separate list.

The following "significant accounting policies" are itemized in the accountant's report: Depreciation "computed on an accelerated method . . .," investment credit "will be passed to the owners . . . taxed as an 'S' corporation," and amortization "on a straight line basis . . .." Depreciation and amortization, whether referring to the method, the useful life of the assets, or the dollar amount, are irrelevant. The reason is found in the definition of cash flow: pre-tax earnings plus depreciation expense plus amortization expense. If depreciation and amortization run higher or lower, the earnings run lower or higher, respectively, by the same amount. The pre-tax cash flow therefore is unaffected by depreciation or amortization. Since cash flow is defined as pre-tax, the amount of income tax also does not matter. It is true that the income tax affects the cash flow after taxes are paid but the amount of tax (and, by inference, the amount of depreciation and amortization) appearing in the cash-flow projections is unimportant and virtually irrelevant for three very pertinent reasons. First, the lending bank cares about before-tax cash flow because that is what is available to pay interest on the loan. As for paying the principal, if the business in question has a poor year causing the earnings to decline, the income tax will decline too, thus helping to pay the principal out of after-tax income. Second, the lending bank is protected by the margin of safety over and above the debt service. That margin has been time-tested by the banking industry on a pre-tax basis. Third, cash-flow projections are designed to bring the hidden earnings out of hiding to show that the business under new ownership really can meet the debt service with ample margin. In real life, the new owner and his or her accountant will put the earnings back into hiding. Thus, to show the income taxes on the cash-flow projections is both incorrect and irrelevant.

The notes and assumptions included the following information:

"Cost of sales . . . was historically about 50% of sales. Year 1 of the projections reflect this 50% factor, year 2 reflects the 50% factor plus $15,000 for the addition of an employee, and year 3 reflects the 50% factor plus $20,000 for wage increases."

After the bank had rejected the loan application it was learned that the $15,000 for an added employee in year 2 was supposed to have been included in the 50% cost of sales, not added to it. The same was true for the $20,000 added in year 3. As a result, the stunted cash flows caused the bank to reject the loan application. It is not known exactly how the misunderstanding came about. One may conjecture, however, that the accountant, somewhat unsure of the importance of the historical 50% factor though understanding quite well the mechanics of calculating it, took his client's direction literally without questioning. The client then, trusting the accountant's competency, did not bother to read the report, or, if he did try to read it, was confused and put off by the arcane nature and difficulty of it. It was the blind leading the blind. In any case, the report was submitted to the bank which examined it and returned it commenting that the bank was doing the buyer a favor by rejecting the loan. The buyer was shaken by the banker's comment and almost backed out of the deal. Relations between the buyer, the seller, and the broker then became strained. Because of the rejection, the seller, on the advice of his accountant, concluded that the buyer had no money and scolded the broker for having brought an unqualified buyer. Relations were eventually resolved when the cash-flow projections were redone by the broker and then submitted to another bank chosen by the broker for its strong commercial loan department. This bank finally did finance the purchase.

The most regrettable aspect of this case is that the accountant failed to warn his client that the cash flow looked terrible. If the accountant had understood cash-flow projections, he would have made an early discovery of the inadequacy by running a few numbers on his scratch pad and he would have discussed with his client before completing the report. He would have prevented the misunderstanding and ill feelings which arose and almost killed the deal. He would also have saved a full month of lost time and he would have completed the job for a lower fee.

The accountant's projections had other shortcomings, but they were comparatively minor and not worth discussing.

Note that the broker had requested the assignment of preparing the cash-flow projections but was rejected because, in the buyer's estimation, the accountant was better qualified. The broker had also requested the assignment of obtaining bank financing and was rejected again because the buyer insisted that he already had a good banking contact, the small branch bank that had financed the buyer's residence. Note also that if the broker had been allowed to do the work he had wanted to do, his commission would have covered both tasks.

In defense of the accountant (a CPA and a partner in a small firm), he probably was not taught in school about estimating the future and he was confronted by a dearth of books dealing as openly with the subject as the book in hand. (Even Pratt's book mentioned above fails to describe preparation of cash-flow projections.) He saw his client's need to get the job done and he did his best to serve that need. In a way, he was a victim too of both the arcane nature of buying and selling a small business and the void of government regulation in the small business market place. For sure, he was not the first accountant or lawyer to fall into the trap and, also for sure, he will not be the last. He is a good accountant by normal standards, he deserved the respect and the trust of his client and the community, and fortunately, to best knowledge, he still has it.

The Difference Between the Past and the Future. The past is a fact which has to be accurately accounted for because people learn from the past and base their decisions on it and because the IRS requires the accounting to be sure of collecting its due. The future is an estimate, based on the past, which can be relied on not to come true. Thus, while well-reasoned projections into the future are invaluable for purposes of planning, pinpoint accuracy is untrue and misleading.

Because the past must be accounted for in detail, the accounting profession attracts persons who are blessed with the ability to track those details with uncompromising accuracy, and to do so while loving what they are doing. Because the future must be accounted for in scope, in thrust, and in magnitude, but not in detail, the profession of estimating attracts persons who are blessed with the ability to understand the past (which, incidentally, promotes appreciation and respect for accounting) and then, so understanding, to project while considering the factors—economic, entrepreneurial, behavioral, political, and so on—which bend the past to become the future, and to do so while loving what they are doing.

The past is a picture well defined, even if sometimes hard to discover. The future is a reflection of the past as seen in a blurred but magical mirror. The professions which account for them are of separate mindsets, as though born into separate worlds.

Revisiting Examples. Following are two real-life examples from previous chapters but augmented with explanations of what went wrong.

> **Example 7.1** (3.2 Revisited.) In Example 3.2, the package liquor store was offered for sale at $225,000 plus inventory, a price which had been suggested by the owner's accountant. It is not known how the accountant determined the price. The prospective buyer's consultant found a handy estimating ratio indicating a price of around $300,000 plus inventory but the consultant's own appraisal was $80,000 plus inventory. Finally, a knowledgeable liquor salesman stated that the store would go for about $50,000 plus inventory. The question is why such differences in prices.
>
> The store had sales around $800,000. In Pratt's book (page 363 in the first edition), statistical data show that package liquor stores have been selling at an average price of 36.6% of annual sales. That would be $293,000 for the store in question, making the offering price seem cheap. Not known, however, are the underlying circumstances for the data in Pratt's book. If much

of it were taken in states where package liquor stores are heavily regulated and licenses comparatively hard to get, retail profit margins for those stores could be high and the stores very profitable. In Missouri there is little regulation. Almost anyone can open a store, and profit margins are low. Therefore, the 36.6% factor probably is not applicable in Missouri.

The buyer's consultant reviewed the same data which had been provided to the seller's accountant. Those data included a lease specifying that $12,000 of the annual rent would be applied to equity in the real estate if the business owner should exercise his option to purchase. The consultant treated the $12,000 as profit (and so stated in the written assumptions) and found a total profit of $26,000 per year. The consultant used a capitalization rate of .33 to get $78,788, and rounded the appraisal to $80,000. Without the $12,000 rent converted to equity, the profit was only $14,000, which capitalizes to $42,424. The consultant would have rounded to $45,000 based on the general appearance and location. The consultant also stated in his appraisal that the store would be worth a higher price to someone willing to work for a lower salary (the prospective buyer was a former president and CEO of a Fortune 500 subsidiary).

Some good lessons are learned from this example. It is tempting to use a number like the 36.6% price-to-sales ratio as a rule of thumb because it is so easy and so convenient. The large error encountered dramatizes the danger in using rules of thumb. Pratt himself gives clear warning of the danger. Another lesson is that, with due respect, accountants (at least those in small firms whom the author is used to working with) do not seem to make good appraisers (nor do lawyers) and they therefore should not be relied on for such advice. (The accountant in question was a CPA.) The final lesson, in a way, is the best. It is found with the liquor salesman who probably never heard of capitalization and who probably couldn't care less. His day-by-day experience in the marketplace makes him a premier estimator, if only by gut feel. If there were a sizeable difference between the salesman's appraisal and the consultant's, the consultant would retreat to his corner to find out what he had done wrong.

Example 7.2 (6.3 Revisited.) In Example 6.3, the grocery store's prospective buyer's offer was far below the seller's listing price, neither was willing to compromise, and the deal died.

The store was listed at $80,000. The broker had advised the seller that since the store had always lost money, he would do well to get back the $40,000 original cost of the equipment and fixtures plus the $25,000 inventory, for a total of $65,000. The buyer's offer was $19,000 determined by his lawyer who allowed nothing for the equipment and fixtures ("used equipment isn't worth anything" said the buyer, quoting his lawyer) and only $19,000 for the inventory ("because some of it will be stale or spoiled," again quoting the lawyer). The buyer said that his lawyer had also advised him "not to pay a penny more." In contrast, the seller's accountant had advised him that the store was worth $90,000 "and not a penny less."

The situation of a lawyer and/or an accountant speaking with finality (instead of with provisionality) on matters they know little about is common to small business sales, and most brokers can tell a story or two about the lawyer or accountant who killed the deal. Thus, this case is a repeat of an old story. But the extremes of the lawyer's and accountant's appraisals in this example coupled with their uncompromising stances suggest what might be going on in their minds. Professional persons untrained in appraising typically take extreme positions when setting values for their clients and they typically state their appraisals with absoluteness: "not a penny more" or "not a penny less." Perhaps untrained persons take positions both extreme and absolute not to protect their clients but to protect themselves from criticism and possible malpractice suits if proven wrong. They take their extreme positions because they sense their own lack of confidence and how liable they are to make a mistake. It is one of the miseries of the small business marketplace that deals are so often broken by such appraisals so that the buyers and sellers who truly need each other are driven apart by the very people paid to help them.

(The principle of protective extremes by those of modest talent can be observed by trading numismatic gold coins with coin dealers. The sharpest, most successful dealers usually buy or sell with the narrowest margins of profit, and the least capable with the widest margins.)

Principles of Appraising. There are certain principles of appraising which keep recurring and which underlie the whole process of appraising. Most of these principles have been at least implied in the preceding material. For improved clarity and understanding as well as for convenience, they are itemized below.

1. The value of a business depends on the purpose of the appraisal. For example, if the appraisal is for a buyer contemplating purchase, the appraised value will reflect his or her ability to manage the business. If the appraisal is for IRS assessment of an estate tax, the appraised value will reflect the historical earnings and/or the liquidation value.

2. The earnings of a business and the resultant ability to service the debt are far more important in appraising the business than the value of its equipment. The equipment, in fact, being already proven useable in place, derives much of its value and sometimes most of it from the value of the business.

3. An appraisal made from more than one approach tends to minimize the possibility of gross inaccuracy. (Note that this principle correctly suggests the absence of precision.)

4. Liquidation value, even though it is usually lower than the otherwise appraised value, should be estimated for its use as a reference point or benchmark.

5. Value tends to increase if the seller does part of the financing.

6. Security and potential growth, each a partial function of the economy, add to or subtract from the value of a business. Security and potential growth may also affect the liquidation value.

7. The value of a business increases to the extent that the negotiated price is contingent on the buyer's performance.

8. The value of a business depends on the buyer's motivation.

9. The value of a business depends on the buyer's negotiating skills.

10. The value of a business depends on the seller's motivation.

11. The value of a business depends on the seller's negotiating skills.

12. Illicit income should be reflected in the appraisal by using probability techniques.

13. Cash-service businesses do not constitute the exclusive domain of illicit income. Illicit practices are also common in businesses where income is thoroughly documented.

14. When in doubt about an appraisal, do one or both of two actions: First, apply for a bank loan. The bank may offer some good advice. (Note, however, that some lending officers have more skill and more vision than others.) Second, obtain an independent second appraisal. An accurate appraisal may save money but, more importantly, it may save the deal.

15. If good cash-flow projections are made, appraisals by other means are of diminished importance, most of the time, greatly so.

16. A negotiated settlement is the best of all possible appraisals be-

cause it accounts for virtually all of the above.

QUESTIONS FOR DISCUSSION
Chapter 7—Appraising

1. Why is appraising an art as well as a science? And why is it controversial?
2. Why should appraised values be declared provisionally?
3. Why is provisionality useful? Why is it important? Could it make or break a deal?
4. What are the three approaches to appraising? Which one is most important for appraising small businesses for the purpose of buying and selling?
5. When does the asset approach become important?
6. Why are market comparisons rarely useful in small business appraising?
7. Define fair market value (FMV). Why is FMV important?
8. What is the general premise underlying appraising a business, especially by the capitalization method? How does the capitalization method apply that general premise to arrive at FMV?
9. In Chapter 2 (page 44), the value of the equipment was described as a function of the business earnings. What was the reason?
10. How were the sales and expenses adjusted in Figure 7.1? Give an example.
11. Briefly describe how Acme's buyer handled the unrecorded earnings. How important were his qualifications for ownership? How important was his keeping an open mind?
12. Briefly state the relationship of expected earnings to the degree of risk.
13. In terms of the degree of risk, tell why appraising is an art.

14. What did you think of Acme's buyer taking time out for a movie to quell the confusion and depression he felt from the complications of appraising? What would you do?

15. How do cash flow projections provide a sanity check on the purchase price and terms?

16. Can cash flow projections be used as an appraisal?

17. Share your thoughts about the whole process of preparing cash flow projections: a) After reading through to the end, did you feel that the process was less arcane and less intimidating than when you started? b) Did you get used to the sleaziness of unrecorded earnings? c) Do you still want to own a business?

18. Why do small businesses have substantially higher capitalization rates than large businesses?

19. How does the author define a small business, and why is that definition important?

20. Name the three invalid zones of small business appraising.

21. What did Real-Life Examples 7.1 and 7.2 show you about the search for truth? How did they relate to the previous question?

CHAPTER 8

Negotiating

Of all the activities required to buy or sell a business, negotiating is the only one marked by four major impediments to success: rank ignorance, aversion to the process, high emotions, and a dichotomy of motives. The first two impediments are due to the American culture wherein negotiating price is infrequent and frowned upon compared to cultures in other countries. The latter two impediments are inherent in the process because of the high stakes involved in buying and selling a small business. Because these impediments play on one another, the overall impediment is greater than the sum of its parts. The possibility of incompetent performance therefore looms large. Sometimes, however, when one or both principals are blessed with common sense, good faith, and mutual respect, they will manage to reach an amicable settlement. Even when the participants are not so blessed, they may muddle through and close the deal. In either of these situations, however, one of the principals may miss a great opportunity for a substantially better price and terms, although, to be sure, one's loss is the other's gain. Sadly, the remaining negotiations will result in broken deals and broken dreams, even when spurred by such powerful motives as a buyer's self-fulfillment (Maslow) and a seller's failing health and burnout.

The purpose of this chapter is to provide at least some of the understanding necessary to open one's mind to the virtue and even the beauty of negotiating and to provide at least some of the knowledge necessary to offer even the most inexperienced person a chance to negotiate effectively.

The chapter is divided into three parts, Philosophy of Negotiating, Twenty-one Basic Rules of Negotiating, and Negotiating the Acme Widget Corporation Price and Terms.

PART 1:
PHILOSOPHY OF NEGOTIATING

This philosophy is to explain what negotiating is, why it is necessary, why it is ethical, and why it is good.

Negotiating is a form of communication in which two or more parties are helped to clarify and understand each other's needs and desires so as to reach agreement on the issue at hand. In the sense that it is a communication towards reaching agreement, negotiating the price and terms of a business for sale is the same as such everyday activities as arranging a time and place for a meeting. The parties involved simply propose and counter-propose until an agreement is reached. In other ways it is completely different. One difference is that buying and selling a business is not an everyday activity and neither (in America) is bargaining over the price. Another difference is that the price of a business is enormously more difficult to determine than a time and place to meet, and still another is that the stakes are fearfully high. Since neither a purchase nor a sale is possible without settling the price and terms, negotiating is both necessary and constructive. It does not matter that one or both parties may negotiate with hostility born of rancor rather than spontaneous cooperation born of good will. Negotiating is still necessary and it is still constructive even if geniality does not prevail. Since it is necessary and especially since it is constructive, it is good.

Negotiating is often marked by spontaneous cooperation but even when it is, it is still an adversarial contest. It is like a war fought by armies on a battlefield but with an important difference: soldiers use guns to shoot bullets of heavy metal intended to cause physical destruction. Negotiators use words to deliver packets of influence intended to cause mental deterioration.

Physical or mental, both are wars of attrition to one degree or another.

Note that negotiating is both constructive and destructive even while leading to agreement. Thus is revealed another view of the treacherous dichotomy of motives. It is treacherous because neither side has to agree to settle. If the damage becomes too great, either side may withdraw from the war, in which case both sides have lost.

Negotiating is ethical when done in good faith. Good faith means making and accepting only those offers and counter-offers one intends to abide by. Good faith means honoring one's concessions once they have been made and accepted. Good faith also means the seller having told the whole truth (within reason) during fact-finding and the buyer having told the whole truth (within reason) when describing his or her qualifications to the seller. Lest high ethics degrade into misguided altruism, good faith does not exclude keeping two appraisals, one to show to one's adversary to coax a lower or higher price, and one for private viewing to set the limits of bidding. Good faith does not exclude accentuating the positive when one is a seller or the negative when one is a buyer. Good faith also does not exclude probing for weakness or exploiting it in hopes of obtaining an enticingly favorable settlement.

One may contend that an honest seller will state a firm price and stand by it while a seller who lowers the price concedes that the price was too high to begin with. No such seller is ethical, and negotiating therefore is unethical, or so the thinking goes. The problem with such thinking is that it fails to account for the enormous subjectivity and complexity of appraising leading to honest differences of opinion and to honest mistakes. It also fails to realize that all values (like all truths) are provisional pending the discovery of additional insights and knowledge. The purpose of negotiating is to explore the subjectivity and complexity of appraising for the purpose of reviewing and adjusting values. That is part of what makes negotiating constructive. Negotiating therefore is ethical.

Negotiating is both beautiful and ugly. It is beautiful when disparate opinions come together, when problems find solutions, and when goals are realized and dreams come true. It is ugly when greed provokes unwillingness to compromise, when irrationality and fear reign supreme, and when incompetence kills the deal.

Finally, negotiating is a mode of truth. It is the truth of competing skills motivated by ethical self-interest which says that the value of a business is based not only on the earnings of the business but also on the skill of the negotiator to emphasize those earnings or any other aspect which contributes to the price and terms. It is the truth of the marketplace where the law of supply and demand is part of the terrain on which the war is fought. It is the truth of the whole myriad of circumstances in an imperfect world that affects one's mind and one's pocketbook and, thereby, one's offer, counter-offer, or acceptance thereof in the heat of battle. And it is the truth of the highest order which transcends all other appraisals because it is the all-inclusive appraisal of finality.

With the prerequisite philosophy accounted for, the basic rules of negotiating now follow.

PART 2:
TWENTY-ONE BASIC RULES OF NEGOTIATING

The 21 basic rules which follow are designed to maximize one's effectiveness in reaching settlement and closing the deal, as well as effectiveness in getting the best price and terms. These rules are neither rules of law nor rules of etiquette although etiquette contributed to their formulation and always should to their application. The rules are based on reason plus experience. One almost could say that they are based on common sense except that some of them require too much insight for most people to determine informally. The value of knowing these rules is partly to be able to apply them as the occasion demands but also to be able to recognize when they are being applied by one's adversary. The rules are easier to understand than the methods of appraising but much more difficult to apply. If appraising is an art, which it is, even more so is negotiating.

1. Decide at the Outset Which Is More Important, Getting the Best Price or Closing the Deal. If the former, an adversarial mind-set may prevail, though not overtly. If the latter, a spontaneously cooperative spirit should prevail, though not unguardedly. Apply the remainder of these rules in accordance with your decision.

Any number of factors will come into play, such as how well the business matches the buyer's dream, how well the buyer matches the seller's dream, the chances of finding something or someone better in the near future, the economic, physical, or emotional need to make the purchase or sale, and so on. If getting a good price seems more important, concessions will be relatively few and small, but the chance of actually making the deal will also be relatively small. If making the purchase or sale seems more important, concessions will increase in size and number and the chances for closing the deal will also increase.

For most small business transactions, closing the deal is far more important than getting a great price. The reasons are the mutual need of the buyer and seller to get on with their lives, and the overriding fact of illiquidity, that good matchups of buyers and sellers are so hard to find. (See section on illiquidity, page 52.)

The following two examples offer some insight into applying this basic rule. At least part of that insight will come from the vicarious experience they provide.

Example 8.1 A doughnut shop is offered for sale at $35,000. The shop was opened just three years earlier with all new equipment. Both the shop and the shopping center in which it is located are attractive. The neighborhood is middle- to upper-middle-income and still growing. Sales have risen slowly but steadily to where the owner draws a $26,000 salary and the business shows a profit of about $6,000. The owner has kept a record of monthly sales and expenses which shows that sales are still rising. The owner tells the broker that the shop cost about $35,000 for equipment and leasehold improvements, that it would easily fetch around $55,000 if he were willing to wait for the right buyer, but that he set a low price to encourage a quick sale and cover his original investment so that he can invest in another, more lucrative opportunity. The broker knows from his own experience with other doughnut shop listings that the seller's claim of a low price is true with no exaggeration.

The broker finds a likely buyer in the person of a young man with an engineering degree who decided to switch careers and who is presently employed as the manager of another doughnut shop. They go on a showing and the buyer expresses strong satisfaction with the location, the layout, the hours of operation, and especially the quality (all stainless steel) and newness of the equipment. Two days later he meets with the broker to make an offer of $21,000 with $16,000 down and $5,000 seller financing. The broker informs the buyer that the shop is a bargain at $35,000 and that his offer is much too low to be seriously considered. The buyer insists that he wants to make the offer as stated. The broker tries to discover the buyer's reasoning but the buyer is guarded and refers obliquely to some advice he has received with no further elaboration. The broker warns him again to no avail, then apologetically carries the offer to the seller. The seller is very polite and states that his offering price is fair and that he will not counter-offer. The seller's message is passed back to the buyer who says he will think it over. The buyer returns two days later and raises his offer to $23,000 with $17,000 down and $6,000 seller financing. The broker warns the buyer again to no avail, then carries to the seller with further apologies. The seller rejects with the comment that if the buyer needs to feel that he was able to negotiate a lower price, the seller might concede one or two thousand dollars just to be done with it but the buyer's offer is so unrealistic that it merits no counter-offer and no further discussion. The rejection is carried to the buyer who politely expresses disappointment and exits.

One day about eight months later, the broker is alone in his office sitting at his desk when a figure appears in the doorway. It is the young engineer with something to say. He has since bought a business in an entirely different field which is hardly making a living for him and which is not nearly as nice or as enjoyable as the doughnut business was. He now realizes that the shop was offered at a fair price and he regrets not having made a decent offer. He concludes by saying to the broker, "I just thought you would like to know." He thereupon exits and is not heard from again.

Example 8.2 A tavern in a lower-income neighborhood is listed for sale at $70,000, real estate included. The tavern is in a freestanding building with an apartment on the second floor. The broker takes a prospective buyer on a showing and the buyer states that this is just what he has been looking for. They return to the broker's office where the buyer signs an offer for the full $70,000. The seller immediately accepts and they have got a deal. The next day the buyer returns to the broker's office and states that when he told his friends what he had done, they all told him he should have offered a few thousand dollars less. Nevertheless, the buyer says, he loves the place and did not want to risk losing it. He feels that the price is fair and he has no regrets.

2. Use an Intermediary if the Negotiation Is Adversarial or Hostile. The intermediary who delivers and receives verbal messages is a buffer who absorbs any abuse given by the principals and who, with good rhetoric and gentle ego, can soften the mistakes being made. Also, an intermediary is a third party who alters the personal chemistry, usually for the better, when hostility prevails. If the skill of the intermediary is not the highest but merely clerical, his or her mere presence will still provide emotional relief to both principals. If the negotiation breaks down for reasons of hostility, however, a skill level greater than clerical is probably required to save the deal, as shown in Example 8.3.

Example 8.3 Agreement has been reached on the price and terms of a restaurant for sale, bank financing has been arranged, the contract and lease have been signed, and all that remains to close the deal are municipal inspections and approvals and miscellaneous details. One of the details involves installing a gas line. The seller, a husband-and-wife team, did their cooking in an all-electric kitchen. The buyer, also a husband-and-wife team, wishes to cook with gas. The buying husband (who is the team leader) telephones the selling wife (who is the team leader) and requests permission to install a gas line a few days before closing so that after closing the buyer can bring in a gas stove and hook it up with minimal loss of time. (Time will be at a premium because the sale is planned to close on a Saturday night and the buyers plan to open the following Monday morning.) All that needs to be arranged is a time after hours so that the buying husband can install the line without disturbing or being disturbed by the employees.

The selling wife says that she will not allow anyone to disturb her employees. Neither the request nor the response is unreasonable. But somehow, in the inscrutable manner of human beings with charged emotions, both the request and the response get blown out of proportion so that the parties break off their discussion in anger. Apparently (as best the story could be pieced together) the buying husband attempts to patch the relationship and to schedule a time to install the gas line but fails. The buyer's lawyer (whose background is unknown) then calls the seller's lawyer (who is a trial lawyer) and they fail not only to resolve the issue but (again, as best the story can be pieced together) they break off the discussion in anger. Next, the seller's lawyer instructs the selling wife not to come to the telephone for anyone on the buyer's side. Then the buyer's lawyer again calls the seller's lawyer in an attempt to patch the deal but the seller's lawyer hangs up on him. Then the seller's broker, a naturally amiable and diplomatic person, approaches the selling wife but is rebuffed. The seller's broker then describes the scene to the buyer's broker, throws up his hands in despair, and announces that he will have no more to do with this deal.

In the meantime, the buying husband, who had quit his job after the contract had been signed, calls the buyer's broker to discuss the problem. In the midst of the conversation, the buying wife picks up an extension and begins to add her comments, one of which is that they have no income and they are fast running out of money. Soon she is screaming such that the broker has to move the handset away from his ear.

The buyer's broker, now that he has been advised of the problem, calls the seller's lawyer, introduces himself, and asks the lawyer for advice on how to restore the deal. The lawyer, despite a somewhat prosecutorial manner and a rapid-fire delivery, is cooperative. He quickly describes the situation as he sees it and emphasizes that the employees are not to be disturbed. The broker then asks the lawyer if he would suggest that he (the broker) call the selling wife so as to be sure to understand her needs and wishes. The lawyer says that yes, that would be a good idea. The broker calls and arranges to meet the wife in her office and then hears 20 minutes of charges, accusations, rhetoric on why it is so wrong to disturb her employees, and so on during which time he sits attentively, offers continuous eye contact, nods in agreement at the right times, and utters not a word except two or three times to say that he did not quite get her meaning on a particular word or phrase. Finally, the wife signals by a long pause and a relaxation of expression that she has said what needed to be said and that it is the broker's turn to talk. The broker asks if she feels that there is some way to work something out without disturbing the employees. She replies that since the restaurant is closed on Sundays, that would be a good time for the buyer to come and install his line. She adds that she could have her manager meet him there with the key to let him in. The broker says that that seems like a good idea and that he feels that the buyer will agree. He then thanks her for her time and her cooperation and departs.

Now it is agreed that the closing should occur in two stages. The first stage will be on a Friday morning at the bank financing the purchase and the second stage at the restaurant Saturday night at the close of business. The seller's lawyer asks the broker if he would be willing to attend Friday morning to act as escrow agent to hold the buyer's payment checks and the seller's bill of sale during the interim between stages, and then make the exchange on Saturday night. The broker happily agrees (as his breast swells with pride) and the lawyer drafts an escrow agreement as described in Figure 5.6. The gas line gets installed a week in advance, the deal closes, and everybody is satisfied.

(Incidentally, the business under the new owners is doing well although it suffered a sharp loss of customers immediately upon transfer of ownership. However, the buyers' hard work and the husband's strong sales effort resulted in steadily rising sales and eventual prosperity. The husband's selling shtick is noteworthy: he would cold-call on businesses with sizeable office staffs and hand the receptionist a slip of paper good for one dozen carry-out, lunch-time sandwiches at absolutely no cost and with no conditions other than an hour's notice to allow time to prepare. Since they made very good sandwiches at modest prices, it did not take long to build a customer base.)

Note that the seller's lawyer and the selling wife were entirely cooperative with the intermediary, mostly because he subordinated his ego to theirs by asking questions rather than by offering a solution, even though the solution was painfully obvious. He also allowed the wife to unload her passions and frustrations while never questioning her logic, such unloading having the status of a psychological imperative. Had she required 40 minutes or an hour instead of only 20 minutes, the intermediary would not have moved a muscle, the unloading was so important. The intermediary's success was also due to the change in personal chemistry at the moment of need. Fortunately, the change in this case was for the better. In another time and another place, the intermediary himself might have become part of the problem, not just because he is human too but also because of the unpredictable variances in human chemistry, underscoring the importance of luck in culminating a deal.

The question arises as to whether almost any person with a modicum of sensitivity to human need might have done as well as did the broker. Probably so, but the broker had the advantage of motivation to collect his commission and the additional advantage of being a natural participant in the deal, invoking less suspicion and more trust perhaps than an outside consultant might have invoked.

This example illustrated two other noteworthy points. One is that most negotiations do not end just because basic agreement has been reached on price and terms. There is a raft of details to be worked out in every transaction, which can lead to the sort of dispute described above right up to the time of closing. The other point is that it does not matter that the individuals involved were intelligent and experienced in business (the selling team and its lawyer enjoy good, well-earned reputations) and it does not suffice to say that they should have done better. When emotions grab hold, intelligence and common sense both fly out the window. That is a primary risk in most negotiations and that is why it is so dangerous to allow inexperienced people to take control.

3. Don't Begin Negotiating Until Fact-Finding Has Been Completed to Your Satisfaction. Although this rule has been stated in previous chapters, it bears repeating because it points to one of the more common mistakes made by buyers and sellers alike. With rare exception, it is tactically wrong to ask any question or make any statement during fact-finding which deals with price and terms, other than the seller's listing or offering price. These are points to be negotiated, not facts to be stated, and because single points can not be reasonably negotiated or determined outside the context of the entire offer.

For example, the seller can not answer the question, "Will you finance the purchase?," without knowing the total price, the down payment, the term of the loan and the rate of interest, the collateral, the assets included in the sale, whether bank financing also will be involved, and so on. Looking at the issue in a different way, if the seller is asking, say, $200,000 cash but, known only to himself, might be willing to accept $175,000, and is offered $200,000 with $150,000 down, that seller has to give serious consideration to the offer. Likewise, that same seller would be tactically wrong to declare that he would accept only an all-cash offer for the simple reason that he might be denying the best offer he is liable to get and, given the illiquidity of small businesses, the only good offer he will ever get.

If the same seller asking $200,000 declares during fact finding that he or she will accept only an all-cash offer, the buyer should ignore the statement. If the seller remains resolute, then, perhaps, the buyer should consider looking elsewhere. An exception occurs if a certain need by either buyer or seller is beyond anyone's control. For example, a contractual obligation of the buyer might preclude his or her coming up with most of the cash for another 12 months or longer, or a terminal illness by the seller might make seller financing understandably distasteful, although it would not necessarily rule it out.

4. Don't Begin Negotiating Until You Have Planned Your Strategy. The first step in planning strategy, as set by basic rule number 1, is to decide which goal has the higher priority, getting the best price or closing the deal. The second step is to review the basic rules as one would review a checklist and to decide which of those rules might apply to the offer or counter-offer at hand. Examples of how to plan will follow. Note that one's strategy should be reviewed before making each counter-offer, and should be reviewed again before agreeing to a final settlement.

5. Begin the Negotiation with a Fully Developed Letter of Intent. A letter of intent is simply a letter from one principal to the other declaring his or her intent to purchase or to sell. There are several reasons for preparing a letter of intent:

Preparing the letter of intent forces the writer to think, minimizing mistakes and increasing chances of consummating the purchase and sale.

Placing the offer in writing minimizes misunderstanding by the recipient, thus increasing chances of consummating the purchase and sale.

The letter of intent sets the tone of the negotiation. Generally, the best tone is a combination of cordiality and formality.

The letter of intent is the first shot fired in the negotiation. When well prepared, it can be a preemptive first strike (as in Example 10.1). (A counter-strike would be to ignore the terms of the sender's letter and to write one's own letter.)

Because it is in writing in a serious and quality format, the offer is more credible and the offerer's terms subtly and inoffensively more firm and therefore more difficult to negotiate against.

The letter of intent summarizes the terms, conditions, and warranties of the purchase and sale agreement. Each term, each condition, and each warranty is a bargaining chip in the negotiation. A thoroughly prepared letter forces the other party to spend his or her chips.

The thorough, aggressive, well-prepared letter of intent can only be viewed with favor by a seller who is being asked to finance.

Since the letter of intent outlines the contract, it is added to the loan application package. The quality of its preparation therefore becomes an inducement for the bank's granting the loan.

The letter of intent provides an outline for both the buyer's and seller's attorneys and accountants, reducing their workloads, speeding the process, and lowering their fees.

The prospective buyer of Acme Widget Corporation has prepared the letter of intent shown in Figure 8.1. If the seller were to write the letter of intent, exactly the same format could be used with minor changes to reverse the flow of thought. Figure 8.2 shows such a letter of intent from the seller.

Figure 8.1 Sample Letter of Intent from Buyer

John Q. Buyer

999 Elm Street

St. Louis, Missouri 63000

314-012-1111

May 5, 2001

John Q. Seller, President

Acme Widget Corporation

123 Business Boulevard

St. Louis, Missouri 63000

Dear Mr. Seller:

This letter expresses my intent to purchase the assets of Acme Widget Corporation, buildings and land excluded, for a total price of $168,000. This price is based on payment of $128,000 cash and a promissory note for $40,000 at closing. This offer is also based on an option to buy the real estate for appraised value with cost-of-living adjustment.

I understand that the sale price would include the tangible assets listed below plus the company name, accounts but not accounts receivable, contract rights, good will, telephone number, and licenses:

2	Compumatic widget-makers
1	Widget tester
1 Lot	Miscellaneous shop and warehouse equipment
1 Lot	Retail store equipment including electronic cash register
1 Lot	Office equipment including computer and peripheral equipment
1	Pickup truck

I anticipate also purchasing your materials and supplies inventory, your merchandise inventory, and your work in progress for an additional price to be determined mutually by your accountant and my accountant as of the date of closing.

My offer is based on the following allocation of purchase price:

Equipment	$100,000
Good will	68,000
	$168,000

My purchase would be based on a number of contingencies including, but not limited to, the following:

- Review of the financial data, books, and records.
- Negotiation of a satisfactory lease on the plant, warehouse, and retail store.
- Your agreement to aid in the transfer of ownership by providing one week of full-time training immediately after closing and a follow-on week of training on a half-time basis.
- Review and approval by my attorney.
- Willingness of the employees to remain after the sale.
- The usual other contingencies such as my ability to obtain the proper licenses and permits, financing, insurance, etc.

I would expect the usual seller warranties such as a non-compete clause, truth and accuracy of books and records, no undisclosed liabilities, marketable title to assets, equipment in working order, shareholder approval of sale, corporation in good standing, etc.

I expect the actual purchase to be made by my corporation, still to be formed. The details can be worked out by our attorneys.

I realize that this letter of intent does not and can not cover all the details of the transaction. However, I hope I have described my offer sufficiently so that you can judge the seriousness of my intent and whether you and I should be able to reach agreement.

I will cooperate with you in every way to work towards a speedy but proper agreement and consummation thereof and I look forward to a very long-lasting and cordial relationship with you.

Respectfully,

John Q. Buyer

Figure 8.2 Sample Letter of Intent from Seller

John Q. Seller, President
Acme Widget Corporation
123 Business Boulevard
St. Louis, Missouri 63000
314-009-2222

May 5, 2001

John Q. Buyer
999 Elm Street
St. Louis, Missouri 63000

Dear Mr. Buyer:

This letter expresses my intent to sell to you or to your corporation the assets of Acme Widget Corporation, buildings and land excluded, for a total price of $300,000. The sale would include a lease with an option to buy the real estate for appraised value with cost-of-living adjustment. I welcome your purchase because I believe that you are well qualified to own and operate the company.

The sale price would include the tangible assets listed below plus the company name, accounts but not accounts receivable, contract rights, good will, telephone number, and licenses:

2	Compumatic widget-makers
1	Widget tester
1 Lot	Miscellaneous shop and warehouse equipment
1 Lot	Retail store equipment including electronic cash register
1 Lot	Office equipment including computer and peripheral equipment

1 Pickup truck

I would also sell my materials and supplies inventory, merchandise inventory, and work in progress for an additional price to be determined mutually by your accountant and my accountant as of the date of closing.

My price is based on the following allocation:

Equipment	$120,000
Good will	180,000
	$300,000

For your protection the sale would be based on a number of contingencies including, but not limited to, the following:

- Review of the financial data, books, and records.
- Negotiation of a satisfactory lease on the plant, warehouse, and retail store.
- Review and approval by your attorney.
- The usual other contingencies such as your ability to obtain the proper licenses and permits, financing, insurance, etc.

The only contingency I would need is review and approval by my attorney.

I would be happy to provide a week of training to facilitate the transfer of ownership. Also, I would expect the employees to be more than willing to remain with you although that is something beyond my control.

I would provide the usual seller warranties such as a non-compete clause, truth and accuracy of books and records, no undisclosed liabilities, marketable title to assets, equipment in working order, shareholder approval of sale, corporation in good standing, etc.

I expect the actual purchase would be made by your corporation, still to be formed. The details can be worked out by our attorneys.

I realize that this letter of intent does not and can not cover all the details of the transaction. However, I hope I have described the sale sufficiently so that you can judge the seriousness of my intent to sell to you and whether you and I should be able to reach agreement.

I will cooperate with you in every way to work towards a speedy but proper agreement and consummation thereof and I look forward to a very long-lasting and cordial relationship with you.

Respectfully,

John Q. Seller

Note that the seller has restated the $300,000 offering price but that he carefully neglected to say anything about seller financing (assuming that he did not make a mistake of omission) thus leaving that possibility open for negotiating. Since he seems to be leaving open the question of financing, there is a hint that he would take a lower price if offered all cash. Perhaps he would do both. Note that the seller mentions that the buyer is well qualified to own and operate the company. That is a nice gesture for setting a friendly tone and it is a further hint of the seller's willingness to finance. Viewed more cynically, it may be a subtle way of suggesting that the buyer will do well enough to justify paying the full $300,000. In any case, the idea of using a letter of intent with all of its advantages to start a negotiation should be clear. The sample letters for Acme Widget could serve as models for virtually any industry and any size business.

Since one of the advantages of the letter of intent is to start the negotiation with a preemptive first strike, forcing the other party to spend his or her bargaining chips in a counter-offer, it would be reasonable for the seller to scale back his letter to exclude most or all of the warranties and contingencies protecting the buyer. Such an approach is aggressive but not unethical. It is hardly friendly, however, and is not generally recommended.

Although it is possible to submit an offer via a signed contract as commonly done in residential real estate, generally it is not practical for several reasons. A business purchase and sale agreement can be lengthy and complex and thus too cumbersome to negotiate with. If prepared by a lawyer, it would run up the lawyer's bill and it would slow the process. It might also intimidate either or both of the parties, casting a pall on the affair. Even if a pre-printed contract is used to submit the offer, the details are numerous and distracting, disadvantages by themselves but especially so in the high emotions of the negotiation. It is usually not necessary to have the lawyer's protection during the negotiation because of the contingency of the lawyer's review and approval. Moreover, the letter is not a contract. It is merely a statement of intention to determine whether a buyer and a seller are in general agreement to make a negotiation worth continuing and a contract worth preparing.

6. Set Your Aspiration Levels High. It has been shown experimentally that negotiators with high goals tend to do substantially better than those with modest or unclear goals. Thus, a seller wishing a high price might start by asking a high price and a buyer wishing a low price might start by offering a low price. Although such goal-setting is not exactly encouraged for small business negotiations because of the greater skill required and the danger of losing the deal, it sometimes can work to obtain a better price and terms than otherwise might be negotiated.

A common technique to get around the bluntness, the hardness, and the jarring effect of the outright low offer is to gently probe to get a sense of the seller's willingness to come down. A buyer looking at a $200,000 offering price, for example, might approach the seller with such words as "I like your business a lot but with all my family responsibilities I probably wouldn't be able to offer much more than around $125,000." With the proper tone of voice, facial expression, and body language, such a probe probably would not be perceived as offensive—a little brazen, perhaps, but not offensive—and it might flush out a motivated seller's secret longing to bail out. The seller then might respond with such words as "Look, you're way too low but I'm willing to work with you," a statement suggestive of a fairly wide range for negotiating the price. Thus, the probe will have done its job to encourage a low offer. Note that the offerer's use of "probably" means that he or she is not absolutely refusing a higher price.

For another way to obtain a low price, see Example 10.1.

7. Don't Be Discouraged by a High Asking Price, a Low Offer, or Counter-Offers with Negligible Concessions.
There are several reasons not to be discouraged. With respect to an asking price which seems high, the seller may be doing what's known as allowing room to negotiate, in which case the price eventually will come down. The seller may erroneously believe that the price is fair, which seems to be the case with Acme Widget, but may be willing to come down when shown a better appraisal. In still another case, the seller may have a justifiable price but may purposely withhold some of the revelations necessary for the buyer to properly appraise, pending the seller's comfort level that the buyer is serious, well qualified, and not an agent of the IRS. In one actual case, the price was way too high ($1,100,000) for what showed on the books (earnings of $90,000) but was promised to be resolved when the buyer (who knew intuitively that everything had not come out into the open) told the seller that he was willing to pay the price if the seller could show that the price was justified, to which the seller replied that then they would have to meet in the privacy of his home, in the basement, at midnight, with the shades drawn.

With respect to low offers and/or small concessions, one reason not to be discouraged is that the other party may merely be probing more or less as described in rule number 6 while at the same time strongly motivated to close the deal. In other words, the dichotomy of motives may be exerting itself. Another reason is that making a small concession is a common tactic when vying for the best settlement. It is a part of the game and one must therefore keep on negotiating. Still another reason is that the other party may not even agree with the small offer or small concession or making a probe but may be under pressure from a partner, a spouse, or an advisor to do as he or she is told. Another reason still is that the other party may simply be an incompetent negotiator muddling through the process.

Part of the trick to negotiating effectively is to determine if and when the other party is ready to make a substantial concession or to back away from his or her demands. In that respect, negotiating can be like a game of chicken where two drivers agree to drive at high speed towards a head-on collision. The chicken is the first one to swerve. A sensitivity to tone of language, tone of voice, facial expression, body language, and so forth can help determine when or when not to yield to the other party's terms, as illustrated below in Examples 8.4 and 8.5. A firm belief in the fairness and the rightness of one's own price and terms or in one's own tactics may also help to deal with a resistant party. In any case, no one ever said that negotiating is for the faint of heart.

Example 8.4 A failed restaurant has closed operations and is listed for sale, to include the equipment and a freestanding building. The prospective buyer will buy some of the equipment, and, to support a new concept, will buy additional equipment from other sources and also do some interior remodeling. The buyer would like to buy the building but no bank will finance the purchase mainly because the concept has not been proven at that location but also because the buyer is young and has not owned before. In addition, the down payment would leave him with no working capital. He is willing to lease, however, if given an option to buy.

The broker writes a tentative agreement outlining all the important terms, including the rent, with no sweeteners. The agreement is verbally and provisionally accepted pending the buyer's review with his financial backer and confidant. After a day or two, the buyer and broker meet, facing each other across a conference table and maintaining good eye contact. The buyer expresses general satisfaction with the agreement, then adds that he understands that lease-option agreements usually allow part of the rent to convert into equity if the option to buy is exercised. Just as the buyer reaches the part about converting rent to equity, his voice inflects and he cracks a wan and quizzical smile, revealing his aversion to negotiating, if not his weakness of resolve. He quickly recovers but it is too late. The clues were too obvious for the broker to miss and the buyer will pay for his mistake.

Example 8.5 A man who had bought a business a year earlier with seller financing learns the hard way that he had botched the appraisal and paid much too high a price (around $300,000). There is virtually no chance that the cash flow will ever become large enough to service the debt. He is not even making a living wage. He is therefore attempting to reopen the negotiation with the seller. His basic argument, his inability to pay the debt, is fortified by the strong possibility that if the seller refuses to renegotiate, the buyer will be forced into bankruptcy. So far, the seller is pitiless and adamant and is making no concession. However, the seller apparently is aware of the buyer's possible bankruptcy, in which case the seller would reap nothing more than a failed and near-worthless business, which the seller would be unable to restore due to his being unqualified to manage (he had inherited the business). He therefore decides to check the legal ramifications and, in apparent continuation of his tough bargaining stance, he hires one of the two largest law firms in the area. Such large law firms typically have one or more clients in the Fortune 100 and offices in other cities, with top-quality lawyers and can be intimidating even though the associates, as contrasted to the partners, are sometimes of no more than average caliber.

The lawyer assigned to the case, an associate in the firm, arranges a meeting with the buyer to discuss the situation. The buyer hires a consultant to prepare an appraisal, plan the negotiation, and attend the meeting. The law firm's office is attractively decorated with thick carpeting and other trappings of prestige, power, and success, and the meeting takes place in a conference room with very attractive furniture. The lawyer, though pleasant and cordial, continues the tough stand taken by the seller but makes one mistake: instead of stating with conviction that this is the way things should be due to the legal and binding contract, he uses the words "we feel that" to introduce his argument that the buyer should pay the original, agreed price and he does so in a compliant tone of voice. Such words and tone are as unconvincing as the argument which follows, and the lawyer has already placed himself and his client at a disadvantage.

In Example 8.5, the obvious mistake was the combination of weak words and compliant tone of voice. A much bigger mistake, however, was the decision to attempt to negotiate payments which the seller, because of the buyer's near insolvency, had little chance of ever collecting and which therefore was a waste of time and legal expense. What should have been done is to acknowledge that the seller was as responsible for the botched appraisal as was the buyer and that the two parties should share the damage. Another probable mistake was the failure to plan the negotiation, as suggested in basic rule 2. Good planning includes considering the alternatives, the alternative in this case being to negotiate the damage which would have given the seller a reasonable chance of collecting something. (The final outcome of the negotiation is not known although it is known that the company was thrown into bankruptcy. It is also not known whether the lawyer had been given a choice to negotiate the damage or, in contrast, had been instructed by his client to enforce the original agreement.)

8. Manage Concessions Properly. The main point of this basic rule is simply to use concessions to one's best advantage. For example, letting one's adversary make the first concession has at least two advantages. One is that getting that first concession puts one ahead in the game of concessions for concessions.

The other is that winning the first concession suggests dominance of one party over the other, puts one's adversary on the defensive, inflicting damage to his or her resolve. In sly contrast, voluntarily making a concession may inflict damage of another kind but with similar effect, the kind that softens an adversary's aggressiveness or induces a lowered guard.

Making concessions reluctantly or grudgingly or in small bits diminishes the other party's patience with the hoped-for effect of that party's eventually succumbing to the accumulated damage and conceding to unwanted compromise. A constant danger is that grudging concessions may have the unintended effect of increasing the other party's resolve.

Knowing how and when to make concessions or to extract them is an art requiring uncommon skill. That is why many if not most buyers and sellers of small businesses (with little or no training or experience) should not attempt to play these games. Even skilled negotiators make mistakes in judgment although, to be sure, their mistakes are relatively few. The best tactic in most cases is to judge whether the concession in question is fair and reasonable and whether the party making the concession can live with that concession without undue cost. This judgment should be made even for concessions which are sought from the other party to avoid failing to reach agreement.

In cases where a concession is judged to be too great in and of itself, getting a concession for a concession may tip the balance of fairness to both parties' advantage. Sometimes a concession can be cut in half and then offered in exchange for half a concession; such dealing being known as compromise. In some cases concessions no one had thought of can be invented to mutual advantage. Example 8.6 illustrates the point.

> **Example 8.6** (This example elaborates on Example 4.1.) A profitable business with good potential growth is offered for sale at $800,000. The potential growth is highly probable, in fact, virtually assured if the buyer is willing to do the modest initial effort of opening a new sales outlet. The $800,000 price was the seller's intuitive estimate, eroded by a professional appraisal of $736,000. The appraisal, however, has been incompetently prepared, a more

reasonable value being in the range of $550,000 to $600,000, the limits depending on whether or not the potential growth should be paid for by a buyer. A prospective buyer makes a diligent and detailed study of the facts, makes an appraisal based on the present earnings, and offers $550,000. The seller, having been shown the inadequacies of the professional appraisal, eventually makes concessions to arrive at $650,000 but will go no lower. The buyer understands the seller's view but feels that doing the work should entitle her to the profits. More importantly, she may decide not to open the new outlet in which case she would not want to pay for it. Nor does she want to pay for something which is still to be proven. Two and a half weeks pass with neither party relenting. To break the impasse, the intermediary suggests a two-tiered price consisting of a firm price of $550,000 plus an additional but contingent price based on a percentage of sales through the new outlet. A cap of $60,000 is set on the contingent price and a time limit for paying royalties of six years. The buyer and seller agree, albeit with some reluctance, and the deal eventually closes.

(Several months after closing, the buyer did open the new outlet. The sales were about 20% less than expected but still very profitable since the overhead of the business was already paid for by the main outlet. One minor disappointment was that the new outlet took some sales away from the main outlet. Overall, the result was still judged a good success. An explanation of the incompetent appraisal is offered in Example 11.4.)

Note that royalties should almost always be based on revenues, not earnings. Earnings are nebulous and subjective since they are so influenced by the owner's salary and perquisites and since they go back into hiding as soon as the sale is completed. Note also that the revenues of the new outlet were easy to identify because they were physically segregated, thus making the compromise feasible.

The key feature of this compromise settlement was that the seller was assured of some payment if the new outlet were opened while the buyer could avoid most of the risk of paying for something that she would never get if the outlet were not opened.

The best part of the above story is that both the buyer and the seller were motivated and they both felt relieved and so happy at having reached agreement. Interestingly, on the day following their having reached agreement, the relief and happiness seemed to recede to a plateau, as though for suspended credulity, until the day when all the papers had been signed, payment had been made, and the entire deal finally closed. Then they both felt like celebrating, the seller especially since the sale had weighed so heavily on his mind.

9. Negotiate in Good Faith. An offer or concession may be rescinded but possibly at the cost of one's integrity with the accompanying losses of good will, credibility, and the deal itself. The basic effect of a rescinded offer or concession is to throw doubt upon the honesty and the integrity of the person who rescinds. In the case of the buyer, a rescinded concession also throws doubt upon his or her qualifications for ownership and for seller financing. For these reasons, concessions should be studied before being made and, once made, should rarely be taken back.

From a legal point of view, an agreement is a contract, whether written or verbal. A concession is an agreement but it is contingent on reaching settlement of the whole negotiation. Even then, in most cases, it is not yet legally binding because most negotiated settlements are contingent on the occurrence of other matters such as review and approval of each party's lawyer and accountant. In other words, each party usually has an easy, legal way to back out of the negotiated agreement, in part or in whole. Legality notwithstanding, rescinded concessions are almost always viewed negatively by the other party, and rightly so.

The question arises as to how to handle a situation where one party feels a necessity to back away from what has been agreed. Example 8.7 is a case in point and further illustrates both the level of emotions when negotiating and the inadvisable use of lawyers and accountants to serve in areas where they have no training or experience.

Example 8.7 A small manufacturing company is listed for sale at a price of $360,000. A year earlier the seller had wanted $600,000 but the broker had refused to list because of excessive price. What had brought the seller's price down was burnout and the accompanying motivation to retire. At $360,000, the price was still high but within the range of reason. A prospective buyer does his fact-finding, then meets with the broker to make an offer of $260,000 via a letter of intent. The broker, who expects the seller to counter-offer at or near his asking price, mails the offer to the seller for his review, then informs him by telephone of the basic terms. Two days later the seller calls to inform the broker that he has received the letter, that he wants to review it with his accountant, and that he would like to meet with the buyer and the broker in his accountant's office on Friday at 9:00 AM. The seller will have his reply ready at that time and he expresses his sincere appreciation for the offer.

On Friday morning the buyer, seller, broker, and accountant meet promptly at 9:00. For the first 15 minutes, the seller tells about the personal side of his business including when he got his first job, his first promotion, when he started his company, how he has fared during all those years, and so on, then caps his story by saying that now he is ready to close his career. At this point, the seller stops talking. There is a silence of 15 seconds or so. He removes his glasses, reaches for his handkerchief, hunches over to bury his face in his hands, and sits for another 30 seconds. Finally, he wipes his face with his handkerchief and blows his nose. In the interim, the others have remained motionless and quiet as though uninvolved. The intimacy is palpable.

Now the seller resumes speaking and says that he has decided to accept the offer. The broker is taken by surprise at the acceptance with no counter, and asks the seller if he has allowed for the broker's commission. The seller assures the broker that he has. The buyer is delighted with the acceptance and thanks the seller for his consideration and effort. The seller, now recovered, begins describing what has to be done to prepare the buyer for takeover. For the next two and a half hours, they converse about all that has to be done. Rapport has been established. When it is almost noon, the principals agree that they have no more questions at present, everybody shakes hands, and the buyer exits. As soon as the buyer is out the door, the seller turns to the broker and states that he cannot live with the agreement. The broker is astonished and asks the seller what he is saying. The seller repeats that he cannot live with the agreed price because, after taxes, he will not have enough to live on, a statement which is questionable because the business has been profitable for 18 years, the real estate is not included in the sale and the seller will draw rent on it, his home is paid for, and his children are raised and off on careers of their own. But the seller repeats that he can not live with the settlement and that the buyer will have to come up with more money. Through the morning, the accountant has said little and he says nothing now about the broken agreement. The seller instructs the broker to inform the buyer that he will have to raise his offer. The broker, normally of level head, is beside himself. He exits and is useless for the rest of the day.

That night, the broker can not sleep for want of a solution to the problem. There is no solution except to call the buyer and tell the truth, a loathsome task which the broker performs the following morning. The buyer is incredulous and asks what is going on. The broker can offer no explanation other than that the seller was overcome with emotion and just did not know what he was doing. But the accountant was there for the entire meeting; the accountant was there, heard everything that was agreed to for two and a half hours and never said a word, says the buyer. That is true, says the broker, but he has no explanation for the accountant's silence. In fact, under the circumstances, he admits, the accountant's silence constituted an approval of the seller's acceptance, tax problems or no. The buyer, to his credit, is polite and controlled despite being very upset at the news. Nevertheless, he tells the broker that as far as he is concerned, there will be no further offer, as he does not know whom to trust, a remark which challenges the broker's integrity as well as the seller's. The broker brings the conversation to a close by saying that he will get back to the seller and see what, if anything, can be done to change his mind. In the meantime, the buyer might give the whole matter additional thought.

The following Monday, the broker calls the seller with the news that the deal is dead. The seller says that he can live with a price of $280,000 if the broker will lower his commission by six thousand dollars. The broker neither agrees nor disagrees but says that everybody needs time to collect their thoughts. Two or three days go by and the broker calls the buyer with the seller's new price. The buyer says that in his mind the deal is still dead because he does not like the way that this affair is being conducted. The broker agrees with him and adds that he is being hurt too by the lowered commission, something he would not normally agree to but might in this case because of the ruination which has occurred. The broker adds that the seller's emotional state is the apparent cause for the mayhem, the accountant's devastating silence notwithstanding. The questions for the buyer to answer now are whether the business is worth $280,000 and if there is anything else that the buyer can get at that price. The broker continues by saying that if the buyer does get back into the deal, one thing is for sure: do not hire that accountant. Nothing more is said. The buyer still does not know whom to believe or trust.

Two weeks go by with no concession by either side. No one is telephoning anyone. Then one day the buyer calls the broker to agree to the higher price, the broker agrees to the lower commission, the buyer and the broker (who have become emotional allies of a sort even though the broker works for the seller) agree with each other that this is a real mess, and the deal eventually closes.

(The buyer's first month in business is struck by the loss of a major customer which itself, in turn, had been struck by a similar loss. The company's product line encounters some disfavor and the buyer suffers a sharp loss his first year in business. He meets the challenge by altering the product line, by searching for new customers, and working seven days a week. His second year breaks even and he is profitable from then on. Eventually he lands a major contract which will allow him to expand both sales and profits, to add state-of-the-art equipment, and to enter the ranks of the prosperous.)

Numerous comments could be made about this case while the performances of all the participants could be variously criticized. Perhaps the broker, for example, should have determined prior to the Friday meeting that the seller had a plan. The broker might also have argued against the seller's raise to $280,000. Perhaps the buyer should have countered, say, at $270,000. And the broker may have earned contempt from his fellow brokers for accepting a lower commission. Such critiques are like those of the armchair quarterback who describes with 20-20 hindsight what should have been done in Saturday's game. The final result was that the deal closed despite its unsavoriness, and both buyer and seller were winners. It is worthwhile to note what was done correctly to repair the damage. The seller, once realizing that he had temporarily lost his mind and accepted an offer that should have been countered, then told the broker that he wanted to counter. The broker correctly assessed the cause of the seller's blunder and so described it to the buyer. He also advised the buyer to consider his alternatives. The buyer's alternative to reopening the negotiation was to start looking elsewhere for the right business to buy, possibly at the loss of a few years' time and the worse possibility of never succeeding. The buyer, therefore, made the correct decision. And this advice: The accountant was a CPA, a partner in a small firm, a director for a bank, and a high-profile auditor for a high-profile client. He thus stood tall in the community. The lesson, often stated in this book and probably not often enough, is that no matter what their qualifications in other fields and no matter what their station in the community, individuals hired to do a job for which they have no training are dangerous.

10. Stress Your Power. One aim of stressing one's power is to establish an intimidating dominance so as to weaken the adversary's resolve. Another is to project the impression that one does not need to close the deal, that one's power will produce other opportunities. For example, a buyer who already owns a business has less motivation to make concessions; he is already at the top of Maslow's Hierarchy. He also presumably (in the seller's mind) has probable knowledge of other businesses for sale competing for his purchase.

A seller's power is enhanced by being in good health and having no need for a quick sale, a condition which results from entering the market a few years before actually wanting to retire, as recommended in Chapter 4. If the business for sale is comparatively less illiquid than businesses in general or especially than those in the same industry, that point is worth conveying because it suggests that the seller has more than one buyer to choose from. A seller who is an absentee owner has inherent power because his or her ability to manage is less affected by problems of health or aging or even relocating, thus reducing the need or urgency to sell.

Power is usually best exploited by letting the source of the power be known quietly, perhaps merely by hinting. Then the adversary is left to evaluate the degree of power and possibly to exaggerate it. In contrast, flaunting one's power may seem crude and offensive rather than intimidating. It may provoke one's adversary to a hardened resolve or to dealing elsewhere.

11. Exploit Your Adversary's Weakness. This rule is the corollary to rule 10 and the inverse of its logic. If power is dominant, weakness is subordinate. If one is weak, one is pushed to compromise the price and to close the deal.

A buyer who has never owned a business is generally more motivated to make concessions than one who has. The motivation resulting from inexperience is a weakness difficult to hide. That makes it easy for a seller to exploit. The buyer's defense is to learn as much as he can about the seller's business and the local economy. Then the buyer can negotiate intelligently while looking for a weakness in the seller.

A seller is weakened by poor health or insufficient working capital. Obviously, the seller in failing health should conceal or minimize his or her condition unless prolonged training or seller consultation would be relied on by the buyer, in which case concealing would be dishonest. If the seller's

Illustration 8.1

weakness is known to the buyer, the seller may shore his position by stating that he or she will not let the business be stolen, that if no reasonable offer is received, the business will be turned over to an auction house. Such statement will leave the buyer to guess whether the seller is bluffing and to guess at the meaning of "reasonable."

When weakness is discovered in one's adversary, especially in a seller badly hurt by something beyond his or her control, the general rule is to express understanding and compassion, even if not deeply felt, and state one's inability due to economic circumstances or family responsibilities to settle at a better price. If one feels guilty for grabbing a bargain from a weak seller, one should remember that one's price is still the best offer on the market and that the seller would be worse off without it.

12. Use Deadlines to Your Advantage. Using a deadline to one's advantage is a special case of exploiting strength or weakness. If one party has a deadline by which time a decision will have to have been made, the other party will use dilatory tactics such as conducting unnecessary procedures, dwelling on minutia, and bowing to other priorities, until his or her adversary mentally collapses and makes a substantial compromise in order to beat the deadline. Deadlines so imminent as to be oppressive are usually not present in purchase and sale transactions but they do occur from time to time, especially to sellers. One example is the seller in the throes of burnout who feels a sense of desperation and who may act irrationally to beat a deadline of his own making to get out of the business. Another example is the seller short of working capital who may have a deadline set by a creditor threatening to foreclose.

A deadline may be indefinite but still forceful. In Example 8.3, the buyer had no income and was under pressure to close the purchase as quickly as possible.

A deadline of special immanence occurs when one travels to another city to negotiate. The visiting party is pressed by the desire to return home as soon as possible to get on with the normal activities of life. The pressure is increased, if traveling by commercial transportation, to make the last departure of the day. The idea is for the party at home to stall so the visiting party will be self-pressured to make concessions that he or she would not otherwise make, just to get the thing over with. If the visiting party senses that such a tactic is being used, it may be countered by saying politely that he or she is running out of time and must move a little faster if the deal is to be put together. If that does not work, the visiting party may quietly pre-empt the other party by starting to pack up and leave well ahead of the scheduled departure, thus negating the other party's tactic and forcing that party either to cooperate or to stop negotiating.

One may strengthen one's position by stating that one has no schedule to meet and plenty of time to find the right deal.

13. Act Aloof. To act aloof is to pretend that one is under no pressure to make large concessions or, for that matter, to make any concessions in order to reach agreement. It is to pretend that one has no dichotomy of motives, that as much as one would like to reach agreement, one can turn away to better things if the deal at hand does not satisfy. It is pressure psychology, pure and simple. When done well, it is inoffensive and subtle. When not done well, acting aloof may be taken as offensive, with the result of the adversary hardening his or her resolve. Acting aloof, therefore, is a good tactic but one best avoided when one is not quite sure how to do it.

14. Act Businesslike. To act businesslike is to maintain a demeanor projecting one's intelligence, maturity, and seriousness of purpose. This creates the impression that one's adversary need not bother using tactics, that they will be seen through easily. Better still, when well done, the businesslike demeanor can be used as a cover for one's own tactics. Again, careful judgment as to one's ability to apply these tactics is strongly advised, as is the adversary's ability to understand what's being done and reacting adversely.

15. Talk Over Each Offer and Each Counter-Offer with a Confidant Before Making Commitments. This rule is one of the more valuable of the basic rules because of the several benefits to be derived and their magnitude.

Discussing with a confidant forces one to think and to analyze. It therefore introduces ideas and tactics which might otherwise be lost and it does wonders to minimize mistakes both in number and in degree.

Using a confidant brings another person into the transaction with insights and creativeness which might otherwise not be discovered. As above, it introduces ideas and tactics which might otherwise be lost and it does wonders to minimize mistakes.

If one establishes at the beginning of the negotiation the necessity of always checking with one's confidant before agreeing to anything, it prevents being trapped in a meeting under pressure to make a concession. A confidant is most useful in the case where the principal parties are in the same room trying to hammer out an agreement; that is when mistakes are most likely to be made. The confidant, of course, should not be in the same room or necessarily in the same building, the idea being that the confidant's remoteness provides the escape so vital to careful negotiating. It does not matter if the confidant is the front person sending and receiving offers and counter-offers and the confidant's principal is behind the scenes. The benefits remain the same. A confidant is also useful when the principal parties are apart and their offers and counter-offers are carried by an intermediary. The opportunity for a mistake is not so great, but all the other benefits apply.

In the case where the seller has a broker working in the seller's best interest, the broker may be the seller's confidant, in which case the buyer is at a disadvantage unless he or she also has a confidant.

The confidant can help when dilatory tactics are in order. The confidant's remoteness is a setup for stalling while preserving one's innocence.

The confidant may be used as a foil. For example, if one wishes to project himself or herself as a giving person while actually being stingy with concessions, one may blame the confidant for the stinginess. Such use tends to heighten the adversary's tension and wear the adversary down in the war of attrition. These roles may be reversed, in which case the confidant is the giving person and the principal is stingy, the deciding factors being what the circumstances might dictate and who feels most comfortable in what role. One advantage to the role reversal is that the giving confidant can also be the intermediary, offering friendliness to the adversary and understanding of the adversary's circumstances while hoping to gain the adversary's confidence and learning his or her position. This is sneaky dealing; unethical if used on unwary consumers and buyers of residential real estate but not unethical when negotiating with business people who presumably are using tactics of their own. Note that the use of a foil has been said to occur in some automobile showrooms. The salesperson (the good person) tells the buyer that the buyer's need for a car and the buyer's willingness to deal are appreciated and that the salesperson therefore will give the buyer a special low price which, if acceptable to the buyer, the salesperson will try to get approved by his or her boss (the bad person) but which approval can't be promised. Thus the buyer is enticed into accepting a special low price which is neither low nor special.

Discussing everything with a confidant and letting one's adversary know that the confidant is active suggests an extra strength for the adversary to deal with. It is the opposite of projecting weakness. The fact of two minds versus the adversary adds a complexity to the adversary's attempt to understand what is happening and further weakens the adversary's resolve.

Using a confidant is especially rewarding for anyone with an aversion to negotiating. The confidant builds confidence while removing part of the distaste. It is an escape from troubled loneliness with a little help from a friend.

Discussing with a confidant provides emotional release, always valuable but especially when emotions tend to be excessive, as they normally are in a negotiation. The emotional release has a double benefit. It removes part of the blockage to logical thinking and it simply makes one feel better.

Finally, there is a joy in sharing one's thoughts with a fellow human being, especially with someone who can be trusted and who is a pleasure to be with. The upbeat feelings stemming from such joy are a positive force in thinking and acting clearly and in maintaining an image of strength.

The value and added power from using a confidant may vary from case to case but the potential value is always as large as the stakes. The stakes are not only the business itself and the price being paid but also the profound effects on the lives of the principals. The confidant can be almost anyone that the negotiator feels comfortable with, whether business colleague, family member, or friend. Some business knowledge is helpful but just as important is the psychological verity that opposites attract (just like polar magnets) offering unique qualities to the negotiating team. Such trustable, psychological opposites are often found by turning to one's mate, as illustrated in Example 8.8.

Example 8.8 A contracting firm is listed for sale at a price of $525,000. The president and majority stockholder is a dignified-looking man who has an exceptionally pleasing manner and who is self-assured in social situations as evidenced by his occasional chairmanship of large industry gatherings. The broker finds a qualified buyer who has several fact-finding meetings with the president and then makes an offer of $290,000. The financial structure of the firm is somewhat muddled with several outstanding notes; the offer correctly reflects the complexity even though it is basically simple and straightforward. The broker carries the offer to the president who invites him into his office. The broker hands the offer to the president, states the $290,000 price, briefly explains the terms, and suggests that the seemingly low offer is merely a starting point and that the buyer is looking for a counter-offer. The president does not respond. Instead, his face elongates, his head tilts down, and he appears unable to comprehend what is happening or what to do next. The broker, sensing the man's apparent aversion to negotiating, quickly offers a suggestion as to how to counter-offer but to no avail. The man simply is unable to handle the situation. A minute or so passes. Then, by chance, the office manager, who also happens to be the president's wife, walks into the room to retrieve a document from a file cabinet. A friendly person, she asks how things are going. The broker seizes the opportunity and briefly explains the offer to the wife, whereupon, with no hesitation and surprising adroitness, she outlines a counter-offer which is entirely reasonable and which takes into account the several outstanding notes. The president seems relieved, if not pleased. He expresses his satisfaction with the result and the deal is on.

In this example, the confidant was discovered by accident but worked to everyone's advantage. That accident, illustrates another of the many ways that luck can either help or hinder purchase-and-sale transactions.

16. Be Flexible: Adjust Your Tactics and Your Priorities to the Situation. A frequent problem for buyers and sellers alike is that they enter the negotiation with preconceived notions about what they must have or what they must do and then are unable to bend to the occasion. Examples are the seller who insists on selling the real estate along with the business so as to be completely free of the thing; the seller who insists on not selling the real estate so as to have incoming rent or to defer capital gains tax; the seller who insists on doing no financing whatsoever even if a bank providing most of the financing insists on greater commitment by the principals; the buyer who insists on seller financing to gain assurance of the seller's belief in the business (an occasional myth held by buyers and their incompetent advisors) or to get a lower rate of interest (also recommended by incompetent advisors); and so on. Buyers and sellers must realize that putting a deal together which completely satisfies both parties is usually impossible; that preconceived priorities are often more emotional than reasonable, and often inadvisable; that the general illiquidity of small businesses dictates that concessions have to be made if deals are to be closed; and that getting on with one's life is probably more important than most of these notions. The idea therefore is to be flexible and to do what is necessary within reason in order to make a deal. Example 8.9 illustrates the point and, once more, how seeking advice from someone with no special training is dangerous.

> **Example 8.9** This example is a continuation of Example 8.4 involving the failed restaurant on which an offer was being made to buy some of the equipment and to lease the building with an option to buy. The broker and the buyer agree on an offer to present to the seller, an elderly widow who, due to infirmity of age coupled with lack of any business ability, has no interest in the restaurant other than to get rid of it for the best possible price. This is the situation:
> - Building vacant for five years.
> - Listed for sale for the last four years.
> - In a changing neighborhood with declining values.

- Uninsurable except at exorbitant rates because it is vacant and because of the neighborhood.
- Has been hit by vandalism and theft. Thieves have ripped out both central air conditioners plus other items such as the electric company's meters, wiring, and conduits.
- Is deteriorating because of roof leaks and a stray animal or two having made it their home.
- Has had no reasonable offers so far.
- Is nothing less than a headache to the widow who has to pay for maintenance and property tax; to the police who view it as a nuisance requiring their time and attention each time there is a vandalism or a theft; and to the broker whom the police always call when there is a problem because his telephone number is on the real estate sign.

The broker would just as soon drop the listing as renew it each year but has continued because of the widow's plight, because of his sense of serving the community, because he has found that other brokers don't want such listings, and because sometimes patience rewards in due time.

The offer is presented to the widow who finds it acceptable except that she refuses to lease the building. Years earlier, she had leased a condominium to tenants who had inflicted damage beyond the amount of the security deposit and she is not willing to repeat what she considers to have been a mistake. The broker explains that such risks are part of doing business and that things tend to even out in the long run. The trick, he explains, is to minimize the risk by choosing tenants who seem responsible. The buyer-tenant in this case, though young, is well qualified, having been employed in the restaurant business for eight years and having worked his way up to managing a local fast food, franchise restaurant. The franchisor, in fact, found this location and will offer such usual franchisor support as the proper training, advertising, and follow-on effort. The deal has the following advantages for the widow:

- It will bring her immediate cash since paying for the roof repair and the new air conditioners will be more than offset by the sale of restaurant equipment.
- It will bring immediate rental income.
- The buyer-tenant will pay for the remodeling and even for repairs to the interior caused by the roof leaks.
- The tenant asks only for a one-year lease because at the end of the year, the business will have established a cash flow necessary to obtain bank financing to purchase the building.
- The buyer has agreed to pay appraised value for the building which is the best price anyone could hope for.
- Since the building will be occupied, the insurance will be affordable and the buyer will pay for that too, protecting the widow's asset.
- Since the buyer has the franchisor's backing, since he will be spending about $60,000 for equipment and remodeling, and since he is well qualified to own and operate the business, his commitment is obvious. Success is likely and therefore well worth taking a chance on, especially since no other offers are in sight.
- The only disadvantage of the deal is that the building will be off the market for one year, a small consequence considering that this is the first offer in four years.

After hearing the broker's presentation of the advantages and being given an outline of these advantages in writing, she is softening her position and consults with her lawyer. The lawyer gives her an absolute no and she turns the deal down. The broker asks why the widow prefers the advice of the lawyer to that of the broker and she replies that he is a prestigious lawyer and on the board of directors of a bank. The broker calls the lawyer, finds him to be monosyllabic and frigid, but coaxes him to give reasons and hears the following: The client wants to sell and it is the broker's job to honor the client's wishes. But the buyer of the business cannot get bank financing without establishing a cash flow at that location, says the broker. He then asks if the lawyer's bank would be willing to finance. The lawyer's reply: "Not without collateral." The widow refuses to reconsider and the buyer-tenant is lost. Three months later, the listing expires. The broker refuses to renew even though the widow implores him to. A year and a half later, the broker drives by the building to find it still unoccupied, still in poor repair, still deteriorating (a small part of the roof has fallen), and with no real estate sign on the premises. A year after that, the broker finds the building all boarded up, the hole in the roof is larger, and still no real estate sign on the premises. Eventually the building is razed, but no explanation for the razing is available.

17. Never Make a Personal Attack. Absolutely Never. A personal attack is any statement or action which denies a person's integrity, destroys his or her dignity, is hurtful either physically or mentally, or is unkind. Disparaging adjectives or name-calling, especially if accompanied by cursing, is forbidden by rules of etiquette and common decency as well as by common sense. So is hanging up the telephone to convey displeasure (as did the seller's lawyer in Example 8.3) or speaking coldly and in monosyllables (as did the lawyer in Example 8.9).

There are several problems with personal attacks. Good will and its benefits—mutual trust, constructiveness, compromise, pleasantness, and so on—are destroyed. In their place remain resentment and disgust. If the person who is the object of the attack is less than patient and understanding, escalation may ensue and, much worse, the deal may be killed, especially if it is on the brink. If the deal is killed, it will be hard to revive. If it is not killed or if it is revived, suspicion will linger and the fun will be gone. Furthermore, the making of a personal attack is devoid of any redeeming value whatsoever (except, of course, for the immense satisfaction of strangling the lawyer in 8.9).

If the parties to the negotiation are conversing and one begins to feel anger and if there is any question of keeping that anger under control, that party should excuse himself or herself immediately and retire until emotional stability has returned (as did the seller in Example 10.1). Saying that one has to take a walk or go to the bathroom is all that is necessary to escape, and any curtness which may result is far less a problem than having made an attack. If an attack should ever be made, the deal might be repaired by admitting guilt and apologizing profusely—probably best in writing followed by a telephone call—but only after both parties have had time to return to their senses. The one making the apology should be prepared to be attacked in return and should let that retribution run its course even though such counterattack is as inexcusable as the original.

Another solution to rising anger before an attack has been made or to reviving the deal after an attack is to employ an intermediary, especially one capable of sensing the damage and the need for repair. The intermediary, or a confidant, can also be used to vent one's anger on, preserving equilibrium in the deal. In this respect, business brokers can be extremely useful or even critical to the success of the deal. Intermediaries keep the principals apart at a time when emotions are at their peak, precluding such potentially deal-breaking incidents as untoward glances and uttered expletives. Intermediaries provide emotional release because the principals will speak their minds—foul language, foul thoughts, and all—to intermediaries with stark directness. Intermediaries, in other words, bear the brunt of the abuse but do so easily because they are not the objects of it. Brokers, because of their experience as intermediaries as well as their third-party status, provide a service which can be very valuable and sometimes even necessary to close the deal.

18. Make Two Appraisals or Two Sets of Cash-Flow Projections. One appraisal is

for persuading the other party and the other is for determining in private the limit of one's bidding. The logic for this tactic is obvious as is the implementation and needs no elaboration. This tactic is perfectly ethical.

19. Keep Notes Delineating Each Term of Every Offer. Most counter- and counter-counter-offers can be made verbally because they involve no more than the price and one or two terms of the agreement. At first, one might simply mark up the letter of intent after each counter-offer but after one or two rounds of negotiating, it becomes easier and less mistake-prone to keep a log of each proposed change along with the date and the time. The purpose of keeping written notes is to avoid losing track and making mistakes. It may also become important in case of litigation. If the negotiation is adversarial in tone, it is advisable to keep notes as to the underlying reasoning, the confidants or other parties contributing to the positions taken by the principals, and any other information which could be useful in court.

20. Emotions Are Sky High During Negotiations; Keep Yours Under Control. The advice for dealing with rising emotions is similar to that for rising anger. If one feels weighed down by heavy emotions, one should stop negotiating and take a break, even for several days if necessary. One may also talk things out with one's confidant, go to the movies, get lost in another city, do anything one feels like doing except continuing to negotiate. One should stay removed until one feels that the problem has subsided. If working under a deadline or under pressure from the other party makes a long break impractical, then, at the very minimum, one should confide in someone whose competency and trust are reasonably assured.

One should also forgive the other party's excesses. Forgiveness can make or break a deal.

21. This Above All: If You Don't Understand Negotiating, Get Help from Someone Who Does. In case the reader has not yet noticed from all of the examples in this book, a disturbingly common mistake is to enlist lawyers and accountants to help appraise the business and to negotiate the price. A probable better solution is to find someone who has some semblance of the right qualifications and to give that person the assignment, even if that person is a stranger. In the St. Louis *Yellow Pages*, there are no listings under the category of "Negotiation Services" but there are under "Mediation Services" and "Arbitration Services." Choosing someone from those categories would at least get help from someone who is more oriented to weighing alternatives and resolving conflicts than to defeating one's adversary. A mediator or arbitrator could also probably handle one's dichotomy of motives. In addition, a mediator or arbitrator would probably know enough to subdue his or her own ego, a trait which often is critical in reaching a settlement and for which lawyers have won few accolades. A mediator usually is preferable to an arbitrator because the mediator helps the parties arrive at a compromise they both decide on and feel committed to, while the arbitrator hands down a decision after hearing the arguments. An alternative would be to hire a business broker for the broker's experience in purchase-and-sale negotiations.

The best time to get help is when help is not needed, before the negotiation begins, for example. Then the help can be sought calmly and deliberately, minimizing the possibility of making a mistake in choosing that help. The help selected can be asked to be available, then paid by the hour when actually used, as one would pay a lawyer or an accountant.

The question arises as to why mediators, arbitrators, or other parties are not usually brought in from the outside to manage a negotiation for one of the parties. One reason is that buyers and sellers probably do not realize that such alternatives exist. Another reason is that calling on a stranger for help is emotionally blocked by fear of the unknown or sometimes by the desire for privacy. Another reason still is not wanting to pay the cost.

To deal with the cost, the buyer and seller could mutually hire a mediator with instructions to be neutral and to bill each for half the cost.

Buyers and sellers should realize that if they need negotiating help and don't buy it, they pay for it without getting it.* In some cases they pay double, or triple, or more. Recalling the many examples in this book showing the results of all sorts of mishandled deals, one should feel a sense of urgency either to understand what's going on or to get help. If one does not feel that urgency, one is a very possible candidate for trouble.

*A paraphrase (if memory serves) from Henry Ford II who said that if a man needs a new machine and doesn't buy it, he pays for it without getting it.

PART 3:
NEGOTIATING THE ACME WIDGET CORPORATION PRICE AND TERMS

Now that the prospective buyer has completed his appraisal and his cash-flow projections, he feels ready to begin negotiating the price and terms. To prepare for the negotiation, he reviews all of his appraisal work and jots down some of the more important data for easy reference:

Recent annual sales under present owner	$415,000
Adjusted sales after deleting owner's personal sales	$403,000
Adjusted earnings	$ 32,000
Present owner's salary	$ 32,000
Buyer's assumed salary	$ 35,000

The above data are based mostly on documentation afforded by the accountant's income statement and are shown in Figure 7.1. The buyer draws a horizontal line underneath these data, then adds:

Extra sales (estimated unrecorded)	$ 30,000
Extra Sales (allowable to risk)	$ 10,000

Appraised value = ($32,000 + 10,000) ÷ .25 = $168,000

The buyer begins thinking about how to handle the negotiation and decides to make an offer using a letter of intent because of the letter's inherent advantages. He also decides to do his best to be as fair and as reasonable as possible, to the seller and to himself. His main reason is that he wants very much to own the Acme company and wants to minimize his risk of losing the opportunity. Also, he believes in fairness and in reasonableness just for their philosophical satisfaction and he further believes that fairness is not wasted on those of like minds but, instead, tends to be repaid. Moreover, he does not feel comfortable using clever tactics. They are not his style nor does he have the talent to employ them. Finally, he has developed a high respect for the seller and feels that the seller holds a similar respect for him. He genuinely hopes that their relationship will endure for years to come. On the other hand, he knows the value of keeping his guard up (having been bitten from behind more than once in his life) and he will take a cautious approach to making any agreements.

The buyer contacts a colleague who has acquisition experience and who agrees to serve as his coach if the need arises. (The colleague works for the same company as the buyer but can be trusted to keep in strict confidence the possibility that the buyer will be resigning in the near future.) The buyer also decides to employ his wife as his confidant. They normally talk over big decisions affecting the family before making commitments. His wife has more imagination than he has and a quicker mind, offsetting his innate stodginess. Moreover, he sees the widget trade from the inside looking out while she, not being employed in the trade, sees it from the outside looking in, providing a fresh perspective. Best of all, she sees *him* from the outside looking in, offsetting his human inability to see himself as others see him. The buyer has kept his wife informed of his general progress during fact-finding and appraising. She was in the car keeping him company and helping to count the customers during the stakeout. Now he only needs to review the above data and his plan to be fair and reasonable with her.

They agree on the fair-and-reasonable approach. They also agree on an offer of $168,000, after he carefully goes through the logic with her, because that is his honest appraisal at present and they further agree that the appraisal is provisional. They agree still further to base the offer on $40,000 seller financing because he honestly believes it will be needed to obtain bank financing. He drafts a letter of intent, his wife edits and approves it as shown in Figure 8.1, and now they must decide whether to hand it to the broker, mail it, or call first and then mail it. They both prefer to avoid any prior discussion with the seller not only to avoid being talked out of anything but also because they realize that an offer needs to be reviewed in its entirety to be properly evaluated. They therefore decide to mail it.

The broker receives the letter and delivers it to the seller who is disappointed by the low amount. Still, the seller calls to thank the buyer for the offer and to suggest that maybe he has not done a good job of showing the buyer where the money is. He suggests a meeting to review the facts. They meet at the seller's office and the seller reaffirms the hidden earnings, the profits from selling excess inventory, and the unrecorded sales made after hours. The buyer replies by handing the seller a copy of the adjusted income statement in Figure 7.1 and mentioning the sales adjustment from $415,000 to $403,000 and the $32,000 profit. Then he describes how he added the $10,000 unrecorded sales to the $32,000 profit, and then divided the $42,000 total by 25% to arrive at the $168,000 appraisal. The seller responds by offering information which he previously had not supplied, that the sales after hours range each year between $25,000 and $30,000 and that the profits from excess-inventory sales add another $2,000 or so to the total earnings.

The buyer is impressed by the seller's statement, partly because it confirms his stakeout and partly because this is the first time that the seller has provided specific amounts. The buyer replies that he does not doubt that some extra sales are being made and that, in general, a seller deserves to be paid for the business his company is doing. The problem, he adds, is that without documentation, the exact amount is a gamble. Having a family to support and a house mortgage to pay, he can allow only a certain amount to enter into his appraisal. He adds that even if he were willing to gamble on the extra sales being $25,000, he still could not base his offer on that amount because without documentation, he would not be able to obtain bank financing. He acknowledges the $2,000 profit from selling excess inventory but adds that he plans not to continue such sales because he doesn't feel comfortable with them. He concludes by saying that he wishes he could offer more because he wants to be fair and reasonable but he just doesn't see how he can justify it under the circumstances.

The seller replies that perhaps they should take one step at a time, that they should concentrate first on whether the extra sales really amount to $25,000 to $30,000 per year and then, realizing that they do, start to worry about bank financing. There is a moment's lull during which the seller waits for the buyer to reply while the buyer waits for the seller to establish the extra sales. The buyer, highly motivated and still feeling somewhat like a supplicant even though he is an equal principal in the negotiation, feels pressured by the silence, so he speaks first. He asks how can the extra sales be established implying that if they could be established, he might raise his bid. This question is what the seller had hoped to hear because he is prepared with an answer.

But the seller is also at a crossroad. Like all sellers who have cheated on taxes, he wants the buyer to believe how much extra money is to be made but he does not want to show hard evidence of that money because of the possibility, remote but frightening, that he could go to prison if caught. The seller, however, is struck by the reasonableness of the buyer's argument that he has a family to support and a mortgage to pay and can not afford to gamble beyond the point of reason. He is also struck by the buyer's sincerity and is moved to believe that the buyer is willing to pay for what the seller sees as the real value of the business.

The seller reaches into his desk and discloses a small stack of 8.5" x 11" accounting sheets. These papers are his confidential record of the after-hours sales he has made for the last ten years. The seller, in other words, has been keeping two sets of books and this is the other set. On each sheet he has used 52 lines (using all 40 lines on one side of the paper and the first 12 lines on the other) to record the sales for each day of the week, Monday through Saturday, with each week's total in the right hand column. Thus, a full year's extra income is recorded on each sheet. He spreads them out before the buyer and points to some of the daily amounts, some of the weekly amounts, and all of the yearly amounts at the bottom of the right-hand columns.

The buyer asks how was the seller able to accurately record these data every business day of the year for ten years seeing as how he could not possibly have been present for each and every extra sale. The seller replies that he got help mostly from a trusted employee who is rewarded each year with an undocumented (and therefore illegal and tax-free) cash bonus of about a thousand dollars. He also got occasional help from his wife and teenagers, all of whom know what's going on. The buyer knows not to ask for a copy of these data but takes a hard look at the sheets to see if they look like they actually have been prepared over a period of ten years or if they were just done yesterday. The older sheets look about as new as the recent sheets, giving rise to suspicion. But the seller has a flair for neatness reflected in his retail store, shop, and warehouse as well as in his dress and grooming and so the new-looking condition of the older sheets can not be taken as inconsistent. The buyer notices that the accounting paper these data are on are not all quite the same shade of green and that there seemed to be at least two ballpoint pens used to record the data and some differences in handwriting due to the wife's, teenagers', and employee's efforts. No other clues as to their genuineness seem to be forthcoming. He wishes that just for a day he could have access to a forensic laboratory, but he keeps that wish to himself. Instead, the buyer tells the seller that these new revelations have given him something to think about and he thanks him for his time and cooperation. He adds that he needs to discuss the situation with his wife and that he will get back with the seller in two or three days.

After discussing the new revelation and noting that the seller's documentation, ersatz though it may be, confirms or at least corroborates the buyer's stakeout, the buyer and his wife decide after much discussion on a new offer allowing $20,000 of undocumented earnings in addition to the $32,000 adjusted earnings. The revised appraisal is as follows:

$$\text{Appraised value} = (\$32,000 + \$20,000) \div .25$$
$$= \$208,000$$

They increase the seller financing to $60,000 and they allocate the $40,000 increase in their offer to good will. They may have trouble getting bank financing but they will worry about that later. They might have to finagle some of the figures. On a copy of the letter of intent, they draw a line through the old figures and write in the new ones. They do not bother to initial the changes; a letter of intent is not a contract. They will mail the markup to the seller but only after waiting a day just to be sure that this is what they want to do.

In the meantime, the seller is reviewing his position. He had made the mistake of not deleting the sales to his personal customers before arriving at his $300,000 asking price (just as the buyer had surmised) and now realizes that he will have to come down on his price. Maybe. This is a real struggle for him because, like other sellers who tend to overrate their businesses, he is loath to change. The problem is more than mere unwillingness to settle for a lower price. Sellers sometimes develop autocratic mind-sets which do not yield easily to differences of opinion, particularly with respect to what their businesses are worth. Some sellers, fortunately, are flexible, entirely reasonable, and a joy to work with. All the others are somewhere in between, as this one seems to be. He suspects that he overvalued his sales and earnings but he still may think of a way to justify what he has done.

Another problem is that sellers have the advantage of knowing exactly how much their businesses are earning, assuming that they are not committing such blunders as counting their salaries or their non-operational incomes as earnings. They therefore have comparatively little doubt to weaken their resolves.

Still another problem tending to make sellers inflexible is the truly substantial taxes they often are faced with. When a business is sold, there is a tax on the difference between what the seller paid for the business and/or how much was spent on capital investments to start or improve the business, and what the seller sells it for. There is also the tax break from the accelerated portion of the depreciation expense. Such tax breaks are not permanent gifts. They are merely deferrals of taxes until the depreciated assets are disposed of. Then all those deferrals come due at the same time and are equal to the accelerated portion of depreciation, and they get taxed as ordinary income. Making matters worse, the current operational income added to the capital gains and accumulated depreciation sometimes puts the business into the top tax bracket and makes the tax bite greater although, for many small businesses, the operating income is kept close to zero. This is the case for Acme.

If the seller plans to disband the corporation after the business is sold, a common practice since the corporate entity often has no further purpose, all remaining cash is distributed to the seller-stockholder as salary or dividends. Then it all gets taxed again at the personal level and perhaps again in an elevated bracket.

For a Subchapter-S corporation, taxes would differ but would still be substantial. If the sale were of corporate stock rather than of corporate assets, the seller's tax burden might be reduced but the buyer probably would not be willing to pay as high a price because of losing the tax breaks afforded by depreciation.

In any case, the seller has already checked with his accountant to learn that his federal corporate taxes will approach $50,000 depending on the sale price and his corporate earnings. Then he will add another $10,000 or so for state and local taxes. And then he'll have to pay his broker ten percent of the sale price. No wonder sellers become upset and hard to deal with during negotiations.

With all of these thoughts flooding a seller's mind in addition to the normal everyday problems of business and personal life and wondering what the future will hold, it is normal and predictable for a seller not to be the most pleasant person in the world to talk to. This seller is no different with respect to the problems he is faced with but he has enough wisdom and presence of mind to try to take things in stride and to take a wait-and-see attitude. Thus, he puts his worries aside as best he can, and waits to hear from the buyer.

When the marked-up letter of intent arrives, the seller is relieved to find the $40,000 increase to $208,000. His relief is not from the price itself (which to him is still too low) but rather from the size of the concession which he immediately understands to mean that the buyer is using fairness and reason, not niggling tactics, and that the buyer is bidding on a business, not haggling for a bargain. Now the ball is in the seller's court and he has to decide what to do.

He calls the buyer and thanks him for the new offer and suggests that they meet for further discussion. The buyer does not warm to further discussion because of the implicit dissatisfaction with his latest offer, not to mention the seller's implicit refusal to budge from his $300,000 asking price. The buyer cheerfully agrees, however, and they meet in the seller's office. The seller has not decided on a counter-offer but, just as the buyer suspected, merely wants to coax a higher offer from the buyer. The seller acknowledges that the loss of his $12,000 in personal sales might merit a lower price if that were the only factor. However, the seller continues, the buyer surely has contacts of his own that will follow him to Acme when he takes charge and that he (the seller) is giving the buyer the opportunity and potential that only a strong company like Acme can offer. There is a short pause, then the seller continues. "You come here with better training and experience than I had when I started in business and you've also got the energy of youth. You'll do better than I did and there isn't much doubt about it." The buyer senses that the seller is manipulating him by using his own strength against him. He replies that he is willing to pay the price for what he gets but that he should not have to pay for whatever talent or sales he might bring to the company. Then, to strengthen his argument while keeping the negotiation on a high plane, he adds, "I'm not sure that I can match your abilities or do anywhere near as beautifully as you've done with Acme. I'm going to have to sweat to meet the challenge."

Now the buyer, despite his usual slowness of wit, has found a hidden resource, an ability to rise to the occasion with the right words at the right time. His wife would be proud of him. This is something new for him and now he senses that he has the momentum to continue with his arguments and so he does even though this is not the way he planned it. He describes to the seller how he arrived at the $208,000 price: He added the $32,000 adjusted earnings to $20,000 worth of extra earnings and took four times the total (the mathematical equivalent of dividing by the 25% rate of earning) to ar-

rive at $208,000. Not many others would pay this much for a business show-
ing a profit of only $32,000, says the buyer. He adds that even the $32,000
is based mostly on the seller's word. "Not that we doubt you," he adds (the
plural pronoun alluding to his wife's backing in the offer), "We believe you

Illustration 8.2

100%; we believe your description of the earnings and we're allowing nearly
all that you've told us about. Our problem is that we just can't go any higher,
partly because we have too much to lose if all the money doesn't materialize
and partly because we're going to have a hard time getting bank financing
when so much of what we're willing to pay for is so completely hidden that
the bank probably won't believe it. You've had a lot of good years but those
lucrative years are what paid you for the business." This last statement is a
subtle reference to all the years of illegal tax-free earnings, a reference which

does not escape the seller nor does the gentility with which it is expressed. Soft though these words may be, they are still strong words which could cause offense if not spoken, as the buyer just has, with low-key intensity, unwavering eye contact, and a countenance reeking with sincerity. The buyer could argue more but decides to quit while ahead. He closes by saying that he hopes the seller will consider all that the buyer has just said and that they will be able to reach agreement.

The seller responds by saying that indeed he will consider what the buyer has said. The seller would like to say more but, like the basketball coach who calls for a time out when the opponents are on a roll, he realizes that taking a break now is his best course of action. He also needs to collect his thoughts. He thanks the buyer for his time and for coming to the office and he promises that he will get back with him shortly. The buyer departs, goes home, reports to his wife (who gives him a big hug), and waits to hear from the seller.

The seller now realizes that the buyer has made it clear that he is not going higher without a telling argument from the seller. The seller must either find that telling argument, look for another buyer, or relent to the buyer's offer. For the first time since the buyer first appeared, the seller starts considering seriously the possibility of a substantially lower price. He counts the factors in the buyer's favor: The obscurity of most of the earnings (even though, to the seller, the earnings are as obvious as the noon-day sun); the buyer's all-around reasonableness; the copies of the adjusted income statement and the buyer's appraisal which spell out mathematically exactly what the buyer is doing and why he is doing it; the buyer's obvious sincerity; the hard truth that all the years of tax-free earnings have, in a sense, paid for the business (especially since most of the illicit earnings have not been squandered but, instead, have gone into hard assets such as his home, securities, an antique automobile, and other havens he would rather not discuss); and the unknown and inestimable prospect of finding a better buyer, especially within a reasonably short time. The seller also reviews his reasons for selling. He is too young to retire but does not wish to spend the rest of his life in the widget trade. He wants to try something different simply for the completeness it will add to his life. Even championship athletes have been known to switch careers in the prime of life. He has another trade in mind in which he already has dabbled and in which he feels he can make more money than by continuing to produce widgets. And it will be fun just for the adventure of it.

The seller takes a hard look at his motivation. How badly does he want out? How certain is it that the other trade will fulfill his wishes of a more complete life and a better income? The seller already knows the answers; he would not have listed his business for sale had he not been sure of what he wanted. It is the immediacy of the buyer's offer that forces him to think again about what he is doing. But the size of the tax bite causes him to hesitate, as does the buyer's price, so much lower than what he had hoped for. He examines the adjusted income statement to find something he can fault the buyer with. The buyer's salary at $35,000 is $3,000 per year higher than his own. A young buyer really should make less than what the seller is making. Reduce the buyer's salary to $30,000 thus increasing the earnings by $5,000, multiply the increase by four to get $20,000, add that to the buyer's $208,000 offer, and the price is up to $228,000. Taking another tack, he asks himself what the business is worth based on the adjusted earnings of $32,000 and the extra money averaging $27,500. Add the two together and multiply by four to get an appraised value of $238,000. (Actually, that price could be bumped higher by adding a premium equal to four times the unpaid taxes on the extra money. But the seller decides that there is a limit to milking the extra money and he puts that idea aside.) Finally, he admits to himself that $238,000 is about the best price he could ever hope to get. Now the buyer's $208,000 offer begins to look better but the seller needs time to think about it.

A few days go by and neither party calls the other. Both parties wonder what the other is doing. The high emotions of the negotiation have subsided to those of yearning watchfulness for signs of restored activity. Such slack periods during a negotiation induce feelings of listlessness combined with an urge to go forward. If only something would happen. It is like being in a sailboat when the wind has calmed, the sea is like glass, and the boat lies dead in the water. More days pass. The buyer discusses with his wife and both agree to do nothing; they have made their case and it is the seller's turn to react. Finally, the seller accepts the situation. He wants to move on to better things. He crosses out the $208,000 price on the marked-up letter of intent and writes $228,000 to reflect the lower salary he thinks the buyer should receive. He makes no other changes except to add a note for the buyer to call for an explanation of the new price. Then he drops it into the mailbox.

The buyer receives the new mark-up, telephones the seller, and receives the seller's explanation. The buyer responds by saying that he is already gambling on all the hidden and undocumented earnings and can't afford to gamble on his salary too. He does not say explicitly that $208,000 is his best and final offer but lets the seller reach his own conclusion. The seller says that he wants to reach agreement but can't let a good company like Acme go for only $208,000. The buyer says that he has already gone out on a financial limb, does not wish to go out further, and that his wife agrees. The seller suggests that they both give the matter further thought. The buyer says that he is not in a hurry and will work to the seller's schedule (a statement which side-steps the seller's point). The seller senses that he has been sidestepped and repeats that both parties need more time to review their positions. The buyer says that he has tried hard to offer a fair price and that he does not know how he can justify anything better. The seller sees the conversation as going nowhere so he says let's both think it over and we'll talk some more later. Thus ends the conversation.

So far, the broker has mostly been kept out of the negotiation. Thus both parties have put the deal at risk by foregoing the benefits of an intermediary, although they have done so without quite realizing what they were doing. The buyer had a colleague for a coach and his wife as a confidant, so he felt no need for further help. The seller did not face up to the prospect of a substantially lower price until the buyer provided hard documentation to back up the $208,000 offer. He too felt no need for help until he reached the present stalemate. Now he calls the broker, describes the stalemate and how they got there, and asks him what he thinks of splitting the difference. The broker likes the idea because it is a simple, straightforward compromise which has the appearance of fairness. (Although he would never say so, the broker also likes it because now he can see his commission beginning to materialize.) The seller asks the broker to prepare a contract on a pre-printed form with a price of $218,000 and present it to the buyer along with an explanation of the price. (The seller could offer directly to the buyer to split the difference but is using the broker to save face and to avoid the awkwardness of relenting. He also is using an aggressive tactic known among seasoned sales persons as the presumptive close.) The broker follows the seller's instructions but is rebuffed by the buyer who explains that he appreciates the seller's concession and the broker's help but he has not agreed to a higher price and he is not willing to sign. The broker reports back to the seller who is dejected by the buyer's refusal to sign. The seller instructs the broker to prepare a fresh contract for $208,000 and to do it before he changes his mind. The broker suggests that it would be quicker to draw a line through the $218,000 price and write in $208,000. The seller says that he wants to start with a fresh piece of paper. (The truth is that the seller does not want to be reminded of what he sees as a defeat. He is still saving face even though his defeat is mostly in his own mind.) The broker does as instructed, the seller signs, the buyer signs, and a settlement is finally reached.

The above negotiation of the Acme Widget Corporation price and terms is a limited composite of what tends to transpire in real life. All of the statements, events, tactics, and emotions which occurred would be unlikely to fall into one transaction. Moreover, the role of the broker was purposely minimized to simplify the example.

This realistic fictional account provides a frame of reference to plan and implement one's own negotiation. It is also valuable for the vicarious experience to be gained. Readers who identified with either of the principals should have felt something of the choices, the thoughts, the fears, and the frustrations which confront the parties to most negotiations and how these affect the emotions and one's capability for objective reasoning.

The buyer in this case was better prepared than the seller. That's because buyers, since they lack the sellers' total knowledge, generally are forced to do something to offset that disadvantage. This buyer did a good job, especially in lining up a coach and a confidant in advance, then using that confidant at each key point in the negotiation. (He did not use the coach at all because he never felt the need, but the coach remained on call just in case.)

Some real buyers would fault the Acme buyer for agreeing to too high a price given the obscurity of the earnings. The Acme buyer, however, was striving to reach the highest tier in Maslow's hierarchy, placing him in an inherently weak negotiating position, while the seller, already in the highest tier, was merely moving sideways. On the other hand, some real sellers would fault the Acme seller's settlement even though, all things considered, he actually got a good price. In any case, negotiating is so controversial that one would have no problem finding someone to disagree with the conduct or judgment of either principal. In any case, the buyer and seller managed to reach agreement, freeing them both so they could get on with their lives. In that most important respect, they were both winners.

To gain the most from the Acme negotiation, the reader might now review the principles of appraising listed at the end of Chapter 7 and then re-read the philosophy of negotiating and the basic rules offered in this chapter. This material should make a lot more sense in a second reading.

QUESTIONS FOR DISCUSSION
Chapter 8—Negotiating

1. The opening paragraph in this chapter referred to the four impediments of negotiating. Have those impediments ever affected you? Did this chapter help you to deal with them?

2. In the philosophy of negotiating, a line was drawn between what's ethical and what's not. Did you agree? How might your own sense of ethics differ?

3. The philosophy declares negotiating to be a mode of truth. How does that declaration mesh with the 16 principles of appraising at the end of Chapter 7?

4. What thoughts underlie the 21 rules of negotiating?

5. Did you agree, more or less, with all 21 rules, or did they

at least make sense to you?

6. Why aren't those 21 rules as easy to apply as they are to understand?

7. Did you realize vicarious experience in any of the Real-Life Examples? Describe any feelings you had.

8. When the author was a young man in graduate school, his industrial psychology textbook offered many real-life examples illustrating the lessons to be learned. (Those examples are what sparked the idea for the examples in this book). With the naivety of youth, he found some of those examples terribly hard to believe because, as he explained to himself, "rational human beings just don't behave that way." Recall Example 8.3. Did you find the behavior of the principals and advisors in that example hard to believe? Did that example leave you with new wisdom, or at least a new kind of understanding?

9. Would people working in other disciplines appreciate, and perhaps learn from, the examples in this chapter, people such as salesmen, politicians, school teachers, criminologists, or playwrights?

10. What are your thoughts about the Acme Widget negotiation? Could you identify with either side? Who was more effective, the buyer or the seller? Did the buyer agree to too high a price, or did the seller give in too easily? Would a buyer less qualified for ownership have agreed to as high a price as did Acme's buyer?

11. Before you read this chapter, what was your attitude towards negotiating? How do you feel about it now? Which of the 21 rules did you find most helpful?

CHAPTER 9

Financing

Once the buyer and the seller reach agreement on the price and terms, the next step towards completing the purchase and sale will be dictated by circumstances. In most cases, financing the purchase will be next for at least three reasons. First, financing is usually the last major challenge to completing the transaction. The buyer and seller therefore usually agree that financing should be secured before spending time and money on the legal, accounting, licensing, and other matters required to close the deal.

Second, obtaining financing, though time consuming, is relatively inexpensive, usually not costing more than a few hundred dollars for the loan application fee, if anything at all. An exception is when no broker is involved or, if one is, the broker's fee does not cover preparation of the loan application package. Such preparation, depending on the complexity and whether or not cash-flow projections have already been prepared, may cost anywhere from a few hundred dollars to a few thousand dollars.

Third, most sellers will avoid becoming further involved until the buyer's ability to pay the price is reasonably assured. Such avoidance is partly because the seller has a business to manage without much time to spare. It is also because the seller, usually older than the buyer, has become jaded through the normal, real-world experiences of broken promises and failed expectations and simply will not be motivated to perform until the bank has approved the loan. Example 4.1 illustrates a possible state of mind for a seller who has experienced failed expectations.

When financing is recognized by both buyer and seller as being little more than a formality and thus well assured, then legal, accounting, licensing, and other matters may be allowed to proceed. If the seller is financing the purchase, for example, or if the buyer already has the cash or at least most of it or has such ample net worth and overall qualifications that financing seems virtually assured, the seller will turn the matter over to his or her lawyer for the proper documentation and security while other matters are attended to.

To assure proper understanding, two terms should be defined: as mentioned in Chapter 2, the term "bank" is used in this book mostly in a generic sense to refer not only to banks per se but to all institutions providing professional financing, including savings and loan associations, finance companies, and credit unions. More importantly, the term "financing" means not only providing cash but also providing such services as screening risks, documenting the loans, and assisting borrowers who fall behind in their payments of principal and interest. As will be shown below, these added services, professionally administered, maximize the chances for success of both the borrower and the lender, as well as of all other parties connected in any way to the deal.

This chapter is in five parts: Bank Financing vs. Seller Financing; Types and Sources of Financing; Professional Lending Standards; Applying for a Loan; and Applying for the Acme Widget Corporation Loan.

PART 1:
BANK FINANCING VS. SELLER FINANCING

Most financing for small business purchases should be sought from professional lenders such as banks, savings and loan associations, and finance companies. That's because these institutions are talented specialists in the art of lending. Moreover, being profit-oriented, they are motivated to keep situations likely to fail from entering their portfolios. Such risky situations include unqualified buyers, businesses of questionable viability, and businesses that are overpriced. By protecting themselves, these specialists also protect their borrowers. In addition, they protect other parties likely to be harmed when businesses fail including sellers who participate in the lending or who merely receive the payments, creditors such as suppliers and subcontractors, employees and their families, customers who rely on the goods and services provided by these businesses, and customers who make deposits or advance payments. In other words, professional lenders benefit the entire community.

The dangers of seller financing should be explicitly noted as a warning:

- Failure to assure an adequate margin of safety of cash flow over debt service.
- Failure even to prepare cash-flow projections.
- Failure to correctly assign a fair market value to the business (as in Example 8.5).
- Failure to understand the risks of the industry or the economy.
- Failure to properly qualify the buyer (as in Example 4.1 or in 9.1 below).
- Failure to assure adequate working capital (a common mistake of small business owners).
- Failure to understand the meaning of a buyer's commitment to the purchase (inadequate cash infusion, no ties to the community, etc.).
- Failure to grant a well qualified buyer forced to temporarily close the business because of illness or disablement a stretch-out of payments or a moratorium when such grant is justified by the circumstances and in everybody's best interest.

It should be clear from the above list that financing is more than a matter of supplying cash and collecting payments of principal and interest. It is also a matter of screening bad risks from good ones and administering the loans to maximize probability of debt payment. This largely maximizes probability of the buyer's success in business.

Since institutional financing generally is safer for buyer, seller, and other parties involved in the business, it is probably less costly, in the larger scheme of things, than seller financing despite the higher interest rate. Exceptions to this rule occur when seller financing is combined with bank financing, subjecting the total deal to professional administration, or in special conditions such as when both principals, not just one of them, are sophisticated enough to know what they are doing.

Myths abound concerning the supposed superiority of seller financing to bank financing. These myths usually are based on the plausible but specious idea that, by nature, profit-making companies such as banks are not concerned about the well-being of their clients, that they provide few if any services to justify their fees, or that their services simply are not useful to the principals in question. For example, some myths are that seller financing is better because the interest rate is lower; because it proves that the seller believes in his own business; and because if the seller finances the purchase and the business gets into trouble, the seller will come out of retirement to help manage the business and rescue the buyer. Other myths are revealed below.

The plausibility of these myths masks the harm which may occur. A lesser harm occurs if a well-qualified buyer insists on seller financing and the seller refuses. The result is that a deal which should consummate is broken, everyone's time is wasted, and the buyer's and seller's dreams are shattered (as in Example 10.2). A greater harm, if a seller does finance, may occur in either of two forms. One is if the buyer is unqualified (as in Example 9.1 below). The result is that the deal is not broken when it should be, the business fails, and everyone gets hurt. The other is if the buyer is qualified, gets into trouble anyway, and is foreclosed on by an impatient or cash-strapped seller when a payment stretch-out or moratorium would serve both parties' best interest. Sadly, the myths are repeated and perpetuated not just by laypeople like ordinary buyers and sellers and their families and friends, but also by professional advisors such as lawyers and accountants.

An objective measure of the success of most banks in screening bad risks is that the reserves that banks set aside for non-performing loans usually total only about one percent of the value of all their loans. This 99% success rate in lending does not translate into 99% success rate for the businesses that banks finance—a business may fail after it has paid the loan or the bank may be paid by foreclosing on the collateral—but it does offer some idea of the loan officers' skills.

The willingness and capability of banks to grant debt-service stretch-outs and moratoriums to troubled borrowers should not be undervalued. The bank's deferment of payments for a struggling business can make the difference between surviving and not surviving. Since the overwhelming majority of their loans are constantly being serviced by payments of principal and interest, banks virtually always have sufficient cash flow to tolerate the small percentage of their loans requiring deferred payments. Moreover, when loan payments are stretched out or deferred, interest continues to accumulate which means that the bank continues to make a profit. If the business fails despite all efforts, the interest rates are designed to make up the losses.

Having made the case for borrowing from professional lenders, fair warning must also be given that the lending industry, just like any other, suffers occasionally from an incompetent or unethical lender who will grant a loan to an unqualified buyer when covered by ample collateral. In the author's opinion, a bank lending to a clearly unqualified buyer should be liable for damages. The author, however, has found no support on this point, not even in an actual case of egregious mishandling (see Example 12.1). Ultimate responsibility still rests with the borrower.

Example 9.1 illustrates what can happen when the seller does not know how to qualify the buyer but is willing to finance the purchase.

Example 9.1 A small manufacturing company with an established product line is for sale. The business was started 30 years ago by a husband and wife team. It has been remarkably profitable almost from the beginning. This couple loves the business and would not sell except for the infirmities of old age. The husband's arthritis is crippling him and preventing his working in the shop for more than two or three hours a day. In the last year or so they have decreased the sales to ease the workload. Neither the husband nor the wife has much business acumen. Their combined talents have been the key to their success. The husband invented the entire product line—a third of which is patented—and designed and built the equipment to manufacture it. Neither are good salespersons, but the product line is so attractive that it practically sells itself at trade shows. His good control of cost, schedule, and quality brings repeat business. The company sells wholesale to retailers and distributors, most of whom are out of state, and also to retail customers on the premises. (The combination of manufacturing, wholesaling, and retailing is similar to that of Acme Widget Corporation.) The wife manages the office and the retail shop and meticulously maintains the books and records.

A buyer is found and a price is negotiated at $280,000 with $60,000 down and a promissory note for the balance. The buyer, whose exact background is not known, is in a maintenance-and-repair trade which provides a carry-over of sorts into manufacturing. The sellers promise to provide adequate training for the buyer. The buyer has other business interests which he plans to keep along with the new acquisition.

Soon after the sale has closed and the buyer has taken over, trouble emerges. The buyer is not coming to work on time, apparently in deference to his other interests. He is even failing to show for the training sessions which the sellers had promised to provide. The husband tries to fill in for the buyer's absences in the shop but finally gives up in disgust. The buyer is on his own, he reasons, so the seller stops bothering to show up.

About the third month after closing, the buyer misses a payment. The seller is told that the buyer is temporarily short of cash but that he will make it up soon. Another month or two go by. One day the seller receives a telephone call at home from an old customer who has made an advance payment but has not received the goods. The husband drives to the shop and finds no activity. The employees have been dismissed. He discovers letters from other old customers who have made payments but received no goods. He then hires a lawyer to regain possession, rehire the employees, and restart the business. The wife writes to the customers to tell what has happened and that she and her husband will honor any payments the customers have made for which they received no goods. The sellers also make up the unpaid gas, electric, telephone, water, and sewer bills.

In a few months, the business is partly back to normal, limited by the husband's infirmity. The sellers have lost all of the $60,000 down payment and then some due to the unpaid bills, dishonored deposits, reduced inventory, and lost rent. They also have lost valuable time in a period of declining health and have received no income.

(A follow-on of Example 9.1 is Example 10.2 which describes what happened when a new buyer rejected bank financing in favor of seller financing.)

PART 2:
TYPES AND SOURCES OF FINANCING

Sources of Financing. The most common sources of professional financing are institutions such as banks, savings and loan companies, and finance companies. The Small Business Administration (SBA) often participates in their lending but virtually all SBA financing is required by SBA rules to be initiated through one of these institutions.

In cases where additions must be made to in-place equipment, the manufacturers and distributors sometimes finance their own equipment. They may provide strong technical support along with attractive financing terms. The manufacturer or distributor may even take back the equipment if not entirely suitable, although a service fee would probably be charged.

If financing for new equipment is not easily available, leasing may be an alternative. Leasing offers several advantages. The amount of cash required to get started is reduced. Exceptionally proficient and timely maintenance-and-repair services may be furnished by the leasing company. The leasing cost is usually tax-deductible in the year spent or accrued. The cost may be applied to equity depending on the arrangement made with the leasing company. Leasing instead of purchasing may increase the ratio of cash flow to debt service. It may ease bank restrictions on the borrower. It may allow trading up if sales grow or if equipment becomes obsolete. The total cost may be less than if purchased. And leasing personnel seem to be imaginative, aggressive, and pleasant to work with.

Although public funds may be restricted to starts of new businesses, it never hurts to call the municipal or state chamber of commerce to discover funds for purchasing or growing existing businesses. Even if no such funds are available, the chamber may offer useful leads.

When other sources of financing are not available or have been used up, credit cards are a useful source despite high rates of interest. The cash is always there for the taking, no questions asked, and with virtually no paper work or other nuisances. The disadvantage is that using credit cards to buy a business detracts from what perhaps is their most useful feature, instant cash for emergencies. Still, financing with one's credit card may be the difference between getting started and not getting started. One must weigh the circumstances and decide.

For many would-be buyers of businesses, borrowing from friends and relatives may be possible and even recommended as a last resort. Friends and relatives, however, are, in a sense, like credit card companies: they may be an easy source of cash, but if their cash is used to buy a business, their availability for emergencies is diminished or lost. In another sense, friends and relatives are unlike credit card companies since friendships are at stake and may be too precious to tarnish or to lose.

Sellers, of course, are a possible source of financing, but they may be dangerous unless the financing is shared with a bank.

Buyers almost always provide their own down payments. Sometimes, through their cash balances or through conversion of other assets into cash, they provide the total funds needed to purchase. Unfortunately, buyers as their own financiers, are, like sellers, amateurs at qualifying themselves to own a business. Their financing, unless it is combined with professional financing, is dangerous to themselves and to the community. It is therefore wise for buyers who are able to pay cash to apply for bank financing anyway to gain the benefits of professional lending.

If a would-be borrower should feel confused about which source of financing to seek, it is important to know that regardless of the type of loan (as explained below) or the amount, the necessary information is almost always just a few telephone calls away. One may begin by calling a local bank commercial loan department and describing the situation. If the situation is not right for that bank but the loan officer is well informed and cooperative, he or she will suggest where the borrower might go to obtain the funds. If the officer is not well informed, the borrower can continue calling banks and other lenders until the right information is found. The borrower may also consult the *Yellow Pages* by looking under "Financing," "Banks," and "Savings and Loan Associations." The St. Louis *Yellow Pages*, for example, has about 75 listings under "Financing" covering a range of sources and types.

"Venture capital," a term which is often vague or dependant on its context, is frequently sought. One useful meaning, not necessarily the most common, will include the following elements: A business with a bright future, though not well established, where investors reasonably may expect to reap returns of around 50% per year compounded annually; the expected return coming mostly from capital gains when the common stock eventually is offered for sale to the public; and likelihood that the investors can recover their investments and profits in from three to seven years. Such ventures are beyond the scope of this book. However, a good book dealing with the subject is the following:

Business Plans that Win $$$, Stanley R. Rich and David E. Gumpert, Harper & Row, New York, NY.

That book also is recommended for the many insights provided for anyone wishing to obtain financing for a business venture of almost any type or size, and also for anyone who wants to grow the business.

Conventional Loans vs. SBA Loans. Two common types of loans are conventional loans and loans with SBA participation. Conventional loans are simple secured loans made by banks to their buyers. For example, the buyer applies for the loan at a bank, the bank evaluates the circumstances of the loan, and the loan is either granted or denied. If the bank is not entirely comfortable with the buyer's qualifications or with the business being bought but feels that the application has considerable merit, it may suggest a loan involving SBA participation. In an SBA Type 7A loan, the bank lends to the buyer while the SBA guarantees most of the bank's loan. In an SBA direct loan, the borrowed funds are supplied entirely by the SBA with no bank participation other than the required act of rejection. However, SBA direct loans are not always available. In an SBA Type 504 loan, funds are supplied by the bank, the SBA, and a quasi-political group with a name like "local development company," "economic council," or something of the sort.

Each type of loan has advantages and disadvantages. The conventional loan is the simplest and the quickest but the one for which banks require the highest standards. Loans with SBA participation are more cumbersome, but, with less rigorous standards, offer financing not otherwise available. The SBA Type 504 loan is the most cumbersome and time-consuming since it requires approvals from all three lenders but it has the great advantage of requiring a relatively small cash infusion from a poorly funded but otherwise well qualified buyer, such infusion amounting to as little as 10% of the total financial package. With such a small down payment from the buyer, the ratio of cash flow to debt service normally would be too low to be viable. In a 504 loan, however, the term of the loan, or at least a part of it, is lengthened to as much as 15 years or longer, lowering the annual debt service and boosting the cash-flow ratio. There are two important requirements for Type 504 loans. One is that jobs must either be created, as in an expansion or startup, or preserved, as in a purchase from a retiring seller who otherwise would close the business. The other requirement is that some assets of the business must be durable enough—machine tools and real estate, for example—to justify the long term of the loan.

One disadvantage of SBA participation has been the discouraging amount of documentation required. In recent years, the SBA has offered a version of the Type 7A loan requiring minimal documentation, referred to as "LowDoc."

One myth about SBA participation is that it amounts to a give-away to minorities. (In this usage, the term, minority, is probably a code word for Afro-American.) Although loans with SBA participation are made to less rigorous standards than are conventional loans, the standards are still high and the loans not easy to obtain. In other words, they are not give-aways.

To qualify for SBA participation in a loan, the buyer must first apply for a conventional loan at two banks or other institutions and be rejected. Then the bank will suggest which type of SBA participation would be most suitable, if any. Some institutions, by virtue of their successful experience with SBA loans, acquire a special status: SBA Preferred Lenders have authority to grant Type 7A loans without making separate applications for each loan. SBA Certified Lenders must apply for their 7A loans but they get approval or disapproval from the SBA in three days or less. Most buyers who have been rejected probably would benefit by next applying at an institution which is either a Preferred or a Certified lender. The commercial loan officers at these institutions know most of the rules and guidelines for SBA financing and can save a buyer considerable time while minimizing frustration.

Although most SBA loans are probably processed through banks, many SBA loans are processed through savings and loan companies and finance companies.

While further details on SBA loans could be offered in this chapter, they are not included (except incidentally below) because the particulars change from time to time (sometimes for the incalculable reasons of politics) and because banks and other institutions can always be relied upon to have the necessary information and are a required part of the process anyway.

Cash-Flow Loans vs. Asset-Based Loans. Cash-flow loans are for those more-

or-less normal situations usually handled by ordinary commercial lenders. These are the main concern of this chapter and this book and probably cover most small business purchases. Cash-flow financing is granted when the cash flow is adequate to service the debt with a comfortable margin of safety, as described in Chapter 7.

Asset-based loans are for unusual and often riskier situations such as high-leverage purchases (purchases made with low down payments) or turn-arounds where the cash flow to repay the loan is in doubt but offset by size-able assets for collateral. Assets often suitable for asset-based loans include inventories of materials or merchandise, accounts receivable, promissory notes, and so forth. Asset-based loans other than for real estate or machine tools usually require much more monitoring by the lender and more reporting by the borrower because the collateralized assets typically lend themselves to quick and easy disposal. If, for example, the asset on which the loan is based is inventory, a truck could be backed up to the rear door at midnight and the inventory moved to another state before the lender knows what happened. Because of their greater administrative expenses of monitoring and reporting, asset-based loans are mostly suitable only for amounts generating enough interest on the loan to justify that expense. Such loans therefore tend to have minimums approaching a million dollars and higher.

Some lending institutions are designed just for asset-based financing and have the special staffing, procedures, and expertise needed for those loans. The loan officers in specialty financing seem to be well informed and more pleasurable to work with. However, even these specialty lenders need an accounting of the projected cash flow to repay the loan. For this reason, the difference between cash-flow financing and asset-based financing is one of degree more than concept.

PART 3:
PROFESSIONAL LENDING STANDARDS

The standards by which lending institutions screen their prospective borrowers may vary in detail from one lender to another due to varying needs and perceptions. These standards also may vary with the passage of time due to normal fluctuations in those same needs and perceptions. Such variances may occur even within a given institution. The standards described here are therefore neither absolute nor rigid but merely an approximation of what the lending industry in general operates by as observed by the author through his experience. These lending standards are divided into two groups, loans in general and purchase loans for small businesses.

Loans in General. All loans must comport with reason. For example, an application for a loan to search for buried treasure or to market an unproven product would be viewed at practically all lending institutions as unreasonably speculative. The application would be rejected.

The purpose of the loan must conform to the law. For example, application for a loan to build an artificially lighted, indoor farm to raise marijuana clandestinely would not be well received.

The ability of the borrower to produce a cash flow comfortably in excess of the debt service must be evident. Because it is, by definition, not evident (not to mention illegal), unrecorded income shall not make up any part of the cash flow.

The borrower's credit rating shall be excellent or nearly so. A good credit rating does little to get the loan but the suspicion and doubt accompanying a poor rating is almost guaranteed to kill it.

Collateral is required unless the borrower is in the public realm and is a very well established institution or company or government agency. Since few buyers of small businesses are public (i.e., listed on a stock exchange, making their finances open for inspection) or well established, almost all must furnish collateral for the loan. Exceptions are the signature loans granted at some financial institutions based on the borrowers' financial qualifications, and credit-card loans.

Collateral shall not serve as a substitute for the borrower's ability to comfortably repay the loan out of cash flow. One of the more common and more specious myths is that banks, since they are interested only in making a profit, will compromise a buyer's ability to produce a cash flow if the buyer has enough collateral to protect the bank. The thinking behind that myth is that the bank, which lures trusting borrowers by holding itself out as a conservative lender in a conservative industry, can gamble on the buyer's ability to operate the business while relying on the buyer's wealth to protect the loan. A moment's reflection, however, reveals that the bank's only opportunity for profit is to collect interest on the principal. If the bank does not have good probability of collecting interest, it is probably wasting its time. Further, if the bank forecloses on the collateral to recover the principal, its profit is gone. Still further, the collateral may have declined in value so as to force a loss instead of a profit, with the expenses of selling the collateral sometimes adding to the loss. Moreover, failed loans are an embarrassment to the bank because they imply the loan committee's poor judgment, even if the failure was entirely beyond the committee's foresight or control. Since banks and other institutions are regularly inspected by state and federal agencies and since the ratio of non-performing loans to total loans is reported to the stockholders, the embarrassment is more real than imagined. It is clear, therefore, that the only purpose of collateral is to minimize a possible but unlikely loss of principal, not to substitute for cash flow. With this understanding of collateral and its purpose, the primacy of the buyer's qualifications to manage the business becomes clearer. So does the primacy of the opening chapter in this book.

The terms of the loan shall be stated in a written contract. The obvious purpose of the written statement is for clarity of understanding, but it also provides necessary documentation to the accountants, the IRS, and, in case of legal action between the borrower and the bank, their lawyers.

The time-frame of the loan shall be commensurate with the purpose of the loan and with the projected viability of the borrower as well as the viability of the borrower's source of cash. For example, if the borrower owns a business, the term of the loan obviously should be no longer than the borrower's lease on the premises. Less obviously, a long-term loan in a rapidly changing industry like electronics or biochemistry would require extra assurance of the viability of the business. A more delicate matter is a long-term loan sought by a middle-aged or older person, the problem being the hard realities of the actuarial tables. To avoid any charge of age-discrimination in such a case, a bank might grant the loan while raising its overall lending standards with an emphasis on collateral.

If the borrower is a corporation, especially a small corporation, the bank almost certainly will require a personal guaranty of the owner, major stockholder, or other guarantor.

Loans for the Purchases of Small Businesses. The above standards for loans in general apply to loans for the purchases of small businesses except as modified or expanded below.

After all expenses and the owner's salary have been paid, the pre-tax cash-flow margin of safety should be in the range of 50 to 100 percent (i.e., a ratio of cash flow to debt service of 1.5 to 2.0), the exact requirement depending on the circumstances and on the loan officer's judgment.

The buyer-borrower must show evidence of ability to manage the business being bought. A successful tenure in the same trade or one closely similar is usually the best evidence. A business plan or loan application package which is comprehensive in scope and substantively written in detail may also serve as strong evidence. A successful tenure combined with a well-prepared business plan constitutes the best evidence possible.

The buyer must evidence commitment to the business being bought. A sizeable down payment constitutes strong evidence. Down payments may range as low as ten percent of the funds required to purchase, but 25 percent to 30 percent is usually more appropriate. Subordinated seller-participation in financing the purchase is welcomed and may be thought of as part of the down payment as long as the buyer's commitment remains well evidenced. Other evidences of commitment are the buyer's agreement to present his or her home as collateral and, to a lesser degree, close family members co-signing the note. Sometimes the assets being purchased show more evidence of the buyer's commitment than other factors. For example, a down payment of $325,000 is proposed for a business consisting of $1,000,000 real estate and $300,000 inventory. Since the down payment barely covers the inventory and since the inventory may easily be turned into cash, the actual risk is only $25,000, just 1.9 percent of the total, hardly a strong commitment.

The term of the loan shall not exceed six years unless a longer term is warranted by the overall circumstances. The reason for the short term is that the longer the term of the loan, the greater the possibility for business or personal problems to develop or for the owner—the key employee—to die or become disabled. By the same reasoning, the term of the loan shall not be extended to improve the ratio of cash flow to debt service.

PART 4:
APPLYING FOR A LOAN

It may come as both a surprise and a relief to discover that applying for a loan is a straightforward effort which may be done almost by rote. Considering the difficult tasks which have been accomplished up to this point; matching the buyer to the seller, fact-finding, appraising (which includes projecting cash flow), and negotiating, applying for a loan is relatively easy. The main tasks are to write a loan application package and to find an interested bank, usually but not necessarily in that order. These relatively easy efforts have difficulties of their own but even these can be dispatched almost by rote.

Preparing the Loan Application Package. A loan application package should contain all the information necessary to make a bank loan officer feel comfortable with the lending situation. It should be written to impress the reader that the writer has told the whole truth with neither reservations nor exaggerations. Not counting the cover letter (which should be brief), the package should consist of two parts, the text which tells the story and the appendices which provide supporting data. The text should be written in a factual tone with no puffing. The text should offer discussion of anticipated problems as well as of the company's bright future. It should be brief, with each statement a nugget of knowledge and with emphasis on economy of words. It should start with a title page, a summary, and a table of contents. Every page in the text should be numbered. (The author prefers ordinary sequential numbering but notes that Rich and Gumpert, mentioned above, differ.) The text probably should not exceed 30 double-spaced printed pages (roughly 10,000 words) but it may be as short as one page if one page is adequate. Since the appendices are reference materials, they may total any number of pages within reason.

The cover letter and the text should be on letter-size paper. Some of the appendices may be on legal-size or other paper but most will usually be letter size. The cover letter should be on high quality bond with rag content. The text and appendices may be printed or copied on good quality copy paper. The text should be printed on one side only; the appendices also on one side only but reasonable exceptions may occur.

The cover letter and text should be prepared on almost any word processor for the obvious advantages of efficiency but also for the higher quality that efficiency promotes. Errors of grammar, punctuation, and spelling are forbidden because of the carelessness and incompetence they project.

Hiring an editor is advised for buyers who are not comfortable with any of the above requirements.

The following recommendations for submitting the package state the author's preferences but he notes that many would differ. The package should be simple, even austere. It may be sent in a plain brown envelope with the cover letter addressed to the bank with attention, if known, to the loan officer by name. Hand-carrying the package to the bank has the advantages of personal contact and the assurance that it has arrived safely. The cover letter is inside the envelope as though it is part of the package even though it is a distinct entity. The cover letter will have the same address as the envelope but the package itself, including the title page, need not mention the bank by name, an advantage if submitting to more than one bank with little, if any, offsetting disadvantage.

The text and appendices need not be in a binder or even be stapled. Instead, they may be and usually should be held together by a large clip or clamp with the cover letter on top. If this arrangement proves too bulky to be easily clipped, the text may be clipped separately from the appendices. If the appendices are bulky, they may be packaged in a separate envelope if the envelope is well marked. A little common sense solves most problems of this type. An advantage of submitting with no binder is that it is easy for the banker to spread the pages on his or her desk to better follow the continuity of thought. It is also much easier for the banker to make extra copies for members of the loan-review committee, especially if the bank's copier can handle a stack of pages and can collate the copies. Further, the report with no binder usually stacks better and takes less space.

If it is deemed necessary to hold the pages together so they do not become misplaced, a staple placed diagonally in the upper left hand corner is usually better than a binder. Stapled reports have just as good if not better appearance than those in binders. Besides, reports in binders are a bother to handle and they do not signify greater authority or seriousness of purpose. Some folks even view them as pretentious.

If the package is prepared by a broker working for a commission dependant on closing the sale, a brief statement by the broker declaring his or her interest in the deal would be appropriate for the sake of ethical standards, though not absolutely necessary.

Applying for the Loan. A major decision is whether to apply for financing at more than one bank at a time, the advantages being to find the lowest interest rate and best terms and to save time in case of rejection. Usually it is much more important to get the loan than to find the sweetest terms. Moreover, although banks welcome loan applications for small business purchases, such loans are not exactly their favorite form of new business. Therefore, concentrating one's efforts at one bank at a time is probably the wiser approach unless working to a financing deadline. The trick is to approach several banks on the telephone with the bare basics of the loan and then to apply for the loan where the most enthusiasm (or the least disinterest) is found. Such telephone canvassing might proceed as follows:

The borrower has telephoned the bank and requested to speak to the person in charge of commercial loans. The receptionist has replied, "Please hold and I'll connect you." A loan officer then answers.

Loan officer:	This is John Smith. How can I help you?
Borrower:	I'm Bert Jones and I'm looking for a loan to buy a retail store. I'll need around ninety thousand dollars and I wonder if your bank would be interested.

From this point on, the loan officer will control the conversation. The borrower has only to answer the loan officer's questions and, while doing so, manage to mention that he already has prepared a loan application package. If the bank shows no enthusiasm, the borrower should ask if the officer could make any recommendations.

After telephoning a few banks, the borrower will know where best to apply for the loan. A personal meeting should be set up at which the loan application package will be handed to the loan officer. The borrower should dress in standard business attire with the emphasis on conservatism. For a man, a blue or gray suit, a fresh white shirt, a necktie, and black shoes are very appropriate. Shoes should be shined, hair combed, and nails trimmed. For a woman, a business suit consisting of skirt (not pants) and jacket should be worn with appropriate blouse, hosiery, and minimal jewelry. Hair should be combed, shoes shined or cleaned, and nails trimmed and painted with clear polish, if at all.

It is important when seeking bank financing to proceed as quickly as possible to minimize degradation of the seller's state of mind while he or she waits with growing impatience for the bank to make a commitment. It is therefore important for the loan officer to estimate the date when the bank will have made a decision. If the bank has not responded by that date, the borrower should telephone to determine the status. It is acceptable, and common, for the bank to slip the schedule for a few days and even to slip the schedule more than once while offering a reasonable explanation. After a second slip, however, the buyer must evaluate the situation and probably should apply at a second bank. The buyer should keep the seller apprised of the status with a brief courtesy call every week to evidence the buyer's continued interest, and to maintain the seller's positive state of mind. Such slips can try everyone's patience.

Once the banker begins to read the loan application package, he or she will begin asking questions, sometimes by telephone and sometimes in writing. If by telephone, the borrower should answer questions as extemporaneously as possible but may also ask for time to prepare answers. If in writing, the answers should be in writing. For purposes of documentation and accuracy of communication, answers given by telephone may be followed up in writing and probably should be. The recommended format will alternate the banker's question and the borrower's answer.

When dealing with banks, it is helpful to know a few things about their competency, their manners, and their procedures. Bank loan officers, like human beings in general, may be divided into three levels of competency: the upper 25 percent, the lower 25 percent, and the 50 percent in between. While the bank's expressed enthusiasm for the lending situation is the primary factor in deciding where to first apply for the loan, the competency and ethics of the loan officer can also be important. Some loan officers will lie when they feel like it or when they think it is in their best interest to do so. Some will lie about the expected decision date for the loan commitment, about the reason for delay, and, if rejecting the loan, about the reason for rejection. It does not matter that such lies may be motivated more out of weakness of intellect than of intelligent self interest. What matters is that such lies occur and there is little or nothing that can be done about it. One may take this into consideration when trying to decide what to do next. Again, forewarning the seller of these possibilities is advised.

A female loan officer is more likely to be adequate than a male. This is based on experience plus at least two reasons: One is the reality that women are generally not treated fairly in the job market. They have to outperform men just to draw the same wages and to enjoy the same ranks. The other reason is that some women, by choice, are secondary breadwinners instead of primary and are not competing on the same track as primary breadwinners.

Loan officers tend not to return telephone calls unless at their convenience, if at all. Such rudeness—this pandemic social disease—seems to have infected women as well as men. If the borrower feels it necessary to contact the loan officer and cannot get through on the telephone, a trip to the bank is in order and will usually get at least a brief conversation.

A good loan officer should have some basic elements of competency. For example: a good officer should have some understanding of the business in question. If lacking even a modicum of understanding, the officer should say so and give the package to another officer or give it back to the borrower with an honest explanation. A good loan officer should allow that not all borrowers meet the standards of textbook perfection. Strengths to compensate for weaknesses should therefore be sought. Some of the early examples in Chapter 1 illustrate the point. A loan officer should visit the business being purchased to assure that it exists and that it has the overall lot of equipment described in the package. A good loan officer can sense the viability of the business. A good officer will question and probe, partly for information and partly to sense the borrower's attitude towards the business, a positive and loving attitude being a strong sign of probable success. A good officer will count as an important strength the support offered by the borrower's immediate family. And a good officer will share his or her doubts with the borrower, partly so that the borrower has the opportunity to reply and, if not able to reply, at least to learn from the experience. With this knowledge of what a borrower has a right to expect, the borrower can better present his or her case to the loan officer and perhaps coax the officer to a better performance. The borrower also may acquire a better sense of whether the loan application was well handled and, thereby, better assess his or her prospects for future applications at the same or other banks.

As already indicated, the borrower can never be sure that the reason stated for the bank's rejection is true. Even if it is, buyer-borrowers must realize that bankers, despite their skills in screening bad risks from good ones, are not entrepreneurs. They certainly are not visionaries and do not always see the rightness in a deal. It is incumbent upon buyers who are rejected to not give up when they feel that the deal makes sense. It is equally incumbent on sellers to have patience with their buyers who are going through rejections and, like their buyers, not give up when the deal makes sense. Example 5.3 illustrates how patience from all concerned parties can bring home the cash even though that was not the main point of that example.

PART 5:
APPLYING FOR THE ACME WIDGET CORPORATION LOAN

Success at one stage of the process (usually worth a mini-celebration) merely introduces the vexing challenge of the next stage. That is where Acme's buyer finds himself now that he has completed the negotiation. Obtaining financing is actually easier than what has gone before, even if it does not seem that way, but it appears to be a daunting hurdle for inexperienced buyers. Acme's buyer is no exception. He could ask his colleague at work for advice but that colleague's experience has all been with corporate acquisitions marked by multi-layered professionalism, the kind of deals that banks welcome with open arms. Acme's buyer is burdened with all the disadvantages of the sole proprietor combined with the disadvantages of inexperience as an owner. And now, trying to borrow money, he finds himself feeling like a beggar with his hat in his hand.

Be that as it may, he has a job to do and he begins immediately after reaching agreement with the seller (and after a night of celebration with his wife) by reviewing his calculations for the ratio of cash flow to debt service and how the increase in price from $168,000 to $208,000 has affected the calculations. His cash-flow ratio was borderline before the price went up. The question now is what to do about it. Before and during the negotiation, he had worried because he had seen so few possibilities toward getting a healthy ratio. But necessity, immediacy of need, and his unflagging motivation to own a business inspire him to several possible partial solutions, one or two of which previously had escaped him.

- Maybe he will not declare the anticipated loss of $12,000 in sales re-
lated to the seller's departure, in which case he also might not declare
the $4,000 in sales that he expects to bring with him to Acme. In-
stead, he could use the same $415,000 in sales that marked the seller's
most recent full year as a baseline for his cash-flow projections. If the
loan officer should ask if any sales will be lost with the seller's departure, he could reply, in devious honesty, that he will bring with him
new customers which will offset the loss of the old and that he will be
scouting for transferable customers between now and when his ownership begins. He may even start his ownership with more business than
the seller had, or so he could reply. This planned deviousness may be
viewed as deceitful since the buyer's true belief would not be in line
with the statement. But could it be viewed as optimism? From a loan
officer's point of view, the difference between deceit and optimism is irrelevant. All that matters is whether the statement conforms to reality,
and, if so, whether or not the statement is reasonably in line with sound
banking practices and sound expectations. The question, however, for
a buyer like this one who cares about living with his conscience, is to
determine the fine line that separates deceit from optimism, from bona
fide optimism. The probable answer is that there is no fine line, that the
two modes of thought overlap in an indefinable zone of fuzz and that
this zone, like most other zones of human thought—as amorphous as
anything in nature—changes interminably with the vicissitudes of human circumstances. This buyer is honest with himself, he knows what
he is doing, and he has decided, possibly, to avail himself of what he
sees as his fair share of reasonable optimism so that he can, in a manner
of speaking, put his best foot forward. One may criticize the buyer's
way of thinking but, he reasons to himself, one must sometimes work
imperfectly in an imperfect world. He has read Machiavelli. The trick
is to do it wisely.
- He may increase his down payment from $70,000 to $75,000, although he will keep this idea in abeyance pending the loan officer's re-

action to the whole loan application package. He will have little left for personal or family emergencies but, he reasons, that's part of the risk in buying a business. Minimizing the risk is that the shortage of funds should only be temporary. After his ownership gets underway the cash flow will increase. As a last resort, he has two sources for emergency cash: his parents and his credit cards. He hopes not to use these.

- He will reduce his salary by $5,000. As he had observed earlier, this is not a real problem in terms of running the household since a reduction in salary in a family-owned corporation is merely an accounting change. Moreover, even if his first year of ownership shows a mediocre profit, the margin of safety in the cash-flow ratio will provide for his family's needs.

- When he calculated the debt service, he did so without allowing that the seller's financing will be at a lower rate of interest than the bank's. The difference in annual debt service on the $60,000 seller financing between the 8.5% bank interest and, say, 6.5% seller interest, is $700, a relatively small but still helpful amount.

- He might stretch the terms of the loans—the bank's and the seller's—from five years to six. The decreases in annual debt service (to the nearest $100) are $4,800 and $2,000, respectively, for a total of $6,800.

- If these ideas do not win the loan, he will ask the seller for a three-month or six-month moratorium before starting monthly payments. The seller will not like that idea but it may be necessary. The seller, having come this far and looking to receive a check for $148,000 less the broker's fee at closing, will probably agree to anything within reason to close the deal.

With the above ideas in mind, the buyer prepares a loan application for the purchase of the Acme Widget Corporation. Excerpts from that loan application appear in Appendix C. The reader should be able to understand most of the package as written, although some discussion is offered at the conclusion.

QUESTIONS FOR DISCUSSION
Chapter 9—Financing

1. Why is bank financing more likely to be successful for the buyer than seller financing?

2. Why is bank financing more likely to be successful for the seller?

3. Financing seems to encourage more myths than anything else in the small business marketplace. Describe and nullify at least three of those myths.

Illustration 9.1

4. Assume that the buyer, after closing the deal, has an accident forcing him to shut down the business for the next three or four months. Which lender, a bank or the seller, is more likely to grant a moratorium on debt service until the buyer recovers sufficiently to reopen the business? Explain why.

5. True or false: Finding a bank that possibly would be willing to finance the purchase of a business is a difficult process?

6. True or false: Getting SBA participation in the bank loan is also difficult?

7. What information should be included in a loan application? How should it be prepared and packaged?

8. The amortization tables tell us that the monthly debt service on a $100,000 bank loan at 10% interest is $2,124.71. The debt service on the same loan from the seller at 8% is $2,027.64, for a difference of $97.07 per month, or a tax deductible $1,164.84 per year. Considering the professional services and benefits provided by the bank, is the higher rate of interest justified?

9. Why is it important for a loan officer to visit the premises of the business being purchased and financed?

CHAPTER 10
Choosing a Lawyer

Once financing has been arranged, it is time to choose a lawyer. Although choosing a lawyer is easy compared to the other tasks required to buy or sell a small business, it is a task usually misunderstood and often bungled. Most buyers and sellers do not understand the benefits of a good lawyer, benefits mostly outside the legal area, and they do not understand the dangers of a bad lawyer, dangers also mostly outside the legal area.

Recall that all human beings can be graded according to their competency: the upper 25%, the lower 25%, and the 50% in between. The purpose of this chapter is to describe some of the inherent benefits and dangers of working with a lawyer, thus motivating the reader to find a lawyer in the upper 25%. This chapter also will provide some of the clues to choosing wisely.

The chapter is presented in three parts: The Benefits and Dangers of Hiring a Lawyer, Qualities To Look for in a Lawyer, and How To Find a Good Lawyer.

PART 1:
THE BENEFITS AND DANGERS OF HIRING A LAWYER

The main benefit of hiring a good lawyer—here defined as one in the upper 25%—is the relatively high probability that the job will be done competently. The main danger of hiring a bad lawyer—here defined as one in the lower 25%—is the relatively high probability that the job will be done incompetently.

The benefits and dangers of hiring a lawyer are of two kinds, legal and extralegal. The legal benefits and dangers are mostly obvious and need only scant mention although, to be sure, they constitute the primary reason to be careful when hiring a lawyer. The extralegal benefits and dangers are mostly not obvious. They tend to be obscured by the legal aspects of the purchase and sale, the arcane nature of the whole affair, and the elevated emotions of the principals. Thus forewarned, the extralegal benefits and dangers constitute all the more reason to be careful when hiring a lawyer.

Benefits and Dangers in the Legal Realm. An example of a basically legal matter is preparing the contract. An example of a basically extralegal matter is appraising the business. Some matters, perhaps most, lap over into both areas. For example, preparing a list of equipment is a legal matter in that it is attached to the bill of sale but it is also an extralegal matter as a normal medium of communication between buyer and seller.

A lawyer's primary duty is to attend to the legal requirements of the deal, including:

- Determine which documents are necessary to close the transaction and to protect the client.
- Prepare those documents or, if prepared by someone else, review and approve them.
- Advise the client as to other activities and matters with legal ramifications. These might include obtaining a building permit if required for leasehold improvements, obtaining proper insurance coverage, hiring a title company, and forming a corporation.

The challenge to the lawyer is to competently perform his or her legal duties with no errors or omissions. Competently done, the probable result is a smooth transaction, at least within the purview of the lawyer, with no undesirable aftereffects. Incompetently done, the likelihood of trouble becomes relatively high.

To take an example from an actual case, a lawyer, whose client was the seller providing part of the financing, prepared the promissory note to be signed by the buyer. Instead of using a pre-printed form (available at most business-supply stores), he prepared his own form but forgot to include an acceleration clause. That mistake was potentially costly. An acceleration clause provides the best and possibly only chance to recover the loan once a troubled borrower has missed an installment. It enables the lender to take immediate legal action to collect the entire loan balance, including future installments, even if only one installment has been missed. Without that clause, the lender can sue only for tardy installments and might have to wait for the accumulation of sufficient arrears to make the action worthwhile.

Pre-printed forms in routine transactions, if correctly selected for the particular transaction, typically offer the advantage of having been time-tested and are almost certainly free of important errors or omissions. Nevertheless, they are shunned by some lawyers who view them as basically adequate but lacking in sophistication and versatility. In some cases, they are probably shunned to impress the client and/or to increase the lawyer's bill.

Assuming that all lawyers must graduate from law school and/or pass a test administered by the state before they can practice law, they all demonstrate a minimum level of competence before they can hold their services out to the public. For this reason, most lawyers, even those in the lower 25%, are probably competent enough to handle a routine purchase of a small business insofar as legal matters are concerned. Most small business purchases and sales do not require exceptional legal competence.

Benefits and Dangers in the Extralegal Realm. Most of the benefits and dangers of dealing with lawyers occur in the extralegal realm. That is where good lawyers tend to rise to the occasion, even in areas where they have no experience, and that is where bad lawyers tend to mismanage.

In the author's opinion, the benefits and dangers in the extralegal realm are about as important as those in the legal realm. This comparative importance becomes easy to see when realizing that, due to the profound effects of closing the purchase and sale on the lives of both the buyer and the seller, preserving the deal, a matter of extralegal importance, is often what counts most. Preserving the deal allows both buyer and seller to get on with their lives. Getting on with their lives means getting on with their chosen careers and their chosen pursuits of happiness. Thus, within the context of the lives of the principals, preserving the deal usually counts more than getting the best price or getting the best terms. Buyers, sellers, and their lawyers need to understand this.

Generally, in the extralegal realm, the benefits tend to preserve the deal while the dangers tend to destroy the deal. These benefits and dangers are wide in scope and large in number because a lawyer's extralegal activities are wide in scope and large in number. Such activities—which, as mentioned above, may lap into the legal area to one degree or another—may include the following:

- Helping the buyer to choose the right business.
- Helping the seller decide when to put the business on the market and when to tell the employees.
- Qualifying the buyer for the seller.
- Appraising the business.
- Negotiating in behalf of the client or assisting in the negotiation.
- Acting as a mediator (which, actually, is part of the negotiation).
- Preparing a letter of intent (also part of the negotiation).
- Acting as the client's confidant.
- Calling for outside experts to assist the client.
- Calling the right people when bureaucracies impede progress.
- Assisting in problem-solving of any kind.
- Assisting with personal difficulties.
- Helping with decision-making.
- Overseeing and administering the entire deal.

Some lawyers may be competent in legal affairs but incompetent in such extralegal affairs as those just mentioned. In fact, such disparity of skills is a common occurrence and a frequent danger. The danger is heightened when a lawyer is eminent for his or her legal skills but when this eminence overshadows, however unintentionally and innocently, the lawyer's extralegal weaknesses. It is this enticing legal eminence too often combined with harmful extralegal weakness that makes choosing a lawyer a subtly dangerous affair. That is why a full chapter is devoted to this task.

Recognizing the importance of the deal in the overall context of the client's life is the lawyer's extralegal duty of highest priority. To repeat the reason: Buying or selling a small business is a major event in the lives of the principals, ranking with graduations, weddings, divorces, and funerals. It has profound and lasting effects on their lives. For the buyer, these profound effects were shown in Chapter 1 in the section titled "Right Reasons for Buying a Business;" not the least of those reasons dealing with Maslow's hierarchy of human needs and being able to do what one loves to do. For the seller, the profound effects were shown in the section titled "Reasons for Selling a Business;" not the least of those reasons being failing health, death of spouse, emotional burnout, or poor profits to the point that the seller can no longer earn a living.

The question arises as to why lawyers, or people in general, fail to see the importance of the extralegal aspects of the small business purchase and sale. The answer is partly because of the human tendency to see a small business as nothing more than a chattel, an ordinary occupation, or a financial investment. The answer also is partly because lawyers lack training in the extralegal aspects of buying and selling a small business. And, sadly, it is partly because some of them lack sensitivity to human needs. This last reason provides a clue to choosing a good lawyer, a clue developed below.

Magnifying the importance of preserving the deal are the illiquidity of small businesses, the months and sometimes years that buyers have invested to find the right seller and can ill afford to lose, and the months and sometimes years that sellers have invested to find the right buyer and which they too can ill afford to lose. To illustrate the dangers of the lawyer who fails either to understand these profound effects or, if he or she does understand, to deal adequately with them, one need only review some of the examples appearing in previous chapters. These examples are valuable even though they were offered to illustrate other points. Particularly noteworthy would be Examples 8.3 and 8.9 showing bad lawyers in action. Further examples will be shown below.

The reader has already seen examples of bad lawyers in action. It is time for an example of a good lawyer in action and the concomitant benefits. Example 10.1 is offered below. This example also will illustrate why the extra effort to find a good lawyer is more than justified.

Example 10.1 A prospective buyer responding to a broker's advertisement announces that he has been searching for this kind of a business for several years and that now that he has found it, is intent on making the purchase. Almost in the same breath, the buyer states that there is something that the broker needs to understand. He (the buyer) generally gets along with people but only up to a point. Past that point, he walks away. Once he walks, he never comes back. Never. The broker expresses his understanding of the buyer's needs, then proceeds to describe the business and answer the buyer's questions. Although the business has not shown a profit in the last three years, the poor performance is apparently explained by the absentee ownership (the owner lives in a distant city) and by suspected ongoing employee theft. The business shows strong potential for a buyer who will manage full time on the premises, as this buyer plans to do.

The buyer is provided ample financial data but the data are hard to understand (partly due to disorderly bookkeeping). The buyer consults with his lawyer who, after examining the data, calls in a respected accountant for analysis. The accountant, with the lawyer overseeing, prepares cash-flow projections showing a lucrative return on investment if the business can be bought for $400,000. If bought at the seller's price of $550,000, the business might still be a good investment but would involve more risk and turnaround speculation than the buyer cares to accept. Further, the buyer can only put $65,000 down and will need seller financing for the balance. Bank financing would be difficult because of the recent failure to show a profit and, possibly, because of a declining neighborhood. After the broker's commission of 9%, the seller will realize only $29,000 cash at closing and will have to pay his legal fees and taxes out of that.

The lawyer writes a letter of intent for the buyer's signature similar to the one written by Acme Widget's buyer in Figure 8.1. That letter, like the one for Acme, is cordial and workmanlike in tone. Then the lawyer writes another letter, also for the buyer's signature, to explain the buyer's low offer and put everything in perspective for both buyer and seller. That second letter, to cover the letter of intent, reads as follows:

Dear Mr. Smith:

I realize that my offer in the enclosed letter of intent falls short of your price and that it will be disappointing to you. I sincerely wish that I could offer the full $550,000 simply because the business seems worth that much and because I want to be as fair as possible. I am limited, however, by modest funds and my family responsibilities. This is the best I can do.

If you would like to put my offer aside while trying to find an offer closer to the true value of your business, I will understand. In the meantime, I will keep my offer open in case you wish to reconsider.

Respectfully,

Charles Brown (signed)

A few days after the buyer mails the offer, the broker receives a long-distance telephone call from the seller. The call is not pleasant. In vituperative terms and with scathing voice, the seller scolds and berates the broker for having sent an unqualified buyer. The scolding lasts for four or five minutes. Then, without the broker having said more than a word or two, the seller says that he will get back later and he hangs up. Only then does the broker realize that this was the seller's way of accepting the offer.

A day or two later, the buyer's lawyer calls the broker to discuss the deal. After only a minute or so, the lawyer interrupts himself to ask the broker if he has spoken to the seller yet. The broker says that he has but that it wasn't very pleasant. Then the lawyer reveals that he too was severely scolded and that he has already gotten it twice. The lawyer adds that he does not understand the seller nor does he relish further conversation with him. All that really matters is closing the deal. The broker agrees and now they have a team of sorts working to the mutual satisfaction of their clients. They also have a bond of sympathy. And they are working for the same goal even though, in a sense, their respective clients are adversaries.

The lawyer takes charge of the deal, prepares the proper documents, mails them to the seller, and negotiates the details with the seller's lawyer. Then a problem arises. The seller informs the buyer's lawyer that he refuses to provide all of the financing. He will settle for the price offered but he wants more cash. The lawyer describes the problem to the broker and asks if he knows of a solution. The broker says no, then they cordially say goodbye. Several days go by with the deal in limbo. Then the broker reconsiders and calls the lawyer to offer to take a note in partial payment for the commission. The lawyer is delighted, predicts that the broker's sharing the financing will unblock the deal, and is proven to be right.

Now the deal is running smoothly, at least legally. Extralegally, it is also running smoothly except that the seller continues to call both the lawyer and the broker to inflict such verbal abuse as neither has heard before and that both find increasingly hard to tolerate. One day, the seller's wife calls the broker and proves to be her husband's match at scathing vituperation. (The broker wonders how two persons of such temperament can exist under the same roof but he puts the thought aside as not being pertinent to the deal.) In any case, one thing is good: the buyer has been spared any of the abuse and the deal is being preserved because of it.

With all the details falling into place—the buyer's lawyer has taken care of permits, the lease, equipment checkout, and so on—the closing is set to occur in the office of a local lawyer who will represent the seller. The seller will fly to St. Louis to attend. (The seller's wife will have signed in advance and will therefore not have to accompany her husband.)

Now the day has arrived for the closing. The attendees are the seller, the buyer and his wife, the two lawyers, the broker, the lessor's agent, an insurance agent, and two others acting in advisory capacities. They are seated around a conference table with the seller at the head of the table and with the buyer at one side with his lawyer next to him. The meeting begins with such routine matters as minor questions to be answered, which documents are to be signed, and so forth. Then the seller brings up the matter of inventory evaluation. It is not nearly enough to pay for the quantity included in the sale or for the quality of it. The buyer's lawyer modestly explains how the evaluation was made. The explanation is unsatisfactory to the seller, one thing leads to another, and the seller launches a scathing attack. The attack itself is not a surprise nor is the severity of it. The surprise is that it does not end but goes on beyond reason—six minutes, eight minutes, maybe longer—but way beyond the point of being a simple emotional outburst. The seller is out of control, the deal now seems threatened, and nobody in the room knows what to do. The buyer's face has already turned red when the seller's attack turns personal and he challenges the buyer to make an explanation. At this point, the seller stops bellowing and waits for a reply whereupon the lawyer, seeing his client's distress, slips his arm around the buyer's shoulders and says, "Charlie, you've waited too long to find this business to lose it now. Let me do the talking." Before the lawyer can say anything, however, the seller resumes his attack with no letup in severity. It has been ten, maybe 12 minutes since the attack began with still no end in sight. Now everyone in the room is stupefied except the lawyer who still has his arm around the buyer but who now places his other hand on top of the buyer's and takes hold. It is clear that the lawyer is going to get that business for his client and that no one is going to stop him.

Now another surprise. The seller himself turns red, he quits his tirade, and walks briskly out of the room without saying a word. The others remain in their chairs, mostly dumbfounded, and wonder what in the world will happen next. After a few minutes, the seller has not returned. The others stand and mill about. Ten more minutes go by, someone looks to no avail down the hallway and in the men's room, then speculation becomes rife on the seller's intentions. No one has an answer so all stand by and wait. Finally, 45 minutes after the seller had walked out, he returns as though nothing had happened, the closing resumes, and it is over in 20 minutes. The buyer has his business, the seller has his payment, the broker has his commission, everybody is at least quiet, if not satisfied, and the deal is done.

Note all that the buyer's lawyer did that was right and some things he did not do that would have been wrong: he recognized his own limitations in financial analysis and hired a good accountant, probably an auditor experienced in digging through mazes of data, to do most of the work, an exceptionally noteworthy action considering that this lawyer was expert in estate planning and taxes. He recognized the value of cash-flow projections in preparing an offer. He recognized the value of a letter of intent. (Incidentally, that lawyer's letter became the model for the letter described in Chapter 8.) He wrote a cover letter which was praiseworthy for the concept but even more so for its execution and its achievement of a preemptive first strike. That cover letter was a psychological gem which, stripped of its polite phrasing, required the seller to take it or leave it, but did it so palatably that the seller accepted a disagreeable offer. The lawyer established a team spirit with the broker. He might have questioned the amount of the broker's commission (as other lawyers occasionally do) but, whatever his thoughts, he wisely kept them to himself. When the seller insisted on more cash up front, the lawyer described the problem to the broker in gentlemanly terms and never even hinted at a solution involving the broker's commission. In other words, he maintained a team spirit and continued to encourage positive thinking by all parties concerned. Moreover, he bore the brunt of the seller's abuse although, to be sure, the broker got battered too. The lawyer remained calm throughout and never let his focus stray from the goal of the transaction: to get that business for his client. At the closing, he monitored his client's feelings, saw his client's distress, gave support when support was called for, and did it under fire. The lawyer helped his client fulfill the dream of a lifetime and to do it at a bargain price.

As a corollary, the lawyer protected the interests of the secondary parties. The employees' jobs were preserved, as were the business's services for the customers. And the community received a much needed lift from the competent new management.

Despite the lawyer's good performance, however, his cover letter is subject to question. The take-it-or-leave-it offer could have been rejected, losing this dearly-sought business for his client. In reply, had the seller rejected, the buyer could have reconsidered and reopened the negotiation, albeit with some loss of credibility. In any case, it is presumed that the buyer and his lawyer discussed these possibilities and acted accordingly. On the other hand, the $400,000 limit may have been genuine for the exact reasons given, in which case it was no bluff. If that is the case, the lawyer is a hero for snatching that business for his financially limited client. Whether or not the offer actually was a bluff, no one will ever know except the lawyer and his client.

(Incidentally, the buyer started his ownership with a bad break: A major piece of equipment ruptured just six weeks after closing and cost $25,000 to replace. That hurt the buyer but made his fiscally conservative offer look good. Fortunately, the buyer exceeded his own sales forecast. New customers were recruited and old customers were lured back to try the new, improved management, and, at last report, he was doing well. As for the broker's commission, the seller was late on the first and last installments but did complete payments eight months after closing, just two weeks later than promised.) Example 10.1 showed how beneficial a good lawyer can be and provided a standard for lawyers to emulate. Example 10.2 very sadly shows the opposite. It also shows why brokers sometimes refer to lawyers as "deal-killers." Although such epithets are not only mostly untrue and unjust, but also immoral because of their false generalization, they are understandable in light of such examples as the following.

Example 10.2 This example is a continuation of Example 9.1 wherein the owners of a small manufacturing company were forced to sell after 30 years in business due to old age and the husband's declining health. The owners, lacking business acumen, had financed the purchase to an unqualified buyer and, in only a few months' time, were forced to take back a damaged business, losing their entire $60,000 down payment and more.

Now the owners list with a broker who, only a few weeks after listing, has the good luck to introduce them to qualified buyers, another husband-and-wife team. The buyers are delighted to find this business not only because it suits their desires so well but also because they have been looking for several years and now are enjoying their first sweet taste of success. The husband will manage the shop and the wife will manage the retail store and office. The salient part of the matchup is that the business needs sales badly while the buying husband has had a long and successful career in sales. Even better, his specialty is making cold calls; with the attractive product line this company has, there is no question that he will bring in new business.

After carefully and cautiously fact-finding the business for about four months—with the buying husband spending many hours in the shop getting a detailed introduction to overcome his weakness in manufacturing—the buyers make an offer and negotiate a cash price of $180,000 contingent on bank financing. Considering that the shop equipment required to manufacture the product line would probably cost at least two or three times the purchase price to replace, and considering that the business has national potential which the buying husband has the skill to exploit (he makes sales calls regularly throughout the United States and Canada), the agreed price is a bargain. The broker prepares a loan application, including cash-flow projections, which is accepted at the first bank he approaches contingent on obtaining SBA participation. The banker, noting how well established the business is, the relatively safe product line, and the good matchup of the buyers to the business, compliments the broker on the matchup and explains that the only reason he insists on SBA involvement is that it is a procedural requirement (at least at his bank) for most depressed businesses.

With financing now practically secured, the broker prepares a contract (on a pre-printed form) for the buyers' signatures, whereupon the buyers hire an accountant and a lawyer. A few days later, the buyers' lawyer calls the broker to discuss the contract. The lawyer's tone is not cordial, but cold and barely civil, and he has a few comments and questions, mostly for clarity on minor items. One of the questions involves his clients' making a $100 earnest deposit. The broker, who sees earnest deposits as useless nuisances except in cases where they have a clearly identifiable purpose, asks the lawyer for his reason. The lawyer gives a vague response. The broker asks if the deposit might be to somehow give weight to the buyers' enforcing the contract should the sellers for some reason wish to back out. The lawyer says yes. Then the broker asks if the sellers, who have spent 30 years of their lives building this business, should be expected to allow themselves to be tied down by a deposit of $100. The lawyer says that yes, that is the idea. The broker says that he will run it by the sellers and see how they feel about it. Not much more is said and the conversation ends. Now the sellers and their broker wait for the signed contract to be submitted or at least to be sent back with changes.

A few days later, the buyers call to inform the broker that they have lowered their offer to $140,000. They also have decided to refuse bank financing, especially with SBA involvement, and will insist on seller financing. The broker notices that something else has changed. He used to have—or at least he thought he used to have—good rapport with the buyers with a friendly, forthright relationship and open flow of ideas. Now the buyers are addressing the broker with a disrespectful tone and snippiness. The broker questions the change in price. They reply that their lawyer told them that brokers always get the highest prices that buyers are willing to pay because that way brokers get the highest commissions. The broker's intuition tells him not to prolong this conversation but he feels justified to ask why their refusal of bank financing. The buyers reply that this is the way they want it. The broker then thanks the buyers for calling and politely says goodbye.

After informing the sellers of the status of the deal (and feeling terrible about it), the broker waits a day to allow his thoughts and his feelings to settle and then calls the buyers' lawyer for explanations. That conversation is best described by the following letter from the broker to the lawyer. The letter is edited for purposes of disguise. Personal names are fictitious.

March 15, 19xx

J. Q. Lawyer
Smith and Jones, Attorneys at Law
xxxx Forsyth Boulevard
St. Louis, Missouri 63105

Dear Mr. Lawyer:

This letter is in response to our telephone conversation of last Thursday when you advised that it would take longer, in case of a default on a business loan, for a seller-financier to take the borrower's home than it would for the SBA. Your reasoning was that the seller would have accepted an unsecured promissory note and would thus be forced into lengthy litigation, while the SBA, having the borrower's home as collateral, would swiftly foreclose and force the borrower out on to the street. You also felt that seller financing could be had at a lower rate and that it would give the seller an incentive to help the buyer, should the business develop problems. Thus you have advised Bob and Mary Butler to avoid the SBA and to obtain seller financing.

To determine the SBA's policies in dealing with defaulted loans, I telephoned the following parties last Thursday and Friday:

Mr. John Tucker
Office of Business Development
xxxx Elm Grove Avenue
St. Louis, Missouri 63100
123-1234
(The OBD is supported by municipal tax funds for the purpose of providing certain kinds of assistance to business people in the City of St. Louis.)

Mr. Al Peters, Assistant Vice President
Friendly Bank of Missouri
21555 Main Street
St. Louis, Missouri 63100
123-2345

Ms. Diane Carter
Small Business Administration
815 Olive Street, Room 999
St. Louis, Missouri 63101
539-6600

Mr. Don Johnson
Business Development Center
Scholarly University
St. Louis, Missouri 63100
123-3456

(The Business Development Center is staffed by University faculty and supported by federal tax funds to provide certain kinds of assistance to business people in the St. Louis area.)

Following is a summary of the comments I received from these parties. Their statements regarding the intent, the purpose, and the policies of the SBA were unanimous. When a borrower defaults on an SBA-backed loan, the initial efforts to collect are done by the banker who tries to work with the borrower. If something cannot be worked out (several months may elapse in the meantime), the bank collects from the SBA which, in turn, takes over in working with the borrower. The SBA fully intends to collect its loans. However, the SBA, being non-profit and in existence solely to assist business owners, will provide several alternatives for a problem loan. These include stretched-out payment plan, moratorium, and liquidation. The SBA prefers that stretch-outs and moratoriums be brief; however, they can last for years if the circumstances warrant. In some cases, the SBA has delayed payment indefinitely to the time when the borrower sells his home at his own convenience. Liquidation is considered a last resort and even then the business is liquidated first, and then the home. Since the SBA is the friendliest of all possible lenders or guarantors (except, perhaps, family), SBA participation is considered a major advantage to a borrower. In contrast, since the sellers in our transaction are in their mid-sixties, their patience, not to mention the patience of their attorney, would likely be considerably less than the SBA's. It would seem, therefore, that insofar as the safety of their home is concerned, the buyers will be much more secure with the SBA.

With respect to the lower interest cost usually associated with seller financing, assume that $60,000 could be seller-financed for five years at 8% instead of 10%. (We must also assume, however questionably, that the sellers and their attorney would agree to an unsecured loan.) The amortization tables give us the following:

$60,000, 5-year loan: at 10% $1274.83/month
                      at 8%   1216.59/month

                    savings = $ 58.24/month

        annual pre-tax savings = $ 698.88

    annual after-tax savings around $ 600

    total 5-year savings around $3,000

I advised Bob and Mary of the possible savings about three

months ago when they were in my office contemplating their first offer. It was my advice then, as it is now, that due to the marginal savings combined with the sellers' very strong desire for cash, a cash offer would be preferable, more negotiable, and would probably result in a lower sale price. Thus, the buyers have already realized the benefits of seller financing by foregoing it in favor of a lower sale price.

With respect to maintaining the sellers' support during the term of the seller financing, the sellers' support is already assured during the first year of new ownership by the terms of the purchase and sale agreement, which you have a copy of. After the first year, even though the sellers intend to remain in St. Louis and to be available from time to time on a consulting basis, I have advised Bob and Mary not to buy this business if they do not feel comfortably capable of exploiting its potential using their own abilities. Granted that it is nice to have the sellers around for a few years in case there is a problem. But if the security of having them around for more than the first year enters into the decision to buy, then it is a bad decision based on false security. It is a bad decision because it places the buyers' focus on the wrong abilities, the sellers', instead of on the right abilities, their own.

Furthermore, there are other motivations, some of them powerful, for the sellers to help the buyers in the event of a problem. The sellers are also the landlords and they wish to collect the rent. The sellers' name will be retained by the buyers, providing the sellers, who are childless, with a form of perpetuity, and a very nice form at that. The continuation of the business also provides the sellers, who have a sense of propriety and rectitude, with the knowledge that their efforts and creations and all of the considerable quality they built into the business during the past thirty years will not be lost to the community. Finally, the buyers, who themselves have a sense of graciousness and respect, have informed the sellers that they will always be welcome to visit.

In the unlikely case that the sellers are for some reason not available, the buyers can always hire a consultant.

There is one other aspect of this purchase and sale which bears mentioning. When a buyer of a business obtains financing through a bank, he may pay a higher interest rate than he otherwise would to the seller but, in exchange, he receives the banker's professional expertise in determining whether the business is viable, stable, and reasonably priced and whether he has the capability of running that business, developing its potential, and repaying the loan. Further, I sensed in our telephone conversation that you feel that the banks and the SBA don't care about the buyer; that as long as they have the collateral, they will lend money to unqualified buyers to buy undesirable businesses and simply foreclose when the business fails and move on to the next customer. My entire experience as a broker and consultant has been to the contrary. As an example, I recently sold a well established and profitable retail business, priced at $20,000 plus $80,000 inventory at cost, to a buyer whose net worth was $600,000. The buyer had an MBA and an excellent track record during twenty-one years in industry. The buyer applied for a $40,000 loan and offered both the business and his personal assets as collateral. Yet he was rejected by two banks because he had no sales experience. A third bank (which, incidentally, was Friendly Bank of Missouri) refused a business loan of any kind whether SBA-guaranteed or not but allowed that, in view of his very sizeable net worth, it might grant a small personal loan to be used as he saw fit. Other examples like this one could be cited but I think you get the point.

To summarize the above, SBA financing is business-like, humane, and designed to be beneficial to the community. Seller financing and concomitant lower interest cost have already been looked at and dealt with and are not necessarily desirable anyway.

In closing, you could do a service to all of the parties involved, including Friendly Bank of Missouri and the SBA, if you would share with us the source of your insights on bank and SBA financing. It might also be helpful to know the source of your statement that most sales of businesses are seller-financed, especially if you include comparative rates of failure between seller financing and bank financing.

Perhaps we could serve our clients better in the future if you and I could discuss any business advice you might be proposing before you propose it. I myself tend to be extremely cautious about proposing legal advice. I would be happy to share my time and my knowledge at no cost to you or to Bob and Mary and they would get the benefit of advice which is more thoroughly thought out and much less contested. The purchase of a business usually inflicts a heavy emotional drain on both buyer and seller. If the banker, accountant, lawyer, and broker can work together, the transaction can be much more smooth and profitable for all parties concerned.

Yours very truly,

J. Q. Broker (signed)

Copy: Bob and Mary Butler

The broker hand-carries the letter to the lawyer's office to be sure that it gets there, to promote a possible chat with the lawyer, and simply to get a look at the lawyer's office. The broker is greeted by the firm's receptionist who informs him that the lawyer is out sick today but that she will see that he receives the letter. The broker thanks the receptionist and exits.

The broker waits a few days in hopes of getting a response either from the lawyer or the buyers but none is forthcoming. The broker calls the sellers and learns that, since the broker's listing agreement has expired, the sellers have listed with another broker. The husband elaborates on what has transpired: he felt so depressed to learn what the buyers had done—especially after all the time he and his wife had spent with them over the last four months—that the same day that the broker had called with the bad news, he had called another broker selected from the *Yellow Pages*. That second broker then brought a buyer with no experience in manufacturing or in sales and who made the following offer: He would buy the business if the sellers would do 100% financing with no money down. In response, the seller told the second broker and his buyer to get out and not to come back. Now he regrets that he listed with the second broker and he apologizes for having done so and for removing him from any possibility—at least for the next six months—of further representing the sellers. The broker tells the seller that he understands the seller's feelings and why he acted as he did and that no apology is necessary. The broker now expresses how bad he feels about what happened, but that he does not know if there is anything he can do to make things right. The two say goodbye and the conversation ends.

A few months later, the first broker calls the selling husband to see how things are going and learns that the sellers have agreed to sell their equipment, inventory, and patents to a company from another city. They will receive a distress-sale price for the business, but have little choice because of the husband's health. The broker again expresses his regrets at the way things went. Their relationship is over.

The lawyer in Example 10.2 made a number of mistakes, all in the extralegal realm, and several of them were big. One of the big ones was his failure to realize the importance to his clients of closing the purchase. Another mistake was his tone of authority on topics he knew little or nothing about. Another was his bias in assessing the broker (a bias somewhat justified, however, by the uneven capabilities and ethics of brokers and their lack of certification). Still another was his bias against the SBA, a mistake compounded by his apparent failure to check out the SBA after receiving the broker's letter. Another still was his failure to comprehend the benefits of bank financing. And still another was his failure to reply to the broker's letter. Finally was his insistence on the seller's accepting an unsecured note.

Three factors mitigated the lawyer's responsibility for the broken deal. One is that the buyers' banker (probably the one handling their house mortgage, not a commercial loan officer) voiced skepticism about the viability of the business. So did their accountant. And the buyers, the bad advice they received notwithstanding, showed a surprising lack of fortitude considering that they had been looking so long for the right business to buy. Perhaps they had remorse about the commitment to go into business which, exacerbated by the bad advice, was the real cause of the broken deal. In any case, the broker felt that the lawyer's performance was flagrantly bad. He therefore complained to the Bar Association. The Bar Association denied the broker's charges. The details are reported in Appendix B.

In spite of all the mistakes the lawyer made, the blame has to be shared by the buyers for their own lack of common sense, their own failure to sympathize with the needs of the sellers, and their failure to question their lawyer, especially after receiving the broker's letter. In a way, perhaps, they did not belong in the world of business, not as owners anyway, since common sense and a respect for the needs of others are so important to success. In light of what happened, the buyers' earlier statement that the sellers would always be welcome to visit—a statement originally viewed by the broker as gracious and wise—might now be seen as shallow and rhetorical and perhaps even self-serving as an opportunity to get free consultations from the owners whenever necessary. From the buyers' viewpoint, therefore, this case may have had the best ending possible, even if they did not realize it. The lawyer is still not excused.

Now that the reader has experienced the work of a good lawyer compared to the work of a bad lawyer, the question is how to tell them apart before becoming deeply involved and committed. That question is the subject of the next part of the chapter.

PART 2:
QUALITIES TO LOOK FOR IN A LAWYER

There are at least eleven qualities to look for in a lawyer and they are discussed in the first eleven sections below. A twelfth section describes some qualities not to look for.

Understanding of the Primacy of the Deal. In Chapter 8, the 21 basic rules of negotiating were presented. The first of those rules was to decide at the outset which is more important and to what degree, getting the best price or closing the deal. A good lawyer will ask that question of the client but, failing that, the client should inform the lawyer. If closing the deal is more important than getting the best price, as it usually is, then that is the lawyer's first priority.

Within the context of being fair and reasonable, virtually everything is subordinate to closing the deal.

Willingness to Compromise. Since closing the deal is usually of primary importance, buyers and sellers need lawyers who are willing to compromise. Even after the buyer and seller have agreed on the price and basic terms, there is always a host of minor terms to be worked out between the lawyers for the principals and also between all the involved parties including the landlord, insurance agents, licensing agencies, and so on. It is a remarkable fact of business life, considering the absolute need for compromise, that lawyers can be perfectly intractable even on matters of small importance and even when the deal threatens to come apart unless agreement is reached. Note Example 10.3:

> **Example 10.3** The buyer and seller of a cocktail lounge have reached agreement on the price and terms and, since financing has been obtained and the liquor license has been applied for, the principals have brought their lawyers into the transaction. The contract has been signed pending the usual contingencies. One of the contingencies is obtaining a lease which, in turn, is contingent on working out an assignment of lease which, again in turn, is contingent on obtaining the liquor license.
>
> An assignment of lease is not a complicated affair but there are three parts to it which require coordination and signatures: the assignment itself which must be signed by the present tenant who is the seller; the acceptance of the assignment which must be signed by the tenant-to-be who is the buyer; and the consent of assignment which must be signed by the landlord. Sometimes the buyer, the seller, or the landlord may insist on a new lease, thus obviating any assignment. The buyer and seller agree that the buyer's lawyer will write the assignment, the seller's lawyer will review it, and, upon the latter's approval, they will submit it to the landlord's lawyer. In St. Louis, liquor license applications are approved by a judge in court session and those applications therefore appear on court dockets. It is imperative that the assignment of lease be coordinated and signed by all three parties prior to the buyer's appearance in court. Nobody knows that better than the lawyers. What follows, therefore, is beyond belief.
>
> About six weeks before the anticipated court date, the broker, not new in the trade and tempered by experience, strongly urges the buyer to instruct his lawyer to get an early start on the assignment, and explains why. The buyer nods his understanding and says he will get right to it. About a week later the broker checks with the buyer and learns that the buyer's lawyer says that there

is still plenty of time and that he will start on it later. The broker expresses some urgency, with only five weeks to go, and repeats his earlier warning that lawyers working with lawyers sometimes require long lead times for work-related reasons such as court appearances, emergencies such as clients in jail or in distress, and heavy work loads. Moreover, for a lease assignment, there are three lawyers to coordinate, not just two, and extra time should be allowed. The buyer says that he will get his lawyer started right away. Another week goes by with no progress. Now there are four weeks left. The broker visits the buyer's lawyer to personally urge him to get started. The lawyer is receptive, and the broker politely explains his concern. The two have a nice chat during which the broker discovers that the lawyer is part of the buyer's family, that he too owns a bar and understands the situation, and that everything will work out just fine.

A week later, the broker calls the buyer's lawyer and learns that he hasn't started yet but will begin next Tuesday. By now the court date has been made firm with just three weeks remaining. The broker telephones on Wednesday and is promised that the assignment of lease will be ready Friday. On Friday he is told it will be ready Saturday noon for sure. The broker goes to the lawyer's office on noon Saturday and, to his relief, the document is ready to go. The broker hand-carries it to the seller's lawyer's office and—this being a Saturday afternoon—has the good fortune to find him there. They have a cordial discussion. The lawyer realizes that only two weeks remain, and he will get right on it. The broker reminds the lawyer that though the seller is too young to retire, he is burned out by the hard work and long hours required at the lounge and really wants to get out of the business. The seller also is tired of working evenings when his wife and children are home and missing out on family activities. The sale is important to the seller, who worries that too much delay will discourage the buyer. The broker adds that if there is anything in the assignment of lease that the seller's lawyer does not agree with, it would be appreciated by all if he could work something out with the buyer's lawyer. The lawyer expresses his understanding and says that he will take care of everything. The lawyer's assurance is warm and comforting and now things seem to be running smoothly.

A week later the broker learns that the seller's lawyer has completely rewritten the assignment but has done so without telling anyone, not even the buyer's lawyer. The broker asks why he did not tell anyone and the lawyer says that now the assignment has been done the way it should be done and that the buyer's lawyer will simply have to go along with it. Next, the broker carries a copy to the buyer's lawyer and reminds him that only one week remains before the court date. The lawyer says that there was nothing wrong with the way he wrote the assignment but that he will examine the new assignment anyway. The broker brings the status to the attention of both buyer and seller and suggests that they get their lawyers moving if they want the deal to close. Both call their lawyers and both are told that everything is fine and that there is nothing to worry about.

Now it is Monday, with closing set for the following Monday morning at the bank. The week passes, neither lawyer calls the other, and nothing is done to resolve the stalemate. On Saturday before the Monday closing, neither lawyer is in his office, both have said they will not attend the closing, neither principal has the necessary document, and the broker is left to ponder what to do to get the deal closed. Fortunately, the broker has kept copies of both versions of the assignment and he stays up late Sunday night to combine what he feels are the best features of each into one document. He types it that night before going to bed.

The following morning, both principals and the broker arrive at the bank on time, everything runs smoothly, and the closing is done except that the landlord's lawyer still has to review the assignment prepared by the broker. (The broker, by the way, has not the slightest intention of telling the lawyers, the principals, or anyone else what he has done.) A copy signed by the principals is carried to the landlord's lawyer's office for his signature as power of attorney. But the lawyer is not in and nobody knows where he is.

Now the deal is hanging in mid-air since the judge will not approve the license without the landlord's signature. All the broker can do is keep pushing as best he can, so he carries another copy—signed by the principals but still lacking the landlord's signature—to the agent (a consultant specializing in liquor licenses) carrying the buyer's license application to court. Then he returns to the landlord's lawyer's office in hopes of getting a signature. There the broker sips coffee, reads a magazine, and waits for the lawyer's return in hopes that he can rush a signed copy to the court in time for the hearing. At 11:30—the powers-that-be smile fortuitously this day—the lawyer walks in, takes the broker into his office, starts reviewing the assignment of lease, then, just two or three minutes later, to the broker's astonishment, gets a telephone call from the judge in the courtroom who has the unsigned document in front of him, who just happens to know both the landlord and the lawyer, and who wants to know why there is no landlord's signature on the assignment. The landlord's lawyer explains that he just a moment ago received a copy of the assignment, he tells the judge that he is sure that something will be worked out, the judge grants the license over the telephone, the landlord's lawyer approves the assignment, no questions are asked of the broker (further evidencing the existence of fortuitous powers), the deal is done, everybody is happy, and the broker, now ecstatic but still nervous, quaffs two beers with his lunch and takes the rest of the day off.

Such stories as the above provide a humor of sorts: The zany, suspenseful deal; insouciant lawyers suited for a Gilbert and Sullivan operetta; two kinds of bars as a milieu for mirth; and all with a happy ending. The buyer was in an unrewarding, dead-end job, and this purchase was his escape. The seller was burned out and wanted more time with his wife and children, and this sale was his escape. They never discovered how close their deal had come to not closing but the reader can be assured that if they had, neither would have thought that this was funny.

Self-Awareness of Limitations. A common deficiency of lawyers is their failure to recognize their limitations. The advice they give is liable to cover any topic whether they are trained in that topic or not. Thus, there is inherent danger in the extralegal advice of a lawyer. It should be clear that the lack of training in the matter under consideration, of and by itself, is not the problem. Lawyers, like professional persons in general, are expected to fill in the gaps in their knowledge to the extent necessary to serve their clients. That's part of what it means to be professional and that's one of the benefits of dealing with a professional. What is dangerous is ill-prepared advice. What is several times more dangerous is ill-prepared advice combined with a tone of authority. Example 10.2 above underscored the point. In Example 6.3 (revisited in Example 7.2), both a lawyer and an accountant spoke as though they were final authorities on valuing a business. "Not a penny more," said one and "Not a penny less," said the other, though they were apart by an order of magnitude. What they should have done was allow that these were their own uneducated estimates and that their clients should seek expert advice elsewhere. As an alternative, either of them could have called in an expert to provide the needed advice, as did the lawyer in Example 10.1.

Low-Key Aggressiveness. The lawyer who devises ways in which to get the best price and terms for his client but who does so without seeming aggressive demonstrates the low-key approach. One advantage of the low key is the better chance for the aggressiveness not to be seen as such by the other party. It thus provides the opportunity, like a Trojan horse, to sneak something past one's adversary. It is a kind of covert attack. If preemptive, the effectiveness may increase. Another, more important, advantage is that aggressiveness designed not to seem aggressive is less likely to rile the emotions. The less the emotions are riled, the more likely the deal will be preserved.

The cover letter in Example 10.1 was a perfect example of low-key aggressiveness. Another, somewhat inelegant but possibly effective example would be a contract prepared by a seller's lawyer devoid of protective covenants for the buyer (or vice versa). The buyer's lawyer of course would insert whatever covenants thought to be needed but would do so with the disadvantage of having to spend bargaining chips with the seller's lawyer to win those covenants. As an alternative, the buyer's lawyer might employ what is the best defense against a one-sided contract, which is to ignore it and write one more favorable. Still, the buyer's lawyer would be at a disadvantage, namely, that he would have to think of the idea of ignoring the contract and writing another. Not all lawyers would. In any case, a contract devoid of protective covenants is generally not recommended because of the possibly fatal loss of trust between the buyer and the seller, or between their lawyers.

A Sense of Human Dignity. At about the 80% point in this book, the high emotions of the small business purchase and sale have been mentioned and illustrated enough times for the reader to have become well acquainted with them. If there is one rule which stands above the others in minimizing undesirable excesses of the emotions and all their tawdry manifestations, it is to preserve the dignity of the individual. The lawyer who treats others, including the client's adversary, as he would have others treat him is about as qualified to preserve the deal as anyone possibly can be. As long as the deal is preserved, even when there are big problems which seem unsolvable, the opportunity to work things out remains alive. If the deal is broken, especially if because the adversary's dignity was ignored or trashed, the opportunity to work things out is probably dead.

Dignity is the state of being worthy and respected. Following are some important devices in preserving dignity:

- To tell the truth and the whole truth about whatever is happening.
- To honor the provisionality of truth, which is to allow that everything is open to discussion.

- To make criticism only if it is constructive and then only in a polite and straightforward manner.
- To refrain from sarcasm.
- To refrain from coercive tactics such as blocking communication or hanging up the telephone on a party to express dissatisfaction.
- To speak and to act as though the decency and integrity of the adversary are presumed even if they are not.
- To manifest empathy.
- To treat others as he or she would be treated.

The lawyer who behaves in such manner encourages feelings of worth in others and he or she encourages thereby the good will which emanates from such worth. Such a lawyer keeps the deal alive even when everything seems to go awry.

It is not a contradiction to be aggressive while maintaining the dignity of one's adversary. See Example 10.1. For some lawyers, such behavior may be a sharp deviation from their normal way of behaving. If so and if they can not adjust, they probably are not suitable for working on the purchase and sale of a small business.

An Open Telephone Line (No Screening). A telephone line is open when the party being called answers the telephone himself or herself or when the receptionist puts the call through without asking who is calling. To ask who is calling is a waste of the caller's time. Because it is a waste, it is also an irritation. Further, to screen a call is an insult and a further irritation because no dignified human being wants to be screened. The screening is made worse when the receptionist does it with feigned courtesy as most of them do: "May I ask who's calling?" but it is still irritating and rude in the constructive form: "May I tell Mr. Jones who's calling?" The erosion of dignity worsens when, after a few seconds, the receptionist informs the caller that Mr. Jones is in a meeting or that he is out of the office, something which the receptionist almost surely knew all along and whose pretense in not knowing is therefore deceitful. Worse still is for Mr. Jones not to return the call, an insult of high order. But worst of all is to have been lied to because that is not only an insult of still higher order but is also a valid ground for suspicion of underhanded dealing. Actually, all of the above insults are grounds for suspicion and it is possible if not probable that they will be so perceived in the high emotions of the deal.

When either principal in the purchase and sale suspects underhanded dealing, the ground is laid for the deal's destruction. It is like the planted handkerchief in Shakespeare's Othello, and no good can come of it. If the seller's lawyer (or, for that matter, the seller himself) has screened any member of the buyer's team including the buyer, the buyer's lawyer, accountant, or banker, when the buyer is in a high emotional state, all sorts of questions may spring from the imagination: Why was I (or my lawyer, accountant, etc.) screened? Why won't he talk to me? Why did his receptionist lie to me? What is the seller hiding from me? Why this dilatory tactic? Has another buyer entered the bidding? More than one? Am I going to have to raise my offer to get this business? Why can't the seller be honest about it?

If the roles are reversed and the buyer's lawyer (or, for that matter, the buyer himself) has screened any member of the seller's team, all sorts of questions may spring from the seller's imagination. Why was I lied to? Why this dilatory tactic? Is the buyer having trouble coming up with the money? Is he bidding on another business? More than one? Is he getting cold feet? Why can't he be honest with me?

Irritations, rudenesses, and insults are dangerous in the high emotional state of the purchase and sale because they are too easily magnified. When magnified, they escalate to destructive levels possibly evoking retaliation. What's worse, the lawyers usually enter the transaction when it is thick and heavy, when details, if not basics, are still being negotiated, when emotions tend to be at their highest, and when intelligence and common sense have flown out the window, as in Example 8.3.

It sometimes happens that a lawyer has a deadline to meet, preventing the lawyer from accepting a telephone call. A lawyer with a sense of human dignity will inform the caller, or instruct the receptionist to inform the caller, that the lawyer has a brief to prepare, a contract to have ready for a 2:30 meeting, or some other duty which cannot wait. Then the caller is asked to leave his or her name and number with a promise that the lawyer will call back. It may be well into the evening or the end of the following day before the return call is made, but the caller's dignity is preserved, and so is good will.

The value of forthrightness with the caller can not be overstated. That value consists not only of the absence of dangerous negatives but also of the presence of beneficial positives. When the caller is told of the lawyer's need to work on a brief or other priority, the caller is treated as a dignified person worthy enough to be told the truth and mature enough to handle it. It is an implied compliment, a very nice compliment, and it builds good will. Moreover, for the lawyer (or the lawyer's receptionist) to share his plight of having a deadline to work to is to promote the caller to a position on the lawyer's team, which is still another compliment. Even more complimentary is to allow the caller the opportunity to deny the lawyer's request to leave a message and wait for a return call. It is a compliment because it recognizes the sense of fairness and the good judgment of the caller. If the caller should actually deny the lawyer's request not to be disturbed, two possibilities exist. One is that the caller has exercised good judgment in which case the lawyer should talk to the caller, however briefly. The other possibility is that the caller has exercised poor judgment in which case the lawyer should allow a few seconds for the caller to state his reason, then firmly reply more or less as follows: "I understand your situation but I honestly have to finish the brief I'm working on and I'll have to call you later this afternoon or tomorrow morning."

If the lawyer absolutely can not take a call, strict honesty is still necessary and still workable. The receptionist must inform the caller that the lawyer is working on a brief and has asked not to be disturbed but has promised to return the call. If no receptionist is present, the lawyer may simply let the telephone ring or use an answering machine. Use of the answering machine as a screening device, however, should be only on an emergency basis. If used routinely for screening, it becomes an insult by proxy because no one is fooled by it when used repeatedly. If to finish a job by a certain deadline the lawyer must refuse all calls except from one particular person, the receptionist can be instructed to put that party through once the party has identified himself or herself. In the case of a caller who doesn't readily identify himself, the receptionist can encourage the caller to leave a message, thus disclosing the caller's identity.

With so many insults arising out of screening calls and with so many compliments arising out of an open telephone line, the lawyer who fails to act on them can only be viewed as either lacking a sense of human dignity or caring little about it. An exception may be a lawyer who does sense all of the above but who feels that, for his type of work or his type of clientele, the time saved or the opportunity to jog his memory or to open his file before taking the call is simply a higher priority. All well and good, but that is the wrong lawyer to handle the high emotions of the participants in the purchase and sale of a small business.

Since an open telephone line is a strong sign of a lawyer with a sense of human dignity, the discussion in this section could have been included in the section above. It was treated separately, however, because it is a special case, because it is an important case, and because telephone screening is so common.

(Note that the author is focused on purchase-and-sale transactions, not other types of transactions, and he therefore allows that the above arguments favoring an open telephone line may or may not always apply. Moreover, in strictly personal matters in the home, a whole new set of rules may be proper. Use of an answering machine to screen calls, for example, may not be a denial of human dignity and may even be justified in the quest for privacy. In that situation, of course, the party doing the screening is preserving his or her happiness, not working for a client.)

Spontaneous Cooperation. There is a class of human beings marked by hesitancy to cooperate, the hesitancy being a result of a kind of unwillingness to work with others, not a result of due caution. The lawyer in Example 8.9 demonstrated his unwillingness to cooperate by his monosyllabic utterances and by his refusal to listen to the broker's plea and to respond intelligently to it. As a result, his client, the elderly and partly disabled widow, was unable to sell the building she had inherited. The building was making her no money, was continuing to physically deteriorate and lose value in a declining market, was nothing but a nuisance to her, and finally had to be razed. That lawyer also exemplified the subtly dangerous state of eminent legal skills combined with deficient extralegal skills.

A Conservative Estimate of the Lawyer's Fee. Once the client has described the situation to the lawyer, the lawyer should provide a conservative estimate of his or her fee. The conservative element in estimating the fee is not, of and by itself, of the highest importance. If the lawyer does everything else right, the client will have been well served. The importance is in providing a clue as to the competence of the lawyer being considered, even if after the fact. Note Example 10.4.

> **Example 10.4** The buyer and seller of a small machine shop have agreed on the price and terms, and bank financing has been virtually assured pending SBA participation. Now it is time to bring in the lawyers. The buyer asks the broker to recommend one. The broker, still fairly new to brokering, has come across only one lawyer so far that he feels is competent enough to recommend. Since he is hesitant to name only one for fear of being suspected of kickback payments or other favors which could be deemed unethical, he offers two names. One is the known quantity. The other is recommended by a colleague whom the broker feels good about but whom the broker does not know well. The broker suggests that the buyer interview both lawyers and then make a decision. The buyer agrees and asks the broker to accompany him.
>
> The interviews are the same. The buyer describes the deal, the broker adds a word or two, the lawyer suggests what legal work probably will be required, and the lawyer estimates the number of hours that the buyer will be billed for. The first lawyer, the one favored by the broker, estimates from 20 to 25 hours based on what he has just been told. He adds that the hours could run

higher but that it is too hard to tell how much higher without getting into the work. He adds that with certain conditions and a bit of luck, the hours could run as low as nine or ten although his estimate remains at 20 to 25. The second lawyer estimates ten to twelve hours but adds that the hours could run higher though it is hard to tell without knowing more. Both meetings are cordial and relaxed and conclude with the buyer saying that he will call with his decision. After the meetings, the buyer asks the broker for his opinion. The broker favors the first one because he knows the quality of his work but adds that the second one seemed capable too, as far as he can tell.

The buyer chooses the second lawyer for his lower estimate. At first, the lawyer keeps the buyer informed of the hours expended, the hours accumulate more or less as expected, and they run into the high teens. The project, however, develops two or three complications, the complications capture everyone's attention, the hours become neglected and unreported, and after closing the purchase, the lawyer bills the buyer for 55 hours. The buyer expresses shock to the broker. The broker suggests that the buyer discuss what happened with the lawyer. The lawyer explains that the complications are what caused the bill to run so high. The buyer expresses anger both at the bill and at not being kept informed of the overrun, and tells the lawyer that the overrun was so large that the lawyer could hardly have not noticed. The lawyer apologizes, the buyer expresses dissatisfaction despite the lawyer's apology, and finally the lawyer lowers the bill to 35 hours. The buyer pays for 35 hours and the dispute is over.

One of the complications developed because the seller, who shared the financing with the bank, demanded either collateral or a guarantor for his loan. To satisfy the seller, a colleague of the buyer agreed to guarantee the seller's loan. The problem was that practically all banks and the SBA insist that seller financing be subordinate to the bank and to the SBA and that the subordination applies to guarantors as well as to collateral. The seller would not agree to subordination of his guarantor. In an attempt to reach agreement, the bank, with 90% of its loan covered by the SBA, agreed to defer to the seller. The SBA, however, balked at being denied access to the guarantor. The dilemma was solved by the buyer's guarantor having his bank issue an irrevocable letter of credit to the seller to cover any default by the buyer. This solution—actually nothing more than a technical side step of SBA regulations—satisfied everyone but not until five lawyers (for the buyer, the seller,

Illustration 10.1

"May I ask who's calling?"

the SBA, the buyer's bank, and the guarantor) had coordinated and agreed.

Such complications as the above are fairly common but hard to predict. That is why an estimate of the lawyer's fee should be conservative. The lawyer's ability to estimate the fee, which includes the ability to allow for complications, is a clue to the lawyer's overall competence. Granted that one cannot judge the lawyer's ability to estimate the fee until after the fact, it is still an inducement to hiring a lawyer who promises by his or her other qualities to rank in the upper 25% of competence.

The buyer's lawyer in Example 10.4 turned out to be basically competent. He was not imaginative (the broker is the one who offered the idea of the letter of credit, a trick he had learned from another lawyer on a previous deal) but he did a reasonably good job overall and he probably would rank in the middle 50% of all lawyers. The only other misstep he made was to take a verbal swipe at the broker with respect to the broker's fee, an interesting irony considering the overrun of his own fee.

For readers who may have speculated who the lawyer was in Example 10.4 who made the better estimate, it was the buyer's lawyer from Example 10.1.

At Least Ten Years' Experience. Most lawyers probably have the legal skills to handle the purchase and sale of a small business even when fresh out of law school. However, the experience of working in the field for a few years is bound to make any lawyer more skilled and much better able to serve his or her clients. Actually, a minimum of 15 or 20 years' experience instead of only ten might be the wiser clue to the lawyer's ability. An older lawyer probably will have better appreciation of the extralegal aspects of working for a client. An older lawyer will have made most of the mistakes he will make during his career, especially on fundamentals, and those mistakes will have been made at someone else's expense. Moreover, there is no reason for a buyer or a seller to hire someone with short experience when there are plenty of experienced lawyers ready to serve. There is too much at stake for such a needless risk and there is no redeeming argument for doing so. An exception is if the young lawyer is monitored by an older, experienced lawyer. Then the client may get the advantage of the older lawyer's experience for the price of the younger lawyer's fee. The client has to be sure, however, that the older lawyer actually does oversee the younger lawyer's work. In one actual case, a young lawyer was purported to be monitored by a higher-up in the firm but actually was not. The result was a waste of everyone's time.

Common Sense. It is a remarkable fact of business life that some lawyers, with all of their high intelligence, education, and experience, lack the common sense of a mature high school sophomore. The buyers' lawyer in Example 10.2 actually expected the sellers, not to mention the sellers' lawyer, to agree to finance 75% of the sale price while accepting an unsecured note. The lawyer's advice was unreasonable by itself but especially so considering that the selling husband's failing health required their becoming entirely free and clear of the business. That same lawyer showed further lack of common sense by offering an earnest deposit of $100. The offer was actually an insult for its small-minded cheapness combined with its failure to consider the needs of the sellers.

The rule to follow is that the deal has to make sense for both parties. Common sense should tell a person that. If the deal does not make sense for both parties, it probably is not workable. It is that simple. The lawyer who fails to understand that rule and who fails to act accordingly is a danger to the transaction and a danger to his own client.

A Sense of Community. A sense of community, like an open telephone line, is a special case of recognizing human dignity. It shows the lawyer's concern about the worth of others and about the special value of good will. A tenant and a landlord had closed their deal when a third party on an adjacent property needed a unilateral concession from the tenant to make his own deal work. The tenant refused but the tenant's lawyer, having a keen sense of community, urged the tenant to make the concession (a minor encroachment of the property line) because it brought major benefits for the third party plus two others including the tenant's landlord while costing the tenant little. As the lawyer also pointed out, it was a reasonable concession if for no other reason than to have a good neighbor and a friendly landlord. The lawyer might have added that hard positions beget hard positions and sometimes retaliation.

Some lawyers express their sense of community by accepting pro bono cases. In a pro bono case, the lawyer forgoes part or all of his or her fee to help an indigent seeking justice or to help a social cause or charity needing legal assistance but lacking the funds to pay for it. Whether or not one supports the idea of helping indigents or advancing social causes, such lawyers, by virtue of their sense of community, probably offer the kind of personality not likely to provoke bad will or broken deals. Such lawyers also probably offer fairness, justice, and decency, all positive factors in preserving the deal. In fact, the term, pro bono, from the Latin phrase, pro bono publico, meaning "for the public good" is an apt description of the kind of lawyer likely suited for the purchase and sale of a small business. Of course, the type of pro bono work should be considered. The buyer's lawyer in Example 10.3 did pro bono work for the Bar Association, which is hardly the same as helping social causes or indigents and which might even be thought of as akin to sucking up to the boss. That lawyer might have been looking for referrals to help his practice. His performance showed why he probably needed them.

A lawyer with a sense of community also demonstrates a vision which sees beyond what is close at hand or near in time. A lawyer or any person with the vision to see ahead is an asset on any team. And who knows but that the lawyer who has proven his sense of community might be able to call in a favor to boost a client. The landlord's lawyer in Example 10.3 received a timely telephone call from a judge in court session, and the lawyer did not even have to ask. It is a safe bet that that lawyer had spread a few favors in his past.

As one buyer once observed, "Let's all pull together. Then we can all make some money."

Some Qualities Not to Look for. There are several qualities which could be perceived as desirable when, in fact, they often are misleading. These qualities therefore should be thought of as having neutral or minimal value. One of these qualities is a plush office in a prestigious office building. Such an office may be decorated with fine art; Oriental rugs (or, as is often the case, imitations thereof); luxurious furniture; a solid wood, front door with carved relief and a large, brass handle (polished up so carefully); designer wallpaper; and a female receptionist smartly dressed and coiffured. Such an office may reek with intoxicating power and authority. Another quality possibly misleading is a warm, friendly, and perhaps even charming personality. Another is a fine suit of clothes. Still another is an authoritative demeanor.

For some lawyers, these qualities are innocuous. They are simple manifestations of the lawyer's simple nature. The paintings are on the wall because the lawyer appreciates good art. The plush office is plush because the lawyer likes plushness. And the lawyer's warm and charming personality is the lawyer's true nature as is his authoritative demeanor. Note, however, that none of these qualities denote any of the qualities mentioned earlier in the chapter, those including primacy of the deal, willingness to compromise, self-awareness of limitations, a sense of human dignity, and so on. For this reason, the plush office, the lawyer's charm, and so forth should be taken lightly as something to enjoy if the truly necessary qualities are present. They have little to do with the lawyer's competency for the purchase and sale of a small business.

It is true that the plush office may evidence enough success in the trade to afford such fine decor and that it therefore shows the lawyer's ability to sell himself and to perform capably in the legal realm. To that extent, the plushness is a point in favor of the lawyer. However, said plushness tells little about the lawyer's fitness for the purchase and sale of a small business.

Since the plush office, fine clothes, and authoritative demeanor project an aura of power, they can be intimidating. They therefore pose a danger that the unwary, inexperienced prospective client is so overwhelmed by the lawyer's ambiance and demeanor that the client's true needs are forgotten or negated by the client himself. The trappings of power may also make one forget that the lawyer paying for those trappings passes on the expense to his or her clients by adding $15 or $20 per hour to the fee.

The lawyer wearing a green sweater and scuffed shoes in an obscure, humble office may be one of the best in town and may put on a suit only when he goes to court. Sometimes one has to ask around to discover such a lawyer. The lawyer's quality may be more than worth the effort.

Another quality not to look for is a lawyer's performance in areas not related to the purchase and sale of a small business. That a lawyer won big alimony in the divorce of someone's sister is not a point in favor of hiring that lawyer. Neither is that lawyer's success in having a driving-while-intoxicated charge reduced to careless driving, or that one's lawyer has been the highly regarded family lawyer for the past 20 years. Note Example 10.5:

Example 10.5 A young woman who successfully started a small restaurant two or three years earlier has saved enough money which, when added to the proceeds of the sale of her restaurant, will enable her to return to college to earn a degree. She lists her restaurant for sale with a broker. Another broker shows the restaurant to a prospective buyer who makes an offer. The offer is written on a pre-printed contract and brought by the selling broker to the listing broker who, in turn, brings it to his client. She accepts the offer but is reluctant to sign because her lawyer told her never to sign anything without his having read it. She is persuaded to sign, however, because of the statement on the pre-printed form saying that the seller's acceptance of the offer is contingent on approval of her lawyer. A signed copy of the offer is then returned to the selling broker who, in turn, brings it to the buyer who is delighted at the acceptance.

The day following, however, the listing broker calls the selling broker to say that the seller's acceptance has been rescinded. He offers the following explanation: when the seller brought the offer to her lawyer, the lawyer, upon seeing that the offer had been signed, scolded her so severely that she began crying. When she pleaded that she thought it would be all right to sign because the offer was contingent on her lawyer's approval, the lawyer replied that he would do the thinking around here. He then directed her to reject the offer. Now the selling broker asks why the rejection if no harm was done. The listing broker replies that he asked the same question but got no answer from the seller other than that he's the family lawyer and we always do what he says.

The selling broker waits a day hoping for a change in direction but none is forthcoming. Then he informs the buyer that the acceptance has been rescinded whereupon the buyer asks what's going on here. The broker tells the story and suggests that the buyer be patient and stand by. The buyer expresses disgust at the way things are being handled and says that he is going to look elsewhere and that if he has any further interest he will call back. The buyer never does call back and neither does the listing broker. The deal is permanently dead.

One may feel disloyal for not choosing the family lawyer. If so, one should realize that a lawyer-client relationship based on person-to-person acceptance has obvious advantage over a relationship set up by someone else. Moreover, no one person is necessarily adequate for every job which happens to come along. Various jobs require various talents, not to mention various mixes of personal chemistries. One's best chance to find competent performance, therefore, is to choose carefully and wisely. There is too much at stake not to.

Another quality not to look for is a low hourly fee. Like the low estimate of hours in Example 10.4, a low fee may be misleading. It may be proportional to the lawyer's meager skills. It may also be related to a highly skilled lawyer's green sweater and humble surroundings. A high hourly fee may be related to the lawyer's charm, warmth of handshake, or ability to intimidate prospective clients. A high fee may also be due to the lawyer's exceptional speed. The hero lawyer in Example 10.1 commands a relatively high fee. He also enjoys a very well-appointed office on an upper floor of an elegant high-rise building in a prestigious part of town, and he serves coffee to his clients in fine china. No Styrofoam in his estate. The bummer, seller's lawyer in Example 10.3 charges about the same fee as the hero while his office has below-average decor.

The message is clear: Look only for those qualities that are truly worth looking for and try to ignore the others.

PART 3:
HOW TO FIND A GOOD LAWYER

Now that one knows what qualities to look for and not look for in a lawyer, the question is how to go about finding one with the right qualities. The following suggestions are not always guaranteed to find a good lawyer, but should maximize one's chances.

One may begin looking for leads by describing the desired qualities to someone who regularly works with lawyers and has had plenty of opportunity to observe. The author, for example, found his lawyer through his contact with the executive director of a charitable organization dealing with lawyers, many of whom do pro bono work. Almost any charitable organization using pro bono lawyers would be a good lead.

Getting a reference to a lawyer from another lawyer would be a dicey move unless one felt comfortable with the referring lawyer. Asking the Bar Association for a referral is not recommended. The buyer's lawyer in Example 10.3 is one reason for avoidance. Another is the experience in Appendix B.

Lacking other leads, one may look in the *Yellow Pages* for a lawyer whose office is near one's home or near the business being bought. This is a cold start but still reasonable for the convenient location.

One's first contact with a prospective lawyer, even if the lawyer is highly recommended, should be by telephone. If the caller asks to speak to Mr. Jones and the answerer responds, "May I ask who's calling?" or "May I tell Mr. Jones who's calling?," the caller may simply say "Sorry, wrong number," and proceed to the next lawyer.

After reaching a prospective lawyer without being screened, the prospective client should briefly describe his or her need and may mention at this point two or three of the qualities sought, especially the primacy of the deal. The lawyer may ask questions or suggest an interview. During the interview, one should mention at least some of the other qualities being sought in the lawyer. One might even hand the lawyer a list. If one is lucky, the interview will provide a good idea of whether or not one has found the right lawyer.

It is perfectly ethical to shop for a lawyer just as one would shop for anything of importance. Shopping for the right lawyer may take time and emotional capital, but the investment is justified. Some of the lawyers interviewed may disagree that shopping is ethical. It is the lawyer's privilege to disagree. It is the prospective client's privilege to move on to the next lawyer.

When the point is reached where the client feels good about a certain lawyer, it is time to hire the lawyer. The lawyer can be counted on to describe what to do next.

One may also wonder if any of the recommended qualities for a lawyer may be compromised. Perhaps so, if most of the other qualities are present. Preservation of human dignity, understanding the primacy of the deal, and common sense should rarely, if ever, be compromised.

If a lawyer is hired but somehow proves not to work well, as in the examples in this book, one should promptly tell the lawyer either to correct his or her performance or the job will be turned over to another lawyer. This is a very difficult decision to make. No one wants to be hard-hearted and intemperate, but too often clients take the easier course of action which is to take no action at all even when the deal is about to die. There comes a time, however, past which the blame for a broken deal passes from the lawyer to the client.

Example 10.6 A divorce has caused a small retail chain to be listed for sale with a broker. The divorce is already final, the stores are in the possession of the former husband, and the proceeds of the sale will be divided in accordance with the divorce settlement. The business is in St. Louis but absentee-owned because the husband now resides in a distant city. Although the divorce settlement allows a flexible deadline for completing the sale, the husband wishes, because of emotional reasons, for the sale to proceed quickly. He also wishes to proceed quickly because sales have been declining steadily due to his absence.

Because the chain is a moneymaker with upscale appeal, the broker, sensing that this is a very desirable business, develops a list of leads, prepares a prospectus, and runs a mail auction to the highest bidder. The winning bid comes in higher than the seller's hoped-for price. The buyer, who also wants to close quickly because he has no income (which is partly why he was motivated to be high bidder), and seller do everything necessary to complete the purchase and sale, and, despite a few delays caused by multiple landlords, multiple insurance requirements, and mailing documents back and forth across the country, everything is running smoothly.

Then a problem develops. The broker has been instructed to work with the seller-husband's St. Louis lawyer but the lawyer has stopped cooperating. The lawyer is refusing all of the broker's telephone calls and refusing to respond to messages even when implored to do so. The broker explains to the receptionist the need for both the buyer and the seller to close quickly or at least to be given a reason for the delay, and he asks the receptionist to please determine the lawyer's status and then to please call him back, all to no avail. The broker tries twice going to the office but is unable to get past the receptionist's desk or to get the lawyer to come out of his office even for just a moment. The deal is not in trouble yet but the buyer is warning that too much delay will cause him to go elsewhere. He is living off of his capital and needs urgently to start making money. The broker calls the seller long distance, describes the problem, and suggests switching to another lawyer. The seller, who by his prompt and enthusiastic cooperation has been great to work with every step of the way, declines switching lawyers and states that his lawyer is too well paid for such crappy service and that he will deal with him immediately. About seven minutes later the broker's telephone rings. It is the lawyer now talking sweetly while taking ample time to review the status of the deal. The balance of the transaction proceeds very smoothly, the lawyer's cooperation from that point on is exemplary, and the deal closes without a hitch.

To repeat the point made above, lawyers can be blamed for a lot, but the client who fails to demand good service is largely to blame for a broken deal even if the lawyer is primarily responsible. What the client must always keep in mind is that the lawyer's boss is the person who pays the bill. The seller in this example understood that point exactly, he did what had to be done, and he wasted no time doing it. Had the lawyer not started cooperating, the

Illustration 10.2

"Mr. Jones is busy. He cannot be disturbed."

seller would have fired him and hired another. This point is more likely to be understood by sellers because of their tendency to be autocratic than by buyers who have not tasted the experience of being entirely in charge of things.

Lawyers are authority figures in American society and are often oppressive whether intentionally or not. It can be hard for a client to fire a lawyer or even to talk firmly to one. It is therefore good for a client to have a confidant. The confidant can help sort things out and imbue the client with the courage to be firm when firmness is called for. There are few things worse in life than to lose something of highest importance due to incompetent service, and then to be billed for such incompetence at a rate of $150 per hour, $175 per hour, or more.

QUESTIONS FOR DISCUSSION
Chapter 10—Choosing a Lawyer

1. Why is it useful to classify lawyers—and professional people in general—into three groups according to their quality of performance?
2. Define a good lawyer and a bad lawyer.
3. What are the two kinds of benefits and dangers when hiring a lawyer, and why is it helpful to know this?
4. Are the benefits and dangers in the extralegal realm about as important as those in the legal realm?
5. If a lawyer is highly competent in the legal realm, does that assure high competence in the extralegal realm?
6. What is the main danger in hiring a bad lawyer?
7. Although it is understandable why lawyers are sometimes described as deal killers, why is such generalization immoral?
8. Does a lawyer doing pro bono work necessarily have a strong sense of community?
9. Who pays the bill for a plush office in a prestigious building?
10. Describe the lawyer's qualities as shown in Example 10.1. Would you make a special effort to search for a lawyer with his talent?
11. How would you search for a good lawyer?

12. Is it ethical to shop for a lawyer?

13. What should you do if your lawyer is not performing to your expectations, and especially to your needs?

14. Why should you think twice before hiring the family lawyer to help buy or sell a business?

15. Who is the lawyer's boss?

CHAPTER 11
Choosing an Accountant

Once financing has been arranged, it is time to choose an accountant. This task is fairly easy compared to the other tasks required to buy or sell a small business and it can be done concurrently with choosing a lawyer.

As noted earlier, all human beings can be graded according to their competency: The upper 25%, the lower 25%, and the 50% in between. The purpose of this chapter is to describe some of the benefits and dangers inherent in working with an accountant and to motivate the reader to find an accountant in the upper 25%. This chapter also will provide some of the clues to choosing wisely.

Compared to the lawyer one hires who is likely to engage in extralegal activities, the accountant will have duties more limited to his or her specialty. The choice of an accountant, therefore, is probably less critical than the choice of a lawyer. Still, it is important to both buyer and seller, although more so for the buyer whose choice of accountant may last for ten to 15 years or more.

Choosing an accountant differs in two ways for the buyer compared to the seller. For the buyer, an accountant should be chosen partly for his or her services up to and including closing the purchase and sale, and partly for services after closing. Usually, the same accountant will be adequate for both phases although the prior phase is probably more important for the sole reason of the need to preserve the deal. For the seller, an accountant may not be needed after the closing unless the seller has ongoing business or personal interests. In any case, choosing an accountant for the seller is usually academic because the seller almost always stays with his accountant of long standing for all of the trust and closeness which have developed. Nevertheless, the seller needs to know the benefits and the dangers, especially the dangers, of working with an accountant as much as the buyer does.

The chapter is presented in three parts covering The Benefits and Dangers of Hiring an Accountant, Qualities to Look for in an Accountant, and How to Find a Good Accountant.

PART 1:
THE BENEFITS AND DANGERS OF HIRING AN ACCOUNTANT

The main benefit of hiring a good accountant, here defined as one in the upper 25%, is the relatively high probability that the job will be done competently. The main danger of hiring a bad accountant, here defined as one in the lower 25%, is the relatively high probability that the job will be done incompetently. The challenge to the accountant is to perform his or her duties with no errors or omissions. Competently done, the probable result is a smooth transaction, at least within the purview of the accountant. Incompetently done, the likelihood of trouble becomes relatively high.

The Scope of Work. To best understand the benefits and dangers, it is helpful to understand the scope of work. For both the buyer and the seller, the accountant's job covers two phases, one phase before and including closing the purchase and sale, and the other phase after closing. Exactly which tasks the accountant performs and to what degree will depend on the individual circumstances.

The accountant's more likely services for the buyer before closing are:
• Advising the buyer of the tax advantages and disadvantages of

forming a corporation versus a proprietorship, a fiscal year versus a calendar year, an accrual basis versus a cash basis, and so forth.

- Explaining depreciation schedules and the need for a list of equipment.
- Reviewing the seller's books and records.
- Working with the seller's accountant to evaluate the work in progress and the inventory, and to allocate the purchase price.
- Assisting the buyer in setting up the books and records and in opening a bank account.
- Describing what services the accountant will be able to provide to the buyer after the purchase has closed.

The accountant's more likely services for the seller before closing are:
- Determining the tax consequences of the sale.
- Working with the buyer's accountant to evaluate the work in progress and the inventory, and to allocate the sale price.
- Describing the services the accountant will be able to provide to the seller after the sale has closed.

After closing, the accountant's most basic job for the buyer as owner will consist of preparing tax returns. However, the buyer may request a number of other services including:

- Compiling conventional balance sheets and statements of income and expense annually and perhaps more frequently.
- Keeping the books (although a competent person specializing in bookkeeping may be less expensive).
- Preparing the payroll (although a company specializing in payroll preparation may be more competent and less expensive).
- Counseling the owner and perhaps the employees on tax matters.
- Preparing various forms required by local, state, and federal governments such as the annual corporate registration (required in Missouri and probably in most other states) and the annual personal property declaration.

• Setting up an employee bonus system or retirement fund.

After closing, the accountant's job for the seller as former owner will be determined by such possible circumstances as seller financing; employment of the seller by the buyer as owner; hiring of the seller by the buyer on an hourly consulting basis; leasing the real estate to the buyer; the seller starting a new business; the seller's retiring; setting up an estate plan; and so on.

The Benefits of Working with a Good Accountant. Some business people choose an accountant for the lowest fee quoted. Those who do probably are not aware of what a good accountant can do for a client. One benefit is that taxes are minimized in accordance with the law. That is a goal of any accountant but the tax laws are so voluminous and complex that accountants with greater skill are more likely to find the lowest taxes. The difference between lower taxes and the lowest will help to offset any difference in fees between a good accountant and a bad one. It may offset the difference several times. It might even offset the entire fee several times.

A good accountant will advise when it is best not to minimize taxes. For example, paying oneself a salary subject to social security and unemployment taxes instead of rent on personally owned assets may be more than offset by future benefits such as qualifying for federal disability insurance as well as drawing from the Social Security pool of funds.

Financial statements with attractive formats and good organization plus the accountant's follow-on discussion help the client to understand what is going on in his or her own business. For example, the owner may be unaware of how costly an optional service or how costly a necessary service buried in the wrong account may be. The accountant's calling attention to the cost of that service may result in significant savings. Whoever keeps the books should be coached by the accountant.

With tax preparation in competent hands, the chances of a mistake resulting in an IRS penalty or audit are minimized, as are tax-related mental stresses. Perhaps more significantly, a good accountant will warn of an expense likely to bring an IRS inquiry while the owner still has a chance to do something about it. Moreover, state and federal tax agents appreciate well-prepared tax returns and they tend to know, respect, and cooperate with the accountants who prepare them thus promoting smoother dealings for all parties.

As with lawyers, the fees charged by good accountants are usually competitive. The fees charged by bad accountants are not always low and sometimes high. (The same truisms apply to physicians and to professional people in general.)

The accountant's competent performance minimizes the owner's distractions and allows the owner to concentrate on managing the business.

For the buyer, the benefits tend to increase chances for survival, especially in the critical first two or three years of ownership. That sole benefit may be the buyer's best benefit of all.

The Dangers of Working with a Bad Accountant. There are two main dangers of working with a bad accountant. One is that poor performance of the above services may result in the owner's distraction from his main duty of managing the business. For the buyer as owner, that danger diminishes chances for survival. The other main danger is in hiring an accountant to provide services for which the accountant is not qualified. Even a good accountant, even the best, is dangerous when performing services for which he or she lacks training or experience. A good accountant avoids those kinds of jobs. Some of the services outside the realm of accounting which accountants often are hired to do are preparing legal documents such as the shareholders' approval of sale; appraising the business; assisting in the negotiation in any way other than as a very limited financial advisor; and forming the corporation. Some of the dangers are illustrated in Examples 6.3, 7.1, 8.7, and, as explained below, 11.1, even though those examples mainly illustrated other lessons.

A special danger exists when cash-flow projections are needed. The accountant is partly qualified to prepare them by virtue of his or her expertise in preparing statements of income and expense. Because of this expertise, the accountant has the misleading appearance of being fully qualified. This enticing appearance led to the harm described in the Chapter 7 critique of an accountant's financial projections where the deal was almost wrecked. Of course, an enticing appearance is not always misleading. The accountant hired by the buyer's lawyer in Example 10.1 did a good job, presumably because the lawyer somehow knew that the accountant had the required skill. Thus it is hard to tell when that special danger may manifest itself and when it may not. (Note, however, the extra lesson from Example 10.1 that one of the benefits of hiring someone in the top 25 percent, as was that buyer's lawyer, is that it leads to finding other performers in the top 25 percent, as apparently was that lawyer's accountant. It is chilling to think of the corollary.) In any case, exceptional caution is the rule when hiring an accountant for any job other than the ordinary day-in and day-out work of accounting.

In the previous chapter, allowance was made that lawyers, because of their professional status, must sometimes take on tasks for which they have no experience. That is part of the value and one of the benefits of hiring a professional. Then why not the same allowance for accountants? Because lawyers seem to have more experience and broader experience in dealing with situations outside the realm of law than accountants have outside the realm of accounting. (Perhaps the broader experience is inherent in the role of being a lawyer.) Besides, accountants have their hands full keeping up with the changes and complexity of the tax laws. During tax season (January through mid-May) they are strained just to keep up with the volume of work and should not be asked or perhaps even allowed to do more than their ordinary tasks.

If a special expertise is needed by the buyer or the seller, the danger of poor performance can usually be minimized by hiring a specialist. For example, if a buyer or a seller should need help to negotiate the price and terms, help can be found in the *Yellow Pages* under "Mediation Services" or "Arbitration Services." This will avoid the kind of problem caused by the seller relying on his accountant in Example 8.7. If legal documents are needed, they should be prepared by a lawyer or at the very least be reviewed by one. Some sellers allow their accountants to prepare legal documents not just to save the expense of hiring a lawyer, but also to sustain their bias against having anything to do with a lawyer including even having one review the documents. If a buyer needs to form a corporation, the work should be done by a lawyer who can offer the proper advice to accompany such an important step. The lawyer, by virtue of training and experience, is informed of all the legal aspects, including legal liabilities, keeping minutes, selecting directors, and so forth.

If one needs help to appraise, a special problem arises. Looking in the *Yellow Pages* for a business appraiser can be as dangerous as hiring a lawyer or an accountant. The problem is that business appraising is as arcane as everything else in the unregulated realm of buying and selling a small business; thus, incompetent appraisers are not shy about advertising their services. For the person who possesses this book, the safest course may be to hand the book to one's accountant with instructions to follow the appraisal guidelines in Chapter 7. As an alternative, one might hire one of the larger accounting firms with national stature or one of the nationally recognized appraising organizations such as the Institute of Business Appraisers or the American Society of Appraisers (page 240).

Adding to the difficulty of determining what the accountant should or should not be hired to do is that the benefits and dangers tend to be obscured by the high financial and personal stakes of the purchase and sale, the arcane nature of the whole affair, and the elevated emotions of the principals.

PART 2:
QUALITIES TO LOOK FOR IN AN ACCOUNTANT

There are at least nine qualities to look for in an accountant or in an accounting firm and they are discussed in the sections below along with some qualities not to look for. All of the desired qualities need not be present but most of them should be.

Understanding of the Primacy of the Deal. In Chapter 8, the 21 basic rules of negotiating were presented and the first of those rules was to decide at the outset which is more important and to what degree, getting the best price or closing the deal. An accountant has little negotiating to do other than when valuing the inventory and work in progress and when allocating the price. An accountant therefore, compared to a lawyer, has relatively little opportunity to hurt the deal. Nevertheless, it is a mistake for either the buyer or the seller to assume that the accountant poses no danger to the deal and it is a mistake to assume that the accountant understands the primacy of the deal. It is therefore the client's duty to himself or herself to explain that primacy to the accountant. If the accountant still does not understand, another accountant should be sought. It is much easier to look for another accountant than it is for the buyer to look for another business to buy or for the seller to look for another buyer.

Two or More Partners in the Firm. Accounting firms typically are structured like law firms, with partners in charge and with associates reporting to the partners. The work is divided, with the associates doing the more routine work and the partners doing the more challenging work.

One advantage of two or more partners is that administrative chores can be divided among the partners, allowing them more time for doing research into the tax laws and for directly serving clients. Another advantage is that the research itself can be divided among the partners with the obvious benefit of shared specialization. Perhaps more importantly, this second advantage can be expressed in another way by saying that research will be done which otherwise would not be done, thus providing more insight and knowledge into the tax laws.

Having multiple partners probably is more significant for an accounting firm than for a law firm because the work done by one partner is more likely to be useful to the clients of the other partners. One reason is that tax laws, dealt with by accountants, have more commonality across the spectrum of client needs than do criminal and civil laws, dealt with by lawyers. Another reason is that the work done by an accountant is less unlikely to be outside the realm of accounting than the work done by a lawyer is to be outside the realm of law.

When a partner is unavailable for reasons of illness, vacation, and so forth, the other partners can serve a client's needs until the missing partner returns.

Another advantage of multiple partners is the constraints placed by one another to limit unacceptable behavior or performance. Such constraints appeared to be missing from the accounting firms in Examples 11.2, 11.3, and 11.4 although those examples were chosen to illustrate another point.

With respect to cheating on taxes, a firm with two or more partners poses two interesting disadvantages. One is that multiple partners increase the danger of exposure. The other is that the constraints partners place on one another may tend to hinder cheating. In fact, a firm with multiple partners is probably less likely to accept a client who cheats than is a sole practitioner. Some accountants are absolute in that they will not accept a client who they believe cheats, even if they are not asked to assist in the cheating. Others, however, may accept the cheating as long as they are not asked to participate. In either case, strange ironies can result:

> **Example 11.1** This example involves the same buyer and broker as mentioned in the critique of an accountant's financial projections in Chapter 7. In that critique, the buyer's accountant had botched the cash-flow projections. This caused the buyer's inexperienced banker to refuse financing because of the poor cash flow shown by the faulty projections. Then the broker saved the day by correctly projecting the cash flow and by obtaining financing from an experienced bank loan officer. Not mentioned in the critique, the broker, now highly regarded by the buyer, had been hired, several months after the buyer's takeover, as an hourly consultant to solve a marketing problem, and the broker had succeeded nicely.
>
> One day about a year later, the owner, formerly the broker's customer but now his client, telephones the broker. The following conversation ensues:
>
> Owner: I've got a tax problem for you.

Broker: Thanks for the call but I don't do taxes. Why don't you call your accountant?

O: I already called my accountant but he refused the job.

B: Your accountant refused a tax job? Do I understand correctly?

O: That is correct.

B: But why?

O: He didn't say why. He just said he wouldn't do it.

B: I don't understand but I still don't do taxes. Why call me?

O: Because you always get the job done.

(Will anyone in the entire world fault this broker for allowing himself to be so easily seduced by his client's flattery that he agrees to an assignment for which he believes he is not qualified?)

The tax in question turns out to be a problem, but a problem of a different kind. It is a business tax levied against inventories of equipment and supplies. The broker has no direct experience with the tax in question but he knows from having resided on the planet for more than a few years that such tax levies are tantamount to engraved invitations for business owners to lie and to cheat. The problem is not merely that the declarations of taxable inventories are on the honor system but that the tax authorities seldom, if ever, come around to check. Also encouraging owners to lie and to cheat is the common perception, probably accurate, that virtually no one tells the truth about these inventories and that therefore no one pays the lawful tax.

Now the broker knows why the accountant refused the job: he would have had a conflict of serving the client while obeying the law. He might also have had moral misgivings although, to be sure, the broker has none. So, not quite sure how to handle the situation, the broker decides to play dumb. He calls the municipal tax assessor to say that he is a consultant who has been asked by his client, a person new in business, to fill out the form for inventory declaration. He adds that he personally is unfamiliar with the tax and that his client's accountant is not available and would the assessor please assist. The assessor is very cooperative and, to the broker's surprise, says that no one he knows of makes an accurate declaration and that a declaration of about 25 to 30% of the real inventory would not raise any questions. The broker thanks the assessor warmly (trying not to be too profuse), follows the assessor's advice, and, once again, has a client who stands with heartfelt appreciation.

Each Partner a Certified Public Accountant (CPA). A CPA is not necessarily a better accountant than a non-CPA, nor is it certain that a CPA will even be competent, especially for the phase prior to the buyer's ownership. Probability, however, is with the CPA because of four criteria: Educational requirements prerequisite to certification testing; the certification test itself administered by the state; continuing education to maintain certification; and implied greater competency by virtue of greater ambition. (Incidentally, the author's accountant happens to be a non-CPA with a master's degree in tax administration. He discovered her while doing an appraisal for a client. She was so competent and cooperative—and charged significantly lower fees—that he decided to switch from his CPA.)

Although an accountant's certification is a worthy plus, the buyer or seller who places too heavy a reliance on it makes a mistake. Simply put, accounting, like all other professions, has its dogs and some of them are CPAs. Note Examples 11.2 through 11.4 which show various types of misbehavior. The reader may speculate on which of these accountants is a CPA and which is not; the answer will be given at the end of the three examples:

Example 11.2 A well-established contracting company struggling to return to profitability after two bad years (due to two large, back-to-back, terribly underestimated winning bids) is listed with a broker who has found a serious buyer. The broker has informed the buyer of the company's problems and so has the seller. The buyer, being very well qualified, is not daunted but wishes to see the just-completed year-end financial statements before placing an offer. He already has statements for three preceding years. The broker relays the buyer's request to the seller who invites the broker to come pick up a copy. When the broker arrives, the seller informs him that his accountant requested that the broker drive to the accountant's office to get the financial statements along with some explanation. The broker meets with the accountant but the accountant talks down to him in the manner of a superior person deigning to talk to an inferior person. The broker, keeping his ego in abeyance and his temper in check, as brokers generally (up to a point) are supposed to do, allows the accountant to play his game without protest in deference to the primacy of the deal but also in hopes of not prolonging the meeting. The accountant hands the broker a copy of the financial statements, then explains that some of the notes accompanying the statements have been deleted because "they are personal" and because "they don't relate to the sale of the business." Therefore, says the accountant, the buyer does not need them and will not get them. The broker thanks the accountant for his advice and the meeting ends. The broker delivers the statements to the buyer along with the accountant's explanation for the missing notes.

Later, the broker receives the buyer's offer but, before delivering the offer and at the buyer's request, visits the bank providing most of the financing to determine the bank's possible cooperation with the buyer. The bank president personally is handling the contracting company's financing (presently about $900,000 which is about in the same range as the negative retained earnings) and greets the broker warmly. The banker is very interested in cooperating with a qualified buyer and cordially discusses various aspects of the deal with the broker. During the normal course of the discussion, the banker refers to the accountant's warning that the viability of the business is in serious question, to which the broker asks what warning the banker is talking about. Why, the warning right there in the year-end financial statements which you said you have a copy of, says the banker, pulling the statements from his file drawer and pointing to the accompanying notes.

After reporting back to the buyer who still is not daunted but who now has reasonable grounds for suspicion about the whole affair, the broker delivers the offer to the owner of the company. The owner counter-offers but the buyer, still extremely cautious and not anxious to make any concessions, takes his time thinking it over. About two weeks pass. One day the buyer calls the broker to say that he just received a lengthy letter from the seller's accountant and that he will forward it to the broker. The letter urges the buyer to follow through on the purchase and tells what an attractive deal it is due to the tax advantage of prior-year losses. The buyer is not persuaded by the accountant's letter. He decides instead to walk, and the deal is dead.

The accountant committed five wrongs. First, he talked down to the broker. That was an inexcusable rudeness; it also impaired the accountant's own ability to work as a member of the seller's team. Further, it was also a mistake, perhaps even in the accountant's own perverted hierarchy of things, in that the broker was older, more experienced, and, unbeknown to the accountant, probably better educated. Second, his withholding of the notes accompanying the financial statements, those notes being an integral part of those statements, was, at the very least, an ethical breach and, possibly, a civil wrong. Third, he lied when he described the omitted notes as being personal and not related to the sale of the business. In the buyer's eyes, the accountant's lie could not help but cast suspicion on the seller. (The broker, however, viewed the seller as an innocent victim of his accountant's defective character, a character viewed in terms of the broker's favorite seven-letter epithet.) Fourth, he committed an ethical breach by going around the broker with his letter directly to the buyer. He did not even grant the broker the courtesy of a copy. Fifth, he contradicted himself when he wrote what a good opportunity it was to own that business while the notes to the financial statements said otherwise. Note that the tax reductions resulting from the prior losses were as much available to the seller as they were to the buyer, affording no special viability to the buyer while, from the buyer's viewpoint, forcing the disadvantage of having to purchase the corporation instead of the assets.

It is true that other factors swayed the buyer's decision to walk besides the accountant's misbehavior. Perhaps the deep troubles of the company along with the bank's need for a personal guarantee—although the personal guarantee might have been left with the seller or shared with him—were the factors most influential. Still, no one needs this kind of an accountant. The harm he did to the deal is incalculable.

Example 11.3 The buyer and seller of a small but profitable manufacturing company have agreed on price and terms and now must obtain bank financing. The seller volunteers the services of his accountant to prepare cash-flow projections for the loan application, and the accountant does a creditable job. Several banks reject (probably because most of the earnings are well hidden in the style of Acme Widget) but finally one expresses strong interest and begins to process the loan. The loan officers are making their own calculations investing considerable time on the application. The bank has just given a green light when the accountant announces an error just discovered in the latest statement of income and expense. The error, to the seller's and the buyer's chagrin, is in the visible earnings, not the hidden ones, and the cash flow now looks weak. The buyer laments the embarrassment he will face in front of the loan officers, an embarrassment made worse by all their work on some wrong numbers, and he wishes audibly that the accountant would have found the error two or three weeks sooner. The accountant replies that, actually, he had discovered the error two weeks earlier but felt that it would be best to repair both the financial statements and the cash-flow projections before saying anything so that everything would be all patched up and ready to go.

In this example, the accountant's mistake in arithmetic was very excusable. Everybody knows that all human beings make mistakes and that dealing with mistakes is part of the job and nothing to get upset about. Even the IRS tolerates mistakes. But note that a mistake has positive value: it provides an opportunity to bring out the character of the person who makes the mistake. A person of strong character will acknowledge immediately upon discovery and then begin making the necessary corrections and adjustments. This accountant's failure to report the mistake immediately to his client, the seller, showed terrible judgment plus weakness of character. His stated reason for delaying the announcement was face-saving and added to his guilt. Fortunately, the bank in question probably wanted that type of loan in its portfolio, especially with a buyer as well qualified as this buyer was. The bank therefore accepted the revised loan application without significant comment, it granted the loan, and the deal eventually closed. Nevertheless, the buyer, who had considered retaining the present accountant when he became owner, decided to hire another accountant despite the seller's recommendation not to change. The buyer made the right decision.

Example 11.4 This example elaborates on the errant appraisal of Example 4.1. The buyer and seller had agreed to share the cost of a professional appraisal for which they hired an accountant who advertised himself as an appraiser and who seemed to be well qualified. This accountant's credentials, in summary, included long experience as an appraiser, much expertise and experience as a courtroom witness, and appraisals conducted for clients in many states and in foreign countries. These credentials, including those of his firm, were explained in detail taking up three of the back pages of the appraisal.

The appraisal report was 8.5 inches by 11 inches with a plastic hinge binding between two heavy paper covers. The main part of the appraisal was 29 pages including the cover letter, title page, table of contents, and substantiation. The remainder of the book consisted of 53 pages, mostly of the last several years' financial statements and tax returns augmented with several pages of statistical data (including some copies of copyrighted material on the restaurant trade by Robert Morris Associates, for which Robert Morris was credited). The substantiation appeared to be a computer printout probably requiring only that the appraiser fill in the blank spaces shown on the computer monitor. The text contained such esoteric terminology as "Developing a Floor and Ceiling-based Compensation Adjustment Factor," and "Reverse compensations differential." The 82-page total of such assemblage made a formidable presentation by any standard. Appraised value was set at $736,000. The cost of that appraisal was $11,000.

The seller submits the appraisal to the broker for his review. The broker studies the appraisal and finds several shortcomings including two big ones: One is failure to declare whether or not the real estate is included in the appraised value. The other is the use of an unexplained multiplier against the gross sales to determine 50% of the appraised value. The broker writes a polite and very detailed letter to the accountant raising these questions. The accountant calls to acknowledge receipt of the letter. The broker takes the opportunity to ask again whether or not real estate is included. The accountant hems and haws, then declares the information to be confidential and further declares that he will answer no questions unless directed by the client.

The first of the two big mistakes, the appraising accountant's failure to declare whether real estate was included in the price, is probably explained by his indifferent use of a computer combined with software he never bothered to analyze and understand. He also never bothered to understand the financial statements prepared by the seller's regular accountant. If he had looked closely, he would have noticed that rent expense appeared only in the last two years, the reason being that the real estate, formerly owned by the seller's corporation, had been sold to the owner personally, just two years earlier. Had the appraiser juxtaposed the four years' worth of data, as did the buyer of Acme Widget, before feeding into the computer, the missing rent expenses in earlier years would have been obvious. Since the real estate value was approximately equal to the business value, the omission was no small matter.

The second big mistake entailed about the same magnitude of value but was conceptually much more damning. The appraiser used three approaches and weighted them to get the $736,000 appraised value. But the heaviest weight (50%) was given to use of an unexplained multiplier against the average gross sales. Use of a multiplier in this manner is nothing more than a rule-of-thumb estimate and a poorly applied one at that. Moreover, no one needs a computer to make that kind of a calculation. A pocket calculator would work just fine. So would a pencil and a piece of paper. In short, the computer printout, the esoteric language, and the 82-page book constituted so much gobbledygook. It was an example of costly incompetence, or perhaps even a fraud.

The accountant in Example 11.2 is a CPA who heads his own firm with one or two associates but no partners. The accountant in Example 11.3 is not certified. He heads a firm with no partners. It is not known whether he has associates. The accountant in Example 11.4 is a CPA who heads a firm with one or two associates and no partners.

Participation in a Peer-Review Program. Private Companies Practice Section (PCPS), part of the American Institute of CPAs, conducts peer reviews of member firms every three years. Their purpose is to promote leadership in "quality, integrity and service." The results are available to the public. In a sense, these peer reviews are similar to accreditation of colleges and universities.

For more information about PCPS, or to obtain a copy of a member firm directory or an individual peer review report, one may call or write to the following:

> Private Companies Practice Section
> American Institute of CPAs
> 1211 Avenue of the Americas
> New York, NY 10036-8775
> 1-800-CPA-FIRM
> Or 212-575-6446 in New York State

Depreciation Schedules Grouped by Type of Asset. One advantage of grouping by type of asset is that the records being kept are easier to understand. If the owner wants to know what equipment he or she owns, a well-kept depreciation schedule provides a ready answer. Grouping assets requires little, if any, extra work by the accountant. Also, grouping by type of asset minimizes the possibility of mistakes such as applying an improper depreciation formula to an asset. Of greater importance is that good record-keeping suggests an accountant with a disciplined and orderly mind, the kind a business owner would want to have on his or her team, and one more likely to be in the upper 25% of the profession.

Following is an example of a sloppy record. It is a list of assets shown on one page of an actual depreciation schedule of a restaurant. The assets are shown in the exact order that they appeared in the left-hand column of the schedule.

Remodeling
Remodeling
Remodeling
Cyclonic vacuum
Building
Walk-in cooler
Carpeting
Microwave
Frymaster fryer
High chairs
Dumpster enclosure

The list is a jumbled mix of real estate, leasehold improvements, dining room equipment, and kitchen equipment, which should have appeared in four groupings instead of just one. The undisciplined mix of assets on this page was typical of the other pages in the depreciation schedule. Moreover, there was one page where the accountant had for some reason jammed more than one entry onto a line and had done so with an illegible scribble one might expect from a below-average high school student.

This sloppy record by itself was of relatively minor importance but it was a telltale clue of a bad accountant who had two other shortcomings. One was his failure in diligently assigning expenses on the check stubs to their proper accounts. This failure led to failure of his client to know with any accuracy where all of his money was being spent. (This failure was discovered by the broker who conducted an appraisal to establish a listing price. The broker had to go through about seven or eight hundred check stubs to get the expenses properly assigned and to correctly appraise.)

The other shortcoming was the accountant's failure to record all of the owned assets on the depreciation schedule. Many were missing, including some of the major cost items. The missing assets suggest strongly that the accountant failed to take full advantage of depreciation expense to minimize taxes. This failure also was discovered by the broker conducting the appraisal. He corrected the problem by rejecting the accountant's list and taking an inventory of equipment to prepare his own list. (Excerpts from the broker's list are shown in Figure 6.3.) This correction was not necessary to close the sale—the broker could have used the existing list—nor did it provide any tax help for the seller. It was done simply for correctness as a matter of principle

Illustration 11.1

"Accountants prefer to talk to accountants. That way,
we know we'll be properly understood."

but it did provide tax help for the buyer as owner and was much appreciated by the buyer's accountant.

This accountant, incidentally, is not certified and he heads his own firm with no partners but about six or seven associates. He also offers to do such legal work as forming a corporation.

Computerized Tax Returns. Use of a computer for processing tax returns results in greater speed and greater accuracy. The advantages include meeting schedules, a more relaxed atmosphere in the accountant's office, especially during tax season, and less cost to the client and/or better all-around service. The value of the computer, however, should not be over-estimated. It can be used to disguise incompetence or to perpetrate fraud, as shown in Example 11.4

A Sense of Human Dignity. The importance of a sense of human dignity, as well as how to manifest it, was described in detail in the previous chapter as applied to lawyers. The same importance and the same details apply to accountants. The one rule which stands above all others in minimizing undesirable excesses of the emotions and all the problems which accompany those excesses is to preserve the dignity of the individual. The accountant who treats others, including the client's adversary, as he would have others treat him, is well qualified to preserve the deal. As long as the deal is preserved, even when there are big problems which seem unsolvable, the opportunity to work things out remains alive. If the deal is broken, especially if because the adversary's dignity was ignored or trashed, the opportunity to work things out is probably dead.

Dignity is the state of being worthy and respected. Following are some important devices in preserving dignity:
- To tell the truth and the whole truth about whatever is happening.
- To honor the provisionality of truth, which is to allow that everything is open to discussion.
- To make criticism only if it is constructive and then only in a polite and straightforward manner.
- To refrain from sarcasm.
- To refrain from coercive tactics such as blocking communication or hanging up the telephone on a party to express dissatisfaction.
- To speak and to act as though the decency and integrity of the adversary are presumed even if they are not.
- To manifest empathy.
- To treat others as he or she would be treated.

The accountant who behaves in such manner encourages feelings of worth in others and he or she encourages thereby the good will which emanates from such worth. Such an accountant keeps the deal alive even when everything seems to go awry.

It is not a contradiction to be aggressive while maintaining the dignity of one's adversary. See Example 10.1. If the dignity of each and every individual touched by one's accountant is not maintained, that accountant is not suitable for working on the purchase and sale of a small business. See Example 11.2.

As noted above, an open telephone line is one way of maintaining the dignity of the individual. It is discussed in detail in the previous chapter in a section titled "An Open Telephone Line (No Screening)." The reader who may have skipped that chapter is asked to at least visit that section (on page 394).

At Least Ten Years' Experience. Since an accountant, unlike a lawyer, may practice his or her trade without being tested and licensed by the state, the value of long experience takes on extra importance. The obvious exception is the certified accountant who, by definition, has an assured minimum competency. Testing and certification aside, the long experience may not be necessary but there is no redeeming reason for not insisting on it, especially when so many accountants are available who have lots of experience. In a firm with one or more principals who have associates, the actual work will be done mostly by an associate who may be fresh out of school. That associate, however, will be monitored by the principal. For the phase prior to closing, most of the actual work probably should be done by the principal, not by an associate. That's because the purchase-and-sale activities of that phase are not the everyday activities of accounting. They are activities well out of the ordinary which should be conducted only by an experienced accountant.

Common Sense. When accountants work within the realm of accounting on such tasks as compiling financial data and preparing tax returns, they have few challenges to test their common sense. Their training and experience enable them to work at high levels of performance. What challenges they do face are within the familiar territory of their everyday work, enabling wise judgment.

Outside the realm of accounting, on matters for which they have little or no training or experience, new challenges arise, and wise judgments are hard to come by. The accountant with common sense will decline requests for advice on such tasks as to appraise a business, negotiate the deal, and prepare legal documents. The client with common sense—having read this book—will not even ask.

For the client who does ask, the first rule of buying and selling a business is that the deal has to make sense for both sides. That is common sense, pure and simple. If one's accountant offers advice that would not make sense for the other side, then one should seek a second opinion.

An accountant or anyone else on the buyer's or the seller's team who shows a lack of common sense probably should be dismissed. There is too much at stake not to.

Some Qualities Not to Look For. The qualities not to look for in an accountant are similar to those not to look for in a lawyer. They include a plush office in a prestigious office building; a warm, friendly, possibly charming personality; fine clothes; authoritative demeanor; and so on. There is nothing wrong with such qualities. On the contrary, such qualities may add to the pleasure of the relationship with one's accountant. The danger is that such qualities can be misleading or even intimidating. They may cause one to choose an accountant for the wrong reasons while ignoring the absence of some important right reasons.

PART 3:
HOW TO FIND A GOOD ACCOUNTANT

Now that one knows what qualities to look for and to not look for in an accountant, the question is how to go about finding one with the right qualities. The following suggestions are not guaranteed to always find a good accountant, but they should maximize one's chances.

In the author's opinion, the three most important criteria for choosing an accountant are two or more partners in the firm, a sense of human dignity, and all partners being a CPA. A fourth criterion, very desirable but subject to compromise, is membership in the Private Companies Practice Section of the American Institute of CPAs.

To find a good accountant, one might begin by contacting the Private Companies Practice Section at the address or telephone number shown earlier in this chapter. With a list of member firms, one can look in the *Yellow Pages* for the firm closest to one's business or home. If none is reasonably close, one might call one of those firms, explain that a PCPS member is not close enough for convenience but could they recommend a good CPA conveniently located. If that approach fails, one may begin contacting CPA firms with two or more partners.

The first contact with an accountant should be by telephone. If the caller asks to speak to Mr. Jones and the answerer replies "May I ask who's calling?" or "May I tell Mr. Jones who's calling?," the caller may reasonably conclude that a sense of human dignity is lacking. One may then grant that accountant's wish to avoid speaking to those to whom he does not wish to speak by saying "Sorry, wrong number," and quietly hanging up. One may then proceed to the next accountant. If calling during tax season, the accountant's receptionist may need to limit the accountant's interruptions. Even so, a good receptionist will explain the accountant's unavailability, then offer to take a message or suggest when best to call back. In either case, the caller's dignity is preserved and an important clue to the accountant's acceptability has been discovered.

Having reached a prospective accountant on the telephone, the prospective client should briefly describe his or her need and may mention at this point two or three of the qualities sought, especially the primacy of the deal. The accountant may ask questions or directly suggest an interview. During the interview, one should mention at least some of the other qualities being sought in the accountant. One might hand a list to the accountant. If one is lucky, the interview will provide a good idea of whether or not one has found the right person for the job.

It is perfectly ethical to shop for an accountant just as one would shop for anything of importance. Some of the accountants interviewed may disagree that shopping is ethical. It is the accountant's privilege to disagree. It is the prospective client's privilege to move on to the next accountant.

One may wonder if any of the recommended qualities for an accountant may be compromised. Perhaps so if most of the other qualities are present, but even then only grudgingly.

When the point is reached where the client feels good about a certain accountant, it is time to hire that accountant. The accountant can be counted on to describe what to do next.

If an accountant is hired but somehow proves not to work well, one should promptly instruct the accountant to correct his or her performance or the job will be turned over to someone else. This is a very difficult decision to make. No one wants to be hard-hearted and intemperate, but too often clients take the easier course of action which is to take no action at all even when the deal is about to die. There is a point in time, past which the blame for a broken deal or whatever other problem might arise passes from the accountant to the client. Note Example 10.6.

QUESTIONS FOR DISCUSSION
Chapter 11—Choosing an Accountant

1. Define a good accountant and a bad accountant.
2. What are at least three benefits of working with a good accountant?
3. What are the two main dangers of hiring a bad accountant?
4. What is the difference between a certified public accountant and one who is not certified?
5. What is the role of the American Institute of Certified Public Accountants (AICPA)?

6. Accountants, unlike lawyers, don't appear stigmatized as deal killers. Yet, they too can cause irreparable harm. What are some of the ways?

7. Why is a firm with at least two partners likely to perform at high levels of competence?

8. Is it ethical to shop for an accountant?

9. Who is the accountant's boss?

CHAPTER 12

Closing

Closing refers to the final event in a purchase-and-sale transaction. This event and how best to deal with it are described in the first part of the chapter, Closing the Purchase and Sale of a Small Business.

Since this is the final chapter in the book, the author—who is not above taking all sorts of license—shall close this book in the second part with something straight from the heart, A Proposal to Regulate the Small Business Marketplace in Missouri; and in the third part with an offering based on his experience, Author's Business Tips.

PART 1:
CLOSING THE PURCHASE AND SALE OF A SMALL BUSINESS

After negotiating has been completed and while financing is being sought by the buyer, the seller usually will lie dormant with mixed feelings of anticipation and doubt until it is certain that the cash will be available. Once the bank issues a written confirmation, however, the seller will come alive to do whatever has to be done to close the sale. That is when closing activities usually begin.

Closing is commonly defined as the final event in the purchase and sale of a business during which the seller receives payment, the buyer receives the property, all of the incidentals are completed, and the transaction is closed. This is usually all in a space of about two hours. Although that definition is a bit oversimplified, it is useful because it provides a convenient point of reference from which closing can be thought of as occurring in three phases, namely, pre-closing, closing, and post-closing.

Pre-Closing. The first thing to do to begin closing is to prepare a list of activities necessary to transfer the ownership and to get the buyer off to a running start. An example of such a list is shown in Figure 12.1. Note that the list identifies the parties responsible for the activities to assure that everything gets done. The list is best prepared by the broker because the broker presumably is best qualified through experience. If no broker is involved, the buyer and seller should prepare the list together. No matter who prepares the list, copies should be sent to the buyer's and seller's lawyers and accountants for their review and approval.

The list in Figure 12.1 was used for an actual purchase and sale. It therefore will not describe everything required for every deal—no list would—but it will serve as a starting point. One may be surprised by the number of items on the list. That list is understated because additional things to do always pop out of nowhere. Examples are unanticipated building inspections by the fire department, the health department, or any other department under the sun—not to mention possibly the various utilities—required to comply with municipal, county, state, or federal rules of transfer. These inspections may reveal surprise non-conformities due to revisions in the building codes that no one had known about and which will require correction before transfer of ownership can be completed. Other activities may arise out of legal complications, as in Example 10.4; or trifling things to do such as making an extra set of keys for the buyer (one buyer, who had just committed $1.5 million, went home with no keys because the seller's spare set had been left at home while his own keys had been taken by his wife); and so on.

Figure 12.1 Things to Do Before Closing

THINGS TO DO

Buyer

- Set up credit card accounts: VISA, Master Card, etc.
- Give new corporate name to bank to set up account.
- Get bank letter of credit for state sales tax number.
- Get sales tax number.
- Buy business insurance. (Name seller as loss payee.)
- Inspect equipment and premises just prior to closing.

Broker

- Prepare closing statement.
- Call telephone company for Transfer-of-Service agreement and for service contract.
- Prep bill of sale.
- Prep list of equipment.
- Notify utilities: Gas, elec, water, sewer.
- Help get retail sales tax number.
- Schedule building inspections for occupancy permit.
- Check possible need for business license.
- Prep contract on preprinted form.
- Prep lease on preprinted form.

Seller

- Provide real estate tax receipts for broker to prep closing statement; also personal property tax receipts.
- Prep list of prepaid expenses to broker for closing statement.
- Prep list of unpaid debts to broker for closing statement.
- Assemble into one place: equipment warranties, instruction books, maintenance records, etc.
- Prep list of suppliers.
- Prep list of employees showing duties of each, hours of each,

which ones have keys to premises, which ones get paid medical insurance and other fringe benefits, etc.

- Notify alarm company of transfer of ownership.

Buyer's accountant

- Allocate sale price with seller's accountant.
- Set up books and records.
- Set values of raw materials inventory, merchandise inventory, and work in progress with seller's accountant.

Buyer's lawyer

- Form corporation.
- Register fictitious name.
- Prep shareholders' approval to purchase.
- Prep directors' approval to purchase.
- Prep directors' approval to borrow from bank.
- Check compliance with zoning laws and with municipal requirements for transfer of business ownership.
- Check environmental regulations, and schedule testing by qualified testing company, if required.
- Make search for existing UCC forms and liens.

Seller's accountant

- Allocate sale price with buyer's accountant.
- Set values of raw materials inventory, merchandise inventory, and work in progress with buyer's accountant.
- Prep schedule of monthly payments and balances for promissory note.

Seller's lawyer

- Prep shareholders' approval of sale of assets.
- Prep directors' approval of sale.
- Comply with bulk sales law or issue bulk sales affidavit.

- Prep security agreement, promissory note, and guaranty.
- Assist buyer's lawyer with fictitious name registration.
- Prep UCC forms and file with Secretary of State and County Recorder of Deeds.
- Make search for existing UCC forms and liens.

After completing the list of things to do and generously estimating how much time will be required to complete all of the activities, set a date for the closing. Six weeks for pre-closing is usually plenty, although allowing two months on the contract is advised. Once the list has been prepared and everyone knows what to do, there is no reason to delay. There is no rule as to who acts as coordinator and monitor. Normally, either the broker or one of the lawyers assumes that responsibility without asking anyone's approval or permission. They just step forward and do it. Authority, in other words, is by force of personality.

Closing. There is no fixed rule to determine where the formal closing should occur, other than to allow the overall circumstances to dictate. For example, the bank providing the financing is often chosen partly because that is where the money is but also because the bank always has adequate facilities and support such as a conference table, copy machine, typist, notary public, bank officer with some experience in closings, and so on. Sometimes the office of either lawyer is chosen and sometimes the business site itself. If the business site is chosen, someone should assure the availability of a copy machine and, possibly a notary public. Surprisingly, title companies are usually not the first choice, although they offer the required support plus exceptional competence in handling closings while having no apparent shortcomings. Title companies come to the fore, however, when ownership of real estate is transferred. They also come to the fore when any question of trust places emphasis on escrow services. For some reason, escrow services are not always available at banks, at least not comfortably so. In any case, title companies, in the author's opinion, are worth every penny of their fees, which can usually be negotiated.

There is no strong reason for a closing not to occur at the broker's office.

Closings, however, engender a state of mind in the principals such that a site more formal or more grand than a broker's office would seem more appropriate. Moreover, the broker as escrow agent is not always fully accepted by the principals. Such was the case in Example 8.3, even though the seller's lawyer had placed the broker under an escrow contract and the broker had enjoyed good rapport with the buyer. The buyer's wife (the one who had screamed into the telephone) withheld the broker's commission check with a comment to this effect: "We'll pay you when we receive the bill of sale and the key to the front door. It's not that we don't trust you; we just want to feel protected." Allowing for the trying circumstances of that case, one cannot help but sympathize with the buyer's wife.

When a retail business is being sold, one of the closing events which necessarily occurs at the business site is valuing the inventory. Buyers and sellers alike have to take care, buyers especially, that the inevitable mistakes that are made are kept small. In one actual case of a package liquor store sale, the seller took the inventory by starting with a list of all the goods carried in that store with their unit wholesale prices, counting bottles and cases and entering the quantities on the list, extending the values, then handing the computed value to the buyer for his inspection. This work took three men several hours to complete. The buyer—making a career change and thus new in the trade—would have been overwhelmed except that he had brought a consultant who knew enough, in the limited time available, to concentrate on the bigger cost items with just spot-checks on the smaller ones. One of the bigger items was about 150 cases of a single brand of can beer which the owner had heavily stocked to get a price break. Ten stacks of about 15 cases each were arranged with one row of four stacks against a wall, then two more rows of three each. One of the stacks against the wall was mostly empty cases, which was discovered when the consultant made a routine check by tearing down parts of the outer rows. The saving to the buyer was less than a hundred dollars, not a large amount in the overall scheme of things. The mere presence of someone knowledgeable acting in the buyer's best interest may have been helpful to minimize the occurrence of other such mistakes. The presence of a concerned observer usually keeps honest people honest.

In another actual case, this one of an electrical service company which carried a large inventory of replacement parts, the seller was showing the buyer through the warehouse when the telephone rang. When the seller stepped into his office to take the call, an employee strolled up to the buyer and suggested looking inside some of the boxes, especially the ones on the top shelves (the top shelves were about eight feet high), and then disappeared. When the seller returned, the buyer asked to look inside some of the boxes. The seller then said that some of the parts were used and he would be willing to discount the inventory by $22,000. Many of the parts turned out to be not only used but useless.

In closings of retail stores that have large inventories of low-cost items, such as grocery stores and drug stores, taking inventory almost requires the same kind of expertise needed to judge quickly the number of birds in a large flock. For such cases, professional inventory-takers are probably in the best interest of buyers and sellers alike.

Closings are almost always attended by both the buyer and seller, plus a third party to assure that everything is done properly. Spouses usually attend because they usually have to sign the documents, although such signings can be done in advance, as in Example 10.1. Whether one or both lawyers should attend is often decided by whether the relationship of the principals has been strained or by other premonitions of trouble. Interestingly, neither lawyer attended the closing in Example 8.3 despite the lingering mistrust.

The closing need not occur in one day. In Example 8.3, the formal closing began at the bank on Friday morning and ended at the restaurant on Saturday night after the doors were locked at the end of the day. In another actual case, closing was dragged out for three weeks while a minor legal complication was fixed. The buyer, with approval of both lawyers, took possession of the business at the start of the three-week period even though he technically was not yet the owner.

There is no guarantee, once the day has arrived for formal closing, that it will actually happen. At one closing, the biggest (due to SBA 504 financing) ever attended by the author in terms of the number of participants (about 15 or so), the formalities had hardly gotten started when somebody realized that the lawyers had forgotten to do their UCC checks. That closing was post-poned for two days, then successfully completed.

In keeping with the feeling of formality and a certain grandness of the event, the principals, without being so advised, sometimes show up dressed as though they were going to church. Sometimes there is a celebration af-terwards and sometimes not. If there is a celebration, there is no rule as to who suggests it, who is invited, who does the inviting, or where it should take place. In one case, the buyer and his wife were so elated to get the busi-ness that they invited their lawyer, their accountant, the broker, the seller, and their spouses to dinner at a fine restaurant where the wine flowed freely. (The seller chose not to attend even though he had received a good price and terms.) After another closing, the one in Example 4.1, the seller and wife felt a tremendously deep sense of relief that it was finally over. They asked the broker to stop by their house to pick up his check and then they guided him to a cushy chair in the softly-lit den with the glow of quiet happiness, reminiscing, and warm conversation for the next hour and a half with two beers. They even gave him a box of chocolates to take home. (The broker still relishes the memory, sometimes almost with tears in his eyes, he so shared their happiness and their relief.)

Post-Closing. The things that fail to get done during pre-closing and closing are attended to in post-closing. Post-closing, in other words, is a clean-up detail. The biggest holdover in terms of cost, and probably the most com-mon, is business insurance. Insurance agents usually have to get premium ad-justments done by the underwriters, and those adjustments sometimes take a month or more to complete. Moreover, these adjustments are not always mathematically correct, in which cases they have to be redone, taking more time. (This was the case in Example 4.1: The insurance adjustments dragged out for about a year before being finally settled and the broker really earned that box of chocolates.) The utility companies may make their final meter readings before, on, or after the day of closing but usually are not off by more than a day or two. Technically, these readings, if early or late, are subject to adjustment. In practice, however, these adjustments, usually small in comparison with the total cost of the transfer, are customarily ignored in deference to the need to get on with things and because, in the post-closing state of mind of the principals, they are just too much of a bother.

With the exception of business insurance, post-closing typically ends within a week or two of closing. Still, all sorts of odds and ends can keep cropping up indefinitely and often the broker is asked to help. In one actual case, the broker's telephone rang at two o'clock a.m. It was the former owner of a retail store which had sold four months earlier. Burglars had broken in and set off the alarm, but the police, not knowing the store had been sold, had gotten him out of bed. He did not have the new owner's name and telephone number at home and he couldn't look it up in the telephone book because the new owner's name was something like John Smith.

In another case, the new owner of a small business with only one part-time employee besides himself, called the broker about 18 months after the purchase to report the following: He was being charged an unusually high percentage for state unemployment insurance. In answer to his complaint, the state had informed him that the former owner, after the business had been sold, had filed for unemployment relief saying that he had been laid off by the new owner. The state had obliged by paying him this relief, rocketing the tax upward. The owner asked the broker to write a letter to the state to explain that regardless of how it might look on paper, this was not a true layoff. All to no avail. The state, maintaining that a layoff is a layoff, would not budge. The new owner sued the state with the broker appearing as a witness but still to no avail.

Closing Documents. A partial set of closing documents is shown in Appendix A along with brief explanations.

PART 2:
A PROPOSAL TO REGULATE THE SMALL BUSINESS MARKETPLACE IN MISSOURI

The author wishes to be clear that, although this proposal is directed to his home state, he hopes devoutly that other states will hear his message and act accordingly.

Why Regulation Is Needed: The Ongoing Harm. The Preface of this book contains a brief account of how the small business marketplace evolved out of a history culminating with the Industrial Revolution and its rapid development in the twentieth century. This marketplace has brought problems which, due partly to its innate technical difficulties and partly to its recent evolution, have yet to be addressed. Now there is a need to solve these problems. That need is evidenced by the shortage of competent advisors to this marketplace, by the activity of advisors who sincerely believe themselves to be competent but who are not, by the myths that abound, by the arcane nature of the market, and by the substantial harm that buyers and sellers and others connected to purchases and sales of small businesses are subject to. That the present time is the right time to begin solving these problems is evidenced by all of the ongoing harm. Some of the examples in this book describe some of that harm. A review of these examples is in order:

In Example 4.1, the seller was buffeted by a real estate agent who failed to qualify the buyer, probably because he did not know how, and by a CPA who sold him a fraudulent appraisal for $11,000, as well as by the normal bumps and shocks inherent in the process. By the time the seller had a good buyer and a good appraisal, he was so emotionally distraught that he almost closed the business, a move that would have cost him half a million dollars.

In Example 5.1, the business broker, a licensed real estate agent, tried to sell the "tool and die" shop by taking prospective buyers on showings as one would take residential property buyers through the living room, bedrooms, and kitchen. The broker had only the faintest idea of what he was trying to sell or how to sell it, and this despite his several years experience selling businesses. His frequent showings caused rumors to spread among the employees which, in turn, caused the owner to fire the broker after the listing had expired. Thus, several months of wasted time and commotion before a new broker was hired.

In Example 5.2, the business broker never thought to ask why the price of the dry cleaner for sale was justified, partly probably because he did not know how to appraise and partly because he did not seem to care or because he simply was not bright enough. That broker wasted everyone's time although he too had several years experience selling businesses.

In Example 5.3, a competent broker who had performed well in a difficult case was cheated out of part of his commission by a collusion of the buyer, the seller, and their lawyers.

In Example 5.4, the seller tried to cheat the broker out of most of his commission. He succeeded, instead, in killing the deal and wasting several months of everyone's time and effort.

In Example 5.6, the business broker, combining bad ethics with rank stupidity, tried to sell an ethnic restaurant without the recipes, then offered to add the recipes at double the price.

In Example 6.1, the buyer of what was perceived as a grocery store but which was really a meat market with related sales was forced to close after only nine months of ownership. No incompetence or bad ethics were involved but no one, the experienced buyer included, had understood the high loyalty of meat buyers to their butchers or, more broadly, the danger of buying a business with an abnormal distribution of sales.

In Chapter 7, a critique of a CPA's financial projections revealed several serious shortcomings which, in summary, showed that he did not know what he was doing. The results of his incompetence were a rejected bank loan that almost killed the deal, and a waste of everyone's time. The telling part of this example is that the CPA was otherwise competent, and a decent human being besides.

In Example 7.1, the liquor store was appraised by a CPA at $225,000 but truly worth only $50,000 to $80,000.

In Example 7.2, the buyer's lawyer said not to pay a penny more than

$19,000 for the grocery store for sale, while the seller's accountant said not a penny less than $90,000. One or both of those advisors gave authoritative advice beyond the realm of his expertise, and the deal was killed before it even got started.

In Example 8.3, the seller's lawyer, whose specialty was trial law, used rough tactics when gentleness and understanding would have been far more appropriate and productive. In the end, no harm was done but only because the broker was skillful enough to repair the lawyer's damage.

In Example 8.5, the buyer, with confidence supported by his lawyer's considered approval of the price, agreed to a deal where he could not earn a living, much less pay the seller's loan. When he tried to reopen the negotiation, the seller's lawyer, perhaps at the seller's direction, refused to lower the price. The buyer then took the only way out which was to declare bankruptcy, and both sides got hurt.

In Example 8.7, the seller enlisted the aid of his CPA to negotiate the price but almost lost the deal because it was so badly bungled.

In Example 8.9, the elderly, infirm widow lost her only real chance to sell when misadvised by her lawyer, whom she described as prestigious. Moreover, the community, in a state of decline, lost the opportunity for the startup of a profitable business. In the end, the building was razed with the probable result that the widow got little or nothing.

In Example 10.1, the buyer's lawyer turned in a stellar performance thus underscoring, by stark contrast with many other lawyers, the advantages of competence and, by inference, the need for lawyers and other advisors to be trained in the art of small business marketing.

In Example 10.2, the buyer's lawyer rejected bank financing with SBA participation in favor of unsecured seller financing. That lawyer also advised his client to reject what was already a bargain price. Thus, the deal was killed, the buyer lost a dream business at a dream price, the sellers were forced by old age and arthritis to sell to someone out of state at a distressed price, the bank lost the checking account and the interest on the loan, the broker lost his commission, the employees lost their jobs, and the community lost a long-standing profitable business.

Continuing Example 10.2 in Appendix B, the broker complained about the buyer's lawyer to the Bar Association but was informed that the lawyer had violated no codes of conduct. Moreover, depending on how one would define the term, the Bar Association's treatment of that broker was uncivil.

In Example 10.3, both lawyers preferred to let the deal die rather than compromise their differences on the lease assignment. The deal was rescued when the broker, who was not a lawyer, illegally completed the legal work necessary to close the deal.

In Example 10.5, the seller's lawyer (the family lawyer) killed the deal for no discernable reason other than ego, and scolded his client for having acted intelligently.

In Example 10.6, the seller's lawyer refused to communicate and even refused to explain why he refused to communicate. The seller, fortunately, knew what to do and the lawyer then behaved responsibly.

In Example 11.2, the seller's CPA deceived the buyer. The buyer accidentally discovered the deceit, and the deal was killed. That CPA also gave bad advice to the buyer, while treating the broker with gross rudeness.

In Example 11.3, the seller's accountant delayed telling anyone of a mistake he had made, allowing the bank to waste its time working on erroneous numbers and risking both the availability of financing and the deal itself.

The harm shown in these examples is only the small amount discovered by the author who is just one broker out of many and whose principals and colleagues were just a few out of many. Although the harm evidenced here is anecdotal and of low quantity and therefore without statistical significance, it implies that the total in the marketplace greatly exceeds that described. In other words, the harm shown here is the tip of the iceberg. In fact, it might only be the tip of the tip of the iceberg.

To Minimize the Harm: Regulate the Marketplace. It is the thesis of this proposal that such harm and malpractice can be minimized by requiring training and licensing for individuals who wish to offer advice in the small business marketplace.

It is therefore proposed that the Missouri Division of Professional Registration create a Board of Certified Business Brokers with authority to establish regulations necessary to bring competency and ethical behavior to the marketing of small businesses.

Illustration 12.1

It is also proposed that the Missouri Division of Professional Registration create a Board of Certified Small Business Appraisers with authority to establish regulations necessary to bring competency and ethical behavior to the appraising of small businesses.

Among the regulations for brokering should be the following:

- A small business shall be defined as one with annual gross revenues less than three million dollars in any one of its most recent three years. (This definition is perhaps more practical for regulatory purposes than the author's definition relating to a single tier of management.)
- Qualified individuals and firms shall be licensed as Certified Business Brokers after receiving training approved by the Board of Certified Business Brokers and after passing a licensing examination approved by the Board.
- Licenses shall be renewed every two years upon completion of continuing education approved by the Board.
- Pre-requisites for licensing training shall include a degree from an accredited four-year college or university; a grade of C or better in a three-credit-hour course in elements of accounting offered at an accredited college or university; and a Missouri real estate broker's license, except that the real estate license shall not be required for lawyers.
- Training shall include, but not be limited to, the following: A survey of small businesses and the skills necessary to manage those businesses, qualifying buyers, psychological factors affecting buyers, psychological factors affecting sellers, listing a business for sale, preparing a business for sale, fact-finding, appraising, negotiating, financing, and closing.
- It shall be a misdemeanor to offer advice or to otherwise participate in the sale of a small business unless the individual or firm is one of the following:
  1. A Missouri-Certified Business Broker,
  2. A business broker certified by a nationally-recognized brokering group such as the International Business Brokers Association,
  3. A principal in the purchase and sale,
  4. A lawyer licensed to practice in Missouri but only with respect to legal advice. Specifically, a lawyer

shall not offer advice in fact-finding, appraising, negotiating, or financing except insofar as legal aspects are concerned.

5. A certified public accountant licensed to practice in Missouri, but only with respect to accounting advice. Specifically, an accountant shall not offer advice in fact-finding, appraising, negotiating, or financing except in determining the validity of actual financial data as opposed to projected financial data.

6. Any of several reasonable exceptions to be determined by the Board, such as the newspaper providing classified advertising, the bank providing financing, etc.

- Business brokers who began their practice prior to the establishment of this Board shall be excluded from the above requirements. However, they shall not use the term certified to describe their services or their competence nor shall they describe themselves or their firms as licensed unless they refer specifically to the type of license such as a real estate license.

- Brokers shall have rights to injunctive relief, property liens, and other devices in order to protect their fees.

- Conversations between Certified Business Brokers, their clients, their customers, and the advisers to their clients and customers shall be privileged in a court of law as are conversations of other professional people such as lawyers, physicians, and clergymen.

- Brokers shall be authorized to conduct any and all activities with respect to buying and selling a small business with this restriction: if legal documents, excepting those named below, are prepared by a broker, they shall be submitted for review and approval of two lawyers, one named by the buyer to act in the buyer's best interest and the other named by the seller to act in the seller's best interest. Excepted documents are those outside the buyer-seller relationship such as a listing agreement and a confidentiality agreement.

Among the regulations for appraising should be the following:

- Qualified individuals and firms shall be licensed as Certified Small Business Appraisers after receiving training approved by the Board of Certified Small Business Appraisers and after passing a licensing examination approved by the Board.
- Pre-requisites for the Appraiser's licensing training shall include a Certified Business Broker's license.
- Training for the Appraiser's license shall cover, but not be limited to, the material in Chapters 6 and 7 of this book.
- It shall be a misdemeanor to offer advice or to otherwise participate in the appraisal of a small business unless the individual or firm is one of the following:
    1. A Missouri-Certified Small Business Appraiser.
    2. A business appraiser certified by a nationally-recognized appraising group such as the American Society of Appraisers or the Institute of Business Appraisers.
    3. A lawyer offering advice only on the legal aspects of the appraisal.
    4. A certified public accountant offering advice only on the actual data on which the appraisal is based.

The rules regulating the small business marketplace probably would be similar to those regulating the real estate marketplace. One obvious problem would be the appointment of members to the Board who have at least ten years experience as Certified Business Brokers. Reasonable substitutes could serve in the beginning years of regulation. Some possibilities would be other members of the Missouri Division of Professional Registration, and well-qualified persons with applicable specialties such as industrial psychology, commercial lending, and so forth.

PART 3:
AUTHOR'S BUSINESS TIPS

The eleven tips which follow are based on experience, partly the author's own and partly the experience of others from whom he has had the opportunity to observe and to learn.

1. Avoid Making Important Decisions When Under Emotional Stress. Under stress, objectivity tends to be lost and wisdom along with it. If making a decision under stress cannot be avoided, one should always consult with a confidant. A confidant with some knowledge or expertise in the matter obviously would be preferred but anyone willing to listen and with whom one could feel comfortable sharing the problem would offer a lot of protection against an unwise decision.

2. Use a Confidant Even When Not Under Emotional Distress. Such use can be productive as well as protective. That is because talking things over is a source of wisdom. And there is always the joy of sharing.

Readers may have noticed that using a confidant has already been suggested in Chapters 2, 4, 5, 8, and 10 and now, twice more, here in Chapter 12. The author's insistent repetition of this advice is driven by his observation of how easily human beings find reasons to avoid acting in their own best interest, both in their business lives and in their personal lives, even when dealing with matters of high importance. Using a confidant provides opportunity for great gain at little or no cost. Everyone should use one. There is no reason not to.

3. Don't Cheat Anybody. Whatever is gained is not worth the enmity, the loss of friendship, and the loss of someone to turn to for favors or advice when needed. The buyer who cheated the broker in Example 5.3 paid dearly for his betrayal not because of any action the broker took but because that betrayal cost the buyer a friend when a friend was needed. By cheating, the buyer deprived himself of Tip number 2.

Honesty simplifies life by reducing the number of things that one must think about. The unassailable rightness of the principle increases self-confidence. It keeps one out of trouble. It even brings in business, at least in the long run.

Best of all is that it is so beautiful to trust and to be trusted. It is so very beautiful. That is largely what makes life worth living.

Obviously, such beauty is lost on many people and so is Tip number 3. That is because nature produces humans with varying genes and varying environments such that some understand and appreciate honesty to a greater degree and some to a lesser degree in the same way that some appreciate art or music to a greater or lesser degree. Dealing with those less appreciative is covered in Tip number 4.

An interesting pattern may occur in those inclined to cheat. They get away with it once, then they try it again. After succeeding a few times and acquiring more skill and self-confidence, they start aiming for bigger things. Finally, the laws of probability catch up and they pay the price. The author has observed two individuals in his business life who had the high intelligence and energy to become millionaires without cheating but who nevertheless made cheating a normal part of their routines. One went bankrupt. The other went to prison. The one in prison will be there for a long time.

The reader understands that the cheating referred to here is one human being to another or one company to another, as contrasted to cheating on taxes. With respect to cheating on taxes, the author remains ambivalent and refers the reader to his statement on that topic in Chapter 1 in the section titled "An Arguable Reason for Buying a Business." The author also refers the reader to "Business Morality in America" on www.monnetpress.com. That article will provide in-depth discussion of cheating in business and further basis for the author's ambivalence.

4. Don't Let Anybody Cheat You. It should be a policy of every businessperson to sue anyone who cheats. One business owner states that when someone tries to cheat him, he goes out of his way to make the cheat pay triple. The small claims courts are exemplary at meting out quick justice. For larger claims, the regular courts can take years and lots of expense but the system works. The broker in Example 5.3 did not see it that way and he settled for a reduced commission because his lawyer advised him that even though he had a sure win in court, it would take two years to collect, it would cost him perhaps more legal expense than he would gain, and in the meantime he would lose the use of the entire commission. Those reasons, in fact, are why the seller, the buyer, and their lawyers colluded to cheat: they felt confident, because the cost analysis was in their favor, that they could get away with it. If the author were in the same situation as was that broker, he would fight the thing in court as a matter of principle, and the cost be damned as long as he was in the right and had a good chance of winning. He would also take into account that the party who cheats has legal costs too and that he could be bluffing, as was the seller in Example 5.4.

(The author, in fact, has been a plaintiff several times and has yet to lose a case. One of those cases took five years and was finally decided by the Missouri Court of Appeals. That case is a reminder of another reason to fight: One of the great things in life is the sense of restitution when receiving a telephone call from one's lawyer beginning with the words "Good news!" followed by the deep satisfaction of knowing that one has beaten someone who tried to cheat, especially when the defendants had lied under oath and the jury had added punitive damages. This case cost the losers almost $100,000 in legal bills. Besides the two mistakes of cheating and doing it to someone who they thought would not fight back, they made a third mistake of major import: They chose a lawyer who himself made three big mistakes. The first was to defend people who were cheating, the second was to try to obfuscate the facts instead of relying on them, and the third was to appeal when he surely knew that appellate courts are loathe to overturn jury decisions because jury decisions are so basic to American justice. On the other hand, perhaps the defendants' lawyer himself was a cheat who, in light of his defendants' ability to pay the bill, decided to take advantage of their greed while ignoring the harm done to the plaintiff by the appeal.)

It is also important to not be shy about letting everyone know that those who cheat will be sued. The mere knowledge of an intended victim's propensity to fight can do wonders. In one actual case, all it took was a short note through the mail explaining why a certain party still owed $1,400 and ending with the subtlest of hints: "As always, it's good working with you. I'm looking forward to our continuing and long-lasting friendship." Two days after the note was mailed, the recipient was on the telephone to say that he does not wish to be sued and that he would like to work out a payment schedule. The debt was paid in full.

5. Maintain Adequate Working Capital. Business schools teach that shortage of working capital is a frequent cause of failure. Even a business that is profitable can get into trouble for lack of ability to meet the payroll or to pay the suppliers enough to maintain inventory. Then they need a broker to find a buyer, at which point an otherwise good business has become another statistic.

The author has seen several cases where a business is profiting nicely under new ownership with the cash rolling in but the owners still manage to get themselves into trouble. Instead of using the cash to pay off the mortgage or at least to save for a rainy day, the owners, apparently thinking that good times last forever and that recessions or setbacks will never come their way, spend the cash on things they don't need. This is partly what happened to the manufacturer in Example 6.8. The worst offenders seem to be machine shop owners who lust for equipment they don't own so they will no longer have to subcontract work. All well and good until sales are down at the same time they have underestimated a large, winning bid (underestimated bids are most likely when sales are down). Experiences such as these explain why banks sometimes restrict their borrowers from making capital investments without the bank's approval. The banks know what they are doing.

In cases where the cash flow is just enough to earn a living and pay the bills and the mortgage, one should live on less than one earns with the difference put into savings. If austerity is required, so be it. The alternative is to risk bankruptcy or being forced out of business for lack of working capital. Note that it has been wisely said that beauty is in the eye of the beholder (Cervantes). Inscribe this in jade: there are few things in life beheld with more beauty than cash on a rainy day.

6. Follow Conventional Business Procedures. Conventional business procedures should almost always be followed as though they are strictly enforced statutory laws. In a way, conventional procedures *are* laws, the laws of business economics, and they are enforced by the cost and the pain of violating them. One general rule is that work requiring special skills should be done by professional people trained and experienced in the required skills. The fees charged by professional people should be viewed as the normal cost of doing business and not as something to avoid just to save money. Lawyers, for example, should be hired to review documents and procedures; they should not be shunned to avoid fees. Business purchases should be financed, at least partly, by banks; they should not be financed wholly by sellers to get lower interest rates. Zoning laws should be checked at city hall, then double-checked. Appraising and negotiating should be done by appraisers and negotiators, not by lawyers and accountants. Bookkeeping should be done by professional bookkeepers, not by family members, unless trained by an accountant.

Another general rule is that delving into new realms of endeavor without proper training may be done but only with due caution. Example 6.8 illustrates the point. That owner expanded into a new product line but did not know how to debug the process. He might have succeeded if he had hired one or two employees experienced in the new line and if he had set aside a small part of his shop for pilot testing using leased equipment. The pilot program itself would have been costly, partly because of the inefficiency inherent in smallness and partly because of the profitable space taken from his established line. With the strong market that he had correctly anticipated, however, the cost of the pilot program probably would have been one of the best investments he had ever made. Whether his avoidance of proper procedures was due to impatience, ignorance, or cheapness (probably the last), he paid the price. The price was misery of high order.

The idea of not delving into new realms without proper training was not lost on the restaurateur in Example 1.3. He regularly adds new items to his menu but never without experimenting in the kitchen until he finds the right recipe. Then he records that recipe in a book.

Another restaurateur (this one discovered in 1975 by the author vacationing in Toronto) understood the idea in reverse. His restaurant serves only two meals. On the first floor (where the author dined), one may order prime rib of beef and nothing else other than the usual trimmings. On the second floor, one may order steak (presumably only one kind of steak) and nothing else other than the usual trimmings. Notice all the competitive advantages implied by such narrow specialization: no menu cost. No lost time with customers reading the menus. No lost time with waiters explaining what is served. Simple, efficient kitchen with minimal equipment. Fewer and simpler duties for kitchen employees who, after a few weeks in the kitchen, are perfectly trained. Easy replacement for employees home ill. Fewer suppliers with fewer checks to write and less bookkeeping. Fewer employees with lower payroll. Price breaks on large-quantity purchases. And less spoilage. These competitive advantages were revealed in the satisfaction of the experience: Fast service. Modest prices. Good portions. High quality of cuts and preparation. And fine decor marked by a surprising array, say, 30 or so, of Tiffany lamps, reputedly genuine. The effectiveness of these competitive advantages was intimated by the description of the restaurant in a Toronto travel guide as a favorite of the residents.

7. Read Every Insurance Policy in Full. Every word should be read. Absolutely every word. Insurance companies and insurance salespeople are like humanity in general: There is the top 25%, the bottom 25%, and the 50% in between, and it is sometimes hard to tell the difference.

In one case, the owner of a one-man brokerage paid for insurance to provide protection for clients and customers who might have entrusted him with funds. His plan was to help his clients feel safe using his brokerage. Having been forewarned by his lawyer, when the policy arrived he read it carefully and felt satisfied until he got to the last page. That was a rider exempting theft by the owner of the brokerage from coverage. The owner then called the agent who explained that owners of companies are assumed not to steal from themselves. The owner reminded the agent that he (the owner) had explained very carefully to the agent that the whole idea was to guard against the owner stealing from his clients, not from himself, and that the agent had understood that when the policy was ordered. The agent had also understood that there were no other employees or colleagues in the brokerage and that the only possible theft would be by the owner. Thus, the policy with that rider did not cover anything. Incredibly, the agent's reply was that he had discussed this with his superior and felt that it was fair coverage. When asked why he did not at least have the courtesy to inform the owner that the he had been excluded, the agent replied that he did not think it necessary. Thereupon, the owner demanded and received an immediate refund and he returned the policy. Then the owner wrote a letter of complaint to the chairman of the board of the insurance company. About a week later, he was notified that an investigation would be made as to any wrongdoing. After three months with no report, the owner contacted the chairman's office and was told that the investigation had been completed and no wrongdoing had been found. But no one ever called me to hear my story, protested the owner. No sir, we checked with the agency that sold the policy and was assured that nothing wrong had been done and that the customer had been satisfied to receive a refund.

If one does not feel qualified to understand the policy or if one does not have time to read it, it should be reviewed by a lawyer. No exceptions. Not even if the name of the company projects lots of warmth with such terms as guaranty, trust, or fidelity.

8. Use a Short-Term Lease with Short-Term Renewal Options. For example, a two-year lease with four two-year options is safer, in case of failure, than a five-year lease with a five-year option. The obvious disadvantage is that the landlord may increase the rent with each renewal. Still, the tradeoff is one to be considered if there is any reasonable doubt about success. It has been argued that one should plan for success, not failure. That argument is fallacious because what one should do is plan for both. With a short-term lease, the cost of failure is minimized without reducing the chance for success.

Another advantage of the short lease is flexibility, should business be so good that one needs to find another location with more space. The restaurateur in Example 1.3 started serving food to delight a gourmet at prices just above modest levels in a store with about 30 seats. Sales grew slowly but steadily for his first 18 months as new customers gradually discovered him. One day, a customer sent a post-card to the restaurant reviewer at the *St. Louis Post-Dispatch*. Fortunately, the restaurateur had only a three-year lease which worked out nicely giving him plenty of time to find a place with almost 100 seats, where he has thrived ever since.

9. Put Verbal Agreements into Writing. First, it should be clear that verbal agreements are just as binding under the law as agreements which have been written and signed. The difference is that verbal agreements are not as easy to prove in court as are written agreements. Nevertheless, verbal agreements are useful because they are easier to make, especially if one party is emotionally reluctant to sign. To put a verbal agreement into writing, one party simply writes a letter to the other party expressing the terms of the agreement in ordinary, straightforward language. Figure 12.2 provides an example.

When making a verbal agreement, it is probably best to condition it with something to allow backing out after giving the matter closer thought. One might say words to the effect that we have a deal but I need to make one last check on my finances. Give me a couple of days and I'll call to confirm.

It is always a good idea to let one's lawyer know about any agreements being made, whether written or verbal.

Figure 12.2 A Letter To Express a Verbal Agreement in Writing

Steve Smith
4590 Orion Avenue
St. Louis, Missouri 63000
(314) 809-0000

April 28, 2001

John Roberts
12345 Star Drive
St. Louis, Missouri 63000

Dear John:

I enjoyed our meeting last Tuesday afternoon and was happy that we were able to agree on the terms of the loan. Just to be sure that I understand properly, I would like to express our agreement in writing.

I will lend $8,000 to you and I will have the check in the mail by May 12. You will repay the loan by next April 3 at the latest. Interest will be 6% per year. I won't need any installment payments so you can mail a check for the full amount with interest to my address at the top of this letter. If you prefer to make installment payments, that would be all right too.

Please let me know if I have not described our agreement properly.

Sincerely,

Steve Smith (signed)

10. Harness Human Emotions. Human emotions are a major factor in the success of most businesses, both large and small. This point is often either not understood or not believed. In the author's undergraduate class in industrial psychology, the instructor provided several examples which, even after 50 years, still remain strongly in mind. One, particularly memorable because it was quantified, was about a homebuilder who had two separate, large development projects simultaneously in work. At Project A, carpenters were assigned into several teams with each team working on one home until finished, then moving to the next. Plumbers were assigned likewise into several teams, which moved from home to home, as were electricians, roofers, and so on. At Project B, everything was the same except that workers were asked to choose their own teammates. Project B built 13 homes for every 12 built by project A. What apparently inspired project B workers to greater effort was the good feelings from being given some control of their work place, from making work more like fun with friends than assignments with anonymous co-workers, and from the spirit naturally arising from real teams.

Such examples showing the positive effect on productivity of catering to emotional needs, some of which are fascinating as well as instructive, have since been repeated. For example, supervising by means of democratic leadership: supervisors would meet with subordinates to hear their suggestions and thrash out solutions while working as a team, instead of solving problems themselves and just giving orders. The obvious advantages to these meetings were that more ideas could be discovered and that once discovered, they could be explored more thoroughly. What was not obvious was that the workers' self-esteem was increased when their opinions were taken seriously, amounting to a promotion to a leadership position. They were given a measure of control over their own lives, a team spirit was built, their lives were made more meaningful by being integrated into the group, and their workplace took on a whole new color.

The psychological elements of these emotionally uplifting tactics can be described in such various terms as adding to the meaning of life (or, possibly, being the meaning of life), respecting the dignity of the individual, caring about the welfare of others and the feelings of others, treating others as one would be treated, nurturing a climate of trust, acting always with a sense of common decency and fairness, and so on. What is particularly fascinating about these tactics is that they work on ordinary people with ordinary talent so that employees in the middle 50% of the work force lift themselves and their productivity into the upper 25%. (See In Search of Excellence, by Thomas J. Peters and Robert H. Waterman, Jr., Harper & Row, 1982.)

(If productivity of the middle 50% can be improved through emotional uplifts, one has to wonder if the morality of the middle 50% could also be improved through emotional uplifts. And what about the morality of the 25% at the bottom. That should be an interesting book for someone to write.)

The owner of the coin laundry in Example 1.8 understood these points. He made people often viewed as weak, useless, and unproductive into managers of a successful enterprise. These managers, in turn, made customers expecting to find nothing more than mechanical devices to wash and dry their clothes into appreciative friends expecting, and finding, caring human beings sharing and delighting in the joy of life.

The restaurateur in Example 4.3 cared enough about his employees as dignified human beings to share with them his plans about selling his restaurant far in advance of when many owners would have spoken. His defections were zero, his transition smooth, and his profits steady right up to the end. This owner was no softhearted patsy molded by self-serving, dominant employees. He was a gentle, caring person but he was also an autocrat who would not hesitate to fire an employee who failed to perform to standards. In other words, he was kind to his employees but he was also kind to himself.

Sometimes the emotional factors work contrary to logic. Sales people should be given quotas beyond those they probably will meet. That way, they will always be under pressure to strive for better performance, or so the logic would dictate. But Peters and Waterman (mentioned above) discovered that salespeople given realistic quotas tend to outsell salespeople given quotas mostly out of reach. Reaching their quotas apparently made these salespeople feel more successful, more self-assured, more secure in their jobs, and more positive. They were happier with their employers and happier with themselves. Harnessing the emotions pays off in dollars and cents. It also pays off with a happier world.

11. Do the Right Thing. (This section is inspired by the 1989 movie of the same title.) In a sense, doing the right thing involves harnessing the emotions as in Tip 10 but is treated here as a special case because harnessing, with all of its benefits, is not the intent; doing the right thing is. The right thing is not necessarily the morally right thing, although it may be, or the more productive thing, although it may be that too. It is simply doing one's part in a kinder, gentler world.

In the movie, an Italian-American white man owns and operates a restaurant in a mostly black neighborhood with mostly black customers. The pictures decorating the walls are all of Italian-American heroes, Joe DiMaggio and so forth. One black customer asks why, in a restaurant with so many black customers, can't they have some black heroes on the walls, Nelson Mandela and so forth. The owner, irritated by the proposal, tells the customer he should get his own restaurant and then he can decorate the walls any way he pleases. Another black customer always carries a radio playing rap music. The owner can't stand it and he tells the customer to shut that thing off and keep it off.

To the script-writer's credit, the story is complex, with cross-currents of emotional forces making the right things to do less than crystal clear, and perhaps even debatable (and making this brief account of the movie over-simplified). In any case, the owner made good pizza which won the customers' patronage, but he failed to do the right things and he never won their hearts. The story ends with disaster.

After the author saw that movie, he was amazed at how true to life it was and that he could name several examples in the world of small business where the difference between doing the right thing and not doing it made the difference between joy and misery. Three of those examples are offered here. If any of these examples seem hard to believe, the reader is reminded that, as mentioned in the Preface, every one of the real-life examples in this book actually happened, just as they are herein described with only enough disguise to assure confidentiality.

Example 12.1 A small restaurant is operated by an owner and his son, with one part-time employee. Nothing about the food makes one wish to eat there a second time and nothing about the decor makes one wish to eat there the first time. This restaurant would not survive in a competitive market. But, being institutional, the customers are somewhat captive and the restaurant makes a good profit. Still, a sizeable potential profit escapes the owner. The restaurant is so unappealing that most of the institutional employees are openly antagonistic and assiduously avoid the place. One describes the decor as "early penitentiary." Another explains the ways in which they avoid it: "Most of the people in my department drive to nearby eateries while the rest of us"—here she refers to an item on the menu board of soup du jour—"the rest of us dine on brown bag du jour."

The profit nevertheless is so good and so well invested by the owner that, after twelve years in the business, the owner buys a second restaurant with twelve employees and about nine times the revenues of the first. The owner pays $700,000 for the business, including the real estate. The son is left to manage the old restaurant while the father takes over the new. The new restaurant is more or less the same type as the old but is not institutional and has several extremely sharp competitors within a three-mile radius.

During the first two days of new ownership, several changes are made. Portions are reduced and prices increased. The employees still may consume all the soda pop, tea, or coffee they desire, but now they must pay for it. Needless to say, the crash begins immediately. Sales plummet from day one, the kitchen manager defects within six weeks (the best employees are almost always the first to go) and the new owner is forced to shut the doors within four months.

Note that this owner did not have to buy a new restaurant to make more money. He could have improved sales and earnings with just a few thousand dollars invested by putting a fresh coat of paint on the walls of the old restaurant, dropping the ceiling, hanging professionally framed pictures on the walls, adding a few potted plants, putting an employee up front with a pleasant expression on his or her face and then—dare one say it—*increasing* the portions, with free desserts on Mondays. In other words, if he had just treated the customers in either restaurant as though he cared about their enjoyment, he would have thrived in the first and he might have survived in the second.

(After the strong stand in favor of bank financing repeated in this book any number of times, the author is embarrassed to admit that the purchase in Example 12.1 was mostly financed by a bank. The details are unknown but one has to suspect that the loan officer never bothered to inspect the old restaurant before approving the loan. If he had just stuck his head inside the front door, he would have seen all that needed to be seen to reject the loan.)

Example 12.2 A business broker, new in the trade, makes prospecting calls to tavern owners to build his inventory of listings. One tavern owner thanks the broker for calling but states that he plans to spend the rest of his life right where he is and he therefore has no interest in selling. The broker compliments the owner by saying that he envies him with his life so comfortably settled. (The reader is assured that the compliment was sincere.) They exchange further brief pleasantries and are about to say goodbye when the owner asks if the broker would be interested in listing a piece of real estate about 75 miles down state. The business broker replies that he would not be able to service a listing so distant but that he knows a real estate broker who could handle it and who would do a good job. The owner gives the broker his name and a brief description of the property, then adds that it should sell for about $550,000. The broker thanks the owner and they say goodbye.

The next day, the business broker calls his colleague, who is delighted to receive the opportunity for such an attractive listing. The following conversation ensues:

Real estate broker: What do you want for this listing?

Business broker: What do you mean?

REB: I mean what do you want out of this?

BB: Just serve the client well.

REB: I mean what do you personally want out of it?

BB: I don't want anything except that you serve the client.

REB: You don't want anything?

BB: Well, you can buy me a cup of coffee after you close the sale and then you can tell me all about it.

REB: You trust me, so I'll trust you.

The real estate broker then describes a listing that he wanted to get but which was rejected by his manager for a technical reason. (The reason was that the landlord would not agree to pay the brokerage firm a commission for placing a tenant.) The real estate broker feels that the business is attractive and would bring a nice commission even without getting anything from the landlord but, he further explains, "I'm not the boss here so I have to let it go.

It's yours to try to get if you want it." Then he gives the business broker the owner's name and number and adds that the listing price will be $550,000. The business broker does get the listing and he makes the sale as described in Example 10.1.

Example 12.3 A broker is in his office one day when the telephone rings. It is an accountant wanting to set an appointment to go over some cash-flow projections for a business he is buying. They meet in the broker's office and it is clear after 15 or 20 minutes that the accountant knows what he is doing. He is also personable. Then they start chatting. The business is a small manufacturer with a well-established product line. The broker states that this is just the kind of business that buyers clamor for but never seem to be able to find. He adds that he could probably sell one every month if only he could get his hands on them and he wonders how this young accountant—he doesn't look a day over 30—came across it.

The accountant tells the following story: A few years ago, the owner ran an ad for a CPA to become the company accountant. I didn't have much experience but I applied anyway and got the job. After I'd been there a few weeks, I noticed this older man who was sort of the low person in the company. He would run errands, distribute the mail, drive the owner around town, and do more or less whatever was asked of him. Even though he got around, he didn't seem to have any friends. The other employees didn't shun him; they just didn't go up to him and he didn't seem to bother going up to them. One day I said hello and he said hello back. We chatted a bit and he didn't reject me so I started trying to go by his desk every day just to say hello or good morning. After a while, we would have a soda together and sometimes even go to lunch. It wasn't anything special but it was all right and he seemed to like it.

One day about a month ago, the owner called me into his office and closed the door. He asked me if I would like to buy the company. I was so surprised. I said that I couldn't afford it. But the owner said back to me, I didn't ask you if you could afford it. I asked you if you would like to buy it. I said, well, it would be nice but I still couldn't afford it. He said yes you can. It's time for me to retire—he's in his seventies—and I need someone to take over. We'll set a price, you don't need anything down, you take the title, and the company generates enough cash flow for you to make the payments. I told him that I liked it but that I was stunned. Why me when he could so easily get somebody to pay cash?

Then the owner told me the following story: I was an officer during World War II with enough rank to command an orderly. When the war ended, I started this company and, knowing that my orderly—who wasn't very adept—would need a job, I asked him to come along. During the war and all the years with this company, this man has been trustworthy and loyal. He's dear to me and you're the only one who ever offered him friendship. Now you know why I want you to own this company.

And now the reader knows why it is not a bad idea to do the right thing.

QUESTIONS FOR DISCUSSION
Chapter 12—Closing

1. Name the phases in which closing occurs, and summarize their activities.
2. Why are most sales of assets rather than of corporate stock?
3. Approximately how many documents are required to close a sale of assets?
4. Who should attend inventory valuation?
5. What is a common post-closing activity, and why?

6. Why is regulation of the small business marketplace so strongly recommended by the author? Do you agree?

7. Would you describe the author's recommended format for regulation as feasible? If not, what would be the likely problems? Would lawyers and accountants lobby against the suggested restrictions?

8. How did you like the author's business tips? Are they too idealistic? What tips would you suggest?

Illustration 12.2

"Hey why don't we go get a soda?"

APPENDIX A:
COMMON CLOSING DOCUMENTS

Listed below are 19 documents commonly required to close the purchase and sale of a small business. They were compiled for an actual closing of a corporate asset sale with seller financing. If the bank had financed as well as the seller, another set of items, 9, 10, 11, 14, and 15, would also have been required in addition to other bank documents. If the transaction had occurred in a state other than Missouri, the list probably would have differed somewhat. If it had been for a proprietorship instead of for a corporation, the list most certainly would have differed. The main point is that there are more documents required to close the purchase and sale of a small business than most individuals would ever imagine. As always, advice should be sought from both a lawyer and an accountant.

1. Combined directors' and shareholders' authorization to sell assets of corporation.
2. Authorization of the board of directors to buy assets of seller's corporation and to lease real estate from seller.
3. Bulk sales affidavit.
4. Inquiry to Missouri secretary of state whether there is on file any presently effective filing statement naming the seller as a debtor and any statement of assignment thereof.
5. Commercial lease.
6. Personal guaranty of lessees (buyers) as individuals to pay rent if their corporation defaults.
7. Memorandum of lease and of option to purchase to notify filing officers.
8. Purchase-and-sale Agreement.
9. Promissory note from buyer to seller.
10. Payment schedule for promissory note.
11. Personal guaranty of buyers as individuals to pay promissory note if their corporation defaults.

12. Bill of sale of personal property.
13. List of equipment (attached to bill of sale).
14. Security agreement granting seller a security interest in the business.
15. Uniform Commercial Code–Financing Statement–Form UCC-1 to notify filing officers of buyer's debt to seller.
16. Bank letter of credit to secure state sales tax.
17. Registration of fictitious name.
18. Agreement transferring telephone number and responsibility for payment, submitted to Southwestern Bell Telephone Company.
19. Closing statement covering all final cost adjustments between buyer and seller.

Buyers and sellers are strongly advised to seek advice from their lawyers. These lawyers will instruct them on documentation requirements, so there is no need to include copies of the above listed documents in this book. However, a copy of Document 8 is included to provide the reader with some idea of a purchase-and-sale agreement that is thorough while being fair to both buyer and seller. This agreement was prepared by the author's lawyer in 1981 and has since been modified only slightly. The author has received occasional compliments on this agreement from buyers, sellers, and, only once, from a lawyer.

The agreement was designed to be printed with blank spaces to be filled in by the broker and then to be reviewed and approved by lawyers for both sides. The blank spaces below have been filled in to show the final agreement between buyer and seller of the Acme Widget Corporation. Italics have been used to simulate handwritten information. In actual practice, the blank spaces on preprinted documents are sometimes filled in using a typewriter. Such practice is discouraged because of the loss of distinction between the preprinted terms of the contract and the terms that have been filled in. Handwriting or hand printing is much preferred. A set of notes typically is added to the agreement to cover the almost-inevitable aberrations, changes, lawyers' additions (which often are mere redundancies), special situations, and so forth that are necessary because of the inflexibility of preprinted forms.

PURCHASE-AND-SALE AGREEMENT

Date_____*August 20, 2001*_____

     This agreement is between _____*John Q. Buyer, Inc.*_____, hereinafter called buyer, and _____*Acme Widget Corporation*_____, hereinafter called seller, for the purchase and sale of the following described business:
_____*Acme Widget Corporation dba Widget Wonder,*_____
_____*123 Business Boulevard, St. Louis, Missouri 63000*_____including the name, inventory, equipment, accounts but not accounts receivable, good will, licenses, assets, telephone number, and contract rights being a part of the business, which business is this day agreed to be sold to buyer subject to approval of seller by_____*August 25, 2001, 5:00 p.m.*_____for the total sale price of _____*Two hundred eight thousand and 00/100** dollars
_____*($208,000.00*)*_____ on the following terms:
             *plus cost of inventory and work in progress

     Earnest deposit made as per this receipt. $ *None*_____

     Cash to be paid on closing date of sale $ *148,000.00*_____
(subject to adjustments as herein provided).

     Liabilities of seller to be assumed by buyer. $ *None*_____
Notes or loans to be accepted by seller as
part purchase money under the terms as set
forth below: $_____*60,000.00*_____

Term___*5*___years; interest ___*6.5*___%;
prepayment privilege: Yes_*Y*_ No ___;
monthly payments of principal and
interest $___*1,173.97*___; security for
said loan shall be ___*Assets of business,*___
___*J. Q. Buyer's personal real estate and*___
___*personal guarantee*___

The sale under this agreement shall be closed subject to terms of
this agreement at the office of Honigmann, Inc., hereinafter called
broker, at 1932 Greenglen Drive, St. Louis, Missouri 63122 on or before
___*October 31, 2001*___.

All adjustments referred to in this agreement shall be made as
of closing.

Title to pass when this sale is closed. Time is of the essence of
this agreement.

CONTINGENCIES OF THIS AGREEMENT:
1. Examination of seller's financial and corporate records by
   buyer, and/or his agents, which review confirms that the
   information provided to buyer is true and correct; and an
   examination of buyer's financial statements by seller, if
   so requested.
2. If the seller's business is subject to a lease, buyer's ability
   to assume the existing lease or to execute an acceptable
   new lease with seller's landlord.
3. Ability of buyer to obtain financing in the amount of
   $___*147,000.00*___.
4. Ability of buyer to obtain necessary licenses and permits
   in order to operate the business which is subject to

this agreement.

5. Buyer's ability to obtain adequate insurance for said business.

6. Review of this agreement by attorneys and accountants for buyer and seller, and determination by them as to the structuring of the transaction, including but not limited to, treatment as a stock purchase or asset purchase, installment method of reporting, and allocation of sale price.

7. Both parties agree to comply with the bulk sales law, if deemed necessary. If the parties agree not to comply with same, seller will indemnify buyer for any loss or damage resulting from noncompliance.

Buyer and seller shall take all reasonable and diligent efforts to satisfy the contingencies set forth above. If any of the above contingencies have not been satisfied by buyer and/or seller, by _____*October 21, 2001*_____, buyer or seller may at its option cancel the agreement because of nonsatisfaction of the above-mentioned contingencies; and earnest deposit (if any) shall be returned to buyer. If buyer or seller has not notified the other of nonsatisfaction of aforesaid contingencies in writing by ___*October 22, 2001*___, all of the above contingencies shall be deemed to have been waived and/or satisfied. Any further contingencies written on the reverse shall be part of this agreement.

See notes added and which are an integral part of this agreement.

WARRANTIES AND COVENANTS:

1. Seller agrees that it will not, without buyer's written consent, directly or indirectly, own, manage, operate, join, control, or participate in or be connected as an officer, employee, partner, or otherwise with any business which competes with the business subject to this agreement within a ___*Ten-mile*___ radius of the business being purchased, for a period of_____*Three*_____years after closing.

2. Seller agrees to train buyer on aspects of operating seller's business for a period of ___*14**___days after closing, at no

cost to buyer.   *First 7 days full time; remainder half time.*

3. Seller warrants that the inventory on closing date will have a cost value of $_____*TBD**_____. If inventory valuation is less than this value, total purchase price will be adjusted accordingly at closing.   **TBD = to be determined at closing.*

4. Seller warrants that accounts receivable on closing date will amount to $_____*None*_____. If said receivables are less than this amount, total purchase price will be adjusted accordingly at closing.

5. Seller represents and warrants as follows:

   a. Seller's financial statements and corporate books are true and accurate according to its best knowledge and belief.

   b. There are no undisclosed liabilities or obligations of seller nor are there any undisclosed written, verbal or implied contracts, agreements, leases or other commitments.

   c. All taxes of every kind and nature whatsoever, including but not limited to withholding, social security, state and federal income taxes, etc., applicable to the period prior to closing, will be paid by seller.

   d. Since the date of the last available financial statements, there have been no changes in seller's business which have materially affected seller's financial condition or assets, other than normal changes in the ordinary course of business.

   e. Seller has good and marketable title to all its properties and assets, free and clear of all liens, security interest, mortgages, and encumbrances as of closing unless otherwise denoted in this agreement.

   f. All of seller's buildings and equipment are in working order and in conformity with all applicable ordinances and regulations, building and zoning and other laws. Any necessary repair of equipment as of closing date will be the responsibility of seller.

g.   The name used by seller in the operation of its business is the only trade name used by seller and such trade name does not conflict with nor infringe upon the trade name or corporate name of others and no claims have been asserted against the seller involving any such conflict, to the best of seller's knowledge.

h.   Seller agrees that pending closing the business will be conducted only in the ordinary course, and that the seller will use its best efforts to preserve the business organization intact.

i.   If the sale contemplated hereunder involves the sale of substantially all of the assets of a corporation, the seller has obtained the necessary shareholder and director approval, as required by law, and will furnish a copy of such approval at closing, or sooner if so requested by buyer.

j.   If the seller or buyer are corporations, the undersigned warrants that the corporation is in good standing and will furnish proof of same at closing, or sooner if so requested.

k.   Seller shall indemnify and hold buyer harmless from all liabilities of seller of any nature whatsoever arising out of the conduct of seller's business until closing.

GENERAL PROVISIONS:

1.   All representations, warranties and agreements made by the seller and buyer in this agreement, or pursuant hereto, shall survive the closing.

2.   This agreement shall be binding upon and inure to the benefit of the heirs, legal representatives, successors and assigns to the parties hereto, as applicable.

3.   All notices, requests and demands and other communications here-

under shall be in writing and shall be deemed to have been given if delivered or mailed, first class postage prepaid, to seller and buyer at their addresses on this agreement, with a copy thereof to the broker at broker's address, Honigmann, Inc., 1932 Greenglen Drive, St. Louis MO 63122.

4. If any covenant, term or provision of this agreement is invalid, illegal or incapable of being enforced, all other covenants, terms and provisions shall, nevertheless, remain in full force and effect.

5. Earnest deposit (if any) to be retained by broker. If buyer shall fail to pay additional earnest deposit when due (if required by contract) or if sale not be closed by date thereof owing to failure of performance of buyer, earnest deposit shall be forfeited by buyer, but buyer shall nevertheless be bound to fulfillment of contract if so determined by seller, but this shall not entitle buyer to enforce sale. Forfeited earnest deposit shall be divided equally between broker and seller as liquidated damages. No other brokers are entitled to any commission on this transaction.

CAVEAT:

1. The parties to this agreement understand that the broker cannot give legal or financial advice. Neither party shall hold the broker liable or responsible for any statement, representation, or performance or nonperformance of the terms contained herein. The broker is merely acting as the broker, and has not given legal or financial advice to either party, nor is the broker responsible for any representations or statements made by the parties to each other. The parties further recognize that if the agreement hereto involves the sale of real estate, it is advisable that a separate contract be prepared relating thereto if this is to be treated as an asset sale.

J. Q. Buyer	*J. Q. Seller*
Buyer	Seller

J. Q. Buyer

Buyer's signature

J. Q. Seller

Seller's signature

Address: _999 Elm Street_

St. Louis MO 63000

Address: _123 Business Boulevard_

St. Louis MO 63000

Telephone: _314-000-8888_

Telephone: _314-888-0000_

APPENDIX B:
A BROKER'S COMPLAINT TO THE BAR ASSOCIATION

This appendix is a follow-up to Example 10.2. The letters in this appendix are edited only for purposes of disguise and brevity; the substance is intact. Following is the letter written by the broker to the Bar Association. The enclosed letter mentioned in the first paragraph is the one shown in Example 10.2.

June 14, 19xx

Mr. J. Q. Executive Director
The Bar Association of Metropolitan St. Louis
One Metropolitan Square
St. Louis, Missouri 63102

Dear Mr. Director:

...[in reference to] a grievance regarding the conduct of an attorney... enclosed is a copy of my letter to that attorney which, I believe, will give you most of the information you need in addition to what is stated here.

The basic facts, very briefly outlined, are as follows: In 19xx, I matched up the sellers (Mr. and Mrs. Thomas) of a business with prospective buyers (Mr. and Mrs. Butler). After several months of investigation, the buyers worked out a tentative agreement on price and terms with the sellers. Bank financing with Small Business Administration (SBA) guarantee was arranged but the attorney for the buyers, Mr. Lawyer, advised his clients to avoid SBA involvement and to obtain unsecured seller financing instead. The sellers refused to grant such financing. The deal thereupon fell apart and the sellers liquidated the business.

My complaints against Mr. Lawyer are several and, although they should mostly be obvious from reading the enclosed letter, some elaboration is in order:

1. Mr. Lawyer failed to reply to my letter. Thus he ignored being told of the erroneous and illogical advice he had given, nor did he express the slightest interest in trying to determine either the truth or the wisdom of the matter.

2. He obviously conducted no research or investigation into the policies of the SBA but nevertheless spoke authoritatively on the subject and, presumably, charged his clients a fee for this disservice. If knowledge of the SBA were arcane or esoteric, Mr. Lawyer might be excused for not knowing (although he still would not be excused for misstating). But that knowledge was just a phone call away as demonstrated in my letter.

3. His advice was predicated on the illogical and unrealistic assumption that the sellers, in their sixties and forced into retirement by failing health and old age, would consent to unsecured financing and would continue to give consultative aid to his clients, the buyers, for a number of years to come, whenever allegedly necessary.

4. Mr. Lawyer approved his clients' giving their personal guarantee as to payment of the loan and he admitted in conversation with me that, therefore, ultimate payment could not be avoided even if the business should fail and even if his clients should have to sell their home in order to make that payment. When I then asked why he insisted on seller financing considering that his clients could still possibly lose their home if they defaulted, he replied that the idea was not to prevent the loss of the home but to delay that loss through the kind of stretched out litigation which would not otherwise be possible with SBA-backed bank financing.

5. Mr. Lawyer failed completely to grasp the almost ideal matchup of his clients' selling skill with the company's main weakness which was in sales. The bank's loan officer (Mr. Peters) noticed the good matchup and made a special mention of it to me. Granted that noticing and understanding such matchups may not ordinarily be an attorney's job. But the matchup was the essence of the purchase and sale (as it should be in every purchase and sale) and it should have been the dominant factor in putting together the deal. It adds to Mr. Lawyer's culpability to have failed to grasp this essence while speaking with authority.

6. Mr. Lawyer, according to his clients, told his clients that brokers try to get the highest possible price when selling a business because that way they get the highest possible commission. The statement is erroneous because it is untrue, because it is a false generalization of brokers, and because it groundlessly infers a certain unscrupulousness to my personal character. Further, juxtapose that accusation with his own admission to the use of drawn-out litigation as a dilatory tactic and then come to a conclusion as to whose integrity is questionable.

7. Mr. Lawyer failed to recognize that, with respect to evaluating a loan in a skillful and unbiased manner, bankers are professionals while sellers, buyers, accountants, and attorneys are rank amateurs. Thus, Mr. Lawyer's recommendation had the effect of throwing away the one party to the transaction most likely to evaluate and administer the loan in an objective and professional manner.

The damages caused by Mr. Lawyer's conduct are that his clients were unduly frightened out of buying the almost ideal business they had been seeking for several years, thus also denied the good potential earnings plus the prestige of owning a fine company which, as far back as the records showed, had always been profitable; my reputation suffered and I was deprived of the rapport I had worked hard to establish with the buyers; the sellers were deprived of the monetary difference between selling an on-going business and liquidating the assets; the lending bank (Friendly Bank of Missouri) lost the account; I lost my commission; the employees lost their jobs; and St. Louis lost the income from a prestigious and somewhat unique business with interstate accounts that was a credit to the community.

It is only fair to point out that Mr. Lawyer's clients were also misadvised by their own banker and, probably, by their accountant. Thus, Mr. Lawyer cannot be held entirely to blame for what happened. But Mr. Lawyer had more control than did the other advisors, made the more destructively irresponsible statements, and should therefore be held primarily responsible for the damage.

To summarize, Mr. Lawyer gave advice which was erroneous, illogical, far beyond the domain of his expertise (the law), unprofessional, unethical, falsely and groundlessly accusative, unresearched to the point of being reckless, and severely damaging to several parties including his own clients. Mr. Lawyer should therefore be punished for what he did. He should, at the very least, be made to pay for the damages he caused.

I hope it is clear that I am in no way disrespectful of the credentials and abilities of Mr. Lawyer or of the legal profession in general. On the contrary, a good attorney can be immeasurably helpful in putting a deal together. But attorneys (and, for that matter, accountants), by virtue of those very credentials and abilities, enjoy a well-deserved position of prestige in our society which attracts the unquestioning trust of their clients and which makes those attorneys all the more responsible for the advice they sell. It is this unquestioning trust which makes it incumbent on attorneys to use all the more care in advising their clients. Mr. Lawyer violated this trust by transgressing far beyond his limitations and by doing so with reckless abandon. If I transgressed my limitations and sold legal advice as Mr. Lawyer sold business advice, you would put me in jail.

It is not valid to argue that there is no law to prevent the dissemination of even the worst imaginable kind of business advice and that attorneys, therefore, like brokers, can give or sell whatever advice they please. Attorneys (and brokers), holding themselves out as experts, have no more right to disseminate advice recklessly than any person has to shout "fire" in a crowded theater.

Thus concludes the presentation of my grievance. I'm sure that you will have questions to ask in order to judge its validity. I will be happy to cooperate.

Thank you for your attention to this matter.

Yours very truly,

BETTER BUSINESS BROKERS

J. Q. Broker (signed)

Enclosure

Shortly after mailing the above letter, the broker receives a letter from The Bar Association of Metropolitan St. Louis saying that the letter has been received and forwarded to the Judicial Bar Committee which will assign a member to investigate. A few days later, the broker receives another letter in an envelope marked CONFIDENTIAL from the Missouri Bar Association which reads as follows:

Dear Mr. Broker:

As Special Representative of the Bar Committee of the 21st Judicial

Circuit, I acknowledge receipt of your complaint. The Committee has appointed the attorney listed below to make an investigation of this matter. The investigator will be in further contact with you as the investigation proceeds. The investigator is:

A. B. Benson
Attorney at Law
00 South Bemiston, Suite 00
Clayton, Missouri 63105
802-9999

Missouri Supreme Court Rule 5.24 provides that investigations of complaints by the Committee are not to be made public. This letter, therefore, along with all future communications with you by the Committee or its representatives should be kept confidential. The Committee takes this opportunity to thank you for your interest in matters pertaining to the ethics of the Bar.

Very truly yours,

C. D. Donovan (signed)
Committee Special Representative

A few days later, the broker receives a call from Benson, the assigned lawyer, who introduces himself, says that the letter was well written, and that he will get back with him later. Six months go by during which the broker hears nothing. He calls Benson, whose manner now is just short of being curt, and is told that the matter will be checked into. A few days later the broker receives a letter from the Bar Association in an envelope marked CONFIDENTIAL. The letter reads as follows:

Dear Mr. Broker:

The Bar Committee of the 21st Judicial Circuit has reviewed your letter of complaint and the report of its investigator. The Committee has determined that there is not reasonable cause to believe that the attorney is guilty of unprofessional conduct; accordingly, the Committee is closing its file.

Missouri Supreme Court Rule 5.24 provides that investigations of complaints by the Committee are not to be made public. This letter is therefore, being sent to you in confidence, for your information only.

Very truly yours,

C. D. Donovan (signed)
Committee Special Representative

Later, the broker calls Donovan for details. The conversation described below was written from notes taken by the broker during the telephone call.

Broker: I would like to know the basis of the Bar Association's decision. Would you describe it for me?

Donovan: No.

B: Am I entitled to ask questions?

D: No.

B: Am I entitled to appeal?

D: Yes, to your private attorney.

B: Your letter said that this matter is confidential. What exactly is confidential?

D: Everything. However, you're allowed to discuss with your private attorney. Will that be all?

B: Will you give me an example of unprofessional conduct?

(Pause)

D: The attorney wins a cash judgment but doesn't turn the money over to his client.

B: But that would be illegal.

D: Yes.

B: But then I don't need the Bar Association. I can turn to the County Prosecutor.

D: Yes. Will that be all?

B: How can I know that my complaint received a fair hearing? For all I know, the lawyer covered up or lied or didn't tell the whole truth. Don't I get the chance to see what he said about me and my complaint?

D: No.

B: In a court, there is cross-examination; are you saying there is none here?

(Pause)

D: Will that be all?

B: I still have no idea of what the Bar Association considers
      unprofessional conduct.

D: Unprofessional conduct is defined by codes. Each
      complaint is compared with the codes. If a code is violated,
      the conduct is judged as unprofessional. The attorney is
      not informed of the reason, not even if punishment is given.

B: Nobody is informed of anything.

D: Will that be all?

B: Yes. Goodbye.

D: Goodbye.

APPENDIX C:
LOAN APPLICATION PACKAGE FOR ACME WIDGET CORPORATION

The loan application package, including the cover letter, appears on the pages which follow. It is followed by a commentary to provide some insight into the buyer's preparation.

To conserve space, parts of the package have been omitted, including the following:

- Part of the narrative and the calculations for projections of income, expenses, and cash flow, which are similar to those in Chapter 7.
- Appendices A through E (their titles are shown only to illustrate typical appendices).

The cash-flow projections are almost identical to those in Figure 7.2 except as follows:

- The columns are headed by column numbers to make them easier to explain in the narrative. (Figure 7.2 was for the buyer's use while these projections are for the bank loan officer's use).
- The year 2000 figures as shown in the accountant's financial data are included in column 2 in place of the adjusted income statement in Figure 7.2 (for the loan officer's easy reference).
- The buyer's salary is reduced to $30,000 (as explained in the commentary following Appendix C).

JOHN Q. BUYER
999 ELM STREET
ST. LOUIS, MISSOURI 63000
314-999-0000

August 7, 2001

John Q. Loan Officer
Friendly Bank of Missouri
999 State Street
St. Louis, Missouri 63000

Dear Mr. Loan Officer:

I wish to borrow $147,000 from Friendly Bank of Missouri for the purchase of a small manufacturing, distributing, and retailing company.

I believe without reservation that the company I propose to purchase is capable of servicing the debt and that I am qualified to own and manage this company.

Enclosed is a package of data describing the circumstances of the purchase and the requested loan. Please refer to the Summary just inside the title page for an overview of the purchase and financing.

You may contact me at the above address or telephone number.

I will appreciate the bank's confidence in this matter. That confidence is important to me.

Thank you for your attention to this request.

Yours very truly,

J. Q. Buyer (signed)
Enclosure

LOAN APPLICATION BY JOHN Q. BUYER

August 7, 2001

SUMMARY

J. Q. Buyer requests a bank loan to purchase the assets of Acme Widget Corporation dba Widget Wonder. The owner of Acme Widget is J. Q. Seller. The proposed application of funds and sources of funds are as follows:

	Application of funds
Purchase price of business	$208,000
Working capital	30,000
Inventories and work in progress	33,000
Acquisition costs and lease deposit	6,000
	$277,000

	Source of funds
Cash infusion by J. Q. Buyer	$70,000
Bank loan	147,000
Subordinated loan from J. Q. Seller	60,000
	$277,000

Included in this loan application package is the text showing that the Acme Widget Corporation is capable of repaying the loan with interest and that Mr. Buyer is qualified to own and operate the business. Also included are appendices to the text with various supporting data.

Mr. Buyer and Mr. Seller will cooperate fully to facilitate the bank's consideration of this application. They may be contacted as follows:

J. Q. Buyer   J. Q. Seller, President
999 Elm Street   Acme Widget Corporation
St. Louis, Missouri 63000   123 Business Boulevard
(314) 999-0000   St. Louis, Missouri 63000
                                 (314) 123-0000

The purchase and sale are being managed by J. Q. Broker who has pledged his cooperation in working to obtain financing and in completing the various other tasks necessary to close. He may be contacted as follows:

J. Q. Broker
Better Business Brokers
888 Merchant Drive
St. Louis, Missouri 63000
(314) 111-8888

TABLE OF CONTENTS

HISTORY OF COMPANY

Acme Widget Corporation was founded in 1972 by J. Q. Founder at its present location. It began as a small manufacturer with only one employee besides Mr. Founder and has grown gradually to its present size with seven employees exclusive of owner and family. Its product line has not changed significantly since inception. Its emphasis has always been on the higher quality widgets appealing to customers in middle and upper incomes.

At first, the company relied only on local distributors to market its widgets to retail outlets. By 1978, sales had become large enough to use one employee as a part-time company sales representative. It then began its own distributing operations and gradually dropped its previous distributors. It has since continued to do all of its own distributing at the wholesale level.

In 1986, Mr. Founder sold the company to the present owner, J. Q. Seller. Sales have since grown from $182,000 in 1986 to $415,000 in 2000.

In 1988, due to many customer requests, the company began retailing from its premises. It did so without significantly competing with local retailers by not attempting to under-price them. Shop-worn, damaged, and other sub-standard widgets are offered from time to time at discounted prices, however.

In 1994, Acme Widget was awarded the annual Blue Ribbon Citation—Small Business Division by the National Association of Widget Manufacturers for its consistent and exemplary dedication to quality. It has since won Blue Ribbon nominations in 1997 and 1998. (The NAWM Small Business Division is for companies with annual sales of less than $5 million.)

PRODUCTS AND SERVICES

To outward appearances, Acme's widgets compare with those made at other companies, but at Acme the emphasis is on reliability and customer satisfaction. To prevent any product with defects from reaching the market, each widget is tested twice on an electronic widget tester and then personally inspected by either the owner or the foreman. Widgets with the slightest misalignment, discoloration, or other blemish are recycled through the manufacturing process. To assure freshness of product, Acme stores no product at its warehouse more than two weeks without recycling, and it monitors freshness of inventories at retail outlets by spot-checking in the field. To maintain customer satisfaction in the rare case when a sub-standard widget would reach a customer's hands (or when a customer merely thinks he or she has received one), Acme's policy is to refund the purchase price or replace any widget returned by a customer and to do so cheerfully with no questions asked. Returned widgets are restored to full quality by recycling through the manufacturing process or, if not recyclable, either sold as shopworn at reduced price or donated to charity.

All Acme widgets carry an unconditional three-month warranty, but Acme's retailers are encouraged to stretch that limit judiciously. The effect is three-fold: Acme customers expecting to pay a service charge three weeks out of warranty are delighted to find free repair or replacement; Acme retailers are delighted because they receive payment for those repairs from Acme while reaping the spill-over of customer good will; and, since such repairs are so infrequent due to the high reliability of Acme widgets, Acme's modest cost for this policy is more than offset by the increased good will of its customers, at both the wholesale and retail level, and by their enduring loyalty.

Another of Acme's services is to customize its products in accordance with individual requests for special sizes, shapes, weights, or colors. These requests account for 11% of total sales and are welcomed at Acme as part of its dedication to service. The nominal charge for customizing barely covers Acme's expense, but this service is more than paid for by the free word-of-mouth advertising and good will which result.

Thus, Acme's key to success is the high quality of both its products and its services.

The proposed purchaser, J. Q. Buyer, understands the importance of maintaining the quality of Acme's products and services. A major reason, in fact, for Mr. Buyer's desire to purchase Acme is that its dedication to quality closely suits his own style of managing.

COMPETITORS

The widget industry in America is marked by three types of manufacturers: national, regional, and local. National manufacturers tend to compete on price due to the inherent economies of large-scale production and to the quest for market share. Their coast-to-coast standardization also appeals to many consumers, particularly travelers and others who seek the assured minimal reliability of national, or at least recognizable brands. Local manufacturers tend to compete on quality of both product and service and, to some degree, uniqueness and its accompanying cachet. Regional manufacturers tend to be hybrids of national and local manufacturers and therefore compete according to circumstances.

In a way, all manufacturers compete with one another since consumers make tradeoffs of quality versus price, utility versus cachet, and so on. The most vigorous competition, however, is between widgets within a manufacturing type. Thus, national manufacturers compete mainly with each other while tending to ignore the local and regional manufacturers. Local manufacturers compete with others in the same local area, and regional man-ufacturers compete as the circumstances demand.

The only local manufacturer in the St. Louis area other than Acme is Gateway Widget Corporation. Thus, Acme and Gateway are in head-to-head competition. To keep abreast of any developments in Gateway's products, Acme regularly purchases and tests samples of Gateway's widgets. These tests have determined that Gateway's widgets are approximately as reliable as Ac-me's and appear to offer good freshness of product. They sell for about three percent less than Acme's but come with only a two-month warranty with no grace period. Unlike Acme, Gateway offers no customizing of widgets. In summary, Gateway offers nearly the quality of Acme at a slightly lower price and therefore provides very strong competition. The two widgets, in fact, comprise the upper market in the St. Louis metropolitan area. They therefore tend to boost each other by comparison, like a Lincoln automobile compared to a Cadillac. The competition between the two is strong but healthy and beneficial for both companies, especially in an economy like St. Louis's with sustained, if not growing, affluence.

One advantage that both Acme and Gateway have over national com-petitors is non-unionization, although Acme and Gateway both pay union hourly scale plus 50 cents. When employees at national and regional manu-facturers are on strike, Acme's and Gateway's employees stay on the job with the promise that their wages will always meet or exceed union scale. Another advantage of non-unionization is that jurisdictional limitations and disputes do not exist. An Acme worker may operate any machine on the premises or perform any task without incurring a grievance. The freedom, when appro-priate, to see a job through to completion or to work without inhibitions is a factor in the good morale enjoyed by the workers and the management at Acme, providing still another advantage over national and regional competi-tors. The good morale, good working climate, and above-scale wages explain the almost non-existent turnover at Acme. They also explain the family-like atmosphere which prevails, why employees willingly accept heavy workloads when someone is out sick, and why Acme earns Blue Ribbon Certification in a competitive market.

Mr. Buyer understands these competitive factors and he will work to preserve the advantages which Acme now enjoys.

MARKETING PLAN

Acme Widget's current marketing plan has two parts. First, it requires regular contacts and occasional visits with Acme's retailers to maintain close relationships while continually reviewing standards of quality. Two employee-representatives make the contacts as part of their duties. This part of the marketing plan has worked well, as evidenced by the low turnover of accounts in recent years.

The second part of the marketing plan requires calling on prospective new retailers to build sales. These calls have usually been made by the owner, Mr. Seller. This part of the plan worked well, as evidenced by the strong growth in sales, until three years ago. Since then there have been almost no efforts to build sales as evidenced by the recent flat growth. Mr. Seller has developed outside interests which have led to his decision to sell the company.

The new owner, Mr. Buyer, will keep the present marketing plan because of its proven effectiveness and will begin, in the second week of new ownership, making sales calls on prospective new retailers. He will dedicate eight hours per week exclusively to that activity in the first year of new ownership and four hours per week in succeeding years.

Since Mr. Buyer will have much learning to accomplish in the first two or three months of new ownership, his eight hours of sales calls will require him to work sixty hours or more in some weeks. He is willing and able to meet that requirement and will have the full support of Mrs. Buyer. The addition of new retailers to Acme's list of customers will require the employee representatives who service those accounts to work overtime. The extra work is expected to be easily handled because the employees welcome overtime work on an occasional basis for the extra income it affords. New employees are not expected to be necessary until after six months of new ownership, if then.

Mr. Buyer, despite his lack of direct experience in selling a tangible product or selling for a profit (he has successfully solicited for charity), has reasonable assurance of success in establishing new accounts for the following reasons:

- The key to getting new accounts is to make cold calls on prospective new customers and to make them relentlessly. In a cold call, the Acme representative enters a business office, asks to speak to the manager in charge of purchasing, and introduces himself or herself while introducing Acme's products and services. The eight-hour weekly time slot Mr. Buyer has set aside for making these calls is absolute.

- Special training is not required if the sales person understands the product, has a sense of communication, and has a sense of both his and the other person's dignity. Nevertheless, Mr. Seller will accompany Mr. Buyer on his initial sales calls to offer coaching and to share sales tips.

- Rejection is always a problem, even for experienced sales people. Mr. Buyer learned about rejection while soliciting for charity. He understands the illogic of it and to never take it personally. He knows the importance of a stable ego and self-generated optimism in dealing with it. He expects much more rejection than success and is mentally prepared for it.

- Business owners as sales persons have several advantages over sales persons who are employed by manufacturers or distributors. Business owners occupy a higher station in the community, commanding greater respect from purchasers. They do not have to telephone the office for approval of special prices or product deviations, making them more convenient and pleasurable to deal with. They share insights with customers that ordinary sales persons are not able to share. They have obvious commitment, implying long-term stability. They have the owner's priority when solving problems. They have obvious responsibility implying reliability of word and deed. And they have pride of ownership gently enhancing their auras of confidence. These attributes are picked up by prospective customers, giving owner-sales people a clear competitive edge over employee-sales people.

Widgets are sold through a broad variety of retail stores (as are such products as ball point pens, magazines, maps, and snacks), providing a large number of retailers to call on. Although many of these retailers already stock nationally recognized brands, some will add a locally produced line if it is a proven seller with a substantial margin of profit.

The eight hours per week on sales calls are expected to produce an increase in sales conservatively estimated at $20,000 in the first year. This estimate is based on empirical sales data at Mr. Buyer's place of employment and it is corroborated by data in a respected trade publication (see Appendix E). In the widget trade it takes 11.5 hours of selling (including 12 minutes driving time per prospect) or 21 cold calls to establish one new account. The average new account produces first-year sales of $1,348. Eight hours per week selling equals 400 hours per year; dividing 400 hours by 11.5 hours per new account yields 34 new accounts and, at $1,348 per account, $45,800 in the first full year. Since the average account in the first year of Mr. Buyer's ownership will produce sales for only half of that first year, the first year increase will be half of $45,800 or $22,900. The $22,900 figure was rounded to $20,000 to allow for reasonable conservatism.

Since Mr. Buyer's sales effort in the first year will produce the $20,000 increase estimated for the second year as well as the increase for the first year, his second-year sales effort will actually be to produce the increase in the third year. His second year effort will also add about $10,000 of new sales to his second year of ownership, but this increase was omitted from the cash-flow projections simply to be conservative. For that reason, his effort in the second and succeeding years will be reduced to four hours per week. This reduction in required effort will serve not only as a welcome relaxation of Mr. Buyer's efforts but will also provide a margin of safety on his expenditures of time and energy.

MANUFACTURING PLAN

The manufacturing plan consists of two parts: One is to assure that both the current quality of the product and the current efficiency of the manufacturing operation are maintained. The other is to staff the shop as necessary to increase output.

To assure continued quality and efficiency, Mr. Buyer will keep the existing manufacturing equipment, shop layout, shop employees, and procedures in place because the existing arrangement has proven efficient and capable of quality work.

To staff the increased production and sales being projected, overtime effort by existing employees is expected to suffice for at least the first six months of new ownership. Mr. Seller states that Acme's employees usually welcome some overtime work on an occasional basis for the extra pay it produces. He knows that long hours for months at a time is not advisable because the employees tend to tire of it and lose their efficiency. Since the employees are currently on a straight 40-hour week and have been for some time, the planned overtime effort is expected to be accepted and welcomed.

After six months of new ownership and increasing sales, a new shop worker may have to be hired. Mr. Buyer's having contacts in the area probably will bring a shop worker who already is proficient at the job. Failing that approach, he will go to the job market for a new hire or to the local trade school for an upcoming graduate. Hiring a new employee in the job market is always a challenge in small businesses where just one or two workers at low efficiency may seriously reduce profits. Mr. Buyer has experience in hiring capable new employees having served on the applicant-review team for four years at his present place of employment. He also has experience in training new trade-school graduates, having been a shop foreman for several years.

FINANCIAL PLAN

The financial plan is centered on the cash-flow projections shown below. These projections show that under the proposed new ownership Acme Widget Corporation will produce sufficient cash flow to service the debt with a substantial margin of safety. The following text explains how the cash-flow projections were prepared and how the funds necessary to purchase were determined. It also shows the proposed sources of the purchase funds.

The cash-flow projections are based on the following assumptions:

1. Inflation will proceed at three percent per year.
2. The first few months of sales growth will be accommodated by present staff, perhaps with some overtime.
3. Present plant and equipment will accommodate growth for at least the first three years.
4. Mr. Seller's departure will cost Acme about $12,000 per year in personality-intensive sales.
5. Mr. Buyer's contacts will gain Acme about $4,000 per year in personality-intensive sales.
6. Mr. Buyer's management skill will not differ significantly from Mr. Seller's.

The cash-flow projections begin with column 1 itemizing the sales and expenses of the company almost exactly as shown on the year 2000 statement of income and expenses as compiled by the company accountant. The only differences are minor changes to the words for clarity and ease of presentation.

Column 2, in combination with column 1, is the 2000 Acme Widget Corporation statement of income and expenses as compiled by the company accountant. Minor changes have been made to the figures to reflect the minor word changes mentioned above but no changes have altered the substance of either the words or the figures.

Column 3 is an adjustment of the accountant's income statement shown in column 2. The adjusted statement is the baseline for projecting the sales and expenses expected under new ownership. The adjustments are explained as follows:

- The $415,000 sales in column 2 was reduced to $407,000 in column 3 to reflect the $12,000 expected loss of sales when Mr. Seller departs and the expected $4,000 increase when Mr. Buyer commences.
- The 2000 advertising expense in Column 2 included $5,000 for radio advertising which produced no results and which was spent only for personal reasons of Mr. Seller. That expense was eliminated in column 3.
- The reduction of automotive expense from $9,000 to $4,000 reflects use of the corporate credit card restricted to business-related driving.
- The reduction of depreciation expense from $15,000 to $9,000 reflects actual wear and tear compared to the accelerated depreciation allowed by the IRS. This adjustment has no effect on cash flow but is shown to provide a truer picture of Acme's profits.
- The reduction of owner's personal insurance expense to $3,000 reflects Mr. Buyer's younger age and smaller family.
- The reduction of legal and accounting expense to $5,000 reflects elimination of $1,000 nonrecurring legal expense.
- Raw materials expense was lowered by $6,000 to reflect a reduced scrap allowance in the shop. (Past scrap allowance was based on manufacturing procedures which have been superseded.) Raw materials expense was lowered by another $1,000 to reflect the reduced sales mentioned above.
- Taxes-and-licenses expense (mostly Social Security and unemployment taxes) was reduced $1,000 in line with the reduced wages.
- The owner's wage was reduced from Mr. Seller's $32,000 to Mr. Buyer's $30,000. Other employees' wages remain the same. Mr. Seller's children's wages of $16,000 were also eliminated.

ACME WIDGET CORPORATION CASH-FLOW PROJECTIONS
UNDER NEW OWNERSHIP
(In thousands)

1	2	3	4	5	6	7
	2000 Income Statement	Baseline (Adjusted Income & Expenses)	Projection Factors	Year of New Ownership		
				1	2	3
Sales	$415	$407	1.08	$440	$475	$513
Expenses						
Advertising	8	3	1.03	3	3	3
Automotive	9	4	1.03	4	4	4
Depreciation	15	9	–	9	9	9
Insurance						
Business	9	9	1.05	9	10	10
Owner's personal	5	3	1.03	3	3	3
Legal & accounting	6	5	1.05	5	6	6
Maintenance & repair	5	5	1.05	5	6	6
Miscellaneous	0	0	1.05	0	0	0
Office supplies	9	9	1.05	9	10	10
Raw materials	46	39	1.08	42	45	49
Rent	27	27	1.03	28	29	30
Taxes & licenses	21	20	1.05	21	22	23
Telephone	3	3	1.05	3	3	3
Utilities	8	8	1.05	8	9	9
Wages						
Owner	32	30	1.03	31	32	33
Other employees	209	193	1.05	203	213	223
Total expenses	$412	$367		$383	$404	$421
Pre-tax net profit	$3	$40		$57	$71	$92
Cash flow	$18	$49		$66	$80	$101

BACKGROUND OF BUYER

After graduating from high school in 1986, Mr. Buyer enrolled in a two-year technical certificate program at Community Trade School. Upon completion in 1988, he began his career by accepting an offer from General Widgets (GW) where he was sent to the company's training center in St. Louis County. After six months of training in manufacturing, testing, maintenance, and repair of widgets, he was assigned to the GW factory in St. Charles, Missouri where he began working as an assembler. In 1991, he became a lead-man, an informal role commonly used to test supervisory aptitude. In 1992, he was promoted to assistant foreman, and, in 1993, to foreman with 18 shop workers reporting to him.

In the meantime, Mr. Buyer completed several business courses, including accounting and marketing, at St. Louis Community College. In 1995, at his request (and with a cut in salary), he transferred to the purchasing department where, as a senior buyer, he acquired experience buying raw materials, component parts, shop equipment, and laboratory equipment. In early 1996, he was assigned to GW headquarters in Pittsburgh for five months of on-the-job training in plant-wide manufacturing planning. He was then reassigned to the manufacturing division in St. Charles, Missouri in his current position as a senior foreman in charge of both consumer and scientific widgets. He now has 35 employees, including two foremen, reporting to him. (The scientific widget represents a growing field for widget applications but which is still too new for companies the size of Acme to enter. It also fuels the long-standing debate about whether a widget is a scientific instrument or an adult toy.)

In 1997, Mr. Buyer was assigned to one of several prospective-employee hiring teams which occasionally assist the personnel department, in showing new prospects around the plant and evaluating their qualifications. He also assists his immediate superior, the assistant director of manufacturing, in reviewing and approving all new hires in the manufacturing division (which assignment affords him the opportunity to renew relationships with his teachers at Community Trade School).

In 1998, Mr. Buyer was appointed to a one-year stint on the company's charity review board. This board monitors the payroll collections and allocates donations to the various charities in the St. Louis metropolitan area. Privately, Mr. Buyer solicits from time to time for a favorite charity on evenings and weekends, which has introduced him to the rigors as well as the pleasures of selling.

Mr. Buyer is married and has two children. (Mrs. Buyer is a homemaker but also does part-time secretarial work out of their home. She does not plan to work at Acme Widget but will make herself available for secretarial and bookkeeping work if and when seriously short-handed. Mrs. Buyer is an active member of a favorite charity to which she donates some secretarial services.)

Mr. and Mrs. Buyer and their children are in good health (although one child suffers from a congenital disability which is under control). All are United States citizens.

COMMENTARY ON THE ACME LOAN APPLICATION PACKAGE

There are several important points about this package. One is the fairly low ratio of cash flow to debt service: $66,000 ÷ $51,000 = 1.29. (The $51,000 debt service was determined just as the $41,000 in Part 2 of Chapter 7 was by simply adding $40,000 to the purchase price.) Had the buyer dishonestly raised his baseline sales to $415,000 as he had thought he might do, his cash flow would have been $73,000 and his ratio 1.43, still not a good ratio but at least in striking range of qualifying for a loan. What changed his mind is partly the disgust he felt at compromising his principles and partly the stout realization that he is the right person to take over this company and to make it grow; there must be a commercial loan officer out there somewhere who will recognize the rightness of the deal. Moreover, if really necessary to satisfy the bank, he will insist on a six-month moratorium on payments to Mr. Seller. Mr. Seller will not be happy about that, but he will have brought it on himself by failing to record his true income.

What the buyer also has sensed intuitively, though not quite consciously, is that motivation moves mountains, for loan officers as well as anyone else. What will motivate almost any commercial loan officer is this buyer's background marked by several strengths which loan officers love to see:

- The buyer's stability evidenced by having stayed with one company throughout his career.
- His solid training at trade school, at the community college, and at GW.
- His steady rise up the ladder of success; his proven ability to supervise employees.
- His apparently stable marriage which allows him to concentrate on managing the business.
- His ability to get along with people evidenced partly by his promotions but also by his appointments to the charity board and to the new-employee review team, both badges of prestige and signals from higher echelons that his star is still rising.
- And his administrative ability evidenced by the comprehensive loan application package he provided. (The bank's loan officer does not need to know that the loan application package was prepared by someone other than the buyer. The buyer still deserves credit for intelligently assigning the task to the right party.)

In addition to the above, the seller's participation in the financing, since it is subordinate to the bank's financing, gives the bank the safest part of the loan, encouraging the bank's approval. Also important is the truthfulness implied by the buyer's acknowledged loss of sales at the seller's departure, the long hours he will work in his first year, and the rejection he will endure while making sales calls.

Major weaknesses in this application are the buyer's lack of experience in making cold calls and the necessity of increasing sales by $20,000 in the first year by making those calls. Offsetting these weaknesses are the overall strength of the buyer's background and the hard statistical evidence he provided which related hours of selling to increases in sales.

The buyer also senses that loan officers have a bag of tricks that they can employ when they want to grant a loan, tricks which may or may not change the mathematics or the economics of the deal but which provide special safeguards which protect the bank and, not incidentally, which also protect the loan officers from criticism when problems develop. The tricks are mostly in the form of special conditions on the loan. One possible special condition would be to require the borrower to obtain the bank's approval before purchasing any new capital equipment. Another is to require bank approval when hiring family members (to prevent nepotism). Still another is to require approval before raising his own salary or increasing any payments beyond the ordinary expenses of doing business. Approvals might also be required for any deviation from the historical norm, such as shifting to a new major supplier, contracting to supply widgets to any new customer requiring more than, say, five percent of Acme's output, and so on.

An idea suggested to the buyer by one of his friends is to discreetly inform the loan officer that, though he can't prove a thing, he suspects strongly that the seller has been skimming sales without reporting them and that this seems to be a common practice in the widget trade. Loan officers are not innocent to the ways of the world and they may take such situations into account, even if they deny doing so.

Note that the cash-flow projections included in the loan application package used the latest income statement prepared by Acme's accountant in column 2 instead of the partly adjusted statement previously used by the buyer. The advantage is the directness of the story line beginning with actual data.

Note also the smooth explanation of some of the illicit hidden earnings such as those in automotive expenses. Actually, the explanation of the scrap allowance was not only smooth but a lie, though a judicious one.

The overall package is basically the kind of loan application that banks like to see. All the necessary topics are covered, with the section on competitors as a bonus.

The appendices are not shown in this book because they would not offer useful insights to the reader. It should be clear, however, that the appendices are essential to any loan application package and, when well chosen, can tip the balance in favor of the bank's granting the loan.

There is no loan application package which can answer everything the banker might think of. Therefore, a prospective borrower should expect to be asked any number of questions and should expect to supply additional documentation. For example, Acme's weak ratio of cash flow to debt service may prompt the loan officer to request an analysis showing at what level of sales decline the company would begin to experience a loss. Needless to say, the buyer should cooperate spontaneously.

The probable final result is that the buyer's strong qualifications plus the well-written application will get him the loan, although he may have to shop for the right bank.

SPECIAL INDEX FOR CHAPTER 2

The terms and concepts in Chapter 2 were presented in a loosely logical sequence for greater understanding of their meanings. Here they are presented in alphabetical order for ease of location. Most are not included in the main index, but those of greater relevance do appear in both indexes.

INDEX

Notes:

1. Entries marked *f* refer to a figure; *t* to a table, and *illus* to an illustration.
2. In some instances, front and back matter have been included in this Index.
3. All of the basic terms and concepts of Chapter 2 are shown in alphabetical order in the Special Index in front of this Index. However, some of those terms and concepts also appear in this Index.